Investment Strategies in Emerging Markets

NEW HORIZONS IN INTERNATIONAL BUSINESS

Series Editor: Peter J. Buckley
Centre for International Business,
University of Leeds (CIBUL), UK

The New Horizons in International Business series has established itself as the world's leading forum for the presentation of new ideas in international business research. It offers pre-eminent contributions in the areas of multinational enterprise – including foreign direct investment, business strategy and corporate alliances, global competitive strategies, and entrepreneurship. In short, this series constitutes essential reading for academics, business strategists and policy makers alike.

Titles in the series include:

Alliance Capitalism for the New American Economy
Edited by Alan M. Rugman and Gavin Boyd

The Structural Foundations of International Finance
Problems of Growth and Stability
Edited by Pier Carlo Padoan, Paul A. Brenton and Gavin Boyd

The New Competition for Inward Investment
Companies, Institutions and Territorial Development
Edited by Nicholas Phelps and Philip Raines

Multinational Enterprises, Innovative Strategies and Systems of Innovation
Edited by John Cantwell and José Molero

Multinational Firms' Location and the New Economic Geography
Edited by Jean-Louis Mucchielli and Thierry Mayer

Free Trade in the Americas
Economic and Political Issues for Governments and Firms
Edited by Sidney Weintraub, Alan M. Rugman and Gavin Boyd

Economic Integration and Multinational Investment Behaviour
European and East Asian Experiences
Edited by Pierre-Bruno Ruffini

Strategic Business Alliances
An Examination of the Core Dimensions
Keith W. Glaister, Rumy Husan and Peter J. Buckley

Investment Strategies in Emerging Markets
Edited by Saul Estrin and Klaus E. Meyer

Multinationals and Industrial Competitiveness
A New Agenda
John H. Dunning and Rajneesh Narula

Foreign Direct Investment
Six Country Case Studies
Edited by Yingqi Annie Wei and V.N. Balasubramanyam

Japanese Multinationals in Europe
A Comparison of the Automobile and Pharmaceutical Industries
Ken-ichi Ando

Investment Strategies in Emerging Markets

Edited by

Saul Estrin

Professor of Economics, London Business School, UK

and

Klaus E. Meyer

Professor of International Business Strategy, Copenhagen Business School, Denmark

NEW HORIZONS IN INTERNATIONAL BUSINESS

Edward Elgar
Cheltenham, UK • Northampton, MA, USA

Published by
Edward Elgar Publishing Limited
Glensanda House
Montpellier Parade
Cheltenham
Glos GL50 1UA
UK

Edward Elgar Publishing, Inc.
136 West Street
Suite 202
Northampton
Massachusetts 01060
USA

A catalogue record for this book
is available from the British Library

Library of Congress Cataloguing in Publication Data

Investment strategies in emerging markets / edited by Saul Estrin and Klaus E. Meyer.
    p. cm. — (New horizons in international business)
  Includes bibliographical references and index.
    1. Investments, Foreign—Egypt. 2. Egypt—Economic policy. 3. Investments, Foreign—India. 4. India—Economic policy. 5. Investments, Foreign—South Africa—Economic policy. 7. Investments, Foreign—Vietnam. 8. Vietnam—Economic policy. I. Estrin, Saul. II. Meyer, Klaus, 1964- III. Series.

  HG5836.A3I583 2004
  332.67'3'091724—dc22

                                                                    2004050613
  ISBN 1 84376 781 3 (cased)

Printed and bound in Great Britain by MPG Books Ltd, Bodmin, Cornwall

Contents

Contributors

PL Beena is Research Associate at the Centre for Development Studies, Thiruvananthapuram, Kerala, India

Laveesh Bhandari is Chief Economist, Indicus Analytics, New Delhi, India

Sumon Bhaumik is Lecturer at the School of Management and Economics at Queens University Belfast and Visiting Fellow at the Centre for New and Emerging Markets, London Business School, UK

Anthony Black is Associate Professor at the School of Economics at the University of Cape Town, South Africa

Alia El-Mahdy is Professor of Economics at the Cairo University, Egypt

Azza El-Shinnawy is Program Officer at the Economic Research Forum for the Arab Countries, Iran and Turkey and a PhD Candidate at the London School of Economics, UK

Saul Estrin is Professor of Economics and Research Director of the Centre for New and Emerging Markets at London Business School, UK

Stephen Gelb is Director at the EDGE Institute: Economic Development, Growth & Equity, Johannesburg, and Visiting Professor of Development Studies at the University of the Witwatersrand, Johannesburg, South Africa

Subir Gokarn is Chief Economist for the Credit Rating Information Services of India Ltd. (CRISIL), New Delhi, India

Heba Handoussa was Managing Director of the Economic Research Forum for the Arab Countries, Iran and Turkey

Maryse Louis is Senior Economic and Data Analyst at the Economic Research Forum for the Arab Countries, Iran and Turkey

Klaus E. Meyer is Research Professor at the Centre for East European Studies at the Copenhagen Business School.

Ha Thanh Nguyen is a Researcher at the National Institute for Science and Technology Policy and Strategy Studies, Vietnam

Hung Vo Nguyen is Researcher at the National Institute for Science and Technology Policy and Strategy Studies, Vietnam

Anjali Tandon is Research Assistant at the National Council of Applied Economic Research, New Delhi, India

Ca Ngoc Tran is a Senior Researcher and Vice Director at the National Institute for Science and Technology Policy and Strategy Studies, Vietnam

Acknowledgements

The research presented in this book has developed over a long period of time, and involved numerous researchers. We first met in November 2000 in London to discuss the key research issues and the general framework. In May 2001 in Cairo we reviewed first evidence from our case research and reassessed our framework and the survey instrument. In September 2001 we met again to finalise the questionnaire instrument and discuss issues of research methodology in a meeting that due to the political situation at the time was somewhat smaller than expected. The survey data were collected in winter 2001/2002, and processed throughout the following year. In March 2003, we presented the results available at the time to a workshop at the London Business School.

This research project would not have been possible without the support of many institutions and individuals. For financial support we thank first and foremost the UK Department for International Development who supported this research under DfID/DRC project no. R7844, the Centre for New and Emerging Markets, London Business School. Additional funding has been received from the Aditya Birla India Centre at the London Business School, which has strongly supported the research on India. The Centre for New and Emerging Markets at the London Business School has been the operational centre for much of this research, and has organised this complex project successfully and with a minimum of fuss.

The field research has been conducted by country teams hosted in leading research institutions in their country: the Economic Research Forum for Arab Countries, Iran and Turkey, (ERF) in Egypt, the National Council of Applied Economic Research (NCAER) in India, the EDGE Institute in South Africa, and the National Institute for Science and Technology Policy and Strategy Studies (NISTPASS) in Vietnam. The lead researchers are authors of chapters of this book. Yet beyond this, we would like to extend our thanks to the leaders of the institutes for their support, and to local research assistants who have been instrumental in collecting the data.

The processing of the data has greatly benefited by contributions by Caitlin Frost and Gherardo Girardi, in London as well as Delia Ionascu and Yen Thi Thu Tran in Copenhagen. Moreover, we wish to thank Anna Malaczynska and Kerrie Quirk for administrative support, and Stella Bailey and Paul Ellis for help in editing and formatting the book manuscript. Leann Player has also played a very special role in editing the whole volume and preparing the entire manuscript in camera-ready form, while Maria

Bytchkova spent months struggling valiantly with difficulties of the data and the bibliography.

We have discussed the design of the study and our interpretations with many of our academic colleagues. *Inter alia* we wish to acknowledge the comments and contributions made by Zoltan Antal-Mokos (Budapest), Alan Bevan (EBRD, London), Simon Commander (London Business School), Jason Hayman (DfID) and Freek Vermeulen (London Business School).

Finally, it should be noted that the views expressed in each chapter do not necessarily reflect the views of the organisations with which each author is associated.

Abbreviations

AFTA	ASEAN Free Trade Area
BCC	Business Corporation Contract
BEE	Black Economic Empowerment
BOT	Build Operate Transfer
CARG	Compound Annual Growth Rate
CAPA	Central Administration of Pharmaceutical Affairs
CCI	Controller of Capital Issues
CEO	Chief Executive Officer
CIABC	Confederation of Indian Alcoholic Beverage Companies
CNEM	Centre for New and Emerging Markets
DPPC	Drug Planning & Policy Centre
ECMS	Egyptian Company for Mobile Services
EPZ	Export Processing Zones
ERSAP	Economic Reform & Structural Adjustment Programme
ESA	Employee Stockholder Association
EST	Edwards Systems Technologies
F & B	Financial & Business
FDI	Foreign Direct Investment
FIE	Foreign Investment Enterprise
FSO	Free Space Optical
GAFI	General Authority for Free Zones & Investment
GATT	General Agreement on Trade and Tariffs
GDI	Gross Domestic Income
GDP	Gross Domestic Product
GEAR	Growth, Employment and Redistribution policy in South Africa
GM	General Manager
GNP	Gross National Product
GPRS	General Packet Radio Services
GSM	Global System for Mobiles
HCMC	Ho Chi Minh City
HDI	Human Development Index

hl	hectolitres
HTM	Hanoi Transformer Manufacturing Factory
IC	Interalsiations Costs
IFU	Industrial Fund for Developing Countries
IMFL	Indian Made Foreign Liquor
ISIC	International Standard Industrial Classification
ISP	Internet Service Provider
IT	Information Technology
IZ	Industrial Zone
JSE	Johannesburg Stock Exchange
JV	Joint Venture
LE	Egyptian Pounds
M & A	Merger and Acquisition
M & E	Machinery and Equipment
MENA	Middle East & North Africa
MIDP	Motor Industry Development Programme
MNC	Nultinatinal Company
MNE	Multinational Enterprise
MOHAP	Ministry of Health & Population
MPI	Ministry of Planning & Investment
NODCAR	National Organisation for Drug Control & Research
NRI	Non-Resident Indian
OE	Original Equipment
OTC	Over The Counter
PA	Partial Acquisition
PE	Private Enterprise
PEO	Public Enterprise Office
PPP	Purchasing Power Parity
PSE	Public Sector Enterprise
R&D	Research and Development
RBI	Reserve Bank of India
Rs	Rupees
SA	South Africa
SBU	Strategic Business Unit
SBV	State Bank of Vietnam
SCB	Scheduled Commercial Bank
SEAB	South East Asia Brewery
SME	Small & Medium sized Enterprise

SOCB	State Owned Commercial Banks
SOE	State Owned Enterprise
TC	Tansactions Costs
TRA	Telecommunications Regulatory Authority
TRIPS	Trade Related Aspects of Intellectual Property Rights
TTR	Trade, Tourism & Recreation
VAT	Value Added Tax
VEAM	Vientam Engine & Agricultural Machinery
WAP	Wireless Application Protocol
WCS	Wholesale Client Services
WEF	World Economic Forum
WTO	World Trade organization
ZAR	South African Rand

1. Investment Strategies in Emerging Markets: An Introduction to the Research Project

Klaus E. Meyer and Saul Estrin

INTRODUCTION

Foreign Direct Investment (FDI) is widely believed to make major contributions to the economic development of emerging markets (for example UNCTAD 2001). At the same time, emerging markets play a pivotal role in the global strategies of many multinational enterprises (MNEs), notably those with ambitious growth targets. Thus MNE and local policy-makers have a common interest in encouraging foreign investment. Their objectives vary: externalities for the local economy or profits and corporate growth. Yet cooperation between local and foreign partners can create beneficial outcomes for both.

This study investigates the foreign investment strategies in four emerging markets, their determinants and their implications for the local economy and for public policy. The outcomes of FDI in terms of both corporate and social performance are highly dependent on how the operation is initially set up. Entry strategies concern the key characteristics of the foreign investment project, including for instance entry mode, timing and location. The entry strategy establishes where, when and how a foreign investor establishes a new operation, setting the stage for the affiliate's own performance and its impact on local partners. This study uniquely incorporates business strategy in the analytical framework and addresses both corporate and social outcomes of FDI.

A wide range of host-country-specific factors influence inward FDI into emerging markets. Foreign investors are attracted to large and growing markets, as well as to host countries' endowments of natural and created assets. In emerging markets, many investors are focused on a particular factor as market-seeking FDI seeks large populations with rising incomes, while resource-seeking FDI seeks labour forces at affordable costs, or specific national resources such as minerals, or oil and gas. Moreover, the institutional context in the location of their (potential) investment is crucial for where and how to establish FDI, and particularly so in emerging economies. Hence, the volume of FDI a country receives is influenced by a wide range of FDI-specific laws and regulations (for example Guisinger et al. 1985) as well as the overall institutional development (Henisz 2000, Bevan et al. 2004, Globermann and Shapiro 2003). Equally, the institutional context shapes the characteristics of inward FDI, notably the preferred entry mode (for example Meyer 2001).

International business and strategic management scholars have analysed the merits of alternative forms of international entry and their implications for corporate performance. The literature has analysed in particular, alternative ownership arrangements (for example Anderson and Gatignon 1986, Tse et al. 1997), and the choice of acquisitions or greenfield entry (for example Hennart and Park 1993, Kogut and Singh 1988). Most studies have focused on project- and firm-specific aspects, such as the investor's global strategy, research and advertising intensity and international business experience, using as their empirical base, primarily FDI between mature market economies where the institutional context is comparatively homogeneous. Recently, empirical studies have begun to analyse entry modes in emerging markets such as Eastern Europe (for example Brouthers and Brouthers 2000, Meyer 2001b, Meyer and Estrin 2001) and China (for example Pan and Tse 2000, Luo 2001, Chen and Hu 2001). Other emerging markets remain under-researched. Moreover, most studies pay only scant attention to local resource endowment and institutional peculiarities, as few have systematically explored the institutional variations between and within emerging markets, and their impact on FDI.

Our study analyses the link between the host-country environment and foreign investment strategies. We use case research to explore and refine the concepts of entry modes, paying special attention to the concepts of resource transfers, ownership and control, and their evolution over the first years of operation of the project. We also use a survey to understand the determinants of entry modes, and the relationship between FDI motivation, entry modes and the performance of the newly established affiliate.

We also examine the benefits the host economy can gain from the interaction with foreign investors, commonly known as spillovers. These arise through a variety of channels, including impact on the balance of payment, employment and investment. Probably the most important ones are knowledge transfer and diffusion that benefit not only the affiliate of the foreign investor, but its local business partners as well. Foreign investors generally transfer resources to their affiliates, thus creating new operations replicating their operations elsewhere in the case of greenfield investment, and restructuring, upgrading and integrating existing businesses in the case of acquisitions. This process affects not only the affiliate, but also local businesses with which they are in contact. Suppliers may be required to achieve higher standards of quality and service, and receive support when striving to accomplish them. Customers may receive higher quality products, complemented with advice on how to improve their application or marketing. Even unrelated firms may benefit from observing new business practices applied in their local context, and learning from this 'demonstration effect' (Altenburg 2000, Blomström and Kokko 2002, Fan 2002). The potential of such impact will be greater the larger the technological gap between source and recipient economy, which makes it particularly relevant in emerging markets.

To understand the mechanisms of spillovers, it is important to understand processes within the investing MNE, and its interaction with the local environment. Policy-makers need to understand MNE behaviour in order to develop policies to influence FDI. Therefore, we analyse spillovers and corporate strategy in a comprehensive framework summarised in Figure 1.1. We use this as the conceptual framework for the case studies in this book.

FDI IN EMERGING MARKETS

Over the past decade, emerging markets have become major recipients of FDI as multinational enterprises have expanded their global strategies to take advantage of business opportunities. Emerging economies are attractive for business because of their sometimes large and often fast growing markets, and because they provide access to resources, notably raw materials and labour not available at the same cost, in mature market economies. Total FDI flows worldwide had grown from US$200 billion in 1990 to US$1,500 billion in 2000, before falling back to US$735 billion in 2001. Of this, developing nations and transition economies account for US$206 billion (28 per cent) in 2001. However, FDI in emerging economies is distributed very unequally, with China receiving the largest share (US$47 billion), followed by Mexico, Brazil and Hong Kong with over US$20 billion each in 2001. The poorest economies of Africa or Latin America, in contrast, receive only negligible sums (all data from UNCTAD 2002).

Despite their attractions, emerging markets pose particular challenges to investors because of the weaknesses in the institutional environment. The legal framework concerning business law tends to be less developed with respect to, *inter alia*, competition policy, regulatory policy, corporate taxation, and definition and enforcement of property rights (not just intellectual property). Moreover, even where the necessary laws are in place, their implementation and enforcement may be inhibited by, among other causes, lack of qualified accountants, bureaucrats and lawyers. Intermediaries and information systems, such as audited corporate accounts and business directories may also be lacking and the laws my be subject to frequent changes, which creates considerable uncertainty for businesses.

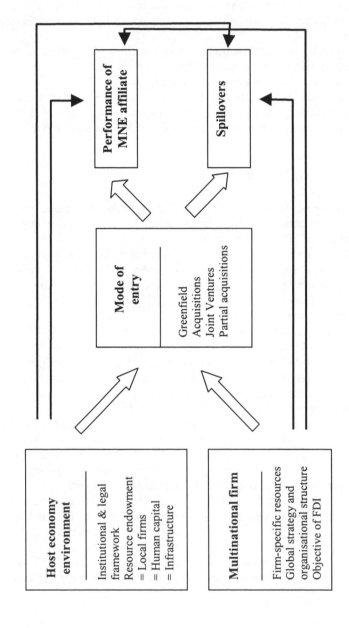

Figure 1.1 Conceptual framework of the study

In addition informal institutions can differ greatly from those of Western market economies. For instance, traditional value systems are more widespread, including collectivist, particularist, and family-oriented values, as well as religion. Relationship-based interactions with business partners are more common, in part due to low trust in both governments and outsiders to the society. Markets – especially for capital and skilled labour – may be thin or illiquid and inhibited by numerous market failures. These 'institutional voids' (Khanna and Palepu 1999) can cause high transaction costs in markets, such that investing firms may prefer to 'internalise' business transactions in situations, where they would use market-transactions in mature economies. At the same time, few local firms match international standards in technology and management. This means that firms following entry strategies in emerging markets face special problems that may require unique solutions.

For this study we have selected four emerging economies that despite significant cultural, geographical and economic differences are quite similar with respect to FDI. Each substantially increased their FDI receipts in the mid to late 1990s although they are still not among the top recipients: India, South Africa, Egypt and Vietnam (Table 1.1).[1] All four countries were relatively closed economies with a large extent of state involvement, but each had gone through substantial liberalisation in the 1990s.

By the end of the 1990s they had achieved macroeconomic stability and economic growth prospects were considered to be favourable. Also, these countries were ranked similarly by the Human Development Report 2002 with positions between 107th and 124th worldwide (Table 1.2). India has operated for many years as a mixed socialist-capitalist economy, but has embarked on major, though gradual, liberalisation of both the domestic economy and its FDI regime since 1991. Egypt formally abandoned the ideas of central planning in 1971, but the process of liberalisation has been very slow and only accelerated in the 1990s; many FDI restrictions have been removed in the 1990s, though others remain in place. Vietnam has belonged to the socialist block since the 1970s, but embarked on gradual reform from 1986, along a similar path to China. South Africa's economy was severely constrained by the international embargo of the apartheid regime, but the regime change in 1994 led to a more open economic system with new business opportunities. Table 1.2 provides an overview of economic and social indicators in each country.[2] The institutional change affecting FDI in each country is presented in greater detail at the outset of each of the country sections of this book.

Market-seeking foreign investors are first and foremost interested in large and fast growing economies. At a time when mature markets in Europe, Japan and (to a lesser extent) North America offer little growth potential, many firms seek business opportunities by serving the growing demand in emerging markets. India is a large economy, with an annual GDP of US$447 billion courtesy of its large population and despite its low average per capita

Table 1.1 Foreign Direct Investment in emerging markets (Annual average)(US$ million)

Year	1982–89	1990	1991	1992	1993	1994	1995	1996	1997	1998	1999	2000	2001	2002
South Africa	49	-5	-8	-42	-19	380	1,241	818	3,817	561	1,502	888	6,789	754
India	113	236	155	233	574	973	2,144	2,525	3,619	2,633	2,168	2,319	3,404	3,449
Egypt	926	734	352	459	493	1,256	598	636	887	1,065	2,919	1,235	510	647
Vietnam	5	16	32	385	523	1,936	2,336	1,803	2,587	1,700	1,484	1,289	1,300	1,200

Notes: We use the latest available revision of the data, i.e. WIR 2002 for data for 1996 onwards.
In the case of Vietnam, this involves a considerable downward adjustment of the data from 1996 onwards, compared to the data reported in UNCTAD 2001.

Source: UNCTAD 1994 to 2003

income. Although ahead of Vietnam, India is a low-income economy with per capita GDP of US$460 at current exchange rates, thus lagging considerably behind Egypt (US$1,490) and South Africa (US$3,020). Vietnam has achieved very high economic growth in recent years with 7 per cent annual growth in the second half of the 1990s, ahead of both India and Egypt. On this score, South Africa performs poorly as its growth rate in recent years is more comparable to that in mature market economies.

All four countries have substantially reduced their inflation rate over the decade to reach single-digit inflation in 2000, and trade has grown, increasing the interdependence with the international economy. However, the trade data show some interesting variations: South Africa is the only country with a trade surplus, with substantive exports of the mining industry and, by the end of the decade, of basic processed goods. In Egypt, the falling price of oil has slowed trade, which thus fell from 52.9 per cent in 1990 to 19.2 per cent of GDP in 2000, while imports exceed exports by over 50 per cent in both years. The volume of trade is largest relative to the country's GDP in Vietnam (96.1 per cent). Turning to social development indicators, Vietnam is performing as well, if not better than the other countries, despite its much lower GDP. Thus, Vietnam is ranked 109th in the Human Development Index developed by the UN, only two ranks behind South Africa (rank 107), and ahead of both Egypt (rank 115) and India (rank 124). The socialist emphasis on education and health care is reflected in a remarkable adult literacy rate of 93.1 per cent and a life expectancy at birth of 69 years. Life expectancy has increased since the 1970s in Vietnam (by 19 years), Egypt (15 years), and India (13 years), while it has in recent years fallen back on 1970s levels in South Africa, mainly due to the AIDS crisis.

However, other indicators of industrial and economic development show South Africa ahead of the other countries, which is indicative of its dual economy: some aspects of the economy resemble a mature market economy, while large parts of the society live under conditions more typical for developing countries. This is reflected in an unusually high Gini-coefficient of 59, high urbanization of 56.9 per cent, higher tertiary (university) enrolment rate of 18.9 per cent (second to Egypt with 20.2 per cent), and a high share of the service sector in GDP (64 per cent). Also, telecommunications in terms of fixed phone lines or mobile phones are far better developed than in the other three countries. Natural resource industries that provide an important basis for economic development include mining in South Africa, oil exploration in Egypt and agricultural products in Vietnam.

India and Vietnam are far less urbanised (28 per cent and 24 per cent, respectively), and agriculture continues to account for a very large share of GDP (28 per cent and 26 per cent). University education is still an exception, and less than 2 per cent have a phone line, while the number of Internet hosts is negligible. Yet, since Internet café's are more common than private connections, many people do have access to the World Wide Web.

Table 1.2 Key economic and social data in Egypt, India, South Africa and Vietnam

	Egypt		India		S. Africa		Vietnam	
	1990	2000	1990	2000	1990	2000	1990	2000
Population, million	52	64	835	1,016	34	43	66	79
GDP, US$ billion	48	95	315	471	113	129	5	31
GDP per capita, US$	926	1,490	377	460	3,325	3,020	78	390
GDP per capita, at PPP int $	2,640	3,690	1,449	2,390	8,524	9,180	n.a.	2,030
Average annual GDP growth (%) *	3.8	5.4	5.4	5.7	0.7	2.6	7.7	7.0
Consumer price inflation	14.0	4.3	10.5	7.6	11.3	6.7	n.a.	3.7
Exchange rates, local currency per US$, average	2.00	3.70	18.10	46.80	2.60	7.60	8.13	14.51
Exports, US$ billion	9.6	4.7	22.5	42.4	28.0	30.0	1.4	14.3
Imports, US$ billion	15.8	13.6	26.9	28.8	21.1	29.7	1.8	15.2
Ratio of trade to GDP (%)	52.9	19.2	15.7	19.4	43.4	46.3	62.0	96.1
Household consumption, % of GDP	72	72	68	68	63	64	90	70
Government consumption, % of GDP	11	10	12	11	20	18	8	7

Gross Fixed Capital Formation, % of GDP	27	24	23	25	19	15	13	25
Life expectancy at birth **	52.1	66.9	50.3	62.9	53.7	53.9	50.3	67.8
Adult literacy rate		55.3		57.2		85.3		93.4
HDI index	0.574	0.642	0.511	0.577	0.714	0.695	0.605	0.688
HDI rank	n.a.	115	n.a.	124	n.a.	107	n.a.	109
Gini index ***	n.a.	28.7	n.a.	37.8	n.a.	59.3	n.a.	36.1
Tertiary enrolment rates, % ****	15.8	20.2	6.1	6.6	13.2	18.9	1.9	4.1
Urban population, % of total **	43.5	42.7	21.3	27.7	48.0	56.9	18.8	24.1
Agriculture % of GDP	19	17	31	28	5	4	37	26
Industry % of GDP	29	33	27	25	40	32	23	33
of which: manufacturing	24	27	17	16	24	19	19	n.a.
Services % of GDP	52	50	42	46	55	64	40	42
Value Added of SOE (% of GDP)	30.0		13.4		14.7		n.a.	
Phone lines (# per 1000 people)	30	86	6	32	93	114	1	32

Table 1.2 (continued)

	Egypt		India		S. Africa		Vietnam	
	1990	2000	1990	2000	1990	2000	1990	2000
Mobile phones (# per 1000 people)	n.a.	21	n.a.	4	n.a.	190	n.a.	10
R&D expenditures as % of GNP	n.a.	1.9	n.a.	0.6	n.a.	0.6	n.a.	n.a
Scientists and engineers in R&D per million people	n.a.	493	n.a.	158	n.a.	992	n.a.	274
Net FDI inflows, % GDP	1.7	1.3	0.1	0.5	-0.1	0.8	0.2	4.1
Stock market capitalisation, US$ billion	1.8	32.8	38.6	184.6	137.5	262.5	0	0
Listed domestic companies	573	1.032	2.435	5.863	732	668	0	0
Average price of traded company, US$ million	3	32	16	31	188	393	n.a.	n.a.

Notes: * averages over the 1990-1995 and 1996-2000, ** data refer to 1975 and 1999, *** Gini coefficient refers to different years between 1993 and 1998, **** data refer to 1990 and 1995.

Sources: IMF: International Financial Statistics; World Bank: World Development Report, Competitiveness Indicators; UN: Human Development Report, various years.

These indicators are of interest to investors because they illustrate the resource endowment, and indicate a growing middle class, which may be demanding Western-style consumer goods. Even in a relatively poor country like India, the large numbers in the urban middle class have purchasing power meriting investment in serving them (Dawar and Chattopadhay 2002).

The last rows in Table 1.2 report data of special interest to financial investors. South Africa has the largest capital market in terms of market capitalisation, which makes it attractive for foreign portfolio investors. However, both India and Egypt have more listed domestic companies, which suggest an active local equity market. In socialist Vietnam no stock exchanges had yet been established. Foreign direct investment, which Table 1.1 shows to be of similar magnitude in the four countries, has quite a different impact relative to the size of the host economy: in Vietnam, it amounts to 4.1 per cent of GDP, while it is only 0.5 per cent in India.

Table 1.3 Country risk indices

	Egypt	India	S. Africa	Vietnam
Overall country risk	3.0	3.1	2.4	3.1
Political risk	3.0	3.5	2.5	3.0
Economic risk	3.0	3.0	2.5	3.5
Legal risk	3.5	3.0	2.0	3.0
Tax risk	3.0	2.5	1.5	3.0
Operational risk	3.0	3.0	2.0	3.5
Security risk	2.5	3.5	3.5	2.0

Note: Risk ratings, with 1=little risk, for 2002

Source: World Markets Research Centre, Country Analysis Report, 2002.

Table 1.3 reports country risk indicators by a risk consultancy agency for the four countries for different aspects of risk. Overall, South Africa is evaluated somewhat less risky for investors, except for security risk, which is high because of the high crime rate. As the EIU (2002) puts it, 'The high level of crime is perceived to be one of the obstacles to economic growth, however, studies of foreign investors' attitudes to crime present a mixed picture.' It can be seen that the other three countries appear rather similar through the lenses of financial risk analysts.

STRATEGIC MANAGEMENT ISSUES

Companies investing abroad have to take many strategic decisions on how to enter a foreign country. This includes, *inter alia*, entry mode, timing, and within-country location, which are often interdependent with operational strategic issues concerning marketing, logistics or human resource management. International business and strategic management scholars have analysed the merits of alternative forms of international entry and their implications for corporate performance. The choice of mode concerns both the resources to be employed in the new affiliate and the ownership and control over these resources. Separate lines of research have analysed alternative ownership arrangements (for example Anderson and Gatignon 1986, Buckley and Casson 1998, Tse et al. 1997), and acquisitions versus greenfield decisions (for example Barkema and Vermeulen 1998, Hennart and Park 1993, Kogut and Singh 1988). Although in practice the decisions are often intertwined, different issues have to be considered.

Our analysis takes the framework in Meyer and Estrin (2001) and the literature on entry mode choice as starting point, but also draws upon literature in international business strategy concerning post-acquisition management (Buono and Bowditch 1989, Haspeslagh and Jemison 1991, Jemison and Sitkin 1986, Birkinshaw et al. 2000), the role of subsidiaries within MNEs (for example Birkinshaw 2000), and the impact of institutions on corporate strategies (Oliver 1997, Peng 2000, Meyer 2001b). Our main focus is on how foreign investors adapt their business to a specific context. Since imperfect institutional frameworks and weak resource bases exist throughout emerging economies, investors have to accommodate these challenges by developing appropriate entry modes.

Entry Modes in Emerging Markets

Foreign investors' entry modes are commonly classified in three types, greenfield (start-up), acquisition and joint venture (JV).[3] A greenfield project entails building a subsidiary from bottom up to enable foreign sale and/or production. Real estate is purchased locally and employees are hired and trained using the investor's management, technology, know-how and capital. Acquisitions are 'purchase of stock in an already existing company in an amount sufficient to confer control' (Kogut and Singh 1988, p. 412). The new affiliate is integrated into the investing company as a going concern that normally possesses production facilities, sales force, and market share. Cross-country acquisitions have become a dominant feature of FDI worldwide, and they are also increasing as a share of inward FDI in emerging markets (see, for example, UNCTAD 2000). In the 1990s, acquisitions in emerging markets were sometimes related to privatisation, especially in Central and

Eastern Europe (for example Antal-Mokos 1998, Meyer 2002, Uhlenbruck and De Castro 2000).

An important distinction in the analysis of entry mode is the origin of the resources employed in the new operation (Meyer and Estrin 2001, Anand and Delios 2002). Whereas a greenfield uses the resources of the investor and combines them with assets acquired on local markets, an acquisition uses assets of a local firm and combines them with the investor's resources, notably managerial capabilities. A greenfield project gives the investor the opportunity to create an entirely new organisation specified to its own requirements, but usually implies a gradual market entry. In contrast, an acquisition facilitates speedy entry and immediate access to local resources, including access to local networks and business licences that help the investor to reduce transaction costs of operating in the emerging market context. However, an acquired company may require deep restructuring to overcome a lack of fit between the two organisations. In some acquisitions in emerging markets, this restructuring is so extensive that the new operation almost resembles a greenfield investment, which Meyer and Estrin (2001) call 'brownfield'. The paucity of firms and the underdeveloped nature of capital markets may also limit the possibility for acquisitions in emerging markets.

The third major mode of entry is a joint venture (JV), which implies creation of a new organisation with resource contributions from two or more parent firms. The parents share strategic and operational control of the firm. A joint venture is created as a new legal entity like a greenfield, but jointly by two or more firms that both contribute resources. Like an acquisition, a JV provides the foreign investor with access to resources of a local firm, whereas a greenfield does not. Joint ventures are designed in a variety of different ways depending on the resource availability, concerns for control, and bargaining power. Last but not least, partial acquisitions (PAs) share some characteristics with both acquisitions and joint ventures. The investor becomes involved with an existing firm rather than a newly created one, but control is shared with other shareholders.

Acquisition versus Greenfield

From a strategic management perspective, the choice between Greenfield and acquisition is foremost a decision over the origins of the resources for the new venture (Meyer and Estrin 2001, Anand and Delio 2002, Danis and Parkhe 2002). A greenfield uses resources of the investor and combines them with local assets, whereas an acquisition uses primarily assets of a local firm and combines them with the investor's. The preferred entry mode thus depends first on the resources needed, which in turn depends on the strategic objectives of the project, and second on the resources that are found (i) within the entering multinational enterprise, (ii) in unbundled form on local markets,

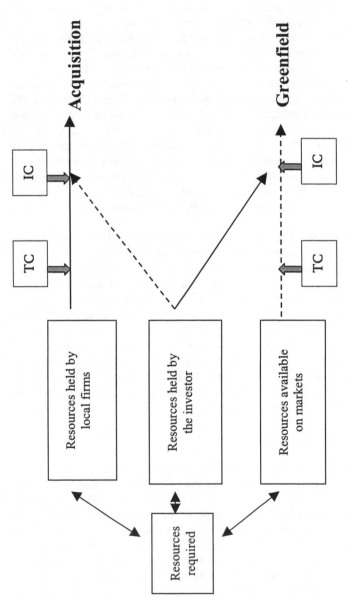

Notes: TC = Transaction costs of the relevant markets, IC = Integration Costs of adapting and integrating resources.

Source: Meyer and Estrin 2001.

Figure 1.2 A Model of Entry Mode Choice

and (iii) in bundled form in local firms (see Figure 1.2). Resources are here defined broadly, including for instance, network capital in form of relationships with other businesses or authorities.

Entry modes are influenced by transaction costs in the pertinent markets, which in turn are shaped by institutions, such as competition policy, profit repatriation rules, protection of property rights, taxation and other aspects of government intervention. Moreover, costs of restructuring and integrating acquired firms affect acquisitions, which in turn depend on, for instance, the strategic, cultural and technological fit. The capability to manage this process is built through prior experiences (for example, Buono and Bowditch 1989, Haspeslagh and Jemison 1991), the strategic and organisational fit between the acquired firm and the acquirer organisations (Kogut and Singh 1988, Birkinshaw et al. 2000), and the cultural distance between the two firms (for example Barkema et al. 1996).

In this study, we draw on both the resource-based view and transaction cost analysis in analysing mode choice. Transaction costs in emerging markets are high due to incomplete and evolving institutional frameworks governing market relationships (for example Peng 2000, Meyer 2001). Acquisitions internalise certain markets and bring together complementary resources, but these resources need to be integrated effectively (for example, Haspeslagh and Jemison 1991). Resource acquisition and absorption is of crucial importance for transformation of enterprises unable to cope with the consequences of liberalisation and privatisation (for example Kogut 1996, Uhlenbruck and De Castro 2000, Uhlenbruck et al. 2003).

Following the framework of Figure 1.2, the first aspect to be investigated concerns the strategic intent underlying the entry. The key distinction is between market-seeking and resource-seeking entry (Dunning 1993). For instance market-seeking FDI pursuing first-mover advantages may seek a local partner to provide market intelligence or access to distribution networks, brand names and market share. Resource-seeking investment may aim to utilise the local human capital to strengthen the global R&D of the investor. Our research thus reassesses how strategic objectives relate to investor's preferred entry mode in the emerging market institutional context.

Greenfield is preferred by investors competing with resources that can be transferred internally and can constitute core competences of the new business unit. These include managerial resources (Penrose 1959), financial resources (Chatterjee 1990), and capabilities with firm-specific public good properties (Caves 1971). On the other hand, resources of local firms can attract acquisition entry, for instance technological assets or market share in the target markets. Finally, local markets provide assets required in greenfield ventures, such as real estate, business licences, local blue-collar workers, and supplies of intermediate goods. Our research thus analyses the role of resources in the host economy, in particular, what kinds of resources controlled by local firms induce foreign investors to pursue a JV or an acquisition entry.

Bringing together resources previously held by different businesses incurs transaction costs either in the market for corporate control, or on local markets for complementary assets. Markets for corporate control are highly imperfect in emerging markets, which raises transaction costs of foreign acquisitions. In emerging markets, the transaction costs in equity markets can be a major constraint on foreign acquisitions. Neither can the markets for complementary resources be presumed to be efficient in emerging markets. Hence, we consider how institutions of the host economy such as infrastructure, the legal system, and regulation of FDI, affect the choice of entry strategy.

The investment is not complete with the acquisition of resources; they have to be amalgamated to create an efficient new business unit within the investors' network. Mode choice therefore has to reflect the costs and time lags required for integration and adaptation. Firms' capability to manage the post-entry integration process thus feeds back into their choice of entry strategy. Greenfield investors avoid the costs of integration, but are more sensitive to relocation costs associated with the international transfer of resources. Thus we explore how factors specific to the investing firm and its potential local target, such as emerging market expertise and psychic distance, affect the entry mode choice.

Generally, our expectation is that less developed local institutions are associated with more joint ventures, while weak local firms would lead investors to favour greenfield entry. This is in addition to investor firm-specific influences on mode choice.

Joint Ventures

A joint venture with a local partner provides access to selected resources contributed by the partner, without the responsibilities that arise from taking over an existing organisation. A new entity is created under joint ownership of two or more parent firms that all contribute in various ways to the organisation. While providing access to selected resources, a JV requires sharing of control, which many MNEs prefer to avoid. Market transactions or internal organisation provide clear governance structures, whereas JVs are subject to possible conflicts between the two parent firms that may pursue objectives that are not entirely complementary. Strategic flexibility may be greatly reduced if strategic decisions need to be cleared by all parents.

A joint venture may therefore easily conflict with other objectives of the entry. If the marketing, logistics and human resource practices have to be negotiated with a local partner, this poses severe constraints on an MNEs' ability to integrate the new operation with its global structures and processes. On the other hand, JVs are a means to accelerate entry and to gain access to crucial complementary assets more quickly than if these resources have to be acquired and built by the foreign firm internally. Hence, if timing is urgent, then market-seeking investors may prefer a JV, at least initially.

Transaction cost economists looking at alternative organisational forms, analyse why firms would prefer a JV despite the apparent disadvantages of shared control (Buckley and Casson 1976, 1998, Hennart 1988). JVs offer the opportunity to establish a business operation in a foreign country when establishment of a wholly owned affiliate is not feasible, or is too expensive. As an intermediate form between market and intra-firm coordination, a JV reduces transaction costs of the market, at the expense of coordination costs between the parents. Multinational firms often consider JVs as a second best mode of entry for emerging markets because they provide only a limited degree of control, which greatly reduces the investor's flexibility. As we have seen, shared control can lead to coordination conflicts between the partners, especially if their objectives are not compatible or cultural barriers inhibit communication. Hence, transaction cost economists argue that JVs are only used if specific conditions apply:

- The project depends on resource contributions from two or more partners;
- The markets for the contributions from the parents are subject to market failure, that is transaction costs are high;
- It is not feasible to internalise the whole operation with one partner taking over the other(s). This would apply for instance when the project is small relative to the parents, or if one of the parents is state-owned.

Anderson and Gatignon (1986) apply transaction costs in a different but complementary way, outlining the conditions when firms would prefer a high control mode, that is a JV rather than a contract, or a wholly owned affiliate rather than a JV:

- If markets fail due to high asset specificity or information asymmetry, and the partner could take advantage of this. This applies even more if the business environment is highly uncertain. Hence environmental uncertainty has a moderating effect on the primary causes of transaction costs, asset specificity and information asymmetry.
- If the firms face major obstacles to communication, or to observe and monitor independent local agents. This could for instance arise due to cultural distance.
- If the local partner could free-ride on the investor's reputation, for example use the brand name without adhering to the quality standards associated with the brand.

In emerging markets, JVs are sometimes a response to legal requirements. For example, India had placed an upper limit on the maximum share of equity that foreigners were allowed to hold in many industries, which was gradually removed over the 1990s. In the case of larger projects, ownership constraints may have to be negotiated with government authorities. The decision to set up a joint venture thus involves adaptation to local institutions, minimisation of transaction costs, optimising control, and access to resources.

Mode Dynamics

Entry strategy decisions are about more than selecting between prototypical organisational forms. The broad classifications of 'acquisition', 'greenfield', and 'joint venture' disguise a wide variety of organisational forms. Many entries can be described as hybrids of different modes, including 'brownfield' (Meyer and Estrin 1999, 2001) and partial acquisition. Moreover, initial organisational arrangements may be temporary, and from the outset, the foreign investor may prepare to replace resources, thus developing a brownfield, or to eventually fully take over a JV or a partial acquisition.

Some projects that are formally classified as acquisition in fact resemble greenfield projects. The foreign investor may initially acquire a local firm, but almost completely replace plant and equipment, labour and product line. The new operation is built primarily with resources provided by the investor. After only a short transformation period, often less than two years, the acquired local firm has gone through deep restructuring, and both its tangible assets, such as physical equipment, and its intangibles such as brand names and organisational culture have been reduced to a supplementary role. Meyer and Estrin (2001) thus propose to distinguish such entries from conventional acquisitions by defining it as follows: a brownfield is a foreign acquisition undertaken as part of the establishment of a local operation. From the outset, its resources and capabilities are primarily provided by the investor, replacing most resources and capabilities of the acquired firm.

This research aims to establish the broader relevance and the performance implication of brownfield entry strategies beyond European transition economies. The existence of brownfield FDI in other emerging markets, its underlying motives and strategies, as well as its implications are important research questions. Thus we explore how prevalent the brownfield phenomenon is across different emerging markets, and under which circumstance it emerges.

The initial ownership set-up of an FDI may change quickly. Control arrangements are known to be unstable, especially in 'staggered acquisitions' (frequently observed in privatisation) or in 'foreigners' fade-out' arrangements. JV may be time-limited from the outset, or unexpected changes in the local firm or in the foreign parent's global strategy may induce amendments of the ownership and control arrangements. Acquisitions may be implemented with stepwise ownership transfer, especially in the context of privatisation of SOEs (Meyer 2002). This study aims at refining the typology of entry modes to incorporate the post-entry dynamics and thus re-examines typologies of entry modes, giving particular attention to the dimensions of resource transfer, control, and time.

From Entry Mode Choice to Affiliate Performance

Foreign investors establish their foreign operations using the mode that most suits their needs, and one would expect that the less they have to compromise on their optimal mode, the better the performance of the operation. Managers themselves generally argue that full control would be preferred in most cases, and that joint ventures risk too many conflicts. However, this sentiment is not necessarily supported by prior empirical literature. On the other hand, acquisitions are reportedly often failing to meet their original objectives, not only in emerging markets but also in a mature market context. This has been attributed to a variety of causes, including managers underestimating the effort required to restructure and integrate the acquired firm. Given the distance of organisational cultures between the emerging markets in this study and the countries of origin of many of the investors, this issue is likely to be of particular concern.

The theoretical considerations suggest that corporate performance will be best when firms have freely chosen their entry mode in accordance with resource and transaction cost considerations, while changes in strategy to accommodate regulatory requirements, for instance a maximum foreign share in equity, would worsen corporate performance. However the study of performance implications of mode choice is complicated by the endogeneity of entry mode choice; in other words the environmental factors influencing performance also influence the selection of entry modes.

IMPACT ON HOST ECONOMIES

FDI influences the host economy in a variety of ways, including technology transfer, technology spillovers, R&D, employment quantity and quality, exports and imports, and competition. This makes it of interest to policy makers in emerging markets, and has triggered considerable research, reviewed by Altenburg (2000) and Blomström and Kokko (2002). This literature has mostly been concerned with testing the hypothesis that FDI has a positive effect on local firms in the industry or in vertically related industries. It finds horizontal spillovers in the same industries hard to establish, except in transition economies (Haddad and Harrison 1993, Aitken and Harrison 1999, Sinani and Meyer 2002).[4] However, there is strong evidence in favour of vertical spillovers (for example Smarzynska 2002). Moreover, the local industry's own technological capabilities and the 'absorptive capacity' (Cohen and Levinthal 1990) are found to be crucial for their ability to benefit from inward FDI (for example Kokko et al. 1996).

This research is largely conducted using official statistical data that do not contain information on many of the constructs that are relevant from a theoretical perspective. For instance, more information is required on the knowledge and resource transfers within the multinational firm, a precondition for technology spillovers to occur. To provide policy advice, it would be necessary to both know whether spillovers occur at an aggregate level, and what would increase them. Hence, conditions prevailing in the local economy need to be incorporated in the analysis, notably the absorptive capacity and the institutional context. Moreover, this literature rarely differentiates FDI projects when assessing its impact on local firms. The literature on FDI and spillovers thus raises many questions, some of which we address in this research, notably concerning the dynamics of resource transfers and the role of entry modes.

Entry strategies profoundly affect the ways in which foreign investors interact with the local economy, and may thus be generating beneficial spillovers. Empirical studies have addressed some of these issues in OECD countries, but no systematic evidence exists for less advanced economies. The *World Investment Report 2000* (UNCTAD 2000) reviews the available literature and infers that the long-term impact of FDI, established by different entry modes, would not differ systematically by most criteria. However, due to path dependency of networks and competence development, acquisitions tend to retain and develop existing supplier links and, as a consequence, continue to share technology with local partners.

In the short term, a number of impact parameters may differ considerably across investment projects. Greenfield investors create new businesses and have positive direct effects on employment and gross domestic investment. They may increase competitive pressures on local competitors, which induce them to improve their efficiency, or be forced to exit the market. Investors typically set up new production facilities with their own management and technology, and import machinery from their own home country. While greenfield projects require more technology and other know-how transfers, the investor is better able to control the diffusion of specialist know-how beyond the affiliate. For example, production with low-cost labour for worldwide markets uses greenfield operations, especially in specifically designed economic zones. Greenfield projects tend to have their strongest economic links with their parent and other affiliated companies, rather than with the local economy.

Greenfield moreover contributes to local capital formation, and thus to gross domestic investment possibly beyond the sum of the FDI reported in balance of payment statistics if additional local sources of funds are mobilised. However, locally raised funds can also crowd out local investment. Greenfield FDI also has direct positive effects on employment levels, since all jobs in a project are newly created. Crowding out effects of local firms that use traditional labour intensive methods of production are however possible.

Acquisitions, on the other hand, are at the time of entry existing enterprises, integrated in the host economy. They may have indigenous R&D operations, local brands, and a local supplier network, and are thus well positioned to act as relatively autonomous affiliates within a diversified MNE. Following the acquisition, traditional business relationships may or may not be continued by the new owners. Yet, even if some acquisitions discontinue local R&D, local sourcing or local brands, on average, acquired affiliates would be more local in these respects than greenfield operations. Evidence on this comes for example from Belderbos et al. (2001) who find a higher share of local content in acquired affiliates of Japanese MNEs, and to a lesser extent in their joint ventures, compared to greenfield FDI. However, crucial for an assessment of the impact is the counterfactual 'what would have happened to the firm without the acquisition?' (for example Zhan and Ozawa 2001). Investors do not necessarily have both options, greenfield and acquisition, to choose between. And, for the local firm the alternative to being acquired may not be prosperity as an independent firm.

From a theoretical perspective, the impact of acquisitions or greenfield investment differs between advanced and transition economies due to, among other factors, the technological gap, quality of resources in local firm, and development of the regulatory and institutional framework. Hence empirical research is required, as inferences from empirical studies elsewhere are only to a limited extent transferable. Table 1.4 presents a preliminary assessment based on the literature, especially UNCTAD (2000). Greenfield investments are more predictable in their development path, while post-acquisition restructuring can proceed in very different ways, dependent on the investor's strategic intent and the envisaged role of the new affiliate within the multinational network. In general, the dominant views in the literature can be summarised as follows:

- In the short term, FDI in the form of acquisitions or greenfield projects differs in its impact on the transfer of financial resources, investment, technology transfer, technology diffusion, original R&D, employment quantity and quality, employee training, exports, imports and competition, and institutional development.
- In the long term, differential impact effects of acquisition and Greenfield investment diminish, leaving no substantial and systematic differences, yet with specific exceptions. Path dependency of networks and competence development lead to persistence of differences in the use of local suppliers, technology sharing with local suppliers, and local R&D.

Table 1.4 Impact of FDI by different modes

	Short-term impact	Long-term impact
Transfer of financial resources	Acquisitions require the immediate transfer of financial resources, whereas transfers for greenfield are more likely to be stretched over time.	Considering subsequent investment and investment in restructuring, both modes may lead to transfer of financial resources to similar extent.
Investment in capital stock	Greenfield adds directly to productive capital stock, while acquisitions would only do so through subsequent restructuring investment, notably in cases of brownfield.	Subsequent investment in acquisitions may exceed that of greenfield projects. Both modes may have an indirect negative effect through crowding out local firms.
Transfer of knowledge to the affiliate	Greenfield normally requires transfer of technology or marketing knowledge (depending on purpose of the FDI), but only what is needed for the specific operation. The knowledge transferred to acquired firms may vary considerably.	Technological upgrading of affiliates is driven by the same strategic considerations and thus unlikely to differ.
Knowledge diffusion	Acquired firms with strong local links are likely to retain them, which facilitates spillovers. If local partners were weak before acquisition, linkages may be discontinued. Greenfield typically has stronger linkages with MNE, less with local firms.	Path dependency of networks and competence development suggests that differences are likely to persist.

Technology generation	Unless there are strong specific R&D capabilities locally, greenfield investors are unlikely to establish local R&D beyond adaptation of products. If an acquired firm has very strong R&D capabilities, these may be strengthened ('asset-seeking FDI'), else discontinuation and centralisation of R&D is likely.	In the long-term, location of R&D is likely to follow availability of R&D resources in the environment. Yet a path dependency effect is likely, that is acquired firms retain R&D, and an early decision of upgrading or discontinuation of R&D may have long-term effects.
Employment (quantity)	In a greenfield, every job is created new. Acquisitions may lead to reduction of employment if motivation is 'efficiency seeking' or 'short-term financial gains', or if the acquired firm has overcapacity. However, this may be 'employment saving' depending on the counterfactual.	Crowding out effects may arise from both acquisition and greenfield. Otherwise, no systematic differences between modes expected.
Employment quality	Greenfield may establish a new and thus more modern work environment, which facilitates higher quality employment, in terms of wages, work conditions, etc. Early unionisation may be less likely. Acquisitions may face inertia as older norms may persist.	No systematic differences between modes expected.
Skills, Training of workforce	Acquisitions face possible initial inertia to skill transfer, possible brain drain by moving people abroad. Greenfield has to recruit top people, often from local firms. Either way, no major differences to be expected.	No systematic differences between modes expected.

Table 1.4 (continued)

	Short-term impact	Long-term impact
Exports	Acquisitions typically continue to serve the existing local markets. Greenfield is often established either to use factor cost advantages for global markets, or to serve the local market.	No systematic differences between modes expected.
Imports	Acquisitions build on local supplier linkages if these are good quality. Greenfield rely to a larger extent on imports (e.g. Belderbos et al. 2001).	Path dependency of networks and competence development suggests that differences are likely to persist.
Market structure	A greenfield entry as such reduces concentration, and enhances competition. The impact of acquisition or brownfield entry crucially depends on the market position of the acquiring firm prior to the acquisition.	International mergers may join foreign affiliates and thus reduce competition, thus acquisition entails a risk of negative impact on competition. Otherwise, the dynamics of competition in the local market may lead to crowding out effects or subsequent entry independent of how the foreign firm entered.
Competitive behaviour	Not expected to vary by mode.	Not expected to vary by mode.

Source: UNCTAD 2000, and own extensions

	Egypt	India	South Africa	Vietnam
Services	ECMS (telecom)	ABN Amro (banking)	ABN Amro (banking)	N
Food & beverages	Heinz (ketchup)	Bacardi-Martini (spirits)	N	SEAB / Carlsberg (brewing)
Manufacturing, intermediate products	N	Packaging (packaging)	NGK / Behr (automotive suppliers)	ABB (electrical components)
Manufacturing, final products	GlaxoSmith-Kline (pharma-ceuticals)	N	EST (electrical equipment)	Honda (motorcycles)

Figure 1.3 Case studies

RESEARCH APPROACH AND OUTLINE OF THIS BOOK

We aim at gaining a comprehensive perspective on the issues and thus use multiple complementary research methods. In each of the four countries of this study, we have conducted three case studies, and a questionnaire survey with at least 150 received responses for each. Moreover background papers review the pertinent institutional and economic environment as well as trends of FDI and their entry modes. Researchers affiliated with leading local institutions, have conducted this research in close coordination with the research team at London Business School.

The case studies were conducted on the basis of a common framework that has been developed jointly, and modified on the basis of initial reports on cases of FDI. This framework established key issues that the field research teams were to consider for each case, including the multinational investor, the local partners, the entry motives and modes, the institutional environment, post-entry restructuring processes, as well as corporate performance and spillovers. In each country, the cases include two manufacturing cases and, except for Vietnam, one service company (Figure 1.3). The case studies consider both local and foreign perspectives and, being prepared by local partners, avoid the common bias of FDI research, focusing on the perspective and information provided by the foreign investor only.

The survey has been conducted with a common research instrument that has been translated to local languages where appropriate. In all countries the sample includes all FDI established between 1990-2000, that have at least 10 employees and foreign equity participation of 10 per cent. To coordinate the research, to discuss the research questions and to design the common research instruments, the research teams met four times between November 2000 and March 2003, including a field research workshop in Cairo that concentrated on local perspectives and information provided by foreign investors.

This book presents the research following the following structure: The next chapter summarises and interprets the data obtained in the survey study in a comparative perspective, and thus sets the stage for discussing patterns for the individual country analyses. Chapters 3 to 10 present the results for each of the countries, following a common structure. Each country is introduced with an overview of key contextual issues that may influence FDI, and a summary of key findings from the survey in that country. The second chapter for each country presents three in-depth case studies of foreign investors. The book concludes with two chapters that draw inferences and practical implications respectively for managers in multinational firms and their local partners, and for policy makers at the national and multinational level.

2. Foreign Direct Investment in Egypt, India, South Africa and Vietnam: Comparative Empirical Results[5]

Saul Estrin and Klaus E. Meyer

INTRODUCTION

In this chapter, we compare and contrast the characteristics, determinants and performance of foreign direct investments (FDI) in the four emerging markets of our study – Egypt, India, South Africa and Vietnam. The findings emerge from a large-scale survey project which was designed to study the business environment; the mode of entry of FDI; the subsequent performance of investing firms; and the broader impact of FDI on the host economies (see Chapter 1). Our analysis in this chapter is primarily comparative and draws on findings from the survey of over 600 firms, comprising 147 from Egypt, 147 from India, 162 from South Africa and 170 from Vietnam. Detailed discussions of the findings from each country are contained in subsequent chapters.

The underlying conceptual framework for our analysis has been outlined with reference to Figure 1.1 in the previous chapter, which draws on the work of Meyer and Estrin (2001). Our approach is to model the strategic choice by a multinational firm about where and how to place their overseas investment as being driven by the various elements of the business environment in the host economy to complement firm and industry specific issues explored in the strategic management literature. This includes a large number of facets, including the level of institutional development, the legal structure, the policy framework and the physical infrastructure. A crucial question for each investing firm concerns the balance of advantage and disadvantage resulting from these factors in each alternative host location. The investing firm needs to be able to purchase or obtain sufficient resources in order to function successfully, and the factors determining where these resources are obtained will depend in part upon the character of the investing firm itself. For example, a firm with considerable multinational experience and rich in intangible assets may be in a position to provide many resources itself, and *ceteris paribus* is more likely to enter as a greenfield operation. Firms with less experience, smaller or less well endowed in intangible assets, may instead choose to purchase a higher proportion of these assets from the host economy. But there remain a number of important choices to make. The resources could be obtained by outright acquisition of an existing firm. This could be done in totality, or only partially. Alternatively the potential entrant could create a new venture jointly with an existing firm. From this decision tree, we identify the four main 'modes of entry' available to investing firms: greenfield entry, acquisition, partial acquisition and joint venture.

In the following section, we describe the characteristics of the four-country enterprise sample in terms of sectoral distribution, size, and parent firm location. We go on in the third section to contrast the modes of entry in the different countries, which we link to the motivations for FDI and to the resources available to the investing firms and from the host economies. Managers' perceptions of the business environment in the host economies are compared and evaluated in the fourth section, which considers input markets and infrastructure as well as political and institutional arrangements. The comparative performance of foreign subsidiaries in the four host economies is the subject of the fifth section, and conclusions and implications for the remainder of the study are drawn in the sixth.

HOST AND SOURCE FIRM CHARACTERISTICS

In this section, we compare the characteristics of the sample in each of the four countries in terms of the sectors, the size of enterprises and the regions from which the parent firms originate. In Table 2.1 we report the distribution of industries by country of the FDI projects. The data refer to the number of firms, not to value of investments. The primary sector investment is found to be everywhere only a small proportion of the foreign investment, representing around 3 per cent of the total. As our sample covers only developing economies one might have expected a high proportion for example in mining. As this is a capital-intensive sector, we find that the primary sector represents a slightly higher proportion of investment to South Africa, measured in terms of capital value (4 per cent). There are also important inter-country differences in terms of the sectors receiving FDI. Investment into Vietnam conforms to a more traditional view of FDI into developing countries, being in manufacturing industry, and within this sector, to basic consumer and intermediate goods. In contrast, investment in manufacturing in India and South Africa has been directed towards the machinery and equipment sector and, to a lesser extent, into intermediate goods. In all four countries, the service sector, (especially finance), is important but South Africa and Egypt have higher proportions of foreign affiliates in this sector than do India and Vietnam. Indeed, more than a fifth of all firms entering South Africa go into the financial and business service sector, as against only 7 per cent in Vietnam and 13 per cent in India. Egypt and Vietnam also have considerable entry into the trade and tourism sector, in excess of 10 per cent of the total in both cases; and entry into infrastructure and construction is also comparatively high in Egypt (18 per cent). Finally, it is worth underlining the high proportion of investment into the IT sector in India in recent years. Since 1991, we find almost 20 per cent of the total number of Indian foreign affiliates enter that industry, which is consistent with the public awareness about the rapid growth of the Indian software industry (see Commander (2004)) and Desai (2003)).

Table 2.1 Cross Country distribution of affiliates by sector (% of affiliates)

Sector	Egypt	India	South Africa	Vietnam
Primary	3	3	3	4
Basic consumer goods	13	12	13	36
Intermediate goods	15	16	14	27
Machinery & equipment	10	26	19	8
Infrastructure & construction	18	6	12	2
Trade, tourism & recreation	15	1	5	13
Financial & business services	18	13	21	7
Information technology (IT)	5	19	8	1
Pharmaceuticals	3	5	5	2

In Table 2.2, we report the size distribution by employment of foreign subsidiaries in each country, using five employment categories ranging from 10 to 50 workers to companies with more than 1,000 workers. Our sampling strategy excludes firms with fewer than 10 workers. We also provide information on the growth of the foreign affiliates by showing employment at the date when the company commenced operations (start of business) as well as in 2001.

Contrary to common perception, most FDI projects in all our sample countries are relatively small, employing fewer than 100 workers on average. This could represent either a lack of comparative advantage in heavy industry or the existence of barriers to entry, for example government regulations or powerful domestic incumbents. The finding suggests that governments should not look immediately to FDI as a motor to create employment in emerging markets, especially in India and Egypt where median employment at the time of entry was only 30 and 40 workers respectively. However, employment in foreign owned subsidiaries in all our countries is growing rapidly. Everywhere except Vietnam, the majority of affiliate firms started with fewer than 100 employees and only in South Africa did more than 25 per cent of firms start operations employing more than 250 empoyees.

Table 2.2 Cross-country size distribution of affiliates (% of affiliates): employment and capital

Employees	Egypt		India		South Africa		Vietnam	
	Start of business	2000	Start of business	2000	Start of business	2000	Start of business	2000
10-50	58	38	65	46	40	31	33	24
51-100	9	19	12	18	16	23	27	24
101-250	15	18	18	19	22	16	21	20
251-1000	12	18	5	16	14	20	17	27
More than 1000	6	6	0	1	9	10	2	5
Total	100	100	100	100	100	100	100	100
Median no. Employees	40	73	30	56	76	90	85	127
Median size of fixed capital stock (US$ million)	N	1.45	N	0.69	N	1.67	N	1.20

This is probably associated with the higher proportion of acquisitions in South Africa. On average, foreign affiliates are somewhat larger in Vietnam than in all the other countries, and this was true from the start of operations. This reflects the more labour intensive production that results from the relative factor endowment of Vietnam, as well as the sectoral distribution, with a higher proportion of basic manufacturing industry.

Looking at the size distribution of foreign affiliates in terms of capital stock paints a similar picture. The median values in 2000 are also reported in Table 2.2. In all the countries, fixed assets of foreign affiliates are valued at less than US$2 million for the majority of firms. The proportion of 'small investments (valued below US$2 million) is the largest in Vietnam and India (67 per cent), though these differences could merely reflect variation in cross-country purchasing power and the sectoral distribution. However, one fifth of all investments into South Africa had fixed assets valued at more than US$10 million in 2001, as against between 10 and 13 per cent in the other three countries. The data on median capital stock is consistent with that on median employment, with South African subsidiaries significantly larger than in the other three countries, especially than in India and Egypt.

In Table 2.3 we compare the distribution of parent firms' home countries. For ease of comparison, we have grouped the enormous numbers of source countries (more than forty) into five. Though the leading source economies are common to all countries, regional factors have significantly influenced the pattern of FDI.

Thus we find the largest proportion of investing firms is almost always from Europe and North America. These two regions account for 80 per cent of total FDI into India and South Africa and 63 per cent into Egypt. However, 78 per cent of investment into Vietnam derives from its 'own' region of East Asia; this is a region which only provides 14 to 15 per cent of foreign affiliates into India and South Africa and a mere 2 per cent in Egypt. Moreover, in Egypt, around one third of total numbers of investments come from the Middle East and North Africa, but this region invests virtually not at all in the other surveyed countries. Regional investors appear to play little or no role in investments to South Africa and India – perhaps because they are not so closely integrated into their regional rather than into the global economy, and because of the size of the home market, especially for India.

ENTRY STRATEGIES

We have argued that firms decide how to enter foreign markets according to the balance of advantage between the alternative ways of creating overseas subsidiaries: Greenfield entry, partnership with a local firm (joint venture) or by acquiring part or all of an existing organisation (partial or full acquisition).

Table 2.3 Cross-country geographic distribution of parent firms
          (% of parent firms)

Home region of parent firm	Egypt	India	South Africa	Vietnam
North America	19	31	23	5
Europe	44	50	57	15
East Asia, inclusive Japan	2	14	15	78
Middle East and North Africa (MENA)	33	4	0	1
Other (including Australia)	2	2	6	2

As the entry mode varies, one would expect the investing firm to be purchasing differing amounts and forms of resources from the domestic markets of the home and host economies and using differing quantities of its own resources. Investing firms might therefore rely on greenfield modes of entry relatively more if resources were more easily available in host economy markets and could be more easily transferred from the investing firm, or if there were fewer opportunities to equip firms in the host economy. On the other hand, acquisition might be used relatively more frequently if there was an abundance of suitable firms available in the host economy, and these had appropriate brands, supply networks, distribution networks and so forth which would be expensive for the entering firm to replicate for themselves.

We report the distribution of entry modes by country in Table 2.4. As we show in the later chapters, entry mode choices in our sample countries are not always unconstrained. In particular, regulations limited full ownership or acquisition in India and Vietnam for some of the period in some sectors. While acquisition is the most significant mode of entry in developed countries (see for example UNCTAD (2002)), it is less common in less developed economies and also in our sample. Thus greenfield and joint venture are found to be the dominant modes of entry in Egypt, India and Vietnam. Taken together, these represent around 80 per cent of all FDI entry in the past decade in these three countries. However, there are some interesting differences in the pattern between these countries. For example, we find relatively more entry via joint venture in India and more greenfield in Vietnam. South Africa is very different to the other three, however, with around one third of all entry by acquisition, and less than a third being greenfield. This contrasts especially with Vietnam, where more than half of all entry is greenfield, or Egypt, where the proportion is 46 per cent.

This seems to suggest that, compared to developed economies, in emerging markets as a whole, foreign entrants rely relatively more on their own resources than on what can be purchased in the local marketplace, either unbundled or as a bundle of resources (that is through acquisition).

Table 2.4 Cross-country distribution of affiliates by mode of entry (% of affiliates)

Mode of entry	Egypt	India	South Africa	Vietnam
Greenfield	46	35	31	56
Joint Venture	37	54	23	32
Acquisition	5	4	31	2
Partial Acquisition	12	6	14	11*

Note: In Vietnam, some joint ventures are created with the transfer of an existing operation to the newly created company. We report them here under partial acquisition, as due to legal constraints we found no partial acquisitions in the sample. (See Chapter 9.)

South Africa differs from this pattern, perhaps because it has a more developed network of incumbent firms and a more developed market, both of which facilitate entry by acquisition. India has more entries by joint venture than any of the other four countries (54 per cent) and this probably reflects the heritage of legal requirements – and the peculiarities of the host business environment.

The literature (see for example Dunning (1993)) categorises the motives for FDI into 'efficiency-seeking', for example for skilled labour, 'resource-seeking' (for raw materials) and 'market-seeking', for example producing for the local market. Our survey yields a categorisation of motives that partially maps into this framework. Questions in our survey allow us to identify the two standard entry motives, and additionally permit us to subdivide the market-seeking category into a further three groups which might be relevant to an emerging market. We report in Table 2.5, data on the share of output exported, at the time of entry and currently, to distinguish between market and efficiency or resource-seeking entry modes. If the primary objective is exporting (in which case the motive for entry was efficiency or resource-seeking), the new subsidiary could have been created either to serve the global market; or a regional market, with the new entry as a hub; or as a source of inputs for the global firm itself, in an integrated vertical supply chain. Given the small share of the primary sector in our sample, we can interpret export-oriented entry as primarily efficiency-seeking. If the primary objective for the new entrants is to serve the host domestic market, the motive for entry is probably market-seeking. We allow for all these categories in Table 2.5.

Perhaps surprisingly, we find efficiency-seeking to have been the dominant motivation for entry in only one of four economies, Vietnam, though it was also important in India. This contrasts with the findings in UNCTAD (2002), which stresses the role of efficiency and resource-seeking

FDI in developing economies as a whole. Perhaps the modest FDI performance of our sample countries noted in the first chapter may in part be explained by the fact that efficiency-seeking entry is relatively less advantageous in them. It also appears that firms made and stuck to the strategic decision about whether production is primarily destined to be exported or for the home market prior to entry, since the proportions of sales exported do not alter greatly between the date of entry and 2001.

If we look first at South Africa and Egypt, the bulk of firms in our survey were set up primarily to serve domestic markets; only around 20 per cent of sales were exported at the start of operations, though this had risen in South Africa by six percentage points by 2001. This focus on domestic market by foreign affiliates is probably associated with the sectoral pattern of FDI: for example, in Egypt, with the concentration on tourism and services. Even in 2001, only around a quarter of FDI in Egypt and South Africa could be viewed as 'efficiency-seeking'.

When we consider the categories of efficiency-seeking entry, a significant proportion in Egypt (nearly half) is found to be serving the regional market, but in South Africa we find relatively more exports are destined for the global market. However, interestingly, we find that in recent years the regional market is also becoming more important, at least relative to when firms first entered in South Africa. Perhaps this suggests that South Africa is beginning to become more integrated into the broader African market since the collapse of the apartheid regime in the mid-1990s.

Surprisingly, given the size of its domestic market, India has a higher share of FDI focused towards exports than Egypt or South Africa, though more than 60 per cent of sales by foreign affiliates remained destined for the home market. Of the 36 per cent of Indian sales that are exported, on average, nearly half are directed into the global economy, while the regional market is much less important. But the survey suggests that India also serves as a relatively important location for production along the supply chain for some multinationals, since around one quarter of the exports by subsidiaries in India are destined for other affiliates of the parent firm. The export orientation to other affiliates is unsurprisingly particularly concentrated in the IT sector, suggesting a lot of investment probably represents relocation of back office and software development activities.

We find investment into Vietnam to have been motivated by rather different factors from those in the other three countries; efficiency-seeking is the majority objective. The average proportion of product exported is 50 per cent, and has been at this level for firms since the start of operations. This orientation towards efficiency-seeking investment perhaps helps to explain the sectoral distribution, which is concentrated on basic manufacturing. It may also be explained by the geographical distribution of parent firms, located largely in the South East Asia. Policy has been focused to promoting exports as well. This interpretation is strengthened when one notes that

Table 2.5 Market focus of affiliates (% of sales)

Market focus	Egypt		India		South Africa		Vietnam	
	Start of business	2000	Start of business	2000	Start of business	2000	Start of business	2000
Percentage of sales exported	23	26	36	37	19	25	51	50
Of which:								
Regional market	10	12	6	7	4	10	25	24
Global market	10	10	20	20	11	12	20	20
Other affiliates	3	4	10	10	4	3	6	6

Table 2.6 Cross-country evaluation of the three most important resources
for success (% of affiliates)

Resource	Egypt	India	South Africa	Vietnam
Brands	32	31	36	20
Business networks	30	27	34	23
Distribution networks	13	20	25	22
Equity	11	30	14	25
Machinery	19	13	19	36
Management	47	34	40	52
Marketing	33	26	32	29
Technology	50	48	39	29

almost half of exports are destined for regional markets and a further 12 per cent to parent firms.[6]

The questionnaire asked firms to rank the resources they regarded as important for their competitiveness. Though we offered fourteen choices, only eight were consistently reported as being critical by our respondents. These fell into five categories: financial (provision of equity financing); technological (technology); intangible assets (brands, business and distribution networks, marketing); tangible assets (machinery) and management. In all four countries, we find that brands, management and technology are always considered to be the crucial resource underlying the success of foreign investments, though the exact ranking differs somewhat from country to country. Brands are seen as the most important resource for success by foreign affiliates in Egypt, India and South Africa, while equity is ranked as the most significant resource for success for foreign affiliates in Vietnam, second most important in India, and third in Egypt and South Africa. Indian respondents rank technology as the critical resource for success, as do Egyptian managers, but it is ranked only third in South Africa and Vietnam. Interestingly, factors that one might expect to be contributed by a host economy partner – for example networks, machinery or marketing – are rarely seen as the critical factors for success in the survey.

One obtains a richer picture by focusing on the leading three rather than the single critical resource for success identified by our respondents. In this case, we see from Table 2.6 that technology is ranked above all other resources in Egypt and India, and it is ranked in second and third places in South Africa and Vietnam respectively. Management, which is rarely considered to be the leading single resource for success, is most frequently included as one of the most important factors, using this criterion, in South Africa and especially in Vietnam, where more than half of our respondents list it in their top three resources. Management is also ranked second in Egypt (where 47 per cent of respondents place it in their top three resources) and South Africa. Other important factors listed in the top three resources include intangibles (marketing and brands). In Vietnam, machinery is also considered important. It is mostly provided by foreign investors and entails embedded technology transfer.

This perception by the managers of key resources for success appears in line with what one might expect given the observed motives for investment and the sectoral distribution of foreign affiliates. For example, in Vietnam, FDI entrants have concentrated relatively more on industrial commodity production for export, so it is not surprising that we find the critical resources to be perceived by managers of subsidiaries as being management, technology and fixed assets; brands have played less of a role. However for the market-seeking investors into Egypt and South Africa, technology and brands as well as management have proved to be the source of competitive advantage. The importance of technology in India as a critical resource for success probably arises because there is relatively more high-tech investment there.

In Figures 2.1 to 2.3, we investigate how firms obtain the resources that they regard as critical for the success of their investments, based on the three most important sources. As one might expect, we find in Figure 2.1 that local firms do not in general supply technology, equity or brands. Though they typically provide distribution and business networks and marketing skills. In Egypt, local firms supply relatively more of the key resources in marketing, management, business and domestic enterprise and distribution networks than in any other country, perhaps reflecting the character of investing firms into the Middle East and North Africa. Local firms supply relatively less of everything in Vietnam, presumably indicating the weaker business environment. The relatively more developed state of the South African business sector is illustrated by the relatively greater local provision of machinery and management, though in fact South Africa and India prove to be quite similar in terms of the local firm contributions over a wide variety of resources. Figure 2.2 provides information on the contribution of the foreign parent firms. Here, we observe the converse picture to Figures 2.1. The foreign firms supply equity, brands, technology and management, but usually rather less in terms of marketing, distribution and business networks. In Figure 2.3 we look at the role of the local market as a source of resources, and observe that these do play an important role especially in the more developed economies of our sample – Egypt, India and South Africa in terms of the business and distribution networks and to a lesser extent of management.

EVALUATION OF THE HOST BUSINESS ENVIRONMENT

Our approach highlights the potential impact of the business environment on foreign investment decisions. We have focused on foreign affiliate managers' evaluations of the quality of the host country's labour force; the quality of the local inputs; and on the institutional environment. Their perceptions measured on a scale from 1 to 5 are summarised in Tables 2.7 to 2.9. Overall, we find considerable within-country variations relative to between-country variations, with standard deviations for most of the indices reported below in the range of 0.9 to 1.2. Differences thus should be seen only as indicative of underlying patterns in the environment.

Table 2.7 reports managers' evaluation of labour markets for four categories of labour ranging from skilled manual workers through to executive management. Perhaps surprisingly for emerging markets, these are all evaluated relatively highly on average, frequently above a level of 4.0.

Moreover, despite the differences in development level and educational attainment, there is surprisingly little variation of these managerial assessments of the business environment across countries and over time. This suggests that foreign firms are either sufficiently small or pay sufficiently high wages to avoid fundamental constraints on the supply side of the labour market. However, Vietnam was rated somewhat below the other countries at the date of starting operations, and it had not closed the gap by 2000. The difference is particularly marked with respect to executive management. It is possible that the Vietnamese scores are affected by the transition from central planning to a market economy, which acted to exacerbate existing shortages in management by creating a demand for market economy based managers and leadership skills.

Considering Table 2.7 in more detail, we find that labour markets are evaluated at around 3.8 to 3.9 in three of the four countries at the start of operations, with Vietnam substantially lower at 3.3, primarily because of weaknesses in the availability of executive managers. The situation is perceived as improving markedly up to 2000 in Egypt, India and Vietnam, with Egypt and India rated on average at that time well above 4.0 in each sub-category (except for executive management in India at 3.9). However, despite considerable improvement in all four categories, labour availability in Vietnam in 2001 is still rated below the levels attained in the other three countries up to a decade earlier.

Though labour availability is rated quite highly in South Africa at the time when foreign affiliates commenced their operations – the levels are comparable to India and slightly below Egypt – the situation did not improve from then until 2001. This has led to deterioration in South Africa's relative position in terms of labour availability by 2000. In all four countries, executive management is evaluated as being the hardest to obtain both at the start of operations and in 2000.

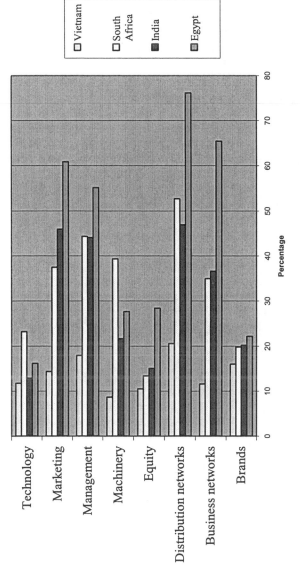

Figure 2.1 Local firms source of three most important resources

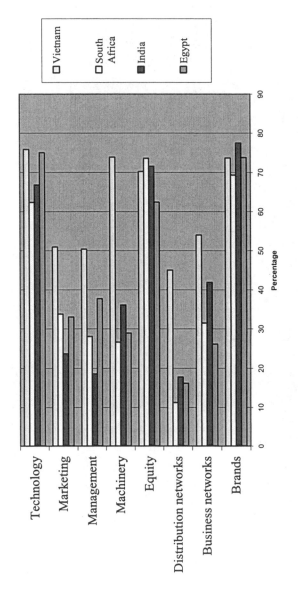

Figure 2.2 Foreign parent source of three most important resources

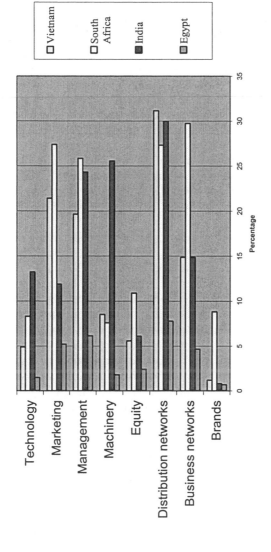

Figure 2.3 Other local source of three most important resources

Turning to local inputs in Table 2.8, we find South Africa to be perceived by managers of foreign affiliates to provide a better business environment across the board in terms of the six indicators reported: quality of raw materials and machinery; the ability to obtain real estate; the quality of professionals; the reliability of information technology and the telecommunications network; and finally, the reliability of utilities, such as electricity. This is true at both the start and the end of the period, though, as in Table 2.7, we observe considerable improvements in the evaluations of local inputs in Egypt, India and Vietnam but very little in South Africa. Hence, by the end of the period, the most advanced other country, India, is attaining evaluations comparable to South Africa at the start.

The most serious problems in the local environment noted by managers of foreign firms in Table 2.8 at the start of operations concern machinery and components in Egypt, telecommunications and IT in India and, raw materials, components and machinery in South Africa and Vietnam. Real estate is also a source of difficulty to inward investors in Egypt, India and Vietnam. The greatest perceived improvement from the date of entry to the current time is perceived to be in IT and telecommunications, especially in India, and Egypt. Problems of machinery and components persist in Egypt and Vietnam, and are exacerbated slightly in South Africa, but we observe some slight improvement in India.

In Table 2.9 we report managers' perceptions about another crucial set of issues for investors into emerging markets – the institutional and policy environment. This is evaluated in three categories: the quality of government at the local, provincial and central level; the predictability of the policy framework; and the quality of the institutional structure. In the latter category we include the legal framework and environmental regulations as well as several important specific issues concerning visas, property and business licensing.

Managers' evaluations of the host economy business environment are somewhat lower on average than we observed in the previous two tables. The average evaluation of the institutional environment in every country is not much above 3 on a 1-5 scale, and, in fact, a number of observations are in the 2's ('not very conducive'). Moreover, except in Vietnam, there is little real evidence of improvement in these crucial areas for foreign investors; indeed the situation is perceived on average as deteriorating very slightly in South Africa and is unchanged in Egypt between the time of entry by foreign affiliates and 2000, though there is modest improvement in India and Vietnam.

When we dig deeper into the detailed questions, we find interesting institutional differences across the four countries. In some aspects the quality of the institutional environments are seen to be reasonable (that is above 3.5), for example in Egypt (environmental regulations) and South Africa (real estate and environment). Indeed in all four countries, one or another indicator of the institutional environment group is ranked above 3.0 (that is visas and environmental regulations in India and Vietnam). However, the general legal framework is perceived to be not conducive (less than 3.0) in Egypt and Vietnam, and only in South Africa does it approach a satisfactory level (nearly 3.5). Moreover improvements to the institutional environment have at the very best been modest, and often non-existent. The only exception is Vietnam, where things had improved somewhat by 2000 in terms of business licensing, real estate and visas. Interestingly, at the time when most of our sample of foreign affiliates started operations, Vietnam ranked very poorly in terms of the institutional environment, but by the end of the period it had overtaken all the other countries in this regard except for South Africa. The same period saw South Africa perceived as deteriorating slightly in terms of the institutional environment, particularly with respect to visas and work permits.

Turning to predictability of the business environment, this was also perceived to be poor by managers of affiliates at the time when operations began in three of the four countries; only in South Africa was predictability above 3.0 on the 1-5 scale and in no countries did it exceed 4.0. Moreover, predictability of the business and policy environment has not been perceived by foreign investors as improving over the period to 2000 in any country but Vietnam. Indeed we find there has been a slight deterioration in the evaluation of the predictability of policy in Egypt and South Africa, though it is found to be improving slightly in India. Even so, the evaluation there remains low – only 2.79 on the 1-5 scale.

Finally, we report the evaluations of the quality of government. Once again, this is found to be very poor in Egypt and for local government in India, but somewhat better in Vietnam and South Africa. India in particular appears to have considerably improved foreign business perceptions of the quality of its central government, but not of its provincial or local government. The perception of quality of all levels of government has improved sharply in Vietnam between the start of its operations of the foreign affiliates and 2000, and interestingly the quality of Vietnamese government is now perceived to be highest of our four sample countries. It might be that the Vietnamese government at all levels has been striving to become more 'business friendly' and open to foreign investors, leading also to the improvements in policy related aspects of the institutional environment (for example visas and real estate) as well as predictability. We find a slight decline in the evaluation of government quality in Egypt and South Africa over this period, paralleling the previously noted decline in predictability.

Our findings in Table 2.9 are symptomatic of the institutional weaknesses perceived by foreign investors into emerging markets and probably explain the relatively poor overall FDI performance in our sample countries, relative to the 'starts' of emerging markets such as China.

Table 2.7 Cross-country labour market evaluations

Type of personnel	Egypt			India			South Africa			Vietnam		
	Start of business	2000	Change	Start of business	2000	Change	Start of business	2000	Change	Start of business	2000	Change
Executive management	3.66	4.01	0.35	3.51	3.91	0.40	3.48	3.56	0.08	2.59	2.87	0.28
Professionals	4.08	4.37	0.29	4.04	4.37	0.33	4.15	4.11	-0.04	3.57	3.82	0.25
Operational management	3.85	4.25	0.40	3.77	4.23	0.46	3.75	3.76	0.01	3.42	3.65	0.23
Skilled non managerial labour	4.17	4.42	0.25	4.01	4.36	0.35	3.95	4.03	0.08	3.79	4.03	0.24
Mean	3.94	4.26	0.32	3.83	4.22	0.39	3.83	3.87	0.04	3.34	3.59	0.25

Note: 1 = never available, 5 = readily available

Table 2.8a Cross-country local input evaluations

Local input	Egypt			India		
	Start of business	2000	Change	Start of business	2000	Change
Utilities	4.07	4.45	0.38	3.52	3.80	0.28
IT and telecoms	3.66	4.42	0.76	3.17	4.14	0.97
Professional services	4.03	4.15	0.12	3.94	4.44	0.50
Real estate	3.98	4.16	0.18	3.83	4.20	0.37
Machinery	2.86	3.19	0.33	3.68	4.21	0.53
Raw materials and components	2.87	3.08	0.21	3.40	3.91	0.51
Mean	3.58	3.91	0.33	3.59	4.12	0.53

Table 2.8b Cross-country local input evaluations

Local input	South Africa			Vietnam		
	Start of business	2000	Change	Start of business	2000	Change
Utilities	4.55	4.63	0.08	3.43	3.86	0.43
IT and telecoms	4.06	4.27	0.21	3.35	3.87	0.52
Professional services	4.44	4.48	0.04	3.69	4.04	0.35
Real estate	4.47	4.51	0.04	3.68	3.83	0.15
Machinery	3.77	3.85	0.08	3.11	3.45	0.34
Raw materials and components	3.51	3.46	-0.05	3.09	3.42	0.33
Mean	4.13	4.20	0.07	3.39	3.75	0.36

Note: 1 = never available, 5 = readily available

PERFORMANCE OF FOREIGN INVESTMENTS

We asked several questions to our respondents about the performance of their subsidiaries, all of which were perceptual and ranked on a scale from 1-5. We explored performance in terms of productivity, profitability and growth in revenue of the subsidiary, and the findings are summarised in Table 2.10. The average scores are fairly high in every country. This may be encouraging

Table 2.9a Cross-country institutional environment evaluations

Institutional factor	Egypt			India		
	Start of business	2000	Change	Start of business	2000	Change
Business licences	3.06	3.12	0.06	2.92	3.38	0.46
Real estate	3.40	3.59	0.19	3.09	3.41	0.32
Visa and work permits	3.36	3.40	0.04	3.12	3.42	0.30
Environmental regulation	3.60	3.62	0.02	3.11	3.13	0.02
General legal framework	2.95	2.92	-0.03	3.03	3.14	0.11
Predictability	2.87	2.67	-0.20	2.71	2.79	0.08
Central government	2.89	2.87	-0.02	3.07	3.33	0.26
Local government	2.97	2.91	-0.06	2.93	3.05	0.12
Mean	3.14	3.14	0.00	3.00	3.19	0.19

Table 2.9b Cross-country institutional environment evaluations

Institutional factor	South Africa			Vietnam		
	Start of business	2000	Change	Start of business	2000	Change
Business licenses	3.70	3.80	0.10	3.21	3.75	0.54
Real estate	4.04	4.10	0.06	2.91	3.32	0.41
Visa and work permits	3.00	2.77	-0.23	3.21	3.62	0.41
Environmental regulation	3.63	3.56	-0.07	3.30	3.47	0.17
General legal framework	3.49	3.33	-0.16	2.88	3.27	0.39
Predictability	3.65	3.58	-0.07	2.80	3.15	0.35
Central government	3.32	3.26	-0.06	3.23	3.59	0.36
Local government	3.39	3.27	-0.12	3.11	3.40	0.29
Mean	3.51	3.44	-0.07	3.10	3.46	0.36

Note: 1 = not at all conducive, 5 = very conducive

Table 2.10 Comparative company performance, cross-country

Performance indicator	Egypt	India	South Africa	Vietnam
Productivity	3.82	3.90	3.84	3.43
Profitability	3.26	3.28	3.46	2.64
Revenue growth	3.42	3.28	3.77	3.02
Mean	3.50	3.49	3.69	3.03

Notes: 1 = performance expectations not met at all, 5 = performance
expectations entirely fulfilled

news for foreign investors into developing countries but such conclusions must be treated with caution since there may be a selection bias; firms that were relatively successful in their FDI entry are the ones more likely to have responded to the questionnaire. Moreover the firms best positioned to succeed in the difficult business environment of emerging markets may be the ones that chose to invest in our sample countries. However, the variations across countries and by sector and entry mode are of interest.

Performance in productivity was on average ranked highest among the performance measures, being evaluated above 3 in all countries and in three of the four countries above 3.5. The only other performance indicator to score above 3.5 in Table 2.10 was the evaluation of revenue growth in South Africa. Interestingly, performance in profitability everywhere is seen on average as quite disappointing, being evaluated below 3.5, though this may reflect gestation periods. These rankings suggest performance is not quite as good as the raw data suggests, and that perhaps a priori assumptions about the business environment in emerging markets are too optimistic, especially if firms are inexperienced. The cross-country variation persistently gives a ranking in which Vietnam is at the bottom in terms of performance, but different countries are at the top, depending on the performance criteria used. India dominates in terms of productivity and South Africa in terms of profitability and revenue growth. This indicates that despite recent improvements in the environment it remains hard to make profits in less developed economies like Vietnam, but is easier in more developed countries like that of South Africa. However, it is interesting that, on average, the cross-country differences are not found to be very great. We also find little variation in performance by sector or entry mode, and these tables are not reported.

A second indicator of the performance of FDI from the perspective of a government in the host economy would be spillovers from the investment. To address this issue, we consider the extent of training, which is potentially of great significance in emerging markets because the training offered to the labour force by foreign-owned firms could be an important source of

Table 2.11 Value of training expenditure, cross-country (% of sales)

Training indicator	Egypt	India	South Africa	Vietnam
Total training expenditure	2.32	2.13	2.54	1.89
Management training	1.67	1.77	1.74	1.58
Non-management training	1.74	1.73	2.21	1.55
Internal training	1.82	1.76	2.17	1.68
Average	1.89	1.85	2.17	1.68

improved labour quality and productivity across the entire economy, as labour flows from the foreign subsidiary to other firms.

The comparative findings are reported in Table 2.11, which show the share of training over the percentage of sales in the four countries in four categories. We find training expenditures to be very modest, in terms of the share of sales, in all the countries, though far from insignificant. Training in all categories represents a higher percentage of sales, and therefore potential for spillovers, in South Africa, followed closely by India and Egypt. There is less training undertaken in Vietnam in all the categories. Thus, interestingly, Vietnam, which attracted a high proportion of resource-seeking FDI, displays weaker performance of the foreign subsidiaries and in one of the possible spillovers to the Vietnamese economy.

CONCLUSIONS

The survey undertaken as part of our project provides a snapshot of FDI's into four comparable emerging markets during the 1990s. The picture that emerges is rather different to expectations derived from the experiences of developed economies. Most foreign direct investments to these emerging markets are small, sometimes very small, and surprisingly high proportions are in the financial and service sector. There is a significant regional pattern to the distribution of donor firms' countries – it is clear that local familiarity, experience with emerging markets and integration into regional trading blocks, plays some role in the FDI process to developing economies.

Contrary to expectations, most FDI to our sample countries is motivated for market rather than efficiency-seeking reasons. This is especially true for South Africa and Egypt. Investments into India follow a split pattern, with most FDI being of a market-seeking character but with a small yet very significant efficiency-seeking sector oriented to export and often integrated into company supply chains in the IT sector. In contrast, Vietnam has a much larger efficiency-seeking FDI sector, representing a majority of all investments. This is reflected in the sectoral distribution of FDI to Vietnam, which is more concentrated in basic manufacturing, and in the regional character of FDI source firms, disproportionately based in South East Asia.

As one might expect in developing countries, appropriate acquisition targets are scarce or capital markets are less well developed and regulations for takeover are more complex. Hence it is unsurprising that the dominant entry modes are greenfield and joint venture in our sample. The only country which looks different in this respect is South Africa, where the industrial and institutional structure is more mature and entry by acquisition is rather more common. The combination of majority greenfield entry, efficiency-seeking motivation, predominant manufacturing and regional integration make the case of Vietnam more comparable to the earlier models of rapid growth through FDI and exports in China, Thailand and Malaysia, than to any of the other countries in our sample.

The survey presents a consistent picture of what the managers of foreign subsidiaries perceive to be the resources crucial to success in emerging markets – brands, management and technology. In general, foreign firms provide the bulk of these inputs, while local firms provide distribution, business networks and marketing skills. Moreover, the perception of the business environment of the host economy is for the most part quite good, though there may be sample selection issues here. The quality of the labour force is found to be fairly good in all four countries, though some problems are noted in the availability of executive management, especially in Vietnam. This is probably because foreign subsidiaries use expatriates, pay efficiency wages or are too small a sector to suffer from economy-wide skill shortages. In terms of the quality of local inputs, most host economies in our sample are again evaluated quite highly by our sample of managers, and perceptions are improving everywhere except in South Africa. The most serious problem with respect to the business environment is perceived to be in the area of the institutional and policy environment. This is evaluated as being significantly worse than the other aspects of the business environment noted above, and is not seen as improving anywhere except in Vietnam during the 1990s. Indeed the situation in South Africa is seen as deteriorating slightly. Predictability of government policy and the quality of central and local government are highlighted as particular problem areas.

Despite this, the bulk of our respondents are relatively satisfied with the performance of their foreign affiliates, especially with regard to productivity and revenue growth. Performance in profitability was evaluated rather less well however, perhaps because of the inevitable gestation lags. Despite the rapid improvement in the institutional environment, it has so far proved particularly hard for foreign firms to meet their profit and other performance targets in Vietnam.

In the remainder of this book, we explore findings of the survey in more detail for each country, and we illustrate many of our major themes –

institutional environment, entry mode, source of crucial resources, and performance – with a number of case studies from each country. The country chapters also discuss in greater depth the institutional and policy environment in each country and country specific findings from the survey. In the final chapters, we bring together the material in separate policy and managerial conclusions.

3. Foreign Direct Investment in Egypt

Maryse Louis, Alia El-Mahdy and Heba Handoussa

INTRODUCTION

In this chapter, we present in greater detail the institutional and policy environment for FDI into Egypt, before analysing the findings from the Egyptian survey. In the first section, we outline the evolving policy environment with respect to FDI into Egypt. We go on to consider methodological issues, in particular the representativeness of our sample with respect to size, sectoral and regional distribution of foreign affiliates. This permits us to introduce the characteristics of the foreign direct investment sector in Egypt. In the fourth section, we present the findings of the Egyptian survey, following the structure employed in Chapter 2. We conclude by evaluating FDI into Egypt during the 1990s. The discussion is developed through the three Egyptian case studies in the subsequent chapter.

POLICY AND INSTITUTIONAL ENVIRONMENT

Economic Environment

Egypt under Nasser followed a highly regulated economic policy, with state control over a significant proportion of the economy and an inward looking trade policy that relied on import substitution. However, an 'open door' policy was adopted in 1974, aiming to reduce state control over an economy that was largely dominated by the state sector. This led to sizeable amounts of foreign assistance, workers' remittances and foreign investment, and a major increase in growth. But, the economy remained inward looking and rapid growth ended in 1986 when oil prices fell significantly. The late 1980s saw an unstable period of decreasing growth rates, increasing inflation and budget and current account deficits. Under the auspices of the World Bank and IMF, the government launched a comprehensive Economic Reform and Structural Adjustment Programme (ERSAP) in 1991.[7]

Despite the apparent success of the ERSAP programme in terms of growth, the economy remained weak and vulnerable to external shocks such as the Asian and Latin American financial crises in 1997 and 1998. There was a recession in 2000 and the economy faced a devalued local currency, an increase in imports, slow growth and an increasing inflation. The September 11th attack on the US thus came at a time when the economy was already suffering.

Egypt was directly affected by the shock; tourism revenues (normally around 25 per cent of total exports and the second largest source of foreign exchange) fell by 26 per cent in 2001/2002 and unemployment in the sector increased. The authorities also faced a large financing deficit that could not be balanced by portfolio and direct investment inflows. GDP grew at less than 1 per cent in 2002, with inflation rising to 4.3 per cent and the budget deficit jumping to 6.2 per cent of GDP. Despite these problems, Egypt has continued to attract foreign investors. In 2000, the FDI flows reached US$1.2 billion, but dropped to US$510 million with the recession in 2001, rising slightly in 2002 to US$647 million.

Our survey of foreign investment firms was conducted between November 2001 and January 2002. From the end of 2000, the Egyptian economy was in a severe recession. In addition to the low growth, we observed:

- An increase in bankruptcy levels among large and small firms;
- A high unemployment rate, estimated at between 8 and 15 per cent;
- A reduction in the amount of FDI flowing into the country, which fell by two thirds, from US$1,500 million in 2000 to about US$500 million in 2001.

The downturn from the September 11th tragedy worsened the negative conditions of the economy. In consequence, a pervasive feeling of pessimism prevailed, not only in the business community, but also among the population at large. This mood of general depression was reflected in the survey – the response rate was relatively low, 10 per cent, and responses often reflected a pessimistic view. The findings of the survey must be interpreted, keeping these factors in mind.

Infrastructure

As a manifestation of its commitment to a growing role for the private sector, after the ERSAP the government started to invest in projects that would crowd-in the private sector; the ERSAP had stressed the role of private investment in growth. New legislation in recent years has contained provisions for the private sector to invest in infrastructure and telecommunications. These moves have been quite successful; the World Competitiveness Report of the World Economic Forum (WEF) ranked Egypt

5th out of 59 countries in terms of having investment in infrastructure as a priority for the government (see WEF 2000).

As a result of these changes, private sector participation in the construction sector has been growing, increasing the growth rate of the sector to an average of 7 per cent between 1999 and 2003. This is in line with the government's long-term plan to increase the habitable area of the country from 3 to 20 per cent by the year 2020 (see Euromoney 2000). Also the government has approved private sector investments in the form of Build Operate Transfer (BOT) projects in power generation, telecommunications, airports and highways that will substantially increase the number and quality of service of infrastructural projects. The implementation of new industrial projects in industrial zones and new communities (such as the 10th of Ramadan and the 6th of October cities) is also being encouraged by offering 10 years of tax exemptions (as opposed to 5 years in other areas). These industrial zones have been specially constructed to host heavy as well as light industrial projects, and contain infrastructure, electricity, water and environmental protection.

One of the main objectives of the ERSAP programme was to reduce the public sector share of the economy. The privatisation programme in Egypt was considered one of the most successful in the world in its starting phase. In 1999, the IMF announced that Egypt's privatisation programme ranked fourth in the world, with proceeds from privatisation amounting to 1.5 per cent of GDP per year (EIU 2000).

Under Law 203 of 1991, 314 public sector enterprises (almost 70 per cent of the industrial sector) were to be moved out of government control. Sixteen independent holding companies were assigned to restructure these enterprises, to operate as private companies with full financial and managerial accountability. The Public Enterprise Office (PEO) established in 1991 was in charge of overseeing public sector reform and privatisation under the supervision of the Minister of Public Enterprise.

Several methods were used in the execution of the privatisation programme:

- Selling 100 per cent of assets to strategic investors (such as Coca-Cola and Pepsi-Cola);
- Selling 95 per cent of the company to Employees Stockholder Associations (ESAs), who then sell them to the employees (ten companies adopted this procedure);
- Selling a significant part of the company's shares through the stock market;
- Selling company debts; and
- Selling a number of small companies and unused public enterprise real estate by auction.

After several consecutive years of success to 2000, during which 180 firms with a value of LE15.8 billion were sold, the pace of privatisation started to slow. In 2001, only 13 transactions were made (sales, leases and liquidations) down from 23 in 2000 and 33 in 1999. This was mainly due to the fact that most of the well-performing companies had already been sold and the remainder were either heavily indebted, over-staffed, using outdated technology or in need of radical restructuring. Another reason for the slowdown in privatisation has been the government's hesitancy to worsen unemployment, which has increased as a result of the privatisation, especially when the economy as a whole is going through a recession. Although the government has relaxed its ban on the privatisation of utilities by selling 15 per cent of the state telecommunications, the privatisation of the four state-owned banks has been stalled.

Governance and Institutions

Good governance and transparent and efficient institutions are key issues to promote and encourage investment. The 1990s in Egypt marked tremendous government efforts to orient economic policies towards an open free market. But this positive record has been slowed by a lack of institutional reforms. One important reason why Egypt has been slow to achieve its economic objectives is due to the cumbersome and ineffective character of the structural and institutional systems (Handoussa and El-Mikawy 2001).

Most surveys have suggested that the ineffectiveness of the taxation system and petty corruption have increased business costs. Distorted competition taxes tend to be very high and the incentives given tend to offset each other and so have little incremental effect. Also, cumbersome procedures of the tax administration and the time-consuming processes add a significant element of uncertainty to private investment in Egypt. Tax evasion is still considered a problem that reflects corruption. Bureaucracy has also been identified as a key constraint by business in Egypt, hindering investment and especially FDI. Starting a new business in Egypt can be extremely difficult when faced with bureaucratic procedures, licences and paperwork.

Egypt still has a large inefficient and underpaid civil service with weak professional incentives and performance, and which is resistant to reform. Interviews with businessmen in Egypt suggest that substantial reforms to government administration are difficult given the immense political power of this sector.

The commercial legal system in Egypt is often accused of being slow and expensive. Corruption in the legal system in terms of irregular payments to judges, experts and personnel is not very common (the WEF report ranked Egypt 30th out of 59 in terms of corruption in the legal system). The clearance rate[8] was reported in the mid-1990s to be 36 per cent (as opposed to 80 or

100 per cent in most developed countries), and the average time period to resolve a case is 6 years. This poor performance is probably due to the limited number of judges and their low remuneration, the exaggerated use of court experts, the lengthy procedures and poor court facilities.[9] Some positive steps have been taken to upgrade the financial sector towards international standards with respect to the variety of services, quality, price and efficiency. These include the introduction of new financial instruments and services, development of stronger institutions through mergers and acquisitions, further strengthening prudential regulations and a monetary policy that is punctually reactive to the market demand. The government declared the Central Bank to be independent from the end of 2001. However the public sector role in the financial system remains dominant, with more than half of the loans in the hands of the four banks that remain state owned.

The persistence of a poorly performing institutional framework is perceived as the main factor that has undermined the process of reforms and limited the flow of foreign investment into the economy. The legacy of public sector domination and of centralisation continues to impact negatively on the functioning of the markets.

Legal Environment affecting FDI

Since the mid-1970s, the government has introduced various laws increasing Egypt's openness to foreign investors. These include: Law 43 in 1974 as amended; Law 230 in 1989; Law 159 for 1981 and the new Investment Law 8 in 1997; Sector Law No. 203 in 1991, Capital Market Law No. 95 in 1992, tax laws No. 96 in 1992, a law regulating the ownership of real estate by non-Egyptians and a law allowing the private sector establishment of airports No.3 in 1997. Further legislative reforms are planned, including a unified companies law institutionalising equal treatment for companies regardless of their country of domestic or ownership status. Reforms are also planned to reduce procedures, define minority shareholder rights, improve rules for mergers and to amend corporate taxes.

However, Handoussa and El-Mikawy (2001) report that the legislative system in Egypt still contains a number of weaknesses:

- The absence of a unified policy framework for the reforms;
- The vague and arbitrary nature of laws, often referring to other laws or parts of laws annulling or amending them;
- The unconstitutionality of many laws;
- The speed with which the laws are passed, reflects negatively on the credibility of the legislative process;
- The frequent amendment of laws, brings into question their credibility.

The Companies Law No. 159 of 1981 is the basic law governing the establishment and operation of companies in Egypt. Investment Law No. 8 of 1997 introduced more incentives to private and foreign investment in Egypt and is considered an improvement to the regulatory framework. Among its most essential provisions is the grant of national treatment to foreign investments. However, official approval remains required for all foreign direct investment firms.

The majority of foreign companies now choose to register under the Investment Law No. 8, under the administrative authority of the General Authority for Investment and the Free Zones (GAFI). The law allows 100 per cent foreign ownership and permits foreign investment in 16 distinct fields, some of which were previously restricted, including industry and mining, tourism and oil production and related services. The Executive Decree of August 1997 added petroleum refining and cinema production. Other fields still require prior approval from interested ministries before an investor can approach GAFI (for example, all military products and related industries; tobacco and tobacco products; any investment in the Sinai).

Investment law No. 8 does not impose any restrictions on the number of Egyptian employees that have to be hired in the foreign company, but Companies Law No. 159 requires that the majority of the directors must be Egyptian and employees must be represented on the board. Under Law No.8, companies – regardless of the level of foreign ownership – have the right to possess and own buildings and land as necessary for exercising and expanding their business. Companies and projects are protected against nationalisation or confiscation by article 9 of the Egyptian Constitution and article 9 of the Investment Law No. 8.

Foreign investors also now have the right to remit profits and to repatriate invested capital. Transfers are made in freely convertible currency and the market exchange rate. Companies under Law 159 however are subject to some restrictions in terms of the amount of capital transferred. The institutional environment is summarised in Table 3.1.

Egyptian law provides the following organisational forms for investors:

- Joint-stock companies and partnerships limited by shares. These are suitable for projects with a capital of at least LE250,000, but difficult to establish without an Egyptian partner;
- Limited liability companies which are suitable for smaller projects of LE50–250,000 of capital;
- Joint partnerships and limited partnerships, which are more suitable for small projects but which would require a minimum of 51 per cent Egyptian shareholding;
- Branches and representative offices for a foreign parent company.

Table 3.1 Comparative matrix of investment laws in Egypt

Category	Law 43/1974 as amended	Law 230/1989	Law 159/1981	Law 8/1997
Fields of activity	Reclamation and cultivation of barren and desert land, industry, tourism, housing and real estate development	Same as Law 43	(Not applicable under this law)	Same as Law 230, plus infrastructure (electricity, water, transport), services for oil drilling and exploration; transport and delivery of gas; financial leasing, risk capital, and guaranteeing subscription to securities. Executive Decree included petroleum refining and cinema production.
Egyptian participation in equity	Mandatory but no minimum specified	Not mandatory	Minimum 49% Egyptian equity	Not mandatory
Capital and profit repatriation	Allowed	Allowed	Not allowed	Allowed
Foreign ownership of land	Not allowed	Allowed	Not allowed	Allowed
Price controls	None	None	Possible	None
Exchange	No exchange controls	No exchange controls	Subject to controls	No exchange controls

Trade	No import or export licences	No import or export licences	Subject to controls	No export/import licensing
Income tax holiday	5 years and up to 8 years 10 and up to 15 years for land reclamation and new cities	5-10 years 0-15 years 15-20 years on low-cost housing	50% tax relief on shares quoted on stock exchange. Projects in 'new communities' enjoy tax privilege of Law 59/1977	5 years 10 years for new industrial zones, remote areas and new projects financed by the Social Development Fund 20 years for outside the Old Valley.
Customs exemption	Customs exemptions on capital goods for some projects	No customs exemptions	No customs exemptions	A unified rate of 5% on value of machines, equipment, instruments imported
Worker participation in profit	At discretion of company	10% of profit with no ceiling	10% of profit up to ceiling of one year's wages	At discretion of company
Implementing body	GAFI	GAFI	Capital Market Authority	The General Authority for Investment and Free Zones

Source: UNCTAD 1998.

Within this framework, the most favourable form of foreign investment is the joint stock company normally set up under Law No. 8. Acquisitions and takeovers must be through GAFI for firms that are established under Law No. 230 and Law No. 8, although foreign takeovers remain rare.

FOREIGN DIRECT INVESTMENT IN EGYPT: AN OVERVIEW AND SAMPLING METHODOLOGY

In this section, we report on our methodology in selecting a representative sample. Fuller information on sampling methodology is reported in Louis et al. (2003). In Table 3.2, we report the distribution of all foreign direct investments into Egypt between June 2000 and June 2002, by sector, size and investment source. The survey target was 150 completed questionnaires of foreign investors in Egypt meeting the following criteria: (i) established between 1990 and 2001, (ii) a minimum of 10 per cent of foreign investment, and (iii) a minimum of 10 employees. We selected a sample of 350 firms randomly, but the response rate was low, so we enlarged the sample size to the 1,500 firms that satisfied the criteria.[10]

The data on the distribution of the population of foreign firms in June 2002 by sector and location show a total number of 4,035 foreign firms from which the 1500 were selected. Our survey was conducted in late 2001 when the total number of foreign firms was 3,824. Data about foreign firms distributed by sector and location were only available for 2002.

Sectoral Distribution

In comparing the sectoral distribution of the sample with that of the base population, we find some differences in the definitions of the sectors. For comparability across the four countries studied, the survey uses the ISIC UN Rev.2 Classification, while the General Authority for Free Zones and Investment (GAFI) uses its own definitions of sectors. The base population sectors are aggregated in such a way that it is not always possible to compare it to the sample sectors, but we present what one can do in Table 3.3.

The manufacturing sector in the base population represents 54 per cent of total foreign firms in Egypt while in the sample it represents only 40 per cent. But the population includes all foreign firms, including those established before 1990, whereas the sample only includes those established after 1990. Moreover, some sectors in the sample are not available in the base population, so the base population sectors could include more sub-sectors than the sample.[11] Table 3.2 showed that FDI directed to the manufacturing sector represents 33 per cent of total FDI stock, which is even lower than the proportion in the sample.

Table 3.2 FDI distributed by sector and origin in Egypt (LE million)

| | FDI | | | | | | June 2002 | |
| | June 2000 | | | June 2002 | | | | |
Sector	Arab	Foreign	Tota	Arab	Foreign	Total	No. of projects	Investment costs
Manufacturing	3,191	5,202	8,393	4,150	6,412	10,562	2,176	59,107
Agriculture	499	211	710	626	242	868	344	7,405
Construction	338	1,782	2,120	382	1,958	2,340	181	19,519
Tourism	3,377	1,363	4,740	3,140	1,881	5,021	360	22,766
Financing	2,953	2,222	5,175	4,356	3,264	7,620	629	34,325
Services	342	515	857					
Sub-total	10,700	11,295	21,995	12,654	13,757	26,411	3,690	143,122
Free zones	2,666	2,926	5,592	3,373	2,441	5,814	345	81,594
Total	13,366	14,221	27,587	16,027	16,198	32,225	4,035	224,716

Source: GAFI, 2002

Table 3.3 Sample properties: industry in base population versus sample

Sector	Base population June 2002		Sample	
	No. of firms	%	No. of firms	%
Agriculture & mining	344	8.5	5	3.4
Manufacturing	2,176	53.9	60	40.3
Construction	181	4.5	21	14.3
Tourism	360	8.9	7	4.7
Financing & insurance	n.a.	n.a.	16	10.7
Services	629	15.6	19	12.8
Trade & distribution	n.a.	n.a.	13	8.7
Transport, storage & communication	n.a.	n.a.	7	4.7
Sub-total	3,690	91.4	149	100
Free zones	345	8.6	0	0
Total	4,035	100	149	100

Source: GAFI 2002

Distribution by Nationality of Investors

In Egypt, more than half of the stock of foreign investors are from neighbouring Arab countries, amounting to 57.1 per cent in 2001 and 57.6 per cent in 2002 (see GAFI (2002)). In the sample, only 31 per cent of the total firms surveyed represent investments from the Arab world. This could be because, given that most of the foreign firms in Egypt are of Arab origin, they are most affected by the business slowdown and hence more reluctant to reply to the questionnaires. The largest Arab investors are from Saudi Arabia, with a share of 14 per cent of total foreign firms in the FDI stock. Europe's share comes second amounting to 26.1 per cent of total firms in 2001 and 25.7 per cent in 2002, but rather more in the sample. This is probably because more recent investment is from Europe, and, with the signing of the partnership with the EU, the share of European investment in Egypt could well increase further. US investment in Egypt amounted to 8.4 per cent of FDI stock and a similar share in our sample. The involvement of firms from South East Asia, for example Japan, into Egypt is very small in both the sample and the population.

Location of Foreign Investments

Almost 73 per cent of our sample firms are located in Cairo. There is no data on the location of FDI firms, but only 26 per cent of all the firms, including both foreign and local firms, are located in Cairo. Thus our sample still looks unbalanced towards Cairo. A possible explanation is the high proportion of non-manufactured firms (89 of 149). Most service firms are located in Cairo, while the location where the service is provided depends on the project. In the construction sector for example, the location of 22 out of the 23 surveyed firms is in Cairo, whereas the projects are often located outside Cairo.

Conclusion

This discussion has highlighted significant methodological problems for research of this sort in Egypt. However, despite some important anomalies between the population data and our sample, we conclude that in most cases these probably represent differences of definition or timing, which are unlikely to cause major biases in our findings.

INTRODUCTION TO THE FIRMS IN THE SAMPLE

Table 3.4 shows the distribution of our sample by sector and employment. The highest frequency of firms is concentrated in three main sectors:

infrastructure and construction, financial and business services and intermediate products respectively. Of those three, intermediate goods-producing companies are the largest in size, in terms of number of workers, with 57 per cent of these companies employing more than 100 workers, while 50 per cent of infrastructure firms are small (10 to 50 employees). This reflects the fact that construction firms find it less costly to sub-contract workers on construction sites than to employ them directly.

For the whole sample, the data reveal that 58 per cent of the companies are of small and medium size (less than 100 workers). This phenomenon – though similar to the general economic structure of firms in Egypt – is surprising given the common belief that FDI companies are usually large in scale in terms of capital and labour. The sample contains very few large firms (>100 workers), all in basic consumer manufacturing and tourism.

Table 3.5 shows that the highest concentration of FDI originates from European countries (43 per cent), followed by Arab countries (33 per cent) and North American countries (19 per cent) respectively. Given the data on FDI stocks, this suggests that more recent investments have tended to come from Europe and North America rather than Arab countries. European firms are mainly concentrated in producing intermediate products; infrastructure and construction; trade and tourism; and pharmaceuticals. This concentration, especially in the case of the first, second and last sectors is consistent with their fields of specialisation and excellence, whereas the investment in tourist companies is more related to the competitive advantage of Egypt. Arab FDI is more evenly distributed among economic activities, with at best, minor concentration in the financial sector, machinery and equipment and infrastructure and construction. Asian investment, though very modest, is concentrated in the machinery sector, and North American companies are concentrated in the financial sector. More than one third of all American investments go to this sector, though it only represents one sixth of total FDI to Egypt. A possible explanation is that the banking, insurance and financial investment have become a thriving and growing field in Egypt since the early 1990s. US firms, with less tradition in the region but international experience obtained elsewhere in banking, have entered the financial sector disproportionately.

As to the concentration of new foreign investments in infrastructure and construction, this could be explained by the fact that there is a growing demand for housing in Egypt, and foreign companies may have ventured into the sector to benefit from this momentum.

The distribution of the companies according to their age, as shown in Table 3.6, reveals that a large proportion (48 per cent) started their businesses between 1995 and 1998.

Several favourable conditions were behind this. First, this period coincides with the successful implementation of the ERSAP, monetary and financial stability, and an excellent international standing, as confirmed by

Table 3.4 Numbers of companies by sector and employment size, Egypt

Local sectors	Employment size of local firm (no. of workers)					
	10-50	51-100	101-250	251-1000	>1000	Total
Primary	1	1	0	1	0	3
Basic consumer	1	4	7	2	3	17
Intermediate	6	3	5	7	0	21
Machines & equipment	4	4	2	3	0	13
Infrastructure & construction	12	3	4	4	1	24
Trade, tourism, & recreation	13	1	2	1	2	19
Financial & business services	10	6	1	5	0	22
Information technology	1	1	1	1	0	4
Pharmaceuticals	2	1	0	0	1	4
Total	50	24	22	24	7	127

Table 3.5 *Number of companies by sector and home country region, Egypt*

Local sectors	North America	Europe	Japan & East Asia	Middle East & North Africa	Other	Total
Primary	0	4	0	0	0	4
Basic Consumer	3	8	1	7	0	19
Intermediate	2	13	0	7	0	22
Machines & equipment	1	4	0	8	0	13
Infrastructure & construction	5	13	0	8	0	26
Trade, tourism, & recreation	2	12	2	6	2	22
Financial & business services	10	4	2	9	1	26
Information technology	4	2	0	2	0	8
Pharmaceuticals	1	3	0	1	0	5
Total	28	63	3	48	3	145

Table 3.6 Number of companies by sector and age, Egypt

| Local sectors | Year of start of operation | | | |
	1990-1994	1995-1998	1998-2001	Total
Primary	0	3	1	4
Basic consumer	7	9	3	19
Intermediate	9	9	4	22
Machines & equipment	5	6	3	14
Infrastructure & construction	7	14	6	27
Trade, tourism, & recreation	4	9	9	22
Financial & business services	5	13	8	26
Information technology	0	5	3	8
Pharmaceuticals	1	3	1	5
Total	38	71	38	147

international rating institutions. Moreover, the implementation of the privatisation programme encouraged foreign investors to buy firms' shares from the stock markets and to enter the Egyptian market in brownfield and acquisition investments. Entry was especially marked in the financial and infrastructure sectors. Also, the new investment law was implemented, giving more incentives to foreign investors and allowing full foreign ownership.

An Introduction to the Investors

Parent firms that have invested in Egypt have the following characteristics. Firstly, the majority (68 per cent) have worldwide employment exceeding 1,000 workers and 40 per cent of them employ more than 10,000 workers. This implies that a considerable number of the foreign companies are affiliated to relatively large parent companies. Although 32 per cent of the FDI parent companies generate no more than 0.1 per cent of the global turnover of their parent companies, there are still 15 per cent of the FDI companies that contribute more than 20 per cent of their parent companies turnover. The latter group is mainly concentrated in companies that produce intermediate products and basic consumer goods, and is usually made up of smaller firms from Arab countries.

Table 3.7 shows that exploitation of intangible assets such as technology or patented brands is probably not a key motive for FDI into Egypt. The majority of the parent FDI companies (72 per cent) allocate less than 2 per cent of their total sales to R&D. Around 54 per cent of parent firms are engaged in infrastructure, trade, tourism and financial activities, which normally do not require high investment in R&D; 30 per cent of these spend more than 2 per cent of global sales on R&D. Firms engaged in manufacturing (consumer goods, intermediate and machines and equipments manufacturing which represent 37.8 per cent of the firms in the sample) are spending more on R&D; 26 per cent of these firms spend more than 2 per cent of global sales on R&D.

The vast majority of the parent companies have experience of investing in other emerging market regions, especially in Latin America and Africa. This probably lends them greater capabilities to adapt to a developing country's environment. Moreover, most of the parent firms are either focused on one main business activity or diversified to related activities. We find conglomerates only among firms in the infrastructure and construction sector.

Choice of Entry Mode

All the main entry modes were feasible in Egypt during the 1990s, and perhaps acquisitions and partial acquisitions represented an easier entry path. Despite this, greenfield and joint ventures are found to be the major modes of

Table 3.7 Number of firms by sector and R&D expenditure, Egypt

Local Sectors	R&D expenditure as % of global sales							Total
	0-0.5%	0.5-1%	1-2%	2-4%	4-8%	8-15%	>15%	
Primary	0	0	0	1	0	0	0	1
Basic consumer	8	0	3	1	3	0	0	15
Intermediate	13	1	2	2	1	0	0	19
Machines & equipment	3	1	0	2	2	0	0	8
Infrastructure & construction	15	2	1	3	1	2	0	24
Trade, tourism & recreation	10	0	1	2	1	2	0	16
Financial & business services	11	2	0	3	1	3	0	20
Information technology	5	0	1	0	0	1	0	7
Pharmaceuticals	0	1	0	0	0	0	0	1
Total	65	7	8	14	9	8	0	111

Table 3.8 Number of firms by entry mode choice and sector, Egypt

Local sectors	Mode of entry				
	Greenfield	Acquisition	JV	PA	Total
Primary	0	1	3	0	4
Basic consumer	12	1	5	1	19
Intermediate	10	1	9	2	22
Machines & equipment	3	0	7	3	13
Infrastructure & construction	13	0	11	3	27
Trade, tourism & recreation	11	2	7	2	22
Financial & business services	10	2	7	5	24
Information technology	4	0	4	0	8
Pharmaceuticals	4	0	0	1	5
Total	67	7	53	17	144

entry; Table 3.8 reveals that greenfield entry represents 46.5 per cent of the total FDI and JVs represent nearly 37 per cent.

This phenomenon could be explained by the fact that acquisitions were mainly channelled through the privatisation process. Hence, when the privatisation programme slowed after 1997, with most successful firms sold, foreign investors started to engage in greenfield investment. Moreover, the total number of privatisations was modest, while growing market needs for new products and services led foreign investors into new economic activities. The new Investment Law No.8 of 1997 also encouraged foreign investment.

These explanations are strengthened by the fact that most of the greenfield and joint venture companies in the sample started operations between 1995 and 1998. Almost 47 per cent of the firms established between 1990 and 1994 were greenfield while another 47 per cent were newly established JVs with a local partner. Between 1995 and 1998, almost half the firms established were greenfield, as privatisation only involved a small number of firms (134) but acquisitions and partial acquisitions represented only 17 per cent of the total.

There is no particularly strong sectoral pattern to the choice of entry mode. However foreign firms producing basic consumer goods (including food processing) slightly prefer to invest as greenfield (63 per cent). Also, most of the newly established pharmaceutical firms surveyed (80 per cent) prefer to invest in Egypt as greenfield. This was not the case in the 1980s, when most pharmaceutical firms entered the market as a joint ventures or acquisition.

RESOURCES FOR SUCCESS

When the affiliates were asked about the most crucial resources behind their successful performance, each firm had to choose and rank the three most important ones. Tables 3.9 and 3.10 reflect their answers.

Key Resources by Sector

Technological know-how was identified as one of the most important resources of success by companies working in producing primary goods, IT, intermediate products, machinery and equipment industries and pharmaceuticals. This result is understandable since one of the main advantages of FDI is its ability to introduce new technologies to emerging markets. The technical know-how helps the incoming companies in securing a niche in the Egyptian market.[12] The managerial capabilities of labour in Egypt ranks second and this applies to almost all companies, while the influence of using brand names comes in the third position. It is especially important to pharmaceutical companies, consumer goods producing companies, tourism and trade, and financial and business services.

Technological know-how is the most important resource for the success of 26 per cent of firms producing basic consumer goods and of 50 per cent of the firms working in the intermediate sector. 'Brands' and 'Technology know-how' were each considered the first choice for 21 per cent of the firms working in machinery and equipment sector. In the infrastructure and construction sector, 63 per cent of the firms agreed that the 'managerial capabilities' was one of the most important resources for success, 26 per cent of those had this as their first choice; 50 per cent of the firms working in the trade and tourism sector considered that brand name was one of the most important resources for their success, 35 per cent of them considering it to be the most important resource. In the financial and business sector, managerial capabilities and business networks were seen as important resources for success by 58 and 54 per cent of the firms respectively. Unsurprisingly, 75 per cent of the IT firms choose the technology know-how as one of the most important resources and 50 per cent of these considered it to be their first choice; 50 per cent of firms chose the business network as one of the most important resources where only 25 per cent of those made it as their first choice. In the pharmaceutical sector, 60 per cent of the firms chose brand names; managerial capabilities and technology know-how to be three most important resources of success and 60 per cent of those chose brand names to be their most important source of success.

Key Resources by Mode of Entry

Both greenfield and JV firms depend largely on the technological know-how, managerial and marketing capabilities as their sources of success, whereas the acquisitions and partial acquisitions rely on brand names. These results are not surprising since for new projects, greenfield and joint ventures, it is very important to introduce new technology to the markets and to have good managerial staff in the initial phase of the operation. In contrast the most important resource for an acquisition or partial acquisition investment, is a pre-existing brand and the distribution network. In Egypt, successful partial acquisitions in pharmaceuticals, beverages, tobacco companies and hotels have been motivated mainly by the objective to acquire famous and successful brand names.

Key Resources by Their Source

As to the sources of the major resources, we find that brand names and technological know-how mostly originate from parent firms, while managerial capabilities and equity shares derive largely from foreign sources and all other resources are provided largely by the local firms (Table 3.10).

Table 3.9 Percentage of respondents selecting the resource as necessary for success, Egypt (%)

Top three resources (1st choice)	Primary	Basic consumer goods	Inter-mediate	Machinery & equipment	Infra-structure & con-struction	Trade, tourism & recreation	Financial & business services	Infor-mation tech-nology	Pharma-ceuticals	Total
Brands	0 (0)	42 (21)	23 (18)	29 (21)	28 (19)	50 (35)	31 (19)	25 (16)	60 (60)	32 (22)
Business networks	50 (50)	5 (0)	32 (9)	7 (7)	30 (7)	30 (10)	54 (23)	50 (25)	20 (0)	30 (12)
Distribution network	0 (0)	11 (5)	18 (0)	43 (7)	4 (0)	10 (0)	12 (0)	13 (0)	0 (0)	13 (1)
Equity	0 (0)	5 (5)	5 (5)	7 (0)	15 (0)	15 (5)	19 (4)	13 (0)	0 (0)	11 (3)
Mach. & equipment	25 (0)	26 (11)	32 (0)	36 (14)	22 (7)	15 (10)	0 (0)	0 (0)	20 (0)	19 (6)
Manag. capabilities	50 (0)	42 (11)	36 (5)	50 (0)	63 (26)	30 (0)	58 (27)	25 (0)	60 (20)	47 (12)
Mrkting. capabilities	0 (0)	32 (5)	27 (5)	33 (7)	44 (11)	45 (10)	31 (8)	25 (0)	0 (0)	33 (7)
Technol. know-how	100 (25)	53 (26)	82 (50)	43 (21)	44 (7)	20 (0)	35 (8)	75 (50)	60 (0)	50 (19)
No. of observations	4	19	22	14	27	20	26	8	5	145

Note: By industrial sector of the respondent

Table 3.10 Percentage of firms that selected resource of primary importance, Egypt

Source of resource	Resources for success					
	Brand network	Business network	Distribution network	Equity	Machinery & equipment	Managerial capabilities	Marketing capabilities	Technological know-how
Local firm	15	70	75	48	55	35	62	18
Parent firm	80	19	0	21	41	23	28	73
Local source	0	10	25	6	4	3	10	1
Foreign source	5	1	0	25	1	40	0	8

Note: By source of resource

The availability of several resources in the Egyptian market represents a major source of attraction to FDI.

Key Resources by Size

The same importance and ranking of the resources for success becomes evident when the companies are considered by size of employment. Brand names seem to be increasing in importance with the size of company increases. Thus we find 83 per cent of the firms with more than 1,000 employees consider brand names to be one of the most important resource for success and 67 per cent of those consider it to be the most important. Business networks however, are only important for small size firms. Machinery and equipment becomes an important source as the size of the firm increases (except for very large firms of more than 1,000 employees). All size groups of firms agree that managerial capabilities are important resources for success. Technology know-how is important for all firms but especially for smaller ones.

INSTITUTIONAL AND MARKET ENVIRONMENT

In this section, we consider the perceptions of the CEOs of our sample of foreign affiliates about the Egyptian business environment. The material is grouped into evaluation of labour markets, factor inputs and the policy environment.

Labour Markets

Table 3.11 indicates that recruiting executive management is difficult and is only sometimes available for all sectors at the initial phase but that there has been an improvement over time. Shortages are particularly marked in financial and business services, and infrastructure. The IT sector also has problems with operations management. However, most of the sectors agree that professionals, operational management and skilled labour are 'mostly available' and that availability is improving.

The Egyptian Input Market and the Business Environment

According to Table 3.12 input markets in Egypt offer sufficiently reliable utility services such as electricity, water, sewerage, telecommunication and IT, professional services and real estate. There are still visible deficiencies however in the availability of machinery and equipment, and raw materials and components, as expressed by companies operating in the production of

Table 3.11 Change in evaluation of local labour market by industrial sector of the respondent, Egypt

Sector	Executive management		Professionals		Operational management		Skilled non-management labour		No. of firms
	Initial	2001	Initial	2001	Initial	2001	Initial	2001	
Primary	3.50	3.75	3.75	4.25	3.75	4.00	4.25	4.75	4
Basic consumer goods	3.32	3.84	4.42	4.68	3.74	4.42	4.21	4.42	19
Intermediate	3.59	3.82	4.05	4.23	3.73	3.82	4.05	4.18	22
Machinery & equipment	4.21	4.50	4.07	4.29	4.07	4.36	4.07	4.57	14
Infrastructure & construction	3.44	3.54	3.92	4.27	3.81	4.19	4.00	4.15	26
Trade, tourism & recreation	4.18	4.50	4.36	4.59	4.18	4.55	4.33	4.57	22
Financial & business services	3.42	3.92	3.77	4.19	3.65	4.15	4.23	4.50	26
Information technology	3.50	4.25	4.25	4.38	3.43	4.14	4.29	4.57	8
Pharmaceutical	4.20	4.60	4.20	4.60	4.60	5.00	4.60	5.00	5

Note: on scale from 1 to 5, 5 = readily available

Table 3.12 *Change in evaluation of local labour by industrial sector of the local inputs, Egypt*

| | Local inputs | | | | | | | | | | | | |
| Sector | Utility | | IT & telecomm. | | Professional service | | Real estate | | Machinery & equipment | | Raw materials | | No. of firms |
	Initial	2001	Initial	2001	Initial	2001	Initial	2001	Initial	2001	Initial	2001	
Primary	4.00	4.25	3.75	4.00	4.00	4.25	4.25	4.25	3.75	4.00	3.00	3.00	4
Basic consumer goods	3.79	4.11	3.68	4.58	4.21	4.37	4.25	4.00	1.79	2.11	2.74	3.00	19
Intermediate	3.77	4.27	3.73	4.18	3.91	3.73	3.35	3.53	2.14	2.27	2.71	2.86	22
Machinery & equipment	4.07	4.43	3.64	4.36	4.00	4.25	3.69	4.31	3.07	3.29	2.92	3.31	14
Infrastructure & construction	3.82	4.37	3.19	4.22	3.96	3.92	3.88	4.16	2.62	3.23	3.31	3.69	26
Trade, tourism & recreation	4.14	4.48	3.86	4.50	4.05	4.41	4.21	4.32	3.24	3.57	2.25	2.25	22
Financial & business services	4.50	4.81	3.69	4.62	4.00	4.31	4.12	4.31	3.91	4.36	3.60	3.80	26
Information technology	4.25	4.63	3.75	4.63	3.88	5.88	4.14	4.14	3.86	3.71	3.33	3.00	8
Pharmaceutical	5.00	5.00	4.60	4.80	4.80	4.40	5.00	5.00	2.60	2.60	2.20	2.20	5

Note: on scale from 1 to 5, 5 = readily available

basic consumer goods, intermediate products and pharmaceuticals. The need to import these items can cause delays, such as shipping problems and discontinuity in production from unpredictable changes in the exchange rates.

In Table 3.13, we report the evaluation of the Egyptian business environment by the managers of foreign affiliates. We find that in most sectors, producers perceive the institutional framework as a whole to be 'somewhat conducive'. There was discontent with certain procedures however:

- Business licences are not easy to obtain;
- The legal framework has also been criticised for its slowness in resolving business disputes and commercial matters such as unpaid cheques...etc;
- Rules and regulations are unstable and hard to predict;
- The role of central government in facilitating establishment procedures, determining economic policies that influence business operations and decisions such as the exchange rate policies, import and export regulations, transfer of profits, etc;
- The role of the local governments, especially in granting approvals, business licences and real estate titles.

The overall sense of pessimism may have been in part due to the recession at the time of the survey. It was much reflected in investors' evaluations of the institutional framework and some institutional environment components were not found to be improving over time, but rather remaining unchanged or deteriorating. Producers of intermediate goods and IT were the most dissatisfied with the institutional framework.

FIRM LEVEL PERFORMANCE

In this section we examine the degree to which affiliates fulfilled expectations in terms of investors' original objectives. Four criteria were chosen to reflect performance: productivity, profitability, revenue growth and domestic market share. Due to the high correlation between profitability and revenue growth, they were used to calculate a 'new performance' index; the average of those two variables, scaled from 1 to 5 where 1 reflects low performance while 5 indicates high performance compared to the original objectives. In Tables 3.14 and 3.15 we report the value of the index, rebasing it to a range of 1 to 3, where 1 represents 1 and 2 in the original 1 to 5 scale; 2 represents 2.5 and 3.5 and 3 represents 4 and 5.

Data in Table 3.14 show how greenfield and JV companies enjoy relatively higher performance compared to acquisitions and PA companies. This confirms the fact that newly establishment firms, either greenfield or JV, are more capable of adapting to the market, despite the difficulties they may face in the installation phase that is in getting up new technologies, and the introduction of new products and services to the market.

Turning to performance by sector in Table 3.15, four sectors seem to enjoy high performance relative to the rest. These are basic consumer goods, intermediate products, infrastructure and construction and financial and business sector companies. These sectors witnessed rapid growth during the nineties, which helped to boost expansion in the construction sector and the exceptional development in the IT and telecommunication sector.

FDI AND SPILLOVERS

In this section we draw together our findings about FDI entry mode, and the impact on spillovers to the host economy. First, we note that the motives for entry are correlated with company performance post-entry. We find in Table 3.16 that firms with a highly domestic focus generally enjoy a higher performance index. Almost half of the firms that have domestic market focus between 25 per cent and almost 100 per cent have the highest performance index. However, only a third of firms that have exactly 100 per cent domestic market focus have a high performance index. Perhaps performance of a firm can improve when focused on the large market that is available in Egypt. However, a 100 per cent focus on the domestic market can prevent the firm from being exposed to international markets and hence could negatively affect its performance.

The relationship between company performance and the business environment as given by: (a) availability of a suitable workforce, (b) availability of the necessary inputs to the production including physical infrastructure and financial services; (c) working in a market where the local industry is relatively inferior to that of the affiliate; (d) availability of an encouraging institutional environment. The findings are reported in Table 3.17, and suggest that a–c are closely correlated to high performance, while d does not seem to differ among the various performance levels. This is understandable since dealing with the institutional environment is usually done in the initial phase of establishing the firm. Hence, it does not really affect the performance of the firm in a later stage, except in the case of extending the business or getting involved in producing new products.

We also find a correlation between high performance and the absence of competitors or their limited number. Only 37 per cent of firms that are facing more than 10 competitors have a high performance index, while 43 per cent of the firms that have between 0 and 5 competitors have a high performance index. Data also reveal that increasing competition from abroad does not affect performance. The performance of these firms improves as their market share grows. This phenomenon is evident in several industries in Egypt.

Table 3.13 Change in evaluation of institutional environment by industrial sector of the respondent, Egypt

	Business licence		Real estate		Visa & work permit		Environment	
	Initial	2001	Initial	2001	Initial	2001	Initial	2001
Primary	3.00	2.50	2.25	2.00	2.75	2.50	3.00	2.75
Basic consumer goods	2.74	2.47	2.36	2.29	1.94	1.88	2.21	1.89
Intermediate goods	3.86	3.32	3.65	2.94	3.11	2.84	2.64	2.64
Machinery & equipment	2.86	2.64	2.75	2.58	2.70	2.70	2.14	2.14
Infrastructure & constr.	2.77	2.89	2.65	2.55	2.58	2.63	2.57	2.65
Trade & tourism	2.80	2.30	2.50	2.30	2.60	2.70	2.10	2.10
Financial services	2.70	2.60	2.30	2.20	3.00	2.90	2.60	2.60
Information Technology	3.10	2.80	2.00	2.00	2.70	2.60	2.70	3.30
Pharmaceutical	2.00	3.60	2.00	2.00	1.70	1.70	1.60	2.00

Table 3.13 (continued)

	Legal framework		Predictability		Central government		Local government	
	Initial	2001	Initial	2001	Initial	2001	Initial	2001
Primary	2.25	2.00	2.50	2.50	3.00	3.75	3.00	3.00
Basic consumer goods	2.42	2.42	2.74	2.74	2.68	2.47	2.47	2.47
Intermediate goods	3.50	3.32	3.25	3.50	3.33	3.52	3.36	3.36
Machinery & equipment	3.21	3.50	3.00	3.07	3.00	2.93	2.93	3.14
Infrastructure & constr.	3.19	3.08	3.31	3.35	3.30	3.35	3.00	3.05
Trade & tourism	3.20	3.40	3.20	3.70	2.90	3.10	2.90	3.00
Financial services	2.90	3.00	3.00	3.20	3.00	3.10	3.10	3.20
Information Technology	3.00	3.10	3.40	3.40	3.90	3.60	4.20	3.70
Pharmaceutical	3.00	3.00	4.00	4.00	3.20	3.20	3.00	3.20

Table 3.14 Performance relative to entry mode choice, Egypt

Respondents performance rating	Number of firms established through mode of entry				
	Greenfield	Acquisition	Joint Venture	Partial Acquisition	Total
Expectations not fulfilled (rating 1-2)	15	1	8	3	27
Expectations partially fulfilled (rating 2.5-3.5)	25	4	16	9	54
Expectations mostly fulfilled (rating 4-5)	25	0	25	5	55
Total	65	5	49	17	136

Table 3.15 Number of firms by performance and sector, Egypt

Local Sectors	Expectations not fulfilled (rating 1-2)	Expectations partially fulfilled (rating 2.5-3.5)	Expectations mostly fulfilled (rating 4-5)	Total
Primary	0	2	1	3
Basic consumer goods	2	7	10	19
Intermediate	2	7	12	21
Machines and equipment	4	5	5	14
Infrastructure and construction	5	9	12	26
Trade, tourism & recreation	8	6	5	19
Financial and business services	4	14	7	25
Information technology	0	4	3	7
Pharmaceuticals	2	1	2	5
Total	27	55	57	139

Table 3.16 Number of firms by performance and degree of market focus, Egypt

| | % of Sales in domestic market | | | | | |
Respondent's performance rating	0	0-25	25-50	75-100	100	Total
Expectations not fulfilled (rating 1-2)	2	3	6	4	12	27
Expectations partially fulfilled (rating 2.5-3.5)	4	3	15	6	23	51
Expectations mostly fulfilled (rating 4-5)	2	3	16	12	21	54
Total	8	9	37	22	56	132

Table 3.17 Change in evaluation by performance, Egypt

| | Expectations not fulfilled | | Expectations partially fulfilled | | Expectations mostly fulfilled | |
Category	Initial	2001	Initial	2001	Initial	2001
Labour markets	3.65	4.07	3.87	4.21	4.13	4.40
Local inputs	3.50	3.65	3.45	3.46	4.09	4.22
Local industry	2.79	2.65	2.68	2.71	2.11	2.25
Institutional environment	2.96	3.04	2.75	2.72	2.66	2.76

One might also expect that the longer an affiliate is in operation, the more chance it gets to raise its performance. This remark is confirmed by the data. Half of the surveyed firms that started operating in the period between 1990 and 1994 have a high performance index of 4 to 5, though this declines somewhat for firms created more recently.

We conclude by considering spillovers from FDI. The majority of affiliates in Egypt (64 per cent) spend less than 2 per cent of their total sales on training, though in a few sectors more than 2 per cent of total sales is allocated for training, in some cases 15 per cent or more. Thus primary commodities sectors (100 per cent of the companies), IT companies (80 per cent of the companies) and the financial and business services (57 per cent of the companies), spend more than 2 per cent of their sales is spent on training. IT and primary goods companies spend 3.76 per cent and 3.33 per cent of sales on training, which is relatively higher than other sectors, but still relatively low with respect to international standards.

Small and medium enterprises (10 to less than 250 workers) are major contributors to training. This may be due to the need of workers in small and medium scale companies to get training to become more capable of dealing with new and advanced technologies.

Diffusion of new technology is another important spillover from FDI. We are able to investigate the role of the parent firm in supporting the affiliate with its needs of the different technological resources. We find in Table 3.18 that the majority of affiliates (68 per cent) 'rarely' or 'never' receive technological resources from the parent firms. Only small percentages of machinery and equipment producers (38 per cent), trade and tourism sector (41 per cent), financial and business sector (31 per cent) 'always' or 'usually' receive technical support. Moreover, 75 per cent of greenfields 'rarely' or 'never' receive technological support from their parent firms, while only 17 per cent of those firms 'always' or 'usually' receive technological support. This could be due to the fact that greenfields, as a newly established business, do not require technological acquisition from the parent firm as it is already established with a minimum acceptable level of technology. As for acquisitions, 71 per cent 'rarely' or 'never' receive technological support while only 14 per cent 'always' receive technological support. This is unexpected, as normally acquiring an already existing firm requires a great deal of technological transfer and reconstruction. Joint ventures and partial acquisition are the luckiest since 25 per cent and 24 per cent of those firms respectively 'always' or 'usually' receive technological support from the parent firms.

We also fail to identify any clear relationship between technology transfer and company performance; the best performing firms have limited access to parent firms' technology. This is surprising since it was expected that there would be a strong positive correlation between high performance and the transfer of technology by the parent firms.

CONCLUSIONS

Egypt has made considerable progress since 1990 in liberalising its business environment and encouraging foreign direct investment. However, our brief summary of the changes suggest that much more remains to be done, especially with respect to governance, transparency of institutions and efficiency of government. Even so, Egypt has managed to attract growing sums from foreign investors during the 1990s, branching out from a largely Arab base to attract significant investment from North America and Europe.

The survey suggests that most investment has been concentrated in three sectors: infrastructure, financial and business services and intermediate products. The majority of entrants are small, though a few large firms have

Table 3.18 Technology acquisition relative to industry sector, Egypt

Sector	Number of firms acquiring technology					
	Always	Usually	Sometimes	Rarely	Never	Total
Primary	0	0	1	2	1	4
Basic consumer goods	2	0	1	4	11	18
Intermediate	1	0	0	6	15	22
Machines & equipment	4	1	0	4	4	13
Infrastructure & construction	2	0	6	2	17	27
Trade, tourism & recreation	6	3	1	4	8	22
Financial & business services	4	4	5	5	8	26
Information technology	0	1	0	3	3	7
Pharmaceuticals	2	0	2	0	1	5
Total	21	9	16	30	68	144

Notes: on scale from 1 to 5, 5 = never

come into basic manufacturing and tourism. The dominant entry modes are greenfield and joint ventures, with acquisitions being rather rare and unknown in infrastructure, IT and pharmaceuticals. They key resources for success are technological know-how and brands. Greenfield entrants stress the importance of technology, management and marketing, while acquisitions see brand names as the crucial resource.

Managers of foreign affiliates assessed the Egyptian business environment relatively positively, though improvements during the 1990s were at best only moderate. Neither labour nor infrastructure is viewed as a major problem for foreign investors, though the influence of the government, the bureaucracy and the frequent and unpredictable state intervention was seen as a persistent problem. Despite this, most firms reported positively on performance, and the survey also isolated significant spillover benefits from FDI.

4. Egyptian Case Studies

Azza El-Shinnawy and Heba Handoussa

INTRODUCTION

This chapter presents three cases of recent foreign investment in Egypt. In the case of the Egyptian Company for Mobile Services (MobiNil), an international consortium takes over a state-run mobile phone service, and modernises its operations in a rapidly growing and transforming market. The local partner subsequently becomes a regional player in Africa and the Middle East. GlaxoSmithKline, a leading pharmaceutical firm, expands in Egypt through multiple acquisitions, while the parent firm itself is subject to M&A at a global level. The leading-brand ketchup manufacturer Heinz has established a production facility for the Middle East jointly with a Kuwaiti multinational specialising in being the local partner for foreign fast-food chains throughout the Arab countries.

THE EGYPTIAN COMPANY FOR MOBILE SERVICES (MOBINIL)

Introduction

Mobile telephony is capturing an increasing share of global telecommunications services, accounting for 23 per cent of global telecommunications revenues (up from 3 per cent in 1990). Mobile telephony is one of the high growth market segments of the Egyptian telecommunications sector, having outpaced the growth of fixed-line telephony, which currently stands at 7.5 million lines, growing at a compound annual growth rate (CAGR) of approximately 14.6 per cent during the period 1995/2000, compared with the staggering CAGR of 169 per cent for mobile telephony during the period 1997/2002 (American Chamber of Commerce in Egypt 2001, p. 14). Since the opening up of the sector to private investment in 1998, the Egyptian mobile telecommunications sector has been host to two of the world's largest mobile operators, namely France Telecom and Vodafone. The two companies, in partnership with their

Egyptian counterparts, have been operating as a duopoly, in what is perceived to be a market of remarkable growth potential relative to Africa and the rest of the Middle East region. Egypt has the third-largest number of mobile subscribers in the region, outnumbered only by South Africa and Morocco. Penetration rates, which currently stand at 5.4 per cent of the population, are forecast to reach 15.5 per cent by 2008 (American Chamber of Commerce in Egypt 2001).

This case study explores FDI in the mobile telecommunications sector in Egypt, by throwing light on the first private operator, namely the Egyptian Company for Mobile Services (ECMS), known in the Egyptian market by the brand name 'MobiNil'.

The Industry

The global wireless communications market has undergone remarkable growth since its initial years of operation during the late 1980s. The most widely used system for mobile communications networks is the Global System for Mobiles (GSM), which is used by roughly 62 per cent of global mobile telephony. In the Middle East region, more than 90 per cent of mobile telecommunications is dependent on GSM 900 networks (American Chamber of Commerce in Egypt 2001, p. 6). The Middle East region accounts for a relatively small share, 2.7 per cent, of the world GSM market. By 2006, the world GSM industry is forecast to service 1.4 billion subscribers, of which the Middle East region is expected to retain a relatively unchanged share of 2.8 per cent (www.gsmworld.com). In the global telecommunications market, three sectors are expected to lead future growth: wireless, data and, to a lesser extent, fixed-line telephony.

Compared to other emerging markets, the Egyptian mobile telephony sector was liberalised early, which allowed the private sector to invest in mobile communication networks, while line telephony to date remains a government monopoly. During the period 1998/2001, the Egyptian mobile telephony market has experienced high growth in terms of the number of subscribers, outpacing world growth rates as well as those in other Middle East and North Africa (MENA) countries. The liberalised status of the mobile sector in Egypt (Table 4.1) combined with its high growth potential, explains why the sector has become one of the FDI magnets.

The Investor

ECMS is an Egyptian Joint Stock Company, established under the Investment Incentives and Guarantees Law No. 8 of 1997, which grants it a five-year tax holiday. The purpose of the company is to establish, manage, operate, develop and maintain a digital cellular mobile telecommunication system (GSM) in Egypt. The authorised capital of ECMS is 1.5 billion

Egyptian pounds (LE), and the issued and fully paid-up capital is LE1 billion (100 million shares at LE10/share).

The three strategic partners in ECMS (France Telecom, Orascom Telecom and Motorola) formed the MobiNil Telecom consortium, which held a 51 per cent stake in the newly formed company. Orascom Telecom acquired 14 per cent of ECMS's shares on the stock market, 2 per cent are held by employees, and the remaining 33 per cent by small private investors. In 2001, the MobiNil Telecom consortium underwent a structural shift in terms of ownership, following the exit of Motorola. When the company was established in 1998, the MobiNil Telecom shares were divided between France Telecom, Motorola and Orascom Telecom. In January 2001, Motorola sold its shares to both France Telecom and Orascom Telecom. Exiting the MobiNil consortium was a strategic decision, to enable Motorola to focus on the market for telecommunications equipment. For Motorola, its stake in a telecom operator with its role as equipment supplier to (potential) competing GSM networks.

France Telecom
In 2001 France Telecom became the majority shareholder, holding 71 per cent of MobiNil Telecom, and indirectly, 36.3 per cent of the ECMS. It is one of the world's leading telecommunication carriers, present in more than 220 countries and territories, serving 90.5 million customers, with total sales revenue in excess of US$26 billion (http://www.MobiNil.com). It either operates under its own name or under the associated brands of Orange, Wanadoo, Equant, or other subsidiaries.

The rapid expansion of France Telecom through acquisitions outside of France as well as outside the European markets came as a reaction to the opening of competition in the French market, and the subsequent pressure on market shares. France Telecom generated three-quarters of its sales by operating as a monopoly in France. In 2002, more than 60 per cent of sales derived from its international operations. The France Telecom Group provides a range of services including: wireless communications, fixed line telephony, Internet access and cable networks. It has become the second-largest wireless operator and the number three Internet access provider in Europe, as well as a world leader in the provision of telecommunications solutions for multinational companies. It is expected that France Telecom will transfer its shareholding in the MobiNil Telecom consortium to the Orange Group, which is the GSM arm of France Telecom.

Orascom Telecom
Orascom Telecom is part of the Orascom Group of companies, which is one of the largest private sector conglomerates in Egypt, operating in the fields of telecommunications, construction and tourist development. It is one of Egypt's information technology leaders, and has become one of the largest

Table 4.1 Overview of telecom regulation of fixed data services (2002)

Incumbent	**Algeria** Algeria Telecom	**Egypt** Egypt Telecom	**Jordan** Jordan Telecom	**Morocco** Maroc Telecom	**UAE** Etisalat
Liberalisation status					
Mobile telephony	Yes	Yes	Yes	Yes	No
Fixed telephony	No	No	No	No	No
Leased lines	No	No	No	No	No
Data	No	No	Competition permitted	Competition permitted	No
ISP	Competition permitted	Competition permitted	Competition permitted	Competition permitted	No
Fixed satellite services	No	No	No	No	No
VSAT	No	Competition permitted	No	Competition permitted	No
No. of mobile operators	2	2	2	2	1
No. of ISPs (2001)	4	38	8	10-24	1

Source: World Bank (2002)

GSM network operators in the Middle East, Africa, and Indian sub-continent, with some twenty-one licences covering the region. Orascom Telecom has established leadership as a conglomerate in emerging markets. By September 2001, it had more than 3.5 million mobile subscribers in 20 countries (www.orascomtelecom.com).

Through acquisitions and tenders, Orascom Telecom has built a regional cellular telephone business, and apart from its 31.3 per cent stake in ECMS, it has stakes in the following companies (EFG-Hermes, April, 2000):

- Fastlink (65 per cent), the first Jordanian cellular phone company
- Telecel (80 per cent), a pan-African company with 11 cellular licences in Africa
- Liberties (65 per cent), operator of the GSM network in Congo Brazzaville
- Chad GSM (80 per cent), operator of the GSM network in Chad.

Orascom Telecom has gained a reputation for GSM operations in emerging markets. Its latest greenfield addition was in Tunisia, where it has been awarded the licence to build and operate a GSM network.

Compared with France Telecom's subscriber base of 90.5 million, Orascom Telecom's 3.5 million subscribers may seem modest. However, Orascom Telecom was a new entrant to the wireless communications business prior to acquiring stakes in ECMS. Subsequently however, Orascom has participated in several mobile phone consortia in Northern Africa and Arab countries. In less than four years it has developed a reputation as 'the' GSM network operator of the MENA region, and has extended its business to Asia with an 89 per cent stake in Mobilink, Pakistan's GSM operator. In 2003, Orascom led the consortium that received the first mobile phone licence for the Baghdad region in Iraq.

While GSM wireless services account for the largest share of Orascom Telecom operations, its businesses also include a host of technology-related activities in the domain of sales, support and services for computer hardware, software, networking equipment, test and measurement equipment, analytical instruments, security systems, and telecommunications products. It is also the distributor for information technology industry leaders such as Hewlett-Packard, American Power Conversion, Microsoft, Oracle, Novell, Netscape, and Lucent Technologies. Orascom Telecom acts as a holding company, with a number of affiliates and subsidiaries. These include Egypt's leading Internet service provider, a software developer/distributor, a computer superstore retail chain, and a stake in a national public pay-phone service provider. As of January 2002, the workforce of Orascom Telecom and its GSM subsidiaries reached over 6,750 employees.

Acquired Local Firm

Wireless communications services are fairly recent to Egypt. Egypt Telecom, the government owned telecommunications company, established the first GSM 900 network in 1996, and was responsible for network management. A French operator maintained the technical sides of operations. Together with Egypt Telecom employees, four public sector banks and two social insurance funds held stakes in Egypt's first GSM network. The network was run as a state monopoly up to May 1998, when it was acquired by the consortium led by France Telecom. In May 2001, the Telecommunications Regulatory Authority (TRA) agreed that Egypt Telecom should offer and operate the third GSM network after the exclusivity period granted to MobiNil and Vodafone expires. Egypt Telecom will operate a General Packet Radio Services (GPRS) network (American Chamber of Commerce in Egypt 2002, p. 44).

Entry into Egypt

The decision of the strategic partners of ECMS to acquire the first GSM network in Egypt was based on two key considerations. Firstly, ECMS operated as a monopoly over the four-month period between gaining the 'key' to the acquired company on 21 May, 1998, and entry of the second GSM provider in November 1998. Being the first private company to enter the market, taking over a subscriber's list of 80,000, as well as a six month waiting list, implied that ECMS's growth potential was substantial. The latest figures provided by ECMS indicate that between market entry in May 1998 and the fourth quarter of 2001, the number of subscribers increased from 80,000 to reach 2 million. The growth performance of ECMS has been impressive by world standards. While global wireless communications has been growing at 12 per cent, between 1998 and 2001 the average annual growth rate of ECMS reached 686 per cent. The staggering growth performance of ECMS is attributed to the low penetration rates in Egypt, and signifies the potential demand that is yet to be met (JP Morgan 2002). Secondly, operating as a duopoly for a five-year period implied that high market shares and subsequent profit margins were to be maintained for a relatively long period. This is reflected in the key performance indicators of ECMS, which exceeded the company's own forecasts.

ECMS signed an agreement and a service-provider licence for 15 years with the Egyptian Telecommunications Regulatory Authority, in May 1998. The licence cost LE1.75 billion, in addition to an annual fee to be paid to Egypt Telecom throughout the duration of the licence. It is expected that a new GSM licence will be granted in the first quarter of 2003. However, to date there have been no significant bids for the licence, and it is probable that the government-owned Egypt Telecom will manage the third network. Entry of the third GSM network is expected to place substantial downward pressure on prices.

The licence fee was financed via a US$490 million loan from Chase Manhattan, ABN Amro, Société Générale and a local bank called CIB. It was imperative that the three strategic shareholders (France Telecom, Motorola and Orascom Telecom) should gain a controlling interest in ECMS to be able to obtain a loan of this size on the international market. In June 1999, the Egyptian Capital Market Authority approved a bond issue by ECMS, with a total value of LE340 million to finance the development of the network. The issuance of the bonds was an important step towards a comprehensive financing package, with Chase Manhattan Bank acting as the global coordinator.

Restructuring

Following the acquisition in May 1998, the first challenge facing ECMS was to restructure the acquired network and to expand its capacity, while operation was already underway. Quoting ECMS's CEO, the process of restructuring resembled the attempt to 'change the engines of an airplane while it was flying'. Restructuring was performed at different levels, particularly with regard to the introduction of new generations of mobile communications technology. There was an extensive restructuring and upgrading of infrastructure, including substantial technology transfer by the two contracted suppliers, Alcatel and Motorola.

The company's human resource base was expanded beyond the 50 former employees of Egypt Telecom. Thus, ECMS did not face the challenge of having to restructure the company's human resource base. The human resource aspect of operations was viewed to have been as 'greenfield as it can get'. The former Egypt Telecom staff who joined ECMS were 'cherry picked' by the new management to avoid any redundancy or layoffs following the acquisition. The ECMS workforce currently stands at 1,700 employees.

Highly qualified top and middle management, engineering, technical, marketing and customer-services staff are presently employed. However, during the initial months of operation, and given the novelty of wireless communications-related services in Egypt, ECMS faced some difficulties in filling some key positions and therefore had to rely on expatriate staff. The picture is completely different now, with the exception of very few posts; Egyptian personnel predominate and the same holds true for ECMS's competitor, Click GSM Vodafone.

Customer-care services were introduced for the first time following the acquisition. ECMS also introduced several innovations such as new differentiated services, particularly for the post-paid lines. The billing system was also completely revamped, and new employees were trained in the use of high technology and in high-standard managerial skills.

When the third GSM operator joins the market, employing the skill levels needed to operate and manage the network will not constitute a serious challenge, as the culture and pool of skills related to mobile communications management and operations is already in place. However, it is likely that the new GSM operator will raid the personnel pool of both ECMS and Vodafone.

ECMS restructured its product range, which prior to the acquisition was confined to the post-paid lines. ECMS provides a differentiated service for the post-paid line, which was given the brand name 'Moga', and a prepaid line service under the brand 'ALO'. Prepaid lines are the fastest growing segment of the wireless communications market in Egypt, and to capitalise on this fast growth trend, ECMS has recently introduced installment schemes to finance the ALO line. The third ECMS product is MobiNil Business, which has a special corporate tariff charge and interconnection fees.

Performance

Compared with other mobile operators in the region, MobiNil is showing significant advantages in terms of key financial indicators. It is among the few operators in the region able to generate a return on invested capital despite its high cost of capital. This fact has added to shareholders' value. Many mobile operators in the MENA region are currently not able to cover the cost of their capital due to the large capital expenditures of the late 1990s (EFG-Hermes Research 2002).

In the third quarter of 2002, MobiNil announced consolidated revenues of LE770 million for the quarter versus LE588 million for the third quarter of 2001. Consolidated revenue for the first three quarters of 2002 reached LE1.9 billion compared to LE1.8 billion for the same period in 2001. The company's EBITDA reached LE431 million representing an EBITDA margin of 56.0 per cent for Q3, 2002. ECMS exceeded the targets for subscriber growth, as active subscribers on September 2002 reached 2.1 million (compared with 1.2 million subscribers with Vodafone) representing a growth of 65.3 per cent in active subscribers from the same period last year (Egyptian Company for Mobile Services 2002).

Competition

ECMS's competitor is Click GSM Vodafone (formerly Click GSM), which was the second GSM operator to be granted a licence to operate in the Egyptian market. Click GSM Vodafone (hereafter Vodafone) started as a joint venture between Vodafone, Airtoch and the two local partners, Alkan and EFG-Hermes. Vodafone is an international brand name in the world mobile communications industry, with operations in 25 countries and a

Table 4.2 ECMS Key performance indicators

	1999	2000	2001	2002*
Revenues (LE 000)	1,500,000	2,117,033	2,320,183	1,948,481
EBITDA (LE 000)	490,400	925,554	1,065,301	1,025,589
EBITDA (%)	32	44	45.9	52.6
Net income (LE 000)	n.a.	291,529	340,815	370,823
Active Subscribers (000)	540	1,210	2,034	2,132

Note: * Q1 to Q3 only

Source: www.MobiNil.com

consumer base of some 65 million subscribers. While Vodafone and ECMS acquired their GSM operating licences at roughly the same time, the former was a typical greenfield project, having to build the network infrastructure before commencing operations in November 1998. Vodafone currently holds a 60 per cent stake in Click.

Competition between the two operators has put downward pressure on prices, particularly on interconnection fees. Vodafone was the first to introduce prepaid services, with the presence of the two competitors driving prices. The tariff structure and connection charge for the two GSM service providers are very similar, and these may seem to imply subtle collusion. However, collusion between ECMS and Vodafone is in fact unlikely, as is the probability of exploiting their duopolistic market position. The Telecommunications Regulatory Authority maintains strict control over the movement of tariffs charged by the two companies.

Resources

ECMS inherited a small GSM 900 network with Alcatel technology from Egypt Telecom, serving only 83,000 subscribers in Cairo and Alexandria, with two switches, and less than 100 stations. Since May 1998, and with the increase in the company's switches and stations, the ECMS network now covers all major cities in Egypt, achieving the required coverage specified in its licensing agreement. ECMS has either replaced or relocated the low quality stations, which caused network inefficiency during the initial acquisition period. At present, all of the company's obsolete stations have been replaced, with current stations reaching 1,131.

The technology needed to support a GSM network has to adhere to standard worldwide specifications, since GSM networks worldwide are interconnected to sustain inter-network traffic. Following the acquisition of the government owned and managed GSM operator, ECMS contracted Motorola to supply the latest technology for its stations and other communications equipment. Motorola was also responsible for the upgrades of existing base stations. The French company Alcatel supplied new switching equipment to support the planned increase in network capacity as well as to enhance the quality and consistency of services provided. ECMS has retired the old generation GSM technology or had it redeployed elsewhere.

When Motorola was first contracted as a vendor, it supplied the latest technology base stations and other vital communications equipment in a large number of areas, which were not previously covered when GSM services were first introduced in Egypt. Motorola was also responsible for the key upgrades of the base station equipment, and hence the quality of service and number of lines available. Together, Motorola and Alcatel supplied new switching equipment to support more mobile lines, increasing the quality and consistency of service to ECMS customers, as well as supporting new subscribers. Alcatel supplied significant upgrades to the existing switching equipment and new high technology base stations. When ECMS took over the government-owned GSM operator in Egypt, one of the first tasks was to survey the infrastructure available, add new capacity and expand the network, to measure up to world standards. The outcome, which is summarised in Table 4.3, was a significant improvement in the quality of services (www.MobiNil.com).

Cairo is one of the most densely populated cities of the world, a fact that could have complicated the expansion of MobiNil's GSM network. However, with Motorola's background in the deployment of GSM networks, the solution to overcoming the problems of underground ducting for telecommunications services was to install the latest Free Space Optical (FSO) transmission systems.

ECMS also launched wireless information services in May 2000, employing Motorolas WAP technology. The Wireless Application Protocol (WAP) allows mobile users to access and interact with information services. ECMS was the first mobile service provider to deliver WAP to the Middle East and among the first to introduce WAP services in the world. WAP also allow for the extension of e-commerce to wireless communications users. ECMS will be introducing the next generation of mobile technology to Egypt, having made the first experimental General Packet Radio Service call in Egypt. This technology will bring close to 10 times more bandwidth to the mobile network.

Table 4.3: ECMS operational highlights (2001 and 2002)

	Added in Q4 2001	2001	Added in Q3 2002	2002
Total no. of sites	106	1,659	54	1,817
Total no. of switches	2	13	0	13
Total no. of cities covered	9	234	11	255
Total no. of highways covered	2	53	2	61

Source: www.MobiNil.com/en/pressandmedia

The company's resources are not confined to the latest world technologies but they also include its human resources, especially those with outstanding managerial skills. A shareholders' agreement, with a built-in conflict resolution mechanism, governs the appointment of key management positions in ECMS. Managerial control is shared between the two majority shareholders, France Telecom and Orascom Telecom. France Telecom appoints the Chief Executive Officer, who is also Chairman of the MobiNil Consortium. The current CEO, a Lebanese national, has a prior track record of employment with France Telecom. The decision to employ a Lebanese national to manage the stake of France Telecom in ECMS proved to be an excellent hedge, which has worked in favour of ensuring cultural harmony when working with Egyptian nationals.

Orascom Telecom appoints the Chairman of the Board, and the Chief Government Affairs Officer. The Chief Financial Officer was appointed by Motorola prior to its departure, and has retained his position beyond its exit.

As mentioned earlier, the technology needed to operate a GSM network is, by 2002, rather standard, and is easy to source, operate and maintain. This fact brings management expertise to the forefront as one of the most important ingredients behind the success of GSM network operations. Clearly, the combination of the management track records of both France Telecom and Orascom Telecom has been instrumental in the operating success of ECMS. In fact, the performance of ECMS may have encouraged the various bids of Orascom Telecom to acquire stakes in GSM networks in Africa and the Middle East.

Counterfactual

Without the acquisition, it was most likely that ECMS would have acquired the second licence offered by the Telecommunications Regulatory Authority, which was taken up by its competitor Vodafone. ECMS would have eventually established the second GSM network in Egypt. The scenario to follow the switch in roles and entry dates would have been the same apart from the reversal of the current brand names of existing operators. Both competing companies in the Egyptian market have forged strong partnerships in which foreign players with strong global presence in the mobile telephony sector provided the know-how, while the local partners provide the necessary local market intelligence and culture-sensitive insight.

Concluding Remarks

The Egyptian Company for Mobile Services (ECMS), known in the market as MobiNil, started as a consortium of France Telecom, Motorola and Orascom Telecom. However, Motorola left the consortium in 2001 to avoid the negative consequences in the telecommunications equipment market as a result of being identified as a shareholder in one of the competing service-providing companies in Egypt.

ECMS acquired the state-run network in May 1998 and enjoyed the advantages of the first mover. It is a joint stock company with 51 per cent of its shares owned by MobiNil, 16.6 per cent by Orascom Telecom and 32.4 per cent by stockholders. Moreover, MobiNil's shares are divided between France Telecom (71.25 per cent) and Orascom Telecom (28.75 per cent).

Not only has ECMS managed to overcome the restructuring challenges in upgrading the 100 inherited stations and recruiting skilled labour in the emerging field of telecommunication, but it has also improved its managerial and technical capacities to meet global standards.

The number of subscribers jumped from 83,000 to 2 million between 1998 and 2001, enabling the company to grow at an annual rate of 686 per cent, on average, during the same period. ECMS has also introduced new services to the local market such as the Wireless Information Services in May 2000. The company also launched the first General Packet Radio Service in 2002. These efforts for continuous improvement were aimed at preserving the company's leadership position and market share in Egypt.

Building on the experiences in EDMS, the local partner Orascom has itself grown into a multinational firm and become a major player in the MENA region. Its successful bid for the central licence in Iraq in 2003 is indicative for its newly gained competencies.

GLAXOSMITHKLINE (GSK) EGYPT

The Industry

The pharmaceutical industry has been classified as a 'sunrise' industry of the future. The term sunrise is the optimistic adjective to describe a range of

Table 4.4 Top five research-based pharmaceutical companies by market capitalisation

	Market capitalisation (US$ million)	Pharmaceutical sales 2001	R&D spent 2001	Pharmaceutical growth (%) 2000-01	Headquarters
Pfizer	249,365	26	4.8	13	New York
Johnson & Johnson	193,162	15	1.1	19	New Jersey
GSK	146,281	25	3.8	12	London
Merck	125,407	21	2.4	5	New Jersey
Novartis	101,686	15	2.2	15	Basel
Egypt GDP	93,800	—	—	—	—

Sources: Pharmaceuticals Executive (2001) Available at (www.pharmaexc.com)

industrial activities that share a set of common characteristics of being '...relatively new, technologically progressive concerns investing heavily in R&D in order to foster not only growth but, more fundamentally, survival given the high vulnerability of their products to rapid technological obsolescence...' (Wells, 1985 p. 11). Sunrise or new-economy industries include companies operating in the fields of electronic data processing, electrical and electronic engineering, aerospace and pharmaceuticals. The pharmaceuticals industry distinguishes itself from other manufacturing activities with its research intensity, as the share of sales allocated to research and development (R&D) has currently reached 18.5 per cent, up from 11.4 per cent in 1970 (PhARMA 2002). These figures are unrivalled by any other new economy industry.

Two types of manufacturing activities characterise the supply side of pharmaceutical production. Research-based companies produce breakthrough drugs, which are patent protected, and normally invest heavily in R&D. Generic manufacturers produce off-patent products, with production costs basically divided between manufacturing and marketing.

Judging by market capitalisation figures, research-based pharmaceutical companies control huge financial resources, a fact which has effectively awarded this group of TNCs, financial power that exceeds the GDP of developing countries. Egypt is a case in point (Table 4.4).

Pharmaceutical products are highly differentiated, and therefore, can only be grouped in sub-markets within which only a reasonable degree of substitutability of one product for the other exists. Competition is assessed within the domains of particular therapeutic groups of drugs. Further distinction is made between in-patent products and generics, as well as between ethical products and over the counter (OTC) drugs. OTC drugs can be obtained without prescription and dispensed outside the regular pharmacy. These distinctions carry significant implications in terms of the cost of production, pricing, entry barriers and competition.

In-patent drugs, referred to as single-source drugs, have a relatively high fixed R&D cost in relation to the total cost of production. In a single-source drug market, higher prices are reinforced by limited competition due to patent protection, which is one of the most significant barriers to entry. Product competition is usually more important than price competition. That is, the ability to create new medicines is more important than the ability to produce them cheaply (Howells and Neary, 1995). Once a product is off patent, drug manufacturers enter what was once a single-source drug sub-market by providing generic versions, which significantly undercut the price of the original brand. In the generic or multiple-source drug market, patent protection is absent and entry barriers are relatively low.

The Egyptian market for pharmaceuticals is estimated at US$1 billion, with local production covering roughly 94 per cent of local demand by volume (American Chamber of Commerce in Egypt, 2001). Sales have increased by over 150 per cent from 1991 to 2002 (Ministry of Health and Population 2002). The Egyptian pharmaceutical market is a predominantly multiple-source drug market, in which the production of generics has proliferated under the auspices of a patent regime (Law 132 of 1949), which only provides patents for processes. Subsidiaries of foreign multinationals produce virtually all of their products under licence for the parent company. On the other hand, domestic private and public firms produce close to half of their products under licence, while the rest fall under the category of generics (Subramanian and Abd El Latif 1997). The case of Egypt is typical of non-major developing country markets, in which generics usually represent more than 30 per cent of the total market by value and 40 per cent by volume (Southworth 1996).

Egypt is a member of the World Trade Organization (WTO), and will, therefore, be obliged to enforce higher standards of intellectual property rights in conformity with the Agreement on Trade Related Aspects of Intellectual Property Rights (TRIPS). The TRIPS Agreement stipulates the provision of a standard 20-year period of patent protection for pharmaceutical products, and is therefore likely to significantly change the pharmaceutical market outlook in Egypt. It is important to note that foreign companies operating in the Egyptian market have collaborated and account for a powerful lobby in urging the Egyptian government towards a speedy respect of the TRIPS Agreement. Generic manufacturers in Egypt (mainly local firms) will have to respect the 20-year period of exclusivity awarded to patent owners. Otherwise, production can only take place under licence from the patent owner.

In addition to being a multiple-source drug market, one of the distinctive characteristics of the Egyptian market for pharmaceutical products is the de facto absence of distinction between ethical and OTC products. This blur has significantly influenced demand for pharmaceuticals. With the exception of a short negative list of products (falling in the general category of narcotics), virtually all pharmaceutical products can be obtained without prescription. Self-prescription is extremely common in Egypt, which explains the very high per capita intake of antibiotics, relative to other markets. Another feature of the Egyptian pharmaceutical market is the relatively low prices of pharmaceutical products, a function of tight government pricing polices for the sector. Pharmaceutical prices in Egypt tend to be among the lowest in the world.

The Investor

The merger between GlaxoWellcome and SmithKline Beecham in January 2001 resulted in the creation of the second-largest pharmaceutical production entity in the world (ranked by global sales), with an estimated 7 per cent of the worlds pharmaceutical market. GlaxoSmithKline (GSK) pharmaceutical sales currently stand at US$24.8 billion, and the company's net profit is US$6.5 billion. While GSK is headquartered in the UK, the company's operations are truly global. GSK has over 100,000 employees worldwide, close to half of which (42,000 employees) work at 107 manufacturing sites in 40 countries (GSK 2002).

The GSK R&D budget of US$4 billion is the largest in the industry. Over 16,000 employees work in the field of R&D. It is important to note that GSK's R&D operations are less globalised than manufacturing and marketing. R&D is located in 24 sites in seven countries, mainly in Europe and the US. In recent efforts to capture a share of emerging bio-technology activities in less developed regions of the world, GSK expanded its R&D activities to China, which is the largest healthcare market in the world.

GSK has a long track record of mergers and acquisitions, the largest of which has been the merger between Glaxo and Wellcome to form GlaxoWellcome in 1995, and that between GlaxoWellcome and SmithKline Beecham, which executed in 2001. The latest merger has targeted the restructuring of manufacturing activities, designed to allow the company to make savings of US$2.57 billion by 2003 (GSK 2002).

GSK has manufacturing facilities in several countries in Africa and the Middle East, including Egypt, Kenya, Morocco, South Africa, Israel, Saudi Arabia and Turkey.

Acquired Local Firm

The history of GSK Egypt dates back to the 1980s, with a series of mergers and acquisitions, see Table 4.5. In 1981, Glaxo acquired minority ownership in Advanced Medical Industries (ABI), one of the local pharmaceutical companies. In less than ten years, this partnership advanced what was a relatively small company, with no profits and a market share of 1 per cent (and a market rank of 22nd) to a consolidate its market presence. In 1990, Glaxo Group Limited acquired a controlling interest of 51 per cent in ABI, taking over the management. Further consolidation followed in 1991, when the Group acquired 69 per cent of the company's stock. In 1992, the company changed its name to Glaxo Egypt SAE with the controlling interest of Glaxo increasing and reaching 87.8 per cent.

Following the merger of Glaxo and Wellcome in 1995, the name of the company was changed to GlaxoWellcome Egypt. During the same year, GlaxoWellcome increased its stake of GlaxoWellcome Egypt to 90 per cent. The remaining shareholders were a small group of institutional investors. Following the merger between GlaxoWellcome and SmithKline Beecham in January 2001, the name of the company was changed to GSK Egypt.

The history of the acquired local company goes back to 1976. Amoun Pharmaceuticals was among the first private companies to be established in the Egyptian pharmaceutical sector after the enactment of the Investment

Table 4.5 Chronology of acquisitions by GSK Egypt 1981-2002

1976	Advanced Medical Industries (ABI) established.
1981	Glaxo acquired a minority ownership in Advanced Medical Industries.
1989	Advanced Medical Industries sold its manufacturing facility in Egypt to Glaxo.
1990	Glaxo Group Limited acquired controlling interest (51 per cent), taking over management of ABI.
1991	Glaxo Group Limited acquired 69 per cent of ABI's stock.
1992	ABI name changed to Glaxo Egypt S.A.E., with controlling interest reaching 87.8 per cent.
1995	Glaxo and Wellcome merger executed and the name of the company changed to GlaxoWellcome Egypt.
1999	GlaxoWellcome Egypt acquired 97 per cent of APIC.
2001	Merger between GlaxoWellcome and SmithKline Beecham, and name of GlaxoWellcome Egypt was changed to GSK Egypt.

Encouragement Law 43 of 1974, which opened the field to private investment. The company was initially founded as an import and distribution company, but developed to become one of the fastest growing companies in the Egyptian pharmaceutical market.

In 1989, Advanced Medical Industries (ABI) – the first of the companies owned by Amoun – sold its private sector manufacturing facility in Egypt to Glaxo. The owner, Dr Sarwat Bassily, already had another manufacturing facility, and his second company Amoun Pharmaceutical Industries Company (APIC) was then ranked fourth among Egyptian pharmaceutical companies.

In January 1999, GlaxoWellcome Egypt acquired 97 per cent of APIC, which at that time held a 3 per cent share of the local market. The acquisition, which cost LE387 million (£70 million), elevated GlaxoWellcome Egypt to pharmaceutical market leader in Egypt, with the company's market share increasing from 6 per cent to around 9 per cent. Amoun currently operates its third company, described below, the two spin-off acquisitions by GlaxoWellcome in 1989 and 1999. The acquisition of APIC by GSK was the third largest acquisition worldwide in the pharmaceuticals industry that year. (See Table 4.6.)

The proceeds of the sale have been used to expand APIC's parent company's new facility in one of the industrial zones around Cairo, which will probably become on of the largest pharmaceutical manufacturing facilities in Egypt. The owner of the acquired company has also retained the brand name of his original company, Amoun. Amoun is a major pharmaceutical exporter in Egypt, exporting to a number of countries, including the USA, Romania, Russia and 14 Arab states.

Table 4.6 Top acquisition deals outside North America and Europe

Value $m	Target name	Country	Bidder name	Country
339	Torii Pharmaceutical	Japan	Japan Tobacco	Japan
132	South African Druggists	S. Africa	Fedsure Holdings	S. Africa
106	**Amoun Pharmaceuticals**	**Egypt**	**GlaxoWellcome**	**UK**
42	Chia Tai Health Products	China	Shanghai Industrial.	Hong Kong
33	Hoechst South Africa	S. Africa	Hoechst	Germany
24	Merind	India	Wockhardt	India
23	Pfizer Korea (Pfizer, Shinwon)	S Korea	Pfizer	USA
14	Roche Products-Hisinchu Factory	Taiwan	Utd Biomedical	USA
14	Hubei Zenith Pharmaceutical	China	Hubei Zenith Group	China
12	Chongqing Medicine	China	Chongqing Taiji	China

Source: PriceWaterhouseCoopers (1999) 'Pharmaceutical Sector Insights'.

The sale by Amoun of its two companies ABI and APIC constitutes a precedent in Egypt where one company twice acquires another company from the same owner. Following the acquisition, GSK Egypt took over the physical premises of APIC, which are located back-to-back with the GSK Egypt factory, another strategic reason to have acquired the company, so as to allow expansion of already existing manufacturing facilities in the same geographic location and close to management headquarters.

The most important intangible asset that motivated GSK's interest in acquiring both ABI and APIC was the market shares held by both companies at the point of acquisition. The sales forces of the two companies and their knowledge of the local market was an extra benefit of the acquisition.

It is also interesting to note that the owner of both ABI and APIC planned to sell assets in one company while having another subsidiary already operating in the market. The notion that TNCs will eventually drive local businesses out of the market as a result of their acquisition strategies has been refuted by the experience of GSK in Egypt.

Motives for Setting up Operations in Egypt

Generally speaking, the decision of a pharmaceutical company to invest abroad is based on the commitment of resources for the purpose of earning a financial return, or with the expectation of gaining future benefits. Generic motives for investing in third country markets include the availability of raw materials, the ability to carry out sophisticated chemical syntheses, and the availability of the workforce (Wescoe 1985).

Another important reason behind the decision of many TNCs to operate in the Egyptian market is related to the nature of the pharmaceuticals market in general. The worldwide market for pharmaceuticals is highly fragmented, which means that there is a considerable degree of variation in the regulatory regimes across countries, which in turn makes it easier to set up manufacturing facilities locally in order to cater to local demand. This is particularly true in the case of relatively large markets.

Like most subsidiaries of research-based pharmaceutical companies located in developing regions, GSK Egypt is only involved in formulation activities, which means that it imports bulk chemicals and processes them in Egypt into their final dosage forms. Hardly any R&D takes place in Egypt, with the few exceptions of the development of some products for local conditions.

When GSK first commenced production in Egypt (as Glaxo) scope for catering exclusively to the local market was very attractive, with a consumer market of some 60 million inhabitants. However, low per capita income was a deterrent against bringing in the whole portfolio of GSK products to the Egyptian market. For this reason, a brownfield entry mode seemed to provide the perfect fit with the strategy of Glaxo at this point in time (early 1980s).

Forming a partnership with an already existing local company enabled the relatively expensive product portfolio of Glaxo to be augmented with the complementary portfolio of the local partner company.

One of the major incentives for the company to choose this model of acquisition is the 'jump-start'. It is much easier for a company to start operating in an already existing framework, with existing licences, approvals, buildings, and infrastructure (even if it is basic) and more importantly an existing market. In the case of GSK it is obvious that the major incentive for the acquisition was not the existing machinery or production line, since there was a major technology transfer, restructuring and extensive replacement of capital equipment. The major incentive was the already existing market share, as well as the fact that the acquired local company was located back-to-back to the GSK factory and management headquarters, which meant that any future expansion could be easily accommodated.

The former managing director, who engineered the two acquisitions of ABI and APIC, was asked about what he would choose by way of entry mode, if given another chance. The prompt answer was: 'greenfield'. From the viewpoint of someone who went through a brownfield experience, greenfield entry in the domain of pharmaceutical production is perceived to best serve the company's objectives and goals for a longer-term vision. Brownfield proved to be time-consuming and burdensome, especially when integrating the administrative bodies of the two companies during the initial phase of the acquisition. Greenfield entry could have helped the business expand without having to put up with an obsolete infrastructure. The burden of restructuring, having to deal with redundant labour, and training needs of the acquired company's workforce are yet another problem associated with brownfield modes of entry. It is important to mention that several of the foreign pharmaceutical companies launched their operations in Egypt as greenfield, foremost among which has been Bristol Myers Squibb, which was the first wholly-owned foreign subsidiary to operate in the Egyptian market.

Entry Formalities

The pharmaceutical-drug regulatory regime in Egypt is composed of three major government bodies. The Central Administration of Pharmaceutical Affairs (CAPA) grants the licence for a company to commence manufacturing; the Drug Planning and Policy Centre (DPPC) is responsible for product registration and pricing; and the National Organization for Drug Control and Research (NODCAR) conducts physical, microbiological, pharmacological and bioavailability testing involving human volunteers. The three bodies fall under the umbrella of the Ministry of Health and Population (MOHAP).

Product registration and pricing are the most cumbersome product entry hurdles facing pharmaceutical companies in Egypt. While registration requirements are fairly straightforward, whereby the provision of a 'free sales certificate' in one of five reference industrialised countries is the basis for obtaining approval, a lag of two to three years usually occurs between the introduction of a product in one of the reference countries and its marketing in Egypt.

No more than four identical products, in terms of therapeutic value and dosage, are allowed to be sold on the Egyptian market, with the exception of products intended for export sales or for public tenders on the local market.

Pricing is the second hurdle. Pharmaceutical products in Egypt are priced on the basis of a cost-plus formula (see Table 4.7), to ensure both the affordability of medicine and to guarantee a positive profit on all drug products sold (Nathan Associates 1995). Moreover, the profit-margin ceiling is 15 per cent for essential drugs, 25 per cent for non-essentials and 40 per cent or more for OTC drugs. Pricing policies and price controls explain which local prices of pharmaceuticals in Egypt are sometimes 80 per cent less than their imported equivalents according to Prime Research (1997).

Restructuring

GSK Egypt has a long track record of restructuring, associated with having gone through two major acquisitions in Egypt as well as two mega-mergers globally. The first episode of restructuring ensued when Glaxo acquired the minority stake in ABI. ABI began to manufacture the products of Glaxo locally, which necessitated adherence to higher manufacturing standards and specifications, as well as training of the sales staff to market the new products.

The second episode of restructuring, which followed the increase in Glaxo's stake in ABI in 1990, and the change of the company's name to Glaxo Egypt, was more comprehensive as the new management restructured the whole firm and substantially increased investment, particularly in the plant and equipment.

There was a complete turnover of employees and a restructuring of the whole management and personnel systems. The company's personnel policy and attitude was marred by the 'jobs for life' culture, which proved highly problematic. The company's headcount, which was 741 at entry, was gradually increased to reach 1,550 by 2000. Between 1990 and 2000 some 380 workers were made redundant and 1,190 new employees were hired. A large-scale programme was instituted to retrain and reorient existing workers and enable them to assimilate the latest imported technology, with a major shift of emphasis from manual to automated systems. As part of the restructuring, both manufacturing facilities and the distribution system were totally rebuilt.

In 1995, the merger between Glaxo and Wellcome in turn necessitated

Table 4.7 Pricing structure for pharmaceutical products in Egypt

Local products	Index	
Ex-factory price	100.00	Price to distributor
+ Distributors' mark-up (12.36%)	112.36	Price to pharmacist
+ Pharmacists' mark-up (25.00%)	140.45	
+ Sales tax (5%) of ex-factory price	145.45	
+ Medical stamp	145.50	Price to public
Imports	Index	
CIF price	100.00	
+ Import taxes (11.55%)	111.55	Landed cost
+ Importers' mark-up (6.4%)	118.65	Price to distributor
+ Distributors' mark-up (7.53%)	127.63	Price to pharmacist
+ Pharmacists' mark-up (13.64%)	145.03	
+ Taxes (1.63% of CIF)	146.66	Price to public

Source: AIDMO (2000)

restructuring on the local front, as a host of Wellcome products were added to the company's product portfolio.

As a result of the acquisition of APIC in 1999, GSK acquired the domestic and export rights to 30 APIC products, including vitamins, antibiotics and analgesics, as well as APIC's production facilities. Up to 300 APIC employees were hired by GlaxoWellcome and were mainly employed in the sales domain. It was also important, however, to retain the sales force of APIC to be able to maintain the links with the acquired company's network of physicians and pharmacists who promote APIC's products. The retention of the 30 APIC products was a strategic decision to complement GlaxoWellcome Egypt's existing business. The nature of the acquisition enabled GlaxoWellcome to supply the Egyptian pharmaceutical market with the broadest range of cost-effective medicines. It also significantly strengthened the company's OTC franchise.

It is, however, important to note that the manufacturing facilities that were acquired from APIC (manufacturing site, machinery and equipment) have not been put to use by GSK Egypt. The post-acquisition assessment of APIC's manufacturing site revealed the need for a significant upgrade in order to fit with GSK manufacturing standards and specifications. The intention following the acquisition was to demolish the APIC site and expand the manufacturing facilities of GSK Egypt.

The most significant of the restructuring episodes, undertaken by GSK Egypt, started in 2000 to prepare the Egypt manufacturing site as one of the supply hubs to 66 markets in Africa, the Middle East and some parts of Europe. This decision was part of a global strategy to restructure GSK's worldwide manufacturing and marketing operations. It will create a specialisation based on the product life cycle, whereby some sites will specialise in the production of drugs in the early phases of their product life cycle, while others specialise in more mature products. Most multinationals operating in Egypt do not use Egypt as an export base to other markets. GDK's new strategy has for the first time placed Egypt as a potential export springboard to neighbouring regions, thus validating the argument that the Egyptian pharmaceutical industry holds strong potential as a low-cost base for the 'production' of pharmaceuticals. It is not known whether this will create a demonstration effect, and be followed by other MNEs.

The SMP has had restructuring implications for the product portfolio of GSK Egypt. A group of products, which were already registered, manufactured and sold in Egypt, were discontinued in favour of importing them at the same cost as those sold on the Egyptian market. A host of new products were added to the local portfolio. Some new products were also added exclusively for export. The process of reconfiguration of the product portfolio of GSK Egypt, in order to prepare the Cairo location to act as the regional supply hub, was initially not welcomed by the regulatory authorities in Egypt. Concern over health care policy objectives, of guaranteeing a sufficient supply of already existing products, was given priority over industrial policy objectives of promoting Egypt as an export base for pharmaceuticals.

The last of the restructuring efforts to date took place following the merger between GlaxoWellcome and SmithKline Beecham in January 2001, to integrate the products of the latter.

Performance

The main activities of GSK Egypt are the manufacturing, packaging, marketing, selling and distributing of GSK products. GSK Egypt also imports and distributes a range of products of the parent company that are not manufactured in Egypt. In addition, GSK Egypt manufactures a range of products under licence from other pharmaceutical manufacturers.

Like most foreign owned subsidiaries, new in-patent products are only manufactured locally after a lag between their initial launch in the major markets of the US and Europe and being manufactured in Egypt. This lag is mainly attributed to the lack of a strong patent regime needed to deter infringing activities, and secondly to the absence of the relevant technology needed to manufacture sophisticated products.

GSK Egypt currently assumes the lead position as the number one pharmaceutical firm in the Egyptian market, (see Table 4.8). A company making a loss of LE2 million in 1991 was completely revamped and was transformed into a profit-generating company in 2001. Total sales increased from LE142 million in 1994 to LE390 million in 2001, and market shares increased from 6 per cent to 9 per cent over the same period.

Table 4.8 GSK market share (%) for selected market (LE million)

	1994	1995	1996	1997	1998	2001
Selected market (LE million)	2.285	2.569	2.735	3.357	3.491	4.334
GlaxoWellcome Egypt	6.2	7.2	7.5	7.8	8.4	9.9*
BMS Egypt	6.2	6.2	6.2	5.5	5.8	5.3
Eipico	4.9	5.1	4.8	5.0	5.1	4.8
Pfizer Egypt	3.5	3.9	4.4	4.1	3.9	3.8
Pharco	3.7	3.8	4	3.6	3.5	3.8

Note: The total shares of GSK plus Amoun
Source: IMS, 2002

GSK Egypt is the only foreign company engaged in export activities in Egypt, mainly to markets in the Middle East and Africa. The large number of Egyptian physicians working in the Gulf region have been playing an important role in promoting the drugs manufactured in Egypt. GSK Egypt seems to have been capitalising on this fact since it started exporting from Egypt during the 1990s. GSK exports are projected to increase substantially, following the full implementation of the SMP.

Competition

There are 29 firms with manufacturing facilities for final pharmaceutical products in Egypt, covering more than 94 per cent of local demand (by volume, GSK Egypt currently ranks first in the Egyptian market in terms of sales value and volume). GSK Egypt's immediate competitors are the subsidiaries of foreign companies operating in Egypt, as well as local private sector companies. Most of these companies (foreign and local private) were established in Egypt after 1974, following the enactment of the Investment Promotion Law 43 of 1974, which was designed to encourage foreign and local private-sector participation in an economy that was dominated by public sector ownership.

Pharmaceutical manufacturers do not compete for the whole range of products available on a market. Instead, competition takes place within the domains of specific therapeutic groups of drugs. Within each of the top five therapeutic groups on the Egyptian market (in terms of sales value), GSK holds a prominent rank among the top five manufacturers.

Because of low per capita income in Egypt (US$1,300), competition between pharmaceutical companies is mainly based on price. Quality is relatively standard in the pharmaceutical industry, with prices becoming the most important factor when prescribing medication, particularly for patients covered by public health insurance schemes. However, foreign companies, like GSK Egypt for example, usually have their products priced at a much higher value than their local counter parts (for drugs with identical generic composition). The lower prices for pharmaceutical products in Egypt are usually charged by the public sector companies, which had the majority of their products priced during a period when price controls were prevalent for public sector output.

In Egypt, it is very difficult to adjust the prices of pharmaceutical products to accommodate inflation and changes in the cost of raw material inputs that are usually very sensitive to any movements in the exchange rate. There have been mounting complaints that the successive devaluations of the Egyptian pound against the dollar have increasingly affected the profitability levels of all pharmaceutical companies operating in Egypt, local and foreign alike. The pharmaceutical industry in Egypt is import intensive (the industry imports more than 90 per cent of all its raw material), and is therefore highly vulnerable to movements in the exchange rate while having prices fixed at the other end of the chain.

In the face of the inflexibility exercised by the regulatory authorities over price revision in the face of inflation and devaluation, drug manufacturers in Egypt have managed to deal with stringent price revaluations by resorting to a process called 'vintaging'. Vintaging means 'that identical products introduced at different times will be sold at different prices, with the more recent "vintage" products being sold at a higher price' (Nathan Associates 1995).

Resources

The GSK plant is located in El Salam City near Cairo International Airport on an area of 55,000m^2, of which the manufacturing plants occupy 15,000m^2. The GSK staff are the most important resource of the company, having currently reached 1,057 employees. GSK Egypt invests heavily in the training of its staff, both at the Cairo manufacturing site as well as at the UK headquarters. GSK Egypt has achieved universal training for its staff at the Cairo manufacturing site, whereby every single employee in the organization has been trained in his or her own professional field.

From the outset, development of the Glaxo Egypt operation has had three major components. First, efforts to establish a total quality management system led to ISO 9002 certification from the British Standards Institution in 1997, the first pharmaceutical company in the Middle East and Africa to achieve this. GSK was also awarded the ISO 14001 in 1997, reflecting their commitment to environmental management. Similar success has been achieved in certification for manufacturing resource-planning processes.

Second, the company invested LE2 million in a development laboratory in 1995 with the principal objective of developing products off patent. Since 1992, 61 product forms have been registered. Four people are presently involved in development and 40 in quality assurance and control. Third, the company has taken its initial steps towards exporting and is the first pharmaceutical TNC in Egypt to market outside the country. Approval has been given to supply Qatar, Yemen and Nigeria, and exports to the latter were worth around LE3 million in 1997. There are hopes that GSK Egypt will be granted the regional mandate to become one of two supply sources for GSK for the Middle East and African market.

As for most pharmaceutical companies, there is no 'direct to consumer advertising', which although it could be done at a relatively low cost through the mass media, is not allowed for the pharmaceutical industry in Egypt. All companies, therefore, have to rely on highly trained sales staff, who make regular visits to physicians and pharmacists to promote the company's products. The sales staff of GSK Egypt is regarded as one of its most important resources and great investment is made in their training.

Concluding Remarks

Glaxo first entered the Egyptian market in 1981 by acquiring a minority ownership in a local company, AB). Ten years later, the group extended its share to reach 87.8 per cent and changed the name of the company to Glaxo Egypt SAE. After the group's global mergers with Wellcome in 1995 and SmithKline Beecham in 2001; the company's name became GlaxoSmithKline (GSK) Egypt.

The brownfield mode of acquisitions provided the company with the jump-start it needed and enabled it to diversify its portfolio of products in a way that reduced the expected risks of low per-capita income and price control prevailing in the Egyptian pharmaceutical market.

The restructuring programme went through several phases following Glaxo Group's global mergers with Wellcome and SmithKline as well as its acquisition of the local company APIC in 1999. The impact of the restructuring efforts was positive enough to increase the company's market share from 1 per cent in 1981 to 9.9 per cent in 2001 and to expand rapidly the range of its offered products.

The achievements of GSK Egypt are not confined to the local market in which it has managed to reach the leadership position. But it has been recognised as the only exporting multinational company in the Egyptian pharmaceutical sector. Furthermore, GSK has successfully invested in both a local development laboratory and in human resources.

CAIRO FOOD INDUSTRIES SAE HEINZ EGYPT

Introduction

Heinz is a global leader in a segment of the processed food industry, and known especially for its ketchup. For its operation in Egypt, it partnered with a Kuwaiti firm, the Kuwait Food Company, which had been established in Egypt for 25 years. The group, also known under its brand name 'Americana', operates as a local franchise partner in the Arab region to global brands in the food and restaurant industries. It contributes both knowledge of the local business environment, and access to franchise restaurants, a key customer group for Heinz's ketchup.

In addition to the local market, Heinz has been developing Egypt as an export base, utilising the favourable climatic conditions for growing tomatoes. It works with local farmers to change their operation modes and logistics to produce tomato varieties, quality and delivery procedures that meet the requirements of industrial food processing.

The Industry

The food processing industry is one of Egypt's oldest manufacturing sectors, relying on the high quality and low-priced agricultural output of the country. The food processing industry accounts for a large yet stable share of output and employment in Egypt, it generates around 15 per cent of Egypt's manufacturing value added and is the second largest industry after the textiles and garment sector. Output was valued at around US$5.2 billion in 1999.

There are 1,299 establishments (15 workers or more) in the food-processing sector, employing 73,000 workers. Over the past decade, the expansion in land reclamation projects has added over 100,000 acres (1,000 hectar) of vegetable and fruit cultivation, which has increased the supply of cost-competitive agricultural inputs to the food processing industry. The Egyptian food processing industry has been a high growth sector, with an annual growth rate of 22 per cent during the decade of the 1990s, mostly in response to the increase in domestic demand (Ministry of Economy 1996).

Processed food in Egypt is not only fast growing, but also undergoing a major transformation in response to changes in consumer demand, both locally and in key export markets. Traditionally, food would be freshly prepared in the household. Yet, changing work patterns of the urban middle class, including higher female work force participation, led to an increased demand for convenience food products like frozen vegetables, pre-cooked meals, etc.

The bulk of processed food in Egypt is manufactured by semi-automated small to medium sized plants. The industry is highly diversified in terms of output, with major product groups including preserved foods such as dried, canned and frozen fruits and vegetables, preserved and processed meat, poultry and fish, milk and dairy products, edible oils, sugar and confectionery products, and fermented and distilled beverages.

Several government authorities regulate the industry. The Egyptian Organization for Standardization and Quality Control of the Ministry of Industry issues industrial quality-control certificates for the food processing industry. New processed-food products launched on the Egyptian market have to obtain a licence from the Institute of Food Industries. The Ministry of Health and the Ministry of Home Trade and Supply also enforce stringent shelf life standards and product specifications for both processed food and agricultural products.

Imports of processed food products into Egypt have to be inspected by five different government bodies, including the Ministries of Agriculture, Health, Supply and Trade, as well as by the Radiation Department and the Customs Authority. Customs duties on imported food products in Egypt range from 5 to 40 per cent, depending on the status of the product as essential or non-essential (Gilada 1999).

Investor: HJ Heinz

HJ Heinz is one of the world's leaders in the branded food processing industry, and is ranked as the 10th largest company in terms of global sales. The company was established in 1869 in the United States as a family run business. The first international expansion by Heinz outside of the USA occurred as early as 1896 with the establishment of its overseas office in London. After years of internal growth, Heinz embarked on a strategy of global expansion and acquired a food processor in the Netherlands, a step that was later repeated in Italy, Portugal, Mexico and many other countries.

At present, Heinz holds the lead position among branded businesses in the majority of the key markets worldwide. HJ Heinz owns several brands including Heinz, Ore-Ida, Smart Ones, Classico, Wyler's Delimex. Heinz also produces several products under licence such as Weight Watchers, and T.G.I. Friday's. The company follows a strategy of related diversification within the food processing industry, and has in recent years focused its product portfolio on sales of peripheral businesses and acquisitions in the core business areas. The core business areas are ketchup, condiments and sauces (28 per cent of turnover, FY 2002), frozen foods (21.2 per cent), tuna and seafood (11.0 per cent), soup, beans and pasta (12.6 per cent), infant foods (9.5 per cent), and pet products (10.4 per cent).

The Heinz's ketchup brand is one of the high performers in the Heinz product portfolio, with market shares of 60 per cent in the US and 66 per cent in the UK. (Heinz *Annual Report* 2002). It is one of the best-known brands worldwide and closely associated with the American way of life.

In a recent strategic restructuring, the company revised its portfolio of products, whereby Heinz spun off the US and Canadian pet food, the US tuna, infant feeding, the retail private soup and gravy, and the College Inn Broth businesses. The spin-off businesses will merge with Del Monte Foods in order to create wholly-owned subsidiaries with stronger and better-positioned companies. The objective is to focus the product portfolio on higher margin, higher growth businesses. The two strategic segments that Heinz currently focuses on are meal enhancers as well as meals and snacks (Heinz *Annual Report* 2002).

HJ Heinz provides more than 5,700 product varieties in more than 50 countries all over the world. In the financial year ending 1 May 2002, Heinz sales reached US$9.4 billion (see Table 4.9), which is more than the entire food industry in Egypt. Worldwide, Heinz employs 46,500 people and generated a profit before tax of US$1.3 billion. Over 40 per cent of its sales, assets and profits are generated outside the USA.

Table 4.9 HJ Heinz: global performance indicators (US$ 000)

	2002	2000	1995	1992
Sales ($)	9,431,000	8,939,416	8,086,794	6,581,867
Cost of products sold ($)	6,093,827	5,788,525	5,119,597	4,102,816
Profit after tax ($)	833,889	890,553	591,025	638,295
Number of employees	46,500	46,900	42,200	35,500
Total assets ($)	10,278,354	8,850,657	8,247,188	5,931,901

Source: Heinz *Annual Report,* 2002.

In 1990, Heinz management explored the Egyptian market and approached the Kuwaiti Food Corporation to form a partnership. The two companies formed Heinz Egypt as a joint venture, which started production in 1992. Heinz Egypt started with imported tomato concentrate, but gradually shifted to local fresh tomato varieties. The initial investment in 1991 was LE37.3 million (equivalent to US$11.4 million based on the ruling exchange rate in 1991) to set up manufacturing facilitates for Heinz products in Egypt, with a focus on tomato (mainly ketchup and tomato paste) products.

In 2002, Heinz Egypt manufactured and marketed tomato-based products, juices, jams and condiments for Egypt and other Arab countries. Manufactured products include Heinz brand, Americana brand and several private labels. The Heinz plant in Egypt has a production capacity of approximately 7,000 tons per annum. Heinz Egypt also exports 35 per cent of its output to markets of the Middle East, mainly to the Gulf Cooperation Council and Saudi markets. Heinz Egypt does not export beyond the regional markets of the Middle East and North Africa. In the Middle East, HJ Heinz has, in addition to the manufacturing plant in Egypt, two manufacturing plants in Israel, established respectively by greenfield in 1999 and by acquisition in 2000. Organisationally, the Middle East is integrated within the European division of Heinz.

The Partner Company

The 'Kuwait Food Company' was established in 1964 as the food-processing arm of the Al Kharafi Group, and is known throughout the Arab world under its 'Americana' brand name. It has been listed on the Kuwait stock exchange since 1981. Al Kharafi Group is a private Kuwait-based group, with diversified interests and activities worldwide. It was established as a trading company more than 100 years ago, and has now developed into an international grade 'A' contractor with an annual turnover in excess of US$2.2 billion. The activities of the group cover construction, manufacturing and commerce. The group has the largest food company in the Middle East. In Egypt, the group has invested US$700 million, divided between the food-processing industry, the tourism sector (which includes the franchise business segment) and infrastructure projects.

Americana was first established as a trading company in Kuwait, but has now developed to become the largest food processing, distribution and retail company in the Middle East. Americana is highly profitable (see Table 4.10) and has some 15,000 employees in its branches located in Egypt, Saudi Arabia, UAE, Qatar, Bahrain, Lebanon, Syria, Morocco and Lebanon.

The operations of Americana include trade and distribution of food products, manufacturing (food processing) and the fast-food franchise business. Food processing activities vary according to the market concerned. For example in Saudi Arabia and in Kuwait, Americana is mainly engaged in the processing of meat products as well as baked products. In the United Arab Emirates, Americana has the largest mineral water production facilities as well as canned beans production. Americana also has the largest cold storage facilities in the Arab world.

Americana is a market leader for franchise business in the Middle East. It is the franchisee for KFC, Pizza Hut, Subway, Hardee's, and T.G.I. Friday's in Egypt, where the franchise business is estimated to be worth some US$158 million and is one of the high performing sectors in terms of generating demand for processed food products. It is expected to be growing at a real rate of 5 per cent. The franchise business is one of the major consumers of Heinz's products in Egypt.

Americana was established in Egypt during the 1970s, following the Investment Incentives Law 43 of 1974, which constituted the legislative foundation of the encouragement of private sector (local and foreign) investment. Incentives provided under Law 43 and its amendments were mainly fiscal in nature, with a five-year tax break on corporate profit,

Table 4.10 Kuwait Food Company 'Americana': financial indicators

Year	Assets (000 KD)	Paid Up Capital (000 KD)	Equity (000 KD)	Net Profit (000 KD)	ROE (%)	ROA (%)
1996	101.84	11.29	37.53	6.46	17.22	6.35
1997	106.28	11.29	42.24	6.89	16.32	6.49
1998	104.18	12.42	46.02	7.64	16.61	7.34
1999	109.05	12.42	54.63	9.60	17.57	8.80
2000	118.01	12.42	58.21	12.07	20.73	10.22

Note: 1 Kuwaiti dinar = 3.36462 US dollar

Source: The Institute of Banking Studies (IBS) in Kuwait,
http://www.kibs.org/kse/kkfcfd.htm

extendable to ten years for projects created in new industrial communities. Most of Americana's business in Egypt is by way of partnerships with American franchises, but in 1991 it also partnered with Cadbury to produce confectionary products in Egypt.

Motives for Setting up Operation in Egypt

Heinz's investment in Egypt has been driven by the objective of accessing local supplies, and by market-seeking motives in view of growing local and regional markets. On the supply-side, Egypt is ranked as the world's fifth largest producer of tomatoes, an attraction for the world's leading producer of tomato-based products. Egypt produces over 5 million tons of fresh tomatoes per year. Climatic conditions in Egypt are very favourable for the cultivation of tomatoes, because the time span during which tomatoes can be grown stretches for 120 days each year. Tomatoes can be cultivated three times during the season: once in winter, once in spring and once during the inter-seasonal period called '*al'ourwa*'. This compares favourably with Europe, where fresh tomatoes suitable for the production of concentrate can only be grown for a total period of 45 days.

Not all tomato seed varieties can be used in the processing of concentrates. In Egypt, the soil is very receptive to the cultivation of the seed varieties that are used in the production of tomato concentrate. Heinz has introduced Egyptian growers to a seed variety called University of California 82, specifically developed to be processed into Brix quality tomatoes. Brix quality tomatoes have a higher solid content, which means that in terms of processing, smaller quantities of fresh tomatoes can be used to produce tomato concentrate.

The sheer quantity of fresh-tomato cultivation in Egypt has meant that prices are extremely competitive. Farm-gate prices for fresh tomatoes in Egypt range between US$250 to US$300 per ton, which is much lower than the competing prices in Italy, Greece, Portugal and Turkey. In terms of production costs, Egypt has one of the lowest average unit costs of production in the region. Yearly performance appraisals conducted for HJ Heinz world-wide manufacturing facilities show that the Egypt manufacturing site is among the best performers in terms of production costs.

Heinz Ketchup is produced almost exclusively with local ingredients procured in Egypt. The main ingredients of tomato products include fresh tomatoes, sugar, vinegar, salt and spices, all of which are available in Egypt. Packaging uses locally manufactured containers for processed food products as the industry is highly developed and competitive in Egypt, and able to meet the specifications required by international manufacturers. Glass containers, labels and cardboard containers are also manufactured in Egypt at very low cost and to high standards. The only imported inputs for Heinz products are the metal bottle-covers, which are yet to be manufactured in Egypt in accordance with Heinz's specifications. The fact that close to 99 per cent of all inputs needed to produce Heinz's products are locally available, has meant that the production process has been shielded against currency fluctuations that may affect imported components, which has affected industries such as pharmaceuticals. Moreover, the quality of local inputs has been the basis for the export success of Heinz Egypt.

On the demand side, Egypt has a very large consumer market with a population of 67 million. The rising per capita income and the shift in consumer tastes in favour of international brand names has increased demand for high-value-added processed food products. A host of multinational firms engaged in the food processing sector are already present in Egypt, either as representative offices or with manufacturing facilities in Egypt, including Nestlé, Fine Food (Unilever), Pepsico-Snacks, Cadbury and may others.

The demand for processed food products in Egypt has been accelerated by the growth of the restaurant and tourism industry. Tourism generates huge demand for processed food products, particularly for the up-market qualities and branded goods. Moreover, the fact that Heinz Egypt has formed a joint venture with the largest franchisee for the fast food business in Egypt has added extra strength to the growth performance of Heinz Egypt.

The Egyptian food processing sector has considerable growth potential owing to the fact that out of the total output of fresh fruit and vegetables, only a small share is being processed into high-value-added processed food products. Of Egypt's output of 5.9 million tons of tomato per year, only 2,300 tons are processed. The growth potential of high-value-added food processed products remains huge, and has attracted a large number of multinational companies to set up manufacturing facilitates in Egypt (Gilada 1999).

Of no less importance is that Egypt has duty-free access for agricultural and processed food products to Arab countries. Heinz Egypt is the supply hub for a group of the company's products (mainly tomato-based products) to the Gulf region as well as to the Levant area. According to the marketing manager of Heinz Egypt, the company exports nearly 30 per cent of its output to neighbouring Arab markets. Heinz Egypt does not sell to EU markets because of an agreement within the Heinz Group.

Egypt has a relatively generous investment climate in the region, particularly in terms of tax breaks on corporate profit. The manufacturing plant of Heinz Egypt was established in one of the new industrial communities around Cairo, and has thus benefited from a tax holiday on corporate profit for a ten-year period after the joint venture began actual production.

Entry

Following the search for a reliable partner in Egypt, Heinz approached Americana, and Heinz Egypt was established and began production as a greenfield project in 1992. While Americana was already one of the key players in the food processing sector in Egypt, the joint venture was considered as a greenfield project, as a newly constituted joint venture was established, with new manufacturing facilities built from scratch.

Initially, the joint venture was 67 per cent owned by Americana, and Heinz held the remaining balance of the shares. While Americana insisted on a majority ownership at the early phase of the joint venture, it gave Heinz the option of increasing its shareholding after the elapse of a five-year period. Currently, Heinz holds a majority of 51 per cent of the shares in Heinz Egypt, while 49 per cent are held by Americana.

The shareholders' structure of Heinz Egypt does not restrict either of the shareholders to specific management controls within the company. In other words, key management positions do not reflect the majority shareholding by HJ Heinz. In fact, certain strategic decisions by the board of Heinz Egypt must be voted on unanimously.

The partnership with Americana has greatly benefited Heinz Egypt. Americana provides extensive knowledge of the dynamics of the food processing industry in Egypt as well as key export markets in the Arab region. Moreover, the access to other businesses of the Americana Group provided the JV with instant market penetration not only in Egypt, but also in other Arab markets, and guaranteed the minimum scale required to make the operation viable.

The joint venture between HJ Heinz and Americana has included an agreement to allow Heinz Egypt exclusive right to sell the range of products manufactured in Egypt in the markets of Egypt, Saudi Arabia, UAE, Qatar, Bahrain, Lebanon, Syria, Morocco and Lebanon. In other words, Heinz

Egypt is the exclusive supplier among the Heinz Group to the aforementioned markets.

Competition

Heinz Egypt controls 90 per cent of the ketchup market in Egypt, and 30 per cent of the market for tomato paste and cooking sauces. Within the market segment for ketchup, competition is relatively limited, as Heinz was the first-comer to the market. However, in the area of tomato paste, Heinz faces considerable competition from existing local companies, which were already in operation prior to its entry to the Egyptian market. The two largest competitors are Kaha and Edfina, the two large public-sector companies in the food-processing sector.

While ketchup – the key product of Heinz Egypt – enjoys the number one position in terms of market share, the company also produces a number of what have been termed 'fighter brands' that compete with products in lower market segments. To defend its market share in the high growth segment of non-branded products, Heinz Egypt produces a group of brands that do not share the same specifications as the Heinz-branded products and are therefore priced considerably lower. For example, ketchup 'fighter-brands' have a higher level of starch as an ingredient, which lowers the cost per pack sold. The same strategy is pursued in other major markets in the Middle East.

Resources and Spillovers

The evolving food-processing industry in emerging markets places new demands on agricultural suppliers to the industry with respect to the quality of the produce, the nature of contractual relationships, and logistics. During its initial years of operation, Heinz voiced concern over what has been termed the 'fresh market' approach. As a producer of tomato products, Heinz had to buy tomatoes from different growers, who more often than not sell their output directly to wholesale or retail traders. Growers in Egypt are not used to the notion of having their crops sold to one buyer beforehand, and prefer to take risks on prices at the point of sale, particularly as prices of tomato in Egypt fluctuate sharply depending on the season. International large-scale manufacturers are not accustomed to this fragmented nature of the market. Unreliable supply of fresh inputs, losses during transport, market segmentation and fluctuating prices are major constraints facing the food processing industry. Under such conditions it is hard to deliver a final product, such as ketchup, at consistent high quality and stable prices.

Heinz Egypt helps in developing standards of tomato agriculture in Egypt (www.amcham.org.eg). It has been successful in improving its supply chain, by introducing contract farming to Egyptian growers of fresh tomatoes. Over its years of operation in Egypt, Heinz has established contractual arrangements with growers, both on the large scale as well as on the very small scale, to buy their output on a yearly basis. Farmers are provided with the necessary seed varieties to guarantee the required output specifications. The parent firm provides resources for seed varieties suitable for cultivation in Egypt.

The company has contracted the output of some 200 hectars. The owners of these agricultural lands benefit from the free extension services provided by a group of Heinz employed agronomists. The outcome of this arrangement has been an increase of 20 to 25 per cent of agricultural yield of contracted land over the average yield of tomato in Egypt. Contracted farming by Heinz Egypt has also introduced growers to the concept of growing fresh vegetables for the sole purpose of industrial production and meeting industrial specifications. Moreover, Heinz Egypt has also introduced safe methods for transporting fresh tomatoes to the manufacturing site, thus reducing wastage in transportation and handling, which elsewhere in Egypt destroys 30 per cent of the annual yield of fresh tomatoes.

The parent company HJ Heinz provides Heinz Egypt with all manufacturing equipment. While the manufacturing process for ketchup, sauces, jams etc. is fairly standard among various manufacturers, certain equipment is exclusively produced for Heinz. The unique manufacturing process for some products, in turn, gives Heinz exclusive know-how and thus market supremacy for these particular products.

Heinz Egypt relies extensively on the training resources of the parent company in the area of production. Employees from the Egypt manufacturing plant are usually trained at the Heinz manufacturing facilities in Italy, with focus on technical skills for new production technologies. To guarantee the specifications required by the parent company, inspection teams from corporate headquarters frequently visit overseas manufacturing plants, including Heinz Egypt.

All Heinz Egypt employees have to go through training once they join the company. Key management personnel travel frequently to attend training courses outside of Egypt. The marketing and training experience of Americana has contributed significantly to the skills of the marketing and sales force of Heinz Egypt. Owing to its early entry, Americana's knowledge and experience of the Egyptian market conditions gave it an edge, in the domain of marketing, over Heinz Egypt. The sales and marketing force of Heinz Egypt attends the same regular generic training courses as the sales and marketing force of Americana. In this way, a synergy has been developed between Americana and Heinz in the area of training.

The brand name is one of the most important resources of Heinz Egypt. In fact, Heinz is often associated with ketchup, perhaps in the same way that the brand name Xerox is associated with photocopying. In export markets, and in addition to the brand name, low-priced inputs play a very important role in the ability of Heinz to export cost-competitive products outside of Egypt.

Heinz Egypt does not advertise extensively in Egyptian media. In fact, the marketing manager of Heinz Egypt has confirmed that this market segment of the food processing industry is not dependent on advertising. Heinz Ketchup is already the number one product on the Egyptian ketchup market, and therefore the returns to advertising are expected to be relatively small.

Given the relatively long history of the food-processing sector in Egypt, the pool of skilled human resources the industry can draw on is fairly large, as is the market in technical specialists. The employees of Heinz Egypt (200 in number) are mainly Egyptian. One of the major strengths of the food processing industry in Egypt is its highly competitive labour force as well as the low priced intermediate inputs. The turnover of Heinz Egypt has currently reached LE60 million, with a net profit (subject to distribution) of LE1 million.

Concluding Remarks

Demand in Egypt is shifting rapidly away from traditional freshly prepared, home cooked food and towards processed food products. Heinz Egypt has been able to sustain a virtual monopoly in the ketchup market, reflected in its high market share, as a result of its advantage based on branding and quality production.

Americana has provided Heinz Egypt with guaranteed demand from the fast food sector, in which Americana is the key player. All Americana franchise businesses use Heinz brands. The market experience of Americana in Egypt and in other Arab countries has been a key determinant of the success story of Heinz Egypt, both in the local and export markets.

The case of Heinz Egypt can illustrate spillovers in two forms in particular. Firstly, Heinz provides knowledge transfer through machinery and training in technology and marketing fields. Secondly, Heinz Egypt has contributed to the modernisation of tomato cultivation in Egypt by creating new forms of cooperation between manufacturers and farmers, and by introducing new seed varieties for industrial purposes.

References for Egyptian Case Studies

AIDMO (2000), *Feasibility Study on Pharmaceutical Industry,* unpublished.

American Chamber of Commerce in Egypt (2001), *The Egyptian Pharmaceutical Industry*, Business Studies Series, Cairo, Egypt.

American Chamber of Commerce in Egypt (2002), *Telecommunications in Egypt*, Business Studies Series, Cairo, Egypt.

American Chamber of Commerce in Egypt, website (www.amcham.org.eg) accessed in spring 2003.

Economist Intelligence Unit (2000), *Egypt Country Commerce*, London: EIU.

EFG-Hermes Research (2000), *The Egyptian Mobile Phone Company, Annual Review.*

EFG-Hermes Research (2002), *Egypt Telecom, MobiNil Research Update.* January.

Egyptian Company for Mobile Services (2002), *Mobinil, Earnings Release Report*, Q4.

Euromoney (2000), *Egypt: Regional Leader and Global Player: A Market for the 21st Century*, Euromoney Books.

France Telecom (2002), corporate website (www.francetelecom.com) accessed in autumn 2002.

General Authority for Free Zones and Investment (GAFI) (2001-2002), *Annual Report*, Cairo: GAFI.

Gilada, N. (1999), 'Fast Food Franchising in Egypt', report prepared for the US Foreign Commercial and US Department of State.

GSK (2002), *Company Profile, 2002* and *Financial Report for 2001* (www.gsk.com).

GSM World (2002), corporate website (www.gsmworld.com) accessed in autumn 2002.

Heinz (2002), *Heinz Annual Report* (www.heinz.com).

Howells, J. and I. Neary (1995), *Intervention and Technological Innovation, Government and the Pharmaceutical Industry in the UK and Japan.*

IMS (2002), *World Review 1999*, London: IMS.

Institute of Banking Studies (2003), Kuwait Stock Exchange Listed Banks and Companies: Yearly Financial Data and Ratios of Individual Companies (www.kibs.org/kse/kkfcfd.htm).

JP Morgan (2002), *Equity Research, MobiNiL, Results Report*, April.

Ministry of Economy (1996), *Egypt Economic Profile,* report published by the Ministry of Egyptian Ministry of Economy, Cairo: Egypt.

Ministry of Health and Population (2002), *Egypt Health Sector Analysis and National Essential Drug List*, Cairo: Ministry of Health and Population.

MobiNil (2003), corporate website (www.mobinil.com) accessed in spring 2003.

Nathan Associates (1995), *Price and Market Liberalization in Egypt,* report submitted to USAID and Ministry of Economy and Foreign Trade Government of Egypt, Cairo: Egypt.

Orascom Telecom (2002), corporate website (www.orascomtelecom.com) accessed in autumn 2002

PhARMA (2002), *Industry Report,* Washington DC: PhARMA.

Pharmaceuticals Executive (2001), Pharmaceuticals Executive.

PriceWaterhouseCoopers (1999), 'Pharmaceutical Sector Insights', Section 2, 1998/9.

Prime Research (1997), *Market Report on the Egyptian Pharmaceuticals Industry*, November 1997, Prime Securities.

Southworth (1996), 'Generic Pharmaceuticals', An FT Management Report published for the Financial Times, England: Pharmaceuticals and Healthcare Publishing.

Wescoe, C. (1985), *Factors in Pharmaceutical Investment.*

5. Foreign Direct Investment in India

PL Beena, Laveesh Bhandari, Sumon Bhaumik, Subir Gokarn and Anjali Tandon

INTRODUCTION

For the first four decades after achieving independence from British colonial rule, the economic polices of the Indian government were characterised by planning, control and regulation. There were periodic attempts at market-oriented reform, usually following balance of payments pressures, which induced policy responses that combined exchange rate depreciation and an easing of restrictions on foreign capital inflows. However, the latter were relatively narrow in scope and had little impact on actual inflows, which remained small. Nevertheless, there were foreign shareholdings in many companies, partly as a result of their pre-independence origins. Moreover, in sectors upon which the government placed high priority, domestic firms were allowed to enter into technology licensing arrangements, which often involved an equity stake as well. But, there was a general sense of discomfort with a foreign presence in industry, particularly in 'non-essential' sectors like consumer goods. This culminated in a series of major policy decisions in the late 1970s that forced companies to restrict their foreign shareholdings to a maximum of 40 per cent. Many companies did comply, but two prominent ones who did not, Coca Cola and IBM, were asked to shut down their Indian operations.

During the early 1980s, following a serious balance of payments crisis and a large loan from the International Monetary Fund, the Indian government relaxed its foreign investment policy. This engendered a number of joint ventures in the automotive industry, involving both financial and technical relationships between Indian and Japanese manufacturers. A few years later, Japanese two-wheeler manufacturers entered the domestic market, again through joint ventures with major Indian producers. Here again, the ventures were followed by a series of arrangements between component manufacturers in the two countries. Other key sectors, like the computer industry, were also provided a more liberal trade and investment environment.

The big opening up came in 1991, following yet another external crisis. This time, the government went much further than before in introducing a series of both domestic and external reforms that fundamentally changed the business environment. One of the key components of this new policy was a significant widening of the range of activities in which foreign firms could enter as well as an easing of the conditions under which they came in.

This chapter first outlines the reform progress and the evolving pattern of FDI over the past decade. We go on to report the key results from our FDI survey.

REFORMS IN THE INDIAN ECONOMY

Prior to 1991, the government exercised a high degree of control over industrial activity by regulating and promoting much of the economic activity. The development strategy discouraged inputs from abroad in the form of investment or imports, while the limited domestic resources were spread out by licensing of manufacturing activity. The result was a domestic industry that was highly protected – from abroad due to import controls and high duties, and from domestic competition due to licensing and reservations.

Industrial policy was dominated by licensing constraints by virtue of which strict entry barriers were maintained. Under the Industries Development and Regulation Act (1951), it was mandatory for all companies to get government approval to set up a new production unit or to expand their activities. Approval was also required if the manufacturer wanted to change the line of production. Moreover, when permission was granted, it was very specific to product, capacity and location. The decision to award a licence involved many stages and became a highly bureaucratic process, with some elements of state capture by incumbent domestic firms. This and other policies led to a very high degree of bureaucratisation of the economy. Also many sectors like textiles were reserved for the small scale sector, thereby making it difficult for domestic firms belonging to these sectors to enjoy economies of scale, and making these sectors unattractive to MNCs.

The government also controlled the exit option for a company. Manufacturers were not allowed to close operations or to reduce their work force without government approval. The intention was to try to avoid unemployment, but it also promoted inefficiency in the industrial economy.

Indian trade policy before the 1990s focused on import substitution. Restrictions on imports were imposed in different forms. In concurrence with the objective of attaining self-reliance, import licensing was imposed to exercise control over the importers. Further, imports were canalised, which meant that certain commodities could be imported by only one agency, which was generally a public sector company.

Import controls and high tariff rates led to high input costs, which made Indian producers un-competitive in the world market. Further, certain items were also subject to export controls with a view to ensure easy availability, low domestic prices and for environmental reasons. As a result, domestic industry operated in an isolated environment with limited exposure to international products and markets.

FDI policy put severe restrictions on foreign investment. Few foreign companies were allowed to retain an equity share of more than 40 per cent, and as a result many did not use their best technologies in India. The economy was deprived of foreign capital and foreign technology and internationally efficient scales and quality of production could not be achieved.

Financial sector policy did not focus upon generating enough capital from within and outside the country. The financial sector was highly regulated by the state. The government had owned all the major banks since nationalisation in 1969 and the early 1980s. It administered low interest rates on borrowings and loans to small industries and agriculture; price controls and credit rationing. Indeed, the basis of planning in India was a Harrod-Domar growth paradigm which made the government focus on mobilisation of savings for investment. The problem was that there was financial repression because of price fixing and directed credit.

Raising equity from the market was also restricted. The government decided both the amount of capital as well as price. Apart from interest rates, initial public offerings and other equity issues required prior government approval through its official arm – the Controller of Capital Issues (CCI). Banks could ignore market forces when taking functional and operational decisions, and private sector participation was discouraged. Profitability of financial institutions remained low owing to government control over interest rates and absence of competitive forces.

In addition to industrial and trade policies, public sector policy exclusively reserved certain sectors for the public sector. The public sector was also present in almost all parts of the economy – petroleum, consumer goods, tourism infrastructure and services, etc. Infrastructure industries such as power, telecom, air transport, etc., were almost wholly public sector controlled.

Reservation contributed to lack of competition, which reduced the incentive to be efficient. Over-manning, poor management, obsolete technology and insufficient research and development activities further contributed to the decay of public sector undertakings. Most important of all, non-commercial objectives and government meddling in day-to-day operations made these companies extremely inefficient.

Small-scale industry policy gave protection from domestic as well as international competition. This was done primarily by reservation of certain product lines exclusively for small industries. The smaller firms benefited from excise concessions and rebates that were determined on the basis of annual turnover rather than investment in fixed capital. Financial aid was also given in form of credit from government owned banks on softer terms. Small firms also benefited from preferential government purchases and input supplies.

To summarise the impact of pre-1990 policies, the Indian industrial structure was weak, both financially and technologically. However, domestic incumbents had been created who were entrenched and this had implications for FDI and for the mode of entry in the 1990s. The major prevailing problems were inefficiencies, high costs, poor management, non-competitiveness, excessive reservation, import controls, lack of export orientation and disincentives to the foreign investors.

Reforms launched in the early 1990s focused on addressing some of these issues. Since manufacturers were highly dependent on domestic growth, a more outward looking policy was adopted. Economic policies were liberalised with a view to encouraging investment and accelerating economic growth.

The new industrial policy announced in 1991 led to delicensing of industry, competition rather than protection as the desired policy environment. The earlier requirement of approvals and licences for any investments and expansions were abolished for all except 18 industries. Within a few years, only five sectors remained under the ambit of industrial licensing.

De-licensing gave companies freedom to take decisions for investments, expansions and plant locations. Bureaucratic practices involved in the investment procedures were reduced significantly. Lowering of entry barriers resulted in greater private sector participation.

Trade reforms addressed the anti-import bias by reducing tariffs, quantitative restrictions and foreign exchange control. From being one of the most protected domestic economies prior to the reforms, the Indian economy has become similar to other developing countries. Trade reforms continued in a sustained manner throughout the 1990s and it is expected that they will go on in the same manner.

The government also liberalised its policy towards FDI. Many constraints that had historically been imposed on portfolio and direct investment were removed. The approval process for technical and financial collaborations was completely revamped. For many industries, the Reserve Bank of India (RBI) would give an automatic approval.

Indian law does not differentiate between an Indian and foreign owned company once it has been incorporated in India. The same procedures govern Indian and foreign owned companies alike. Like Indian companies, foreign owned companies also do not now require a licence for production in most manufacturing sectors.

Technology transfers were also made easier by removing many mandatory approval requirements. Another measure to bring in FDI was reduction of controls on technology and royalty payments. Restrictions on foreign collaborations investment (both financial and technological) were by and large removed.

India's financial sector went through a wide variety of reforms during the 1990s (see Sarkar and Agarwal 1997), aimed at correcting the biases in the lending policies of government owned banks and financial institutions. Under new polices, the banks were free to decide lending and deposit rates. This was accompanied by a significantly proposed reduction in pre-emption of bank loans, both by the government and the priority sector. Both these gave the banks freedom to opt for the most rewarding investments. Capital market reforms coupled with the removal of restrictions on firms reduced entry barriers for the private sector. As a result, today there are many private operators in the sector – banks, financial institutions, NBFCs and insurance companies have a significantly higher private representation.

The reforms in the public sector enterprises (PSEs) were intended to be three-pronged; privatisation, greater autonomy and reduction of the monopoly power of the public sector. However, much has not been accomplished. First, privatisation has not been very successful. Minor proportions of a few companies' total equity was 'dis-invested', only one company out of a total of 242 public sector companies owned by the government has been completely privatised. Second, though some attempts were made at giving greater autonomy to PSEs this has largely been unsuccessful (Bhandari and Goswami 2002).

Third, the public sector environment was highly un-competitive vis-à-vis the rest of the world. Abolishing its monopoly was thought to be a solution that would force public companies to adopt better management practices. Sectors reserved exclusively for public sector were de-reserved (except for some social and security sectors). This was a policy measure to bring in private performers in competition with the PSEs. Compared to the first two, these measures have been much more successful.

The policy reforms with respect to the small-scale sector have not been as significant. Small industries traditionally benefit from the preferential treatment given by the government in many ways, including reservations and tax concessions. Protective polices continue to shield small manufacturers from competition from the medium and large ones. As a consequence, much of the small sector depends on subsidies, concessions and reservations for its survival.

India removed most quantitative restrictions from 1 April 2001. Under such circumstances, the small manufacturers face serious challenges from international producers who have open access to the domestic market. International companies that can benefit from large scale may therefore have a major advantage over the domestic small manufacturers with fragmented capacities.

FOREIGN DIRECT INVESTMENT

FDI Trends

As the restrictions on foreign investments were reduced or removed, there was a sudden spurt in foreign net inflows. The number of approvals of foreign technical collaborations registered a dramatic increase in the new policy regime, and the number of foreign technology approvals went up. The value of FDI approvals also increased significantly in the post-reform period. 1997, US$15.8 billion of FDI was approved in contrast to US$0.3 billion approved in 1991. Figure 5.1 highlights the increase in net FDI inflows after 1991. Net FDI inflows were only US$0.074 billion in 1991 increasing to US$3.6 billion by 1997, though falling in later years (US$2.6 billion in 1998). After 1991, foreign investment followed a steep upward curve: from 1981 to 1990, FDI grew by 23 per cent annually; this increased to 44 per cent annual growth during 1991 to 2001. Only US$0.1 billion of foreign capital was invested in 1991, compared with US$4.28 billion in 2001 (World Bank Development Indicators).

However, FDI still constitutes a very low share of total investment in India. By 1998, this ratio was 2.5 per cent – much lower than that of most other Asian countries. In many other post-reform economies, FDI has been seen to increase substantially when there has been large-scale public sector privatisation. In India this has not happened as yet; indeed domestic firms in India have proved capable of absorbing large state-owned firms that are being privatised, for example BALCO and VSNL. But the share of FDI, as a percentage of gross domestic investment (GDI) and GDP, has been growing. While the share of FDI in GDI was only 0.2 per cent in 1990, it increased to 3.98 per cent by 2001, while FDI as a percentage of GDP increased from 0.05 per cent in 1990 to 0.90 per cent in 2001.

Although, inflows of foreign investments did gear up, they were not very impressive in comparison with some other countries. (See for example UNCTAD 2003) for a comparison of India with China.) India's FDI share in the developing world was only 0.4 per cent in 1991. A marginal improvement was seen by 2001, when the share had increased to 1.7 per cent.

Distribution of FDI

In the absence of details of actual FDI inflows into different sectors, the present sector-wise discussion depends on approval data only. The bulk of the approvals from early 1990s to 2002, were directed towards infrastructure and energy sectors. More approvals were made in non-manufacturing sectors. An analysis of half-yearly figures from the SIA Database reveals increasing shares of the metallurgy, power and fuel sectors in total number of approvals. Large falls were observed in transport, industrial machinery and food processing. The services sector including telecommunication increased its share during the initial years of 1992 to 1994. Its growth was limited by the domestic climate in the later years.

A ranking of cumulative investment approved during the period 1991 to May 2002 reveals that the USA was the largest investor in India with an investment of Rs570 billion. Mauritius, the UK, Japan, Korea (South), Germany, Netherlands, Australia, France and Malaysia follow in that order. The USA had a smaller share of FDI into India after 1997. Mauritius ranked next to the USA in its cumulative investments since 1993. By 1997, the inflows from this country accounted for almost 20 per cent of FDI inflows, probably because of its status as a tax haven. Most of the approvals were in power, fuel, telecom and transport sectors.

Ownership Classification

The more liberal environment resulted in greater equity participation from abroad. Approvals for collaborations involving some amount of equity increased both in number and percentage. Nearly 70 per cent of collaborations were independent of any equity in 1991. Their share declined in successive years. Further, most of the approvals were for majority stakes in the host company. While there were only 4 per cent majority approvals in 1991, the share increased to almost 16 per cent by 1997. The most dramatic change was witnessed by the subsidiary (wholly owned) segment, which had carved a share of 17 per cent over seven years. Relatively greater investments were approved for absolute ownership during 1995 to 1997, when power and services sectors were opened up.

The reduction of rigidities in the investment procedures led to an increase in the number of international collaborations. Initially, there was a spurt in the number of joint ventures between international and Indian companies. This was for two reasons. Firstly, approvals in many industries were possible only if an Indian company was also involved as a promoter. Even in cases where it was not necessary to have an Indian partner, the existence of one greatly facilitated the initial approval process. Secondly, operating in the Indian market was highly different from that in the other countries. Partnering with an established Indian company benefited the new entity in setting up labour relations as well as marketing. However both these factors have become less important since the 1991 reforms.

The government no longer insists on Indian partnership for FDI in most industrial sectors and operating in India is now more transparent. As a result,

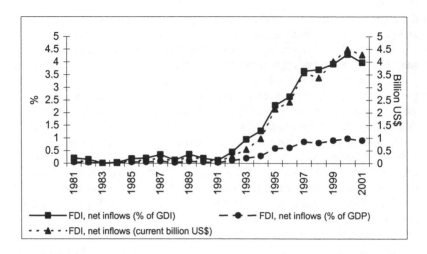

Source: World Development Indicators, CD-ROM, 2002, World Bank Little
         Data Book, 2001 and www.worldbank.org

Figure 5.1 Foreign direct investment in India

joint ventures in the form of technological collaborations also declined during
the period.

In the recent past, more ventures have been motivated by greater foreign
equity shares in the target firms. This is due to raising of the upper cap on the
equity limits. Further, more investment decisions were focused on the
benefiting from the already built-in domestic distribution networks. This is
evident from a slight increase in the approvals for marketing of international
products in India.

Prior to the reforms, the government supported technology inflows by
means of technical collaborations between Indian and foreign companies, and
tended to restrict financial participation by foreign companies. The
restrictions on financial investments were dropped in the 1990s. For example,
new sectors were opened for automatic approvals up to 74 per cent of the
total equity. A combination of factors discussed above, as well as preference
for greater control, led to a situation where more foreign companies opted for
capital investment rather than purely technological alliances.

Until 1993 most collaborations tended to be purely technical in nature.
The situation reversed by 2002 when the share of financial approvals reached
82 per cent leaving behind purely technology transfer approvals at only 11
per cent.

Table 5.1 Foreign ownership by level of control, India (in % of total FDI in the year)

Year	Non-equity	Minority	Majority	Wholly-owned	Average equity
1991*	69.0	27.0	4.2	0.0	35.6
1992	55.0	31.0	13.0	2.0	41.1
1993	50.0	32.0	13.0	5.0	35.4
1994	44.0	34.0	17.0	6.0	47.4
1995	54.0	47.0	18.0	9.0	45.3
1996	33.0	34.0	20.0	13.0	49.7
1997#	30.0	29.0	27.0	17.0	65.8
All	43.5	32.7	16.2	7.7	47.5

Notes: Non-equity collaborations are primarily technical collaborations, which have no equity ownership by the international collaborator. * Aug-Dec, # Jan-Aug.

Source: Basant 2000.

Mergers and Acquisitions

Mergers and acquisitions (M&A) activity grew at an unprecedented rate during the 1990s, rising from US$35 million in 1992 to a peak of US$1.520 million in 1997, and staying in excess of US$1 billion between 1999 and 2001. Many such arrangements were worked out between Indian and foreign firms and the bulk of these involved multi-national companies (MNCs), though M&A activity between Indian companies was also quite significant. Basant (2000) reports that between 1991 and 1997, 252 mergers and 145 acquisitions occurred. More than 85 per cent were between private Indian firms, and almost 60 per cent of 145 acquisitions between 1991 and 1997 were by private Indian firms. Foreign private acquisitions accounted for 32.4 per cent. 221 out of 252 mergers (88 per cent) belonged to the Indian private sector. Foreign private firms followed with a share of 7.5 per cent. Non-Resident Indian (NRI) mergers were only 0.4 per cent, while joint ventures between Indian and foreign firms were a little higher at 1.6 per cent; 60.7 per cent of the acquiring firms were Indian private companies. In about 32 per cent of the cases, the acquirer was a foreign company. NRIs acquired 4.1 per cent of Indian firms while joint ventures between Indian and foreign firms had a share of only 1.4 per cent. Thus, merger and acquisition activity substantially increased in India in recent years, though foreign investors participate only in a minority of deals (although these may include some of the largest deals).

FDI SURVEY IN INDIA

With the help of data collected from 152 MNC affiliates established in India in the last decade, the remainder of this chapter outlines the role of FDI in the Indian economy. The data were collected by way of stratified random sampling, to ensure that none of the sectors are over- or under-represented in the sample, relative to the population, and that there is no selection bias of any other kind. The majority of firms belong the manufacturing sectors, including machines and equipment (26 per cent), intermediate goods (16 per cent), and basic consumer goods (13 per cent). Information technology and software firms account for 20 per cent, while business services account for 13 per cent (Chapter 2). The machines and equipment sector has been over-sampled, and the intermediate goods sector has been under-sampled. However, there is no selection bias at the 2-digit level of ISIC classification.

Characteristics of MNC investing in India

Only a small fraction of the MNCs investing in India are large, the proportion of MNC affiliates with 250 or more employees in the sample being 16 per cent. On the other hand, small firms, those having between 10 and 50 employees, account for 42 per cent of the firms in the sample. The size of the affiliates in India seems to be positively correlated with the overall size of the MNCs. An overwhelming majority of them are small, about 76 per cent of them having fewer than 10,000 employees worldwide (Table 5.2). Most of the larger affiliates are concentrated in the infrastructure and machinery and equipment sectors. Interestingly, however, the machinery and equipment sector also accounts for a significant proportion of the very small firms. The intermediate goods sector and the IT sector account for the bulk of the other very small firms. A significant proportion of the MNC affiliates in India, namely, 23 per cent, contribute to a significant proportion of the worldwide turnover – greater than 5 per cent – of the parent MNCs (Table 5.2). However, about 47 per cent of the affiliates constitute a small fraction of the global turnover of the parent companies. Most of the firms contributing significantly to the parents' global output are in the IT and machinery and equipment sectors.

Most of the firms investing in India are from the USA and Western Europe, together accounting for 78 per cent of the firms in the sample. MNCs from Germany (11 per cent) and the UK (9 per cent) are the leading European investors. This pattern of investment is consistent with India's trade patterns. Between 1990-91 and 1998-99, the EU accounted for 26 to 27 per cent of India's exports, and 24 to 29 per cent of India's imports. The USA, on the other hand, accounted for 14 to 21 per cent of India's exports and 8 to 12 per cent of her imports.

Table 5.2 Characteristics of investing MNC, India

	(Unit)	Categories						
Worldwide employment	(000)	(<1) 38.3%	(1 - 10) 37.0%	(10 - 100) 19.8%	(>100) 4.9%			
Local contribution to global turnover	(%)	(0 - 0.1) 20.8%	(0.1 - 0.5) 26.7%	(0.5 - 2) 13.3%	(2 - 5) 15.8%	(5 - 20) 17.5%	(>20) 5.8%	
R&D expenditure	(% of turnover)	(0 - 0.5) 38.1%	(0.5 - 1) 12.4%	(1 - 2) 6.7%	(2 - 4) 16.2%	(4 - 8) 11.4%	(8 - 15) 3.8%	(>15) 11.4%
advertising expenditure		49.5%	10.7%	10.7%	3.9%	10.7%	9.7%	3.9%
Emerging regions experience	(count)	(None) 22.5%	(1) 34.9%	(2) 20.2%	(3) 10.1%	(4) 12.4%		

Much of the European investment is concentrated in the intermediate goods and machinery and equipment sectors. The majority of the North American firms, almost all of which are from the USA, on the other hand, have invested in the IT and financial services sectors. Much of the investment of Japanese and East Asian firms have been concentrated in the 'old economy' machinery and equipment sector and in the 'new economy' IT sector.

In light of the fact that economic reforms in India began in earnest as late as 1991, it is hardly surprising that not many MNCs invested in India until 1994, i.e., during the first four years of economic liberalization, and investment into India picked up only after 1994. Indeed, only 25 per cent of the firms in the sample invested in India prior to 1995. This is consistent with the slow yet steady liberalization of FDI regulations and the capital account of the balance of payment in India since 1991. Most of the early entrants into India were in the intermediate goods, machinery and equipment and IT sectors. These three sectors, along with financial services, continued to account for most of the post-1995 MNC investment in India.

Most of the MNCs investing in India do not have R&D intensive products; parents of about half the firms in the sample invest less than 1 per cent of their global sales in R&D activities (Table 5.2). The MNCs with R&D intensive products have invested largely in the IT and pharmaceutical sectors.

The MNCs parents of about 50 per cent of the firms in the sample spend more than 1 per cent of their global sales on advertising, while only about 13 per cent of the parents spend more than 8 per cent (Table 5.2). Given that high advertising related expenditure is associated with consumer goods products, this is consistent with the pattern of MNC investment in India, with the majority of investment in the intermediate goods, IT and machine and equipment sectors.

About 57 per cent of the MNCs in the sample either did not have any emerging market experience before entering India, or their experience was limited to one of the four major regions with developing countries/emerging markets, namely, Asia (other than Japan), Eastern and Central Europe, Latin America and Africa. The proportion of MNCs investing in India without significant emerging market experience – about 76 per cent – is especially striking for the financial services sector. However, two-thirds of the MNCs investing in the pharmaceutical sector had significant operational experience in all four regions.

Entry Strategies

Most of the MNCs enter into India either with greenfield projects or with joint ventures with local firms. Indeed, greenfield and JVs account for 83 per cent of entries captured in the sample. MNCs investing in the basic consumer goods sector prefer greenfield to JV, as do those investing in the pharmaceutical sector. MNCs investing in the machines and equipment sector, however, prefer JV to greenfield. Entry mode for these three sectors is entirely consistent with the hypothesis that MNCs with high proprietary 'technology' would prefer to enter an emerging market on their own. There is, however, no discernible pattern for the other sectors.

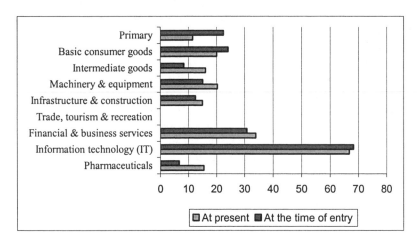

Figure 5.2 Proportion of output exported in India

Nearly 70 per cent of the output of the IT sector is exported (Figure 5.2), while another quarter of it is 'produced' for either the parent MNC or other affiliates of the parent MNC. This is consistent with India's reputation as an IT hub catering to the rest of the world. MNCs in all other sectors sell 60 per cent or more of their output in the local market, confirming the popular wisdom that the size of the Indian domestic market plays a significant role in attracting FDI.

On average, MNCs that entered India by way of JVs cater more to the local market, while MNCs with greenfield entries cater more to overseas markets. About a third of the JVs in the sample sell more than half their output in the local market, and about 37 per cent of them sell 10 per cent or less. The corresponding numbers for greenfield projects are 20 per cent and 50 per cent. This is consistent with the literature which argues that MNCs aiming to cater to the local market are more likely to tie up with local partners to help mitigate costs associated with understanding markets and developing business contacts and distribution networks. MNCs with focus on the global market, on the other hand, are more likely to retain complete control to ensure that the quality of the products meets global standards, and that the contractual agreements with global buyers are met.

Importance and Sources of Resources

Brands are viewed by a significant proportion of the MNCs in India as the most important resource necessary for success. Most of these firms belong to the primary, basic consumer goods, financial services and pharmaceutical sectors. With the exception of distribution networks (for pharmaceutical sector), equity (for primary and infrastructure sectors) and technology (for the primary and machinery and equipment sectors), no other resource is as important to the MNC affiliates in the sample. However, if one takes into account the three most important resources necessary for success, as chosen by the firms' management, managerial and marketing capabilities also emerge as important resources. It should be noted that aside from equity and technology, most of the resources deemed important by the MNC affiliates are intangible. *Ceteris paribus*, this suggests that in India the potential gains from a tie up with a local firm can be significant.

In keeping with the literature on agency and transactions cost, a majority of the MNCs that entered India by acquisition, rate brand as the most important resource necessary for success, while a third of the MNCs entering by way of a JV, accord a similar status to business networks. If, as before, one takes into consideration the three most important resources contributing to a firm's success, managerial capability emerges as another resource important to the acquiring firms. Technology is deemed important for success by a majority of the firms, irrespective, of their choice of mode of entry.

The eight resources deemed most important for success by the MNC affiliates are brand, business network, distribution network, equity, machinery and equipment, managerial capability, marketing capability and technological know-how. Importantly, most of these are intangible resources. The MNC parents contribute 80 per cent of brand value, 85 per cent of equity and 73 per cent of technological know-how, on average (Figure 5.3). At the same time, 70 per cent of the business networks, nearly half of the managerial capability, about two-fifths of the distribution networks and almost all of marketing capability are sourced locally.

In other words, the MNCs provide most of the tangible resources and source most of the intangible resources from India. This is consistent with the fact that JVs constitute a significant proportion of the firms in the sample. Further, given that distribution networks and marketing capabilities are two of the key intangible resources sources that are sourced locally, it can be hypothesised that most of the MNCs aim to sell their products in the Indian market.

Brand, equity and technological know-how are the resources that are deemed important for success by a majority of the MNCs in the sample. Of these, technological know-how is important to firms of all sizes, the measure of size being the number of people employed by the local affiliate. Brand, on the other hand, is more important for larger affiliates while equity is more important for the smaller affiliates.

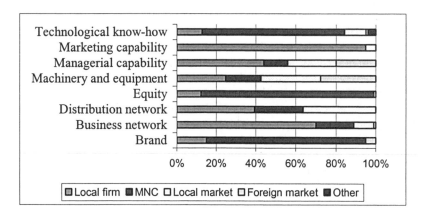

Figure 5.3: Source of key resources in India

FACTOR MARKETS AND INSTITUTIONAL ENVIRON-MENTS IN INDIA

The MNCs in the sample feel that there has been a noticeable improvement in the quality of labour available locally across the board (Figure 5.4). The average quality of labour registered a 0.40-point improvement, on a 5-point scale, for executive management, professionals, operations management and

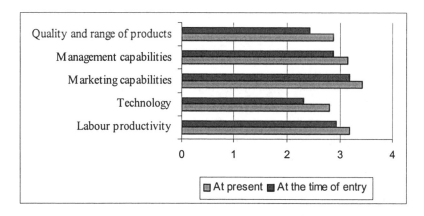

Figure 5.4 Perceptions about the local industry in India

skilled non-managerial labour. MNCs investing in the primary, intermediate goods and IT sectors experienced the most significant improvements in labour quality.

The perception about the across-the-board improvement in the quality of labour available locally is also invariant with the mode of entry of the MNCs. Interestingly, however, the MNCs that are in JV with local firms experienced the least improvement in labour quality. This may be a manifestation of the agency costs associated with local partnership.

The MNCs in the sample experienced a noticeable improvement in a variety of local resources – IT, professional services, real estate, machinery and equipment and raw materials, but the perceived quality/reliability of utilities still lag the quality/reliability of other inputs. The most significant improvement was experienced, not surprisingly, with respect to IT: a 0.91-point increase on a 5-point scale. MNCs that invested in the primary, intermediate goods, financial services, IT and pharmaceutical sectors experienced the greatest improvement in quality of local resources, while those that invested in the infrastructure sector experienced the least improvement in quality.

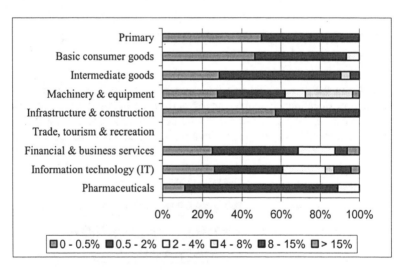

Figure 5.5 Proportion of revenue spent on training by local affiliate in India

The perception about the institutional environment in India, however, too is not as optimistic (Figure 5.3). Respondents felt that there was virtually no improvement in the legal-institutional framework relevant to business during the 1990s. The only perceptible improvements were with respect to procurement of business licences, real estate and visa and work permits. The

MNCs that invested in the pharmaceutical and machinery and equipment sectors experienced the greatest upturn in the business-related institutional environment.

The MNCs that entered India by acquisition had the worst experience with respect to the country's institutional environment. They felt that the legal-institutional environment in India deteriorated during the 1990s. MNCs that entered India by all other modes, including JV, however, experienced an improvement in the legal-institutional environment. While the experience of the JVs highlight the importance of local partnership in emerging markets, the experience of the MNCs that entered by way of greenfield is perhaps a reflection of a selection bias – these MNCs entered on their own because they were capable of functioning successfully under the Indian legal-institutional set-up.

MNCs from North America reported the greatest improvement in the legal-institutional environment; the experience of MNCs from Europe and East Asia (including Japan) was not as good. Both the North American and European MNCs reported the greatest improvement with respect to business licences and visa and work permits. The East Asian MNCs, in addition, felt that there was an improvement in the support of the central government's institutions and policies for FDI, as well as in the legal-institutional framework associated with procurement of real estate.

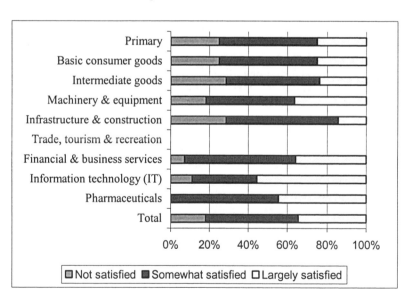

Figure 5.6 Performance of MNC affiliates relative to expectations in India

MNCs investing in all sectors were favourably impressed with the direction and pace of change in the quality of range of products produced in India (Table 5.3 and Figure 5.4). With some exceptions – intermediate goods and financial services sectors – the perception was that the pace of change in the quality of management was far less muted. In other words, there is *prima facie* evidence that the spillover effect of FDI in India has largely been in the form of better quality of products, rather than in the form of improved managerial abilities. Interestingly, while the MNCs in the sample felt that the productivity of local labour improved, on average, those investing in the IT sector experienced a decline in labour productivity. This is consistent with the views about the impact of *en masse* migration of high quality IT professionals to North America and Europe, and the inability of the local educational system to rapidly replenish the stock of such professionals.

The MNCs that entered by way of JVs perceive the greatest improvement by far in range and quality of products, as also in managerial and marketing capabilities of local firms, the level of technology used and labour productivity. This suggests that JVs contribute most to FDI-related spillovers in India.

TRANSFER OF TECHNOLOGY AND KNOW-HOW

A negligible proportion of the firms spend a significant fraction of their turnover on training (Table 5.5). Indeed, only about 6 per cent of the MNCs in the sample spend more than 8 per cent of their turnover on training, while a meagre 12 per cent spend more than 4 per cent. Even in the IT sector, only 17 per cent of the MNCs that invested in India spent more than 4 per cent of their turnover on training. By contrast, three-quarters of the MNCs spend less than 2 per cent of their turnover on employee training. In other words, abstracting from the relative contribution of different entry modes to spillovers, the absolute level of knowledge and know-how spillover from FDI is not significant in India.

Even MNC affiliates whose parent firms have R&D intensive products do not spend a noticeable proportion of their turnover on training. Only 15 per cent of such MNC affiliates spend more than 4 per cent of their turnover on training. This suggests that by and large MNCs use India as a manufacturing base for low-end generic or downstream products. This is consistent with the experience of the IT industry, which has not moved significantly up the value-addition ladder.

Although firms across the board offer little or no training to their employees, there is a weak relationship between training and performance of the MNCs in India. The firms that were most dissatisfied with their own performance are also the ones that offered noticeably less training to their employees, as compared to the other firms.

PERFORMANCE OF MNC AFFILIATES

Overall, most MNCs were satisfied with their own performance, relative to their initial expectations (Figure 5.6). However, the aggregate numbers mask a significant amount of heterogeneity across firms. MNCs in the sample that entered India by way of greenfield projects were by and large happy with their performance; the measure of experience being an index that accords equal weights to the MNCs' experience with respect to labour productivity, revenue growth and profit growth. About 40 per cent of them feel that all or nearly all their expectations have been satisfied. In comparison, MNCs that entered by way of JV were less successful; only 28 per cent of them feel that all or nearly all their expectations have been satisfied. Overall, only 16 per cent of the MNCs report that their expectations have been largely or entirely unmet.

A significant proportion (nearly 40 per cent) of the early entrants, i.e., those that entered India prior to 1995, have had their expectations with respect to performance met. By contrast, only 29 per cent of the late entrants, i.e., those that entered after 1998, were satisfied. This may be a reflection of the change in the a priori expectations of the MNCs about investment in India over time.

The largest number of well-performing firms are in the machinery and equipment and, not surprisingly, IT sectors. A large proportion of the MNCs in the financial services and pharmaceutical sectors, about 35 and 44 per cent respectively, are also satisfied with their performance. The machinery and equipment and the intermediate goods sectors account for most of the under-achieving MNC affiliates in the sample.

MNCs in the sample are more likely to have been satisfied with their performance if they are very export-oriented than if they are focused on the domestic market. About 52 per cent of highly export-oriented MNCs are very satisfied with their performance. By contrast, only about 33 per cent of the MNCs with domestic market focus feel that all or nearly all their expectations have been fulfilled.

As seen before, all MNCs experienced an improvement in the quality of local labour during the 1990s. However, the MNCs that were least satisfied with their performance experienced the most significant improvement in the quality of non-managerial skilled labour and, at the same time, the steepest decline in the quality of executive management (Table 5.3). This possibly suggests that 'failure' of MNCs in India is closely associated with management problems, as opposed to problems with the non-managerial labour force.

MNCs that are dissatisfied with their performance in India experienced noticeably less improvement in the reliability of utilities, compared to other MNCs. However, on average, satisfaction with performance and experience with local resources have a non-monotonic relationship. Indeed, while MNCs

Table 5.3 Assessment of the Indian business environment and FDI
*   performance*

Performance	Not satisfied		Somewhat satisfied		Largely satisfied	
	Initial	At present	Initial	At present	Initial	At present
Labour market						
Executive manager	3.32	3.81	3.37	3.82	3.81	4.16
Professionals	3.68	3.19	4.07	4.38	4.23	4.58
Operations management	3.68	4.24	3.71	4.12	3.98	4.37
Skilled non-managerial labour	3.68	4.38	4.07	4.35	4.14	4.48
Local inputs						
Utilities	3.45	3.76	3.39	3.69	3.88	3.91
IT and telecommunications	3.32	3.82	2.98	4.07	3.37	4.40
Competent professionals	3.91	4.36	3.85	4.40	4.19	4.62
Real estate	3.68	3.95	3.76	4.16	4.09	4.34
Machinery and equipment	3.55	4.14	3.59	4.16	3.98	4.38
Raw materials and components	3.53	4.05	3.33	3.90	3.61	4.10
Local industry						
Quality and range of products	2.18	2.86	2.29	2.75	2.74	3.00
Management capabilities	2.86	3.41	2.93	3.25	3.00	3.05
Marketing capabilities	2.64	3.36	3.39	3.45	3.16	3.38
Level of technology	2.23	2.86	2.39	2.84	2.60	2.89
Labour productivity	2.77	3.50	3.15	3.27	3.00	3.08
Institutional environment						
Business licences	3.55	3.20	3.02	2.55	2.72	2.49
Procurement of real estate	3.05	2.81	2.80	2.42	2.88	2.65
Visa and work permits	2.73	2.67	2.98	2.54	2.84	2.70
Environmental regulations	3.27	3.35	2.76	2.70	2.86	2.89
General legal framework	2.86	2.77	3.05	2.86	2.74	2.83
Predictability and stability of rules	3.00	3.18	3.39	3.27	3.05	3.08
Central government	3.00	2.68	3.19	2.78	2.74	2.70
State government	3.00	3.05	3.26	3.00	2.63	2.70

Notes: Average perceptions of MNCs about the Indian labour market, local inputs, local industries and the local institutional environment. The perceptions were measured on a 5-point Likert scale.

that are completely or almost entirely dissatisfied and those that are by and large satisfied with their own performance experienced similar (average) levels of improvement in the quality of the local resources – 0.44 points on a 5-point scale – the middle of the road MNCs have distinctly better experience with the quality of the same resources. The latter experienced an average improvement of 0.58 points on the aforementioned 5-point scale. This surprising result might be a reflection of the high a priori expectations of the 'successful' MNCs about the rate of improvement in the quality of the local resources.

The degree of satisfaction of the MNCs with their own performance has an unambiguous negative relationship with the perceived change in the quality of the local industries to which the MNCs belong. This is possibly a reflection of the more realistic a priori expectations of the 'successful' MNCs about the quality/extent of local competition they were likely to face, and hence the extent to which they would be able to extract rent using their proprietary products and brands.

Firms across the performance spectrum witnessed improvement in the legal institutional environment pertaining to procurement of business licences, real estate and visa and work permits. In addition, a large number of the MNCs perceived an improvement in the FDI-related policies of the central and state governments. Firms who were entirely or almost entirely satisfied with their own performance did not perceive any significant improvement in the government's policies. Indeed, the firms at the two ends of the performance spectrum felt that the state government's policies actually became less investor friendly over time, albeit marginally.

CONCLUDING COMMENTS

India has come a long way since 1991 in so far as quantum of FDI inflow is concerned. But it is still a mere US$4 billion per year, and seems to have stagnated at that level. FDI inflow in 2002 was just 3.2 per cent higher than FDI inflows in 2001. The popular wisdom is that MNCs are discouraged from investing in India by bureaucratic hurdles and uncertainty about the sincerity of the government(s) about economic reforms.

However, to date, there has been very little discussion about two important issues, namely, the experience of MNCs that have invested in India and the relationship between their performance and experience with the operating environment, and the extent of spillovers in the form of transfer of technology and know-how. The importance of the former is that the satisfaction of expectations of the MNCs that are already operational within India is, for obvious reasons, an important pre-condition for growth in FDI inflow. Transfer of technology and know-how, on the other hand, is at least as likely to have an impact on India's future growth as the quantum of FDI inflow. Indeed, to the extent that India's future growth will depend on the global competitiveness of its firms, the importance of such spillovers can be paramount.

Data obtained from the 147 MNC affiliates in India directly address both these issues. MNCs that have invested in India are, by and large, satisfied with their own performance, the measure of experience being an index that incorporates into itself the MNCs' experience with respect to labour productivity, revenue growth and profit growth. Indeed, the majority of the firms in both old economy sectors like machines and machine tools and new economy sectors like IT, feel that their expectations with respect to these parameters of performance were largely met. Importantly, neither the central nor the state and local governments were viewed as obstacles to carrying on business in India.

However, there is little room for complacency. Firms whose expectations with respect to performance have not been met experienced a noticeable decline in the quality of executive management in India, and were largely dissatisfied with the extent of improvement in the reliability of utilities. Further, late entrants into India were found to be less satisfied with their own performance, on average, than the early entrants, perhaps reflecting the fact that the growth of labour productivity, revenue growth and profit growth of MNCs did not keep pace with the *ex ante* expectations about the rapidly growing Indian economy.

But the optimism on this front has to be tempered by two observations, namely, that most of the firms investing in India have small R&D budgets, relative to their turnover, and most of them do not provide significant training to the employees in their Indian affiliates. This casts doubt on both the extent of transfer of cutting edge technology to India, and the extent of spillovers by way of enhancement of skills of the labour force.

As with the overall economic reforms programme, India's performance with respect to FDI remains a mixed bag. A stagnation of the quantum of FDI inflow coexists with the perception that quality of labour and other inputs, as well as the legal-institutional environment relevant to the MNCs, have improved noticeably during the 1990s. The average MNC remains satisfied with growth in labour productivity, revenue and profits, and remains willing to transfer technological resources to the Indian affiliate. At the same time, however, supply of key resources like power remain unreliable, and the extent of spillover effects in terms of both quality of technology and know-how remain uncertain. The appropriate mood, perhaps, is one of cautious optimism.

6. Indian Case Studies

P.L. Beena, Subir Gokarn and Anjali Tandon

INTRODUCTION

The Indian case studies illustrate in particular the influence of industry-specific regulation and the nature of competition on entry strategies. The case of Bacardi-Martini illustrates the relationship between the regulatory environment and its disparity across states with the strategic decisions taken at corporate level. The Packaging case, which is reported anonymously, illustrates a staged acquisition of a private business previously owned by a domestic conglomerate, and acquired by a global player in the specific industry. The ABN Amro case illustrates the expansion of a foreign-owned bank during the stepwise liberalisation of the financial services industry, among other strategies by acquisition of the retail operation of another foreign investment bank.

BACARDI-MARTINI INDIA LTD

The joint venture Bacardi Martini India Ltd. (BMIL) was established in 1998 between the multinational wines and spirits major, the Bacardi-Martini group and a relatively small Indian distiller, Gemini Distillers. Bacardi-Martini itself is the outcome of a 1992 merger between Bacardi, well-known internationally for its rum, and Martini & Rossi, which established its reputation in the wine business before going on to acquire a presence in other segments of the alcoholic beverages market. Both were family-owned and controlled firms. Bacardi had its roots in Cuba, before moving its base to the Bahamas and has a very large presence in North America. Martini & Rossi originated in Italy and grew to become a pan-European entity. During the 1980s, the two companies entered into marketing and distribution alliances to take advantage of each others' continental presences. These alliances were formalised by a merger in 1992.

In the early 1990s, when India opened its alcoholic beverages industry to foreign investment, a number of global majors entered. Foreign shareholdings in this industry were restricted to a maximum of 74 per cent.

As a consequence, compounded by specific characteristics of the industry, entry in India was exclusively through the joint venture route.

The significance of this case is twofold. First, it demonstrates the impact of the local regulatory environment on the investment decisions and strategic choices made by the foreign entrant. This is of course an industry characteristic, and the implications of the analysis are general. Second, there is a very important distinction between BMIL and other entrants. BMIL's main product in India is rum, which is distilled from molasses, an intermediate product in the sugar cane – sugar linkage. The predominant product segment of the other entrants is whisky, which is typically distilled from grain. As it happens, the overwhelming majority of India's alcoholic spirits production (which does not include beer and wine) is distilled from molasses. Even Indian whisky is largely a mix of alcohol distilled from molasses with appropriate flavours and colours. More expensive brands are blended with varying proportions of grain-based alcohol, but even these do not meet the international standard for 'whisky', which defines the product as exclusively grain-based. In this context, BMIL, the only significant rum producer to have entered the Indian market, is the only one of these ventures whose main product is consistent with the conventional domestic feedstock. This increases the possibilities of externalities from backward linkages.

The origins of this case study are somewhat unconventional. While the country team was exploring possibilities, the lead researcher was working on a project commissioned by the Confederation of Indian Alcoholic Beverage Companies (CIABC), an industry association representing the foreign and larger Indian companies in the business. The objective of the project was to demonstrate the collective benefits to state governments from harmonising their various tax regimes for alcoholic beverages, which were extremely disparate. In the process, some understanding about the nature of the existing regulatory regime was gained. The project also provided the researcher several opportunities to interact with managers from both the foreign and Indian companies, which contributed to an understanding of the relationship between the regulatory environment and its disparity across states on the one hand and their strategic choices on the other. In addition to several conversations with the two top managers of BMIL during the course of the other study, structured interviews were held with both of them in December 2002.

The discussion of this case is structured as follows. The second section describes the regulatory environment in which the industry operates and how this could potentially affect the strategy of the foreign investor. The third section provides a brief picture of the structure of the alcoholic beverages industry in India, with the idea of establishing the competitive space in which BMIL operates. The fourth section analyses BMIL's operations in terms of the general analytical framework, focusing on the issues that emerged as significant during the discussions and interviews.

The Regulatory Framework

The tax system
India has a federal fiscal system, with three tiers of government – central, state and local – possessing the constitutional right to levy taxes. Each tier is constrained in terms of what activity it can tax and what kind of tax it can impose. The bulk of revenue at the central and state levels is collected by indirect taxes – excise taxes levied on the value of production of goods at the centre and sales taxes levied on the value of transactions of both goods and services at the level of the state. There are a few exceptions to the exclusive power of the central government to collect an excise tax (i.e. a tax at the point of production). Alcoholic beverages are by far the most important exception. Therefore, each state government has the exclusive right to collect taxes from alcohol either produced or consumed within its borders. For the Indian states collectively, alcohol taxes represent the second largest source of revenues after sales taxes. In recent years, while the latter have contributed about 60 per cent of aggregate state tax revenues, the former have accounted for about 15 per cent.

At the core of the tax regime on alcohol are three elements. The first is tantamount to a specific (dependent on alcohol content) excise tax levied at the point of production. The second is a licence fee levied on trade in alcoholic beverages, either retail or service. The third is a tax related to the movement of products across states – an export fee in the state in which it is produced and an import fee in the state in which it is consumed.

In practical terms, however, the discretion states have over this tax base has resulted in a proliferation in the number and complexity of the levies imposed under each of these broad categories. CIABC estimates that there were 117 different types of levies on alcohol over all the states. The end result of the evolution of the tax and regulatory regime across different states has been a significant dispersion in the effective tax incidence on alcoholic beverages across states, and consequently, in retail prices.

Other regulatory instruments
The tax system is accompanied by a variety of regulations at each stage on the sequence from production to consumption. At the production stage, the basic requirement in all states is a licence to set up a facility, which may be a brewery, a distillery or a blending and bottling plant. The licence specifies production capacity. The issue of new licences is typically dependent on perceptions about the adequacy of existing capacity. There are added considerations in the states that produce sugar cane, from which molasses, the basic feedstock for distilleries, is extracted. Molasses is the source for both industrial and potable alcohol. There is a concentration of distilleries in these states, which supply industrial alcohol to downstream users and potable alcohol to blending and bottling plants both within the state and in other

states. Given constraints in the area under sugar cane and production and yield risks, expansion in distillery capacity is likely to contribute to price volatility as well as supply uncertainty to existing facilities. There is, therefore a 'risk management' element in the licensing structure. The price and other conditions attached to the licence vary from state to state.

At the consumption stage, there are licence fees, which differ for retail and service establishments. All states impose a set of restrictions, which vary widely, on location and timing of such establishments. The mechanism of licensing itself varies across states. Some states have a system of fixed licence fees, while others auction licences. Further, many states have restrictions on ownership at different stages of trading activity. For example, some states allow private ownership of retail establishments, while restricting wholesale procurement and distribution activity to public enterprises, owned by the state government. At least one state allows private activity in the wholesale trade, while restricting retail activity to public enterprises.

Inter-state movements of alcoholic beverages are also subject to regulations both by the producing state and the consuming state. This is apart from the regulations governing movement in molasses and alcohol. An important component of movement regulation is the notion of brand registration. Typically, a brand that is not produced in a state has to satisfy certain conditions before being allowed to distribute in that state. For example, it may be asked to prove that it sells a certain minimum volume in the rest of the country before being registered in a particular state. Finally, all of these state-specific instruments are supplemented by national restrictions on advertising and promotion of alcoholic beverages.

This brief and perhaps oversimplified description of the variety of taxes and other regulatory instruments prevailing across Indian states is relevant to this case study for a number of reasons. First, the independent pursuit of alcohol policy by various states has resulted in a significant fragmentation of the national market. Each state effectively constitutes a separate market, with its own distinct features. Local knowledge about the markets in which an entrant aims to compete is critical to the likelihood of success of a strategy. More specifically, knowledge about the regulatory complexities in each state is a vital input into evaluating the potential of each market and designing a strategy that optimises revenue and profitability in the markets that the entrant has decided to focus on.

Second, also related to the fragmentation of the market, the returns to any national-level investment, such as advertising or other brand-building efforts, are likely to be significantly diluted. Movement and distribution restrictions are always potential disruptors of any attempt to quickly cash in on a brand-building campaign by setting up and sustaining supply chains. This is particularly important for multinationals, whose brand identities are already established in the domestic market, even though the majority of customers many not have ever consumed the products that they offer. Brand identities have to be reinforced or repositioned as a prelude to their entry into the market. From a cost viewpoint, it clearly does not make very much sense to develop several different state-level campaigns to do this. Reconciling the national-level brand-building strategy with the state-level supply and distribution constraints is, therefore, a priority.

Third, the fiscal significance of alcohol-related revenues inextricably links this entire industry with the political-bureaucratic process. Major decisions relating to licences, tax rates and licence fees are all influenced, if not dominated, by political considerations. Long-standing political connections are perceived as a valuable asset in this business.

The Structure of the Indian Alcoholic Beverages Industry

The structure of the industry is clearly influenced by the regulatory environment and the consequent fragmentation of markets. There are basically five categories of alcoholic beverages – beer; wine; Indian Made Foreign Liquor (IMFL), which includes whisky, rum, vodka and other similar spirits; country liquor, which is the indigenous equivalent of IMFL – essentially, flavoured alcohol, with an alcohol content somewhat less than the standard for IMFL; and, toddy, which is a mildly fermented juice extracted from palm and may be considered the indigenous equivalent of beer, in terms of alcohol content. The regulatory framework covers all these categories. Besides these, there is a significant presence of illicitly brewed alcoholic beverages, which escapes the tax and regulatory net.

The IMFL segment has the largest sales volume overall, and is divided into a number of price niches. The lower-end niches are catered to by regional or local players (confined to a state or even a part of a state), whose products carry brand labels, but do no promotion at all. Their selling point is price and availability. The middle niches attract regional players and most of the national players, so conscious branding activity takes place here, even though price is still perhaps the dominant factor, i.e., brand premiums, if they do exist, are relatively small. However, volumes tend to be large and the larger players just cannot ignore the opportunity. In the higher-end segments, the large, national players have a dominant presence. In this segment, brand premiums are significant and producers exploit every opportunity they have within the regulatory constraints to promote brands. Volumes obviously decline, significantly as prices increase, but margins are high and worth going after, even with relatively small volumes.

This is the segment in which the typical foreign entrant competes. There has been some entry in the beer market (SAB Miller and Fosters, for example). However, the overwhelming focus of foreign entrants – Seagrams, Pernod-Ricard, IDV, for example, has been on the higher-end IMFL segment especially, the whisky segment. Firms like IDV have made forays into the middle range whisky categories, but, by and large, the emphasis is on small volumes and high brand premiums.

They face intense competition from domestic players, who, as indicated earlier, straddle both the higher-end and the middle segments. They thus benefit from both higher volumes and established brand loyalties.

BMIL's Strategy: Goals, Resources and Spillovers

As mentioned above, the target segment of the majority of foreign entrants into the Indian market has been the higher-end whisky segment, with some exceptions. BMIL's goals were unique in this respect. It entered with its flagship brand Bacardi White, which, in the Indian context was in a previously unknown market segment. Historically, rum produced in India has been dark. Its positioning in the market was somewhat below the middle range domestic whiskies. It is a product closely associated with the military services, to which it is issued as part of their regular monthly supplies, exempt from the tax burden that civilian consumers have to bear. There was an attempt to create a market for white rum by a major domestic spirits manufacturer in the early 1990s, but it was not successful. The introduction of Bacardi white rum into the Indian market, at a price significantly above the highest-priced brand of domestic (dark) rum, was tantamount to establishing an entirely new market niche.

Choice of mode
Bacardi's organisational history is that of a family owned and managed company, and its merger with Martini & Rossi did not significantly change that. Clearly, given a choice, it would have preferred to come into India through the wholly-owned subsidiary route. This could have involved acquisition of an existing firm which held a valid licence for the manufacture of alcoholic beverages. The limits on foreign ownership in this industry were the primary motivation for its decision to enter through a joint venture. Having made this decision, however, the choice of the partner was driven by strategic considerations.

Ownership structure
BMIL is a 74 : 26 joint venture between Bacardi-Martini (through Bacardi International of the USA) and Gemini Distilleries of Mysore, Karnataka. Bacardi International acquired 74 per cent stake in the going concern, with an overall valuation of Rs320 million in 1995. In 2000, with BMIL's operations gaining in steadiness, its US parent decided to infuse an additional Rs290 million into the Indian subsidiary producing and marketing the popular Bacardi rum. The money was brought in through issuance of non-convertible, non-cumulative preference shares. The shareholding of Bacardi International in BMIL remains unchanged at the existing level of 74 per cent. Since the

resident shareholder's equity holding cannot be lowered than 26 per cent at any point in time, it chose the preference share route to infuse funds into the venture.

Strategic considerations for choice of partner

The parent company considered three possible partners, two located in the state of Karnataka and one in the state of Maharashtra. Both states are major sugar cultivators and therefore have significant distillery capacity. Both are also relatively prosperous and relatively large consumers of alcoholic beverages. Due diligence and valuation exercises were undertaken. The final choice of Gemini Distilleries was influenced by the strength of the political connections of the owner, who at the time was a member of the Indian Parliament. The parent had no expectations of the local partner with respect to any managerial or technical inputs. However, there was an expectation that the partner would be valuable in dealing with regulatory and 'environmental' issues. The partner was seen as the venture's interface with the political and administrative systems. Its role has continued along these lines through the course of the venture, including obtaining the necessary approvals and permissions within the state of Karnataka as well as in other states (as a member of parliament, the owner is a national-level politician).

Resources from the parent

The infusion of financial resources by Bacardi-Martini into the joint venture was used mainly to bring in new equipment, including a maturation facility, which was critical to the positioning of the product in the Indian market. An important input from the parent firm was the waste treatment facility, using anaerobic technology, which was introduced for the first time into the Indian distillery industry. This technology was originally developed in-house by Bacardi as a proprietary process, but has since been divested to another company. The process produces methane gas, and can be used to fuel boilers or to co-generate electricity. The project was expected to promote this technology in a number of industries including food and beverage, pharmaceuticals, pulp and paper, petroleum and chemicals. Whether this has since happened is not clear, but discussions with the head of technology indicated that environmental regulations were pressurising domestic producers to upgrade their waste treatment facilities and that having a working model of this technology made it easier for them to assimilate it.

Local resources

The local partner's inputs into the venture have already been addressed. Their value is a direct function of the complexity of the regulatory framework within and across states and the continuous interface that a producer has to have with government. However, outside of the partner's contribution, other local resources were also significant. The raw material was completely indigenous; although there were some yield problems with the local molasses, these did not detract from its quality and acceptability even for the standards that the venture was aiming for.

Most significantly, managerial resources were almost exclusively local. The CEO, who initiated Bacardi-Martini's presence in India with the commencement of the search for a local partner is Indian, with several years of experience both in the alcoholic beverages industry and the local operations of a major consumer goods multinational. The head of technology is also Indian, with long experience of the industry in a number of the major domestic players. One of the critical competences in this product is the final blending of stocks of different maturities. In the parent company, blending is a closely guarded skill, confined to the inner circle. The initial blending expertise was, therefore, inevitably from outside the country, but the situation changed relatively quickly. The master blender is currently Indian, having received training in the parent company's establishments outside the country.

Expansion strategy

In 1998, Bacardi International made an effort to take over domestic alcoholic beverages major Jagatjit Industries. The offer by Bacardi for Jagatjit fell through, reportedly because of disagreement over the acquisition price. In 2001, Bacardi International acquired American Beverages (Mauritius). This company had 51 per cent shareholding in Whyte & Mackay India with another domestic major, Radico Khaitan as the local joint venture partner. The two companies, Whyte & Mackay India and BMIL, operate as independent entities while attempting to exploit scale economies in sales and marketing.

In 2000, BMIL entered into a marketing pact with the Scotland-based Grants to market the Scottish firm's whisky brands in the country. The deal was to help bring two whisky brands – Glenfiddich and Grants – to the country. This was part of Bacardi's plans to bring all categories of liquors in India. It markets Grants' brands in the same way as other brands.

Both these moves have established the Bacardi-Martini group's presence in the whisky segment of the Indian market, where it is in direct competition with all the other foreign players that have entered the market, as well as with the premium products of the domestic players. Other than the acquisition-based expansion into the highly competitive whisky segment, BMIL also attempted to create a new market niche for low-alcohol drinks, introducing their international brand 'Breezer' into the Indian market.

Marketing strategies

There are two distinct strategies discernible in the company's marketing plan. One is centred around the 'Bacardi' identity, which encompasses the premium rum and the Breezer products. In promoting these products, BMIL followed the international positioning of Bacardi – youth-oriented and aspirational. Sponsorship of events, particularly concerts that attract young people, is an important component of this strategy. Bacardi does this around the world and has pursued a similar strategy in India. The other strategy relates to the whisky segment, in which its association with Whyte & Mackay and Grants gives it access to a wide price range of products.

Outcomes

Being a closely held company, BMIL is not required to publish financial information and was unwilling to provide information on sales volumes or financial achievements. However, the company indicated that it has maintained 'growth' in excess of 30 per cent per year. Certainly, its marketing strategy for the Bacardi label is relatively high profile and anecdotal evidence suggests that the flagship product has gained significant acceptance in the major Indian markets.

In the interview, the country head outlined his perception of BMIL management's fulfilled and unfulfilled expectations from the India venture. On the fulfilment side, he indicated that establishment of the Bacardi brand and the success with the creation of the market for the premium white rum. He also noted that this was achieved by a largely domestic human capital resource. On the negative side, he felt that the business continued to be at the mercy of arbitrary tax policies of state governments (he was a prime mover of the tax harmonisation project mentioned in the introduction).

Conclusion

Bacardi-Martini's choice of the joint venture as a mode of entry into India was inevitable because of the policy restriction on foreign ownership in this industry, but its choice of partner had obvious strategic elements. The choice was motivated largely by the complexity of the local regulatory environment, which differed from state to state and effectively fragmented the market. In these circumstances, local knowledge, and more so relationships with the bureaucracy and the political class were perceived as assets. The expectation from the local partner focused exclusively on the management of these relationships. Technical and managerial resources were contributed exclusively by the foreign partner.

However, as in the ABN-Amro case, the joint venture relied almost exclusively domestic managerial resources. In fact, it is debatable whether Indian managers can be considered a 'local' resource, because they appear to be quite mobile globally. The employer therefore has to compete not just with local firms (or local affiliates of foreign firms) but also with firms in other locations. However, if this resource cannot be considered fully mobile, it seems to be an important source of cost advantages for foreign entrants, who bring in technology and capital but have no need to bring in high-cost expatriate managers. The fact that even a highly exclusive skill like blending is also in domestic hands underlines the importance of the cost/productivity advantages that local human capital resources provide to foreign entrants.

The technology that the venture brought in for waste treatment is the source of potential positive externalities. Regulation is forcing domestic producers in this as well as other process industries to upgrade waste treatment technology. The existence of a working model in the country, as well as people who have experience with it is probably an important element in making the transition easier.

Finally, one important global resource that the company contributed was its marketing strategy. This appears to have helped in creating a new market for its flagship product, and associating it with the same set of values that it identifies itself with internationally. Global media exposure appears to have played a part in this, but active local promotional efforts among the target segment of consumers seems to have worked as well. For at least some products, the message truly appears to be universal.

PACKAGING

In this case, a multinational enterprise that specialised in a specific segment of the food packaging industry acquired a business in its sector from a major Indian business group with most of its activity in another industry. The packaging industry is highly dependent on domestic production due to transportation costs and integration in the supply chain of the local food industry. The industry supplies other companies where timeliness and quality are of great importance. In consequence, supply disruptions due to, for instance delayed processing of imports at Indian ports, could cause substantial losses to the industrial customers.

A large business group headquartered at New Delhi established the firm after World War II. While the main activity of the group is in the paper industry, this particular firm operated in an unrelated industry. It had four production units, two in northern India and one each in western and southern India.

The foreign firm is a world leading MNE in its segment of the international packaging industry. Its headquarters are based in a western country, but the Indian affiliate reports to its regional headquarters that are closer to India. The CEO of the subsidiary is however from a third country and is drawn from the western activities.

The Indian company was among the leading firms in the industry in India, but small by international standards. Its quality and output was well received in the market and it had a stable share in a moderately growing market. In this particular product segment, the company was in the top three in terms of sales. The top five companies together control about 90 per cent of the market. Moreover, smaller firms using a recycling based production process take up part of the market. Despite their small size, these companies are highly competitive and limit the effective market for the larger producers.

With the reforms following 1991, the government relaxed conditions for international collaborations. The Indian business group and the international packaging MNE saw it in both their interests to establish technical collaboration. They did so in 1991 when the MNE introduced new technology in the Indian company. Under the technology agreement, the Indian company paid 2 per cent royalty on exports. However, no royalties were charged for domestic sales.

The reforms affected the company in another way. With relaxed FDI policy, many MNEs entered India and many more were expected to set up operations in the near future. This meant that their international suppliers were also interested in setting up a base in India. This particular MNE also supplied to other major MNEs internationally and this following-the-customer-motive may have contributed to its early entry to India. Despite the reforms, setting up a greenfield unit in India takes a long time. Consequently many MNEs would have preferred to take over Indian companies rather than rapidly entering the Indian market, had this been permitted. Since the government at that time tended to be less open to acquisitions, many foreign companies entered into joint ventures with Indian partners.

The MNC bought 51 per cent stake in the Indian company, establishing a new legal entity under a new name. The company now paid a 3 per cent royalty on domestic sales in addition to the 2 per cent royalty payment on exports to the international MNE. The Indian business group had several reasons to wish to sell its packaging business:

- The group was itself going through a major restructuring, where different parts were being divided between various family members. This created a negative perception in the market.
- The restructuring process coincided with a recession in the Indian economy. Hence positive effects could not be realised in the short run. The investors thus rated the company as uncompetitive.
- The packaging company had a low degree of synergy with most of the other activities of the business group. It lacked a dedicated approach and had traditionally resorted to backward vertical integration. The group wanted to sell off side businesses such as this packaging unit, and focus on its core activities.
- The company needed funds for its investment and services segment. The cash flow from realisation of the sale was to form the basis for the needed investment.
- The company was facing a major liquidity crunch, as most of the other companies of the group were not performing financially well; consequently availability of the funds also might have been an issue.

- For the purpose of monitoring its side business, the company had set a 25 - 25 rule. Probably, the packaging business was sold after it failed to meet the criteria.

At an early stage, the international MNE was not a very aggressive partner in the joint venture and it continued to be run in the same manner as before. Senior, middle and junior level employees of the company remained. The international partner transferred a few key technical personnel to India, however, no major changes occurred in the management structure, or the way decisions were taken.

The employees representing the international partner increasingly felt that a more aggressive path needed to be developed to permit robust growth in the changing competitive environment. They foresaw a need for relatively large investments in upgrading machinery and expanding plant capacity. The Indian group however was either unwilling or unable to come up with the funds required for this investment. By 1997 it was decided that the foreign partner would fully take over the company, but keep all the employees and restructure the company according to its perceptions of the Indian market. The factors that facilitated the acquisitions were:

- Need for investment in plant and machinery;
- Insufficient financial resources of the Indian partner;
- Lack of synergies for the Indian partner but a core activity for the international company;
- Relaxed government controls on FDI acquisitions.

The multinational enterprise had multiple motives to acquire the Indian packaging firm in full:

- Despite losses, the new firm that was formed continued to be the largest supplier of the key products in this industry in India;
- It had valuable client relationships with, among other firms, several foreign MNEs in the food and pharmaceutical industries;
- The acquisition provided a good fit with the MNE's global strategy, and allowed it to expand its market reach in its core business to India. It was trying to reach the Indian markets owing to the relaxed conditions for investments. In fact, in 1997 it entered a similar venture in another state in India, and in 2000, it initiated talks for further acquisition-based growth in India.

The Indian company received government approval for a complete takeover by its foreign partner in 1997, yet it took three years to implement the takeover. Since then the employees of the MNC have been completely in charge of the company. The firms invested in upgrading plant and machinery in one of the three plants after the acquisition, with moderate changes in the others. While the financial investment has not been huge by the standards of this industry, employees reported that the major change has been in the 'style' of the operations of the company.

On the other hand, almost half of the top twenty managers have left the company. They were replaced by new employees, who are predominantly Indian and were recruited from different industries. The regional headquarters has also sent in its technical people who oversee the operation of the plants. However, there is not much interaction between the international and Indian organisation. The international and regional headquarters do not provide any significant help to the Indian operations. The help has been limited to technical assistance and some transfer of financial resources.

The new employees report some difficulty in interacting with the older employees. The latter are reported to have a more 'relaxed' and 'less aggressive' attitude. There has been less change in middle and junior levels of the hierarchy. This mix of old and new therefore exists both at the plant and machinery level, as well as at the employee level. And it appears to not have been smooth.

Despite the technology transfer, newer equipment, and transfer of skills in the form of international expatriates, customers report a fall in quality. Employees within the company accept this fall and ascribe this to the making the 'old' and the 'new' work together.

Curiously, commentators also point to the poor 'India' skills of the international personnel from the regional headquarters, whereas those from western global headquarters are relatively more successful. These authors have also come across such arguments from other sources. That is, it is easier for western expatriates to function in India than for those more experienced with working in East Asia. Many expatriates report that conditions in India are more like Eastern Europe than Southeast Asia. This has also made the transition more difficult.

ABN AMRO INDIA

Introduction

ABN Amro Bank has been doing business in India since the early 1920s. Its relevance as a case study in a project on entry strategies is, therefore, subject to question. However, in the context of the evolving policy scenario in India, with reference to both foreign investment and the financial sector, it would be fair to say that the process of reforms initiated in 1991 significantly changed the operating environment for foreign banks. During the early 1990s, many lines of business in the broad category of financial services were opened up to foreign entities. There are, of course, many regulatory constraints still in place, which have played an important, even predominant, role in shaping the present structure of the bank's Indian operations.

The case study is structured as follows. An overview of the financial sector in India, focusing on its dynamics over the decade of the 1990s. ABN Amro's expansion and diversification strategy in the context of the sectoral developments, drawing on inputs from the interviews with bank managers, where necessary, and resource dimensions of the entry are addressed.

The Recent Dynamics of Indian Banking

The Indian financial system was fairly liberal until the late 1950s with no ceilings on interest rates and low reserve requirements. However, the government tightened its control in the early 1960s by means of controlling the lending rates and higher liquidity requirements. By this time all banks other than SBI and its seven associate banks were under private ownership. In order to serve the masses with a better credit planning, the government nationalised 14 of the largest private banks in July 1969. Further, six more private banks were nationalised in April 1980. However, the small private banks were also allowed to play while the expansion of existing foreign banks was stringently restricted (Sarkar 1999). These nationalised banks though played a positive role by dispensing credit to the small borrower under social obligations but at the expense of achieving profitability and efficiency. By the mid-1980s the banking sector was gradually liberalised in order to channel scarce invisible funds to the most productive uses and reduce the cost of investable funds. The liberalisation of the financial sector was even more necessary in view of the adoption of the macroeconomic stabilisation and structural adjustment programmes initiated in the early 1990s.

At the core of the restructuring initiated in 1992, deregulating the financial sector and particularly the banking segment was a major activity. One of the major policy changes was raising the interest rate on deposits, which was intended to lead to an increase in the rate of savings. The deregulation of the lending rates, lowering of reserve requirements and introduction of internationally accepted prudential norms was intended to increase the supply of credit and raise the quality and quantity of investment. The new policies also directed the nationalised banks to rely on the capital market for supplementing their equity base. The reforms aimed at creating a competitive environment by allowing entry of new private and foreign banks.

The banking sector is dominated by scheduled commercial banks (SCBs), which account for nearly 95 per cent of all banking operations. Among the scheduled banks are the public sector banks namely the State Bank of India and its seven associates, 19 nationalised banks, 32 private domestic banks (24 old and 8 new) and 42 foreign private banks along with 196 regional rural banks. By the year 2000, the number of scheduled commercial banks increased to 297, from 274 in 1987.

The removal of entry restrictions in 1993 sparked the entry of new private and foreign banks. Nine domestic and 21 foreign banks were started over a period of seven years, between 1993 and 2000. Though there were more foreign players in terms of number, their market share in terms of total assets account for only 8.3 per cent of the total assets of all SCBs during the period 1999-2000 (RBI 2001, p. 46)

The number of foreign banks in India has almost doubled from 24 to 45 during 1993 to 2000. The presence of more firms among the foreign banking sector has also reflected on the concentration ratio, the share of the top five foreign banks in terms of total assets has declined. The ratio was 0.99 during 1991 to 1992; it fell to 0.60 in 1995 to 1996 and then declined sharply to 0.28 in 1999 to 2000. From this we conclude that the new policy has had a positive impact in increasing competition among the foreign bank operators.

It is worthwhile to look at the performance of foreign banks in terms of select indicators and compare it with all SCBs during the period 1990 to 2000. In terms of conventional criteria, foreign banks have been functioning relatively better as compared to all SCBs. While over the period 1990 to 2000 the net profit to total assets of foreign banks has been 0.83 per cent, it has been only 0.18 per cent for all SCBs. Net profitability of foreign banks has increased to 1.12 during 1995 to 2000 from the level of 0.46 during 1990 to 1995.

An analysis of financial data from domestic and foreign banks suggests that the latter performed better compared to all SCBs in terms of profitability despite incurring a relatively high intermediation cost and interest cost. This profit making behaviour of the foreign banks can be explained by the trends in net interest incomes. The net interest income to total assets has been high for foreign banks as compared to all SCBs through the decade.

Finally, the foreign banks have been keeping higher reserve surpluses to meet exigencies. This is evident from the ratio of provisions and contingencies to total assets, which is higher for foreign banks. During 1990-1995, this ratio was 3.19 per cent for the foreign banks and 1.79 per cent for all SCBs. During 1995-2000, the ratio of provisions and contingencies to total assets declined slightly for the foreign banks and all SCBs, though it remained higher for the foreign banks.

There are a number of implications from this comparative picture of the evolving structure of Indian banking for the strategic analysis of foreign banks. First, in the post-liberalisation business environment, foreign banks as a group are on a relatively more robust footing. Their realisations are higher, their costs lower and their ability to meet prudential requirements greater. The reasons for this are partly historical and are not particularly important in and of themselves. But they are significant to the extent that they constrain the competitive responses of domestic public sector banks. As the concept of financial intermediation evolves, reducing or eliminating the boundaries between different sets of activities, the foreign banks are, as a group, relatively better placed to expand their activities to take advantage of new opportunities.

Second, with reference to the issue of appropriateness of this case study in an entry strategy context, the significance of the change in the environment meant that every player had to re-evaluate their business opportunities and re-orient their strategies to exploit the opening up of the environment. In that sense, even though ABN Amro has been in India for a long time, its perceptions about the market, like those of other banks, would have been transformed after 1991 and its subsequent business decisions can reasonably be compared to more classic 'entry' decisions. The main difference, of course, would be the strength of its prevailing local knowledge, which would influence its prioritisation of local alliances, in its expansion strategy.

Third, there is a significant limitation in confining the description of structural change to banking, when expansion strategies of major players involve straddling many, or all, segments of the financial services spectrum. However, the perspective taken here is that of an organisation that has essentially been in a relatively narrow banking niche using its established strengths to expand into other areas of banking as well as other financial services. In the next section, we make some comparisons between ABN Amro and other organisations pursuing similar strategies for leveraging from a relatively narrow business to a universal presence.

ABN Amro's Global Strategy

The ABN Amro Bank is a conglomerate bank with international services that span consumer banking, structured finance, transaction banking, debt underwriting and distribution, broking, corporate finance, investment banking and fleet management. It expanded its operations to 74 countries and territories by 2000, from 52 countries and territories in 1991. The number of branches also increased from 1,928 in 1991 to 3,594 branches by the year 2000. Similarly, the employment at the ABN Amro Bank was 56,747 employees in 1991, but almost doubled to 115,098 by 2000.

In 2002 the bank ranked fifth in Europe and sixteenth in the world on tier 1 capital with a total asset of over €543.2 billion. Over the past ten years its assets have grown at an average growth rate of 13 per cent, with a sharp increase in the second half of the 1990s. However, the financial performance of ABN Amro in terms of rate of return (profit before tax to total assets) has not shown a similar hike over the same period. The average profitability ratio was 6.3 per cent during 1991-95 and this increased only at a marginal level (7.9 per cent) in the later half of the 1990s.

Initially the bank was organised so as to expand its operations in the maximum number of countries. Such a structure was revamped with the new strategy in 2000, which embodied a vision to maximise the shareholder value. This year also marked the end of the Universal Banking concept of the ABN Amro Bank. Consequent to its newly adopted strategy the bank restructured its organisation into three strategic business units (SBUs) that were aimed to focus on client groups. The three SBUs were namely wholesale clients, consumer and commercial clients and private clients and asset management. These SBUs were focused on major international corporations and institutions, individuals and small to medium-sized business enterprises, asset gathering activities and fund management respectively.

Also in the year 2000, the bank restructured itself towards a more market-oriented strategy in order to reach its client groups. While the bank operated in 76 countries and territories during 1999, it operated in 74 countries and territories in 2000. Although the number of countries and territories has gone down by two over a period of only one year, the number of branches and offices has gone up. In 1999, the bank had 3,583 branches and offices world over which increased to 3,594 in the following year. This can be accrued to the branches and offices belonging to the newly acquired firms and businesses in the operating countries in 2000. In fact, ABN Amro expanded its operations through many mergers, acquisitions and alliances. For instance, it acquired Alleghany Asset Management which is a major asset manager with over 550 institutional clients in the USA and principal offices in Atlanta and Chicago. This deal itself contributes almost 40 per cent growth in ABN Amro's global assets under management and allows ABN to distribute Alleghany funds worldwide and Alleghany to distribute ABN funds. Another acquisition was Michigan National Corporation, a commercial bank holding company based in the state of Michigan, with assets of US$11.6 billion, 3,600 staff members and more than 180 offices. In June 2000, ABN Amro Lease Holding acquired the Dial group with operations in France, Italy, Spain and the UK.

Further, as part of their new governance structure the bank introduced the concepts of interest rate risk, operational risk, market risk, country risk and credit risk in order to preserve the quality of its products and survive in an uncertain market environment. The bank also introduced value-based measures for compensation and a new remuneration structure for top management. All these factors had a major role in better performance of ABN Amro in the absolute sense. However, the efficiency ratio has declined for the bank due to high operating costs. This was the result of higher expenses owing to internal growth, information technology projects, acquisitions and higher performance-related bonuses.

Table 6.1 Compound annual rates of growth of banks in India (%)

	Deposits		Advances		Total assets		Investments	
	ABN	Foreign banks	ABN	Foreign banks	ABN	Foreign banks	ABN	Foreign banks
1991-92 to 1999-00	33.15	33.22	45.43	38.43	41.61	36.54	41.63	38.98
1991-92 to 1994-95	32.23	71.29	60.06	74.30	40.12	71.59	14.68	71.82
1995-96 to 1999-00	55.75	15.56	42.99	13.88	44.67	16.84	79.67	30.10

Source: Prowess

ABN Amro in India

The ABN Amro Bank had a significant presence in the foreign sector of the Indian banking industry. It was traditionally known as the 'Diamond Financing Bank' due to its services to the diamond clients in the two major metros of the country Kolkata and Mumbai. Consequent to the merger of ABN (Algemene Bank Nederland) and Amro (Amsterdam Rotterdam) worldwide in 1991, the ABN Bank in India turned into a full-fledged bank in the name of ABN Amro Bank.

It took off in a big way with a comprehensive range of services. It has shown a tremendous growth especially after the mid-1990s. For instance, it ranked third amongst all the foreign banks in terms of total assets in 1991 to 1992. It however, lost its rank to the new foreign entrants that emerged after the deregulation of the banking sector. It ranked ninth during 1995 to 1996. By the late 1990s, ABN Amro Bank began to strengthen its position in India and ranked sixth in 1999-2000. Thus, even when the C_5 ratio was on a fall, the ABN Amro Bank could manage to improve its ranking in terms of its market share based on total assets. In India, the foreign competitors of ABN Amro Bank include Citibank NA, HSBC, Bank of America NT & SA and Standard Chartered.

The overall growth of ABN was relatively high as compared to foreign banks through the 1990s. In general, the growth rates presented in Table 6.1 show a higher growth in deposits, advances, total assets and investments of the ABN Amro Bank compared to the overall growth of the entire foreign bank segment during 1991 to 1992 to 1999 to 2000. Though the performance of ABN in India during the first phase of the 1990s i.e. 1991 to 1992 to 1994 to 1995 was not all that encouraging, it has picked up in the later half of the 1990s i.e. over the period 1995-96 to 1999-2000 (based on Prowess data). For instance, the deposits of the international bank (ABN Amro) grew at a compounded annual rate of growth (CARG) of 55.75 per cent during 1995-96 to 1999-2000 while the corresponding rate for all foreign banks was only 15.56 per cent. This was in contrast to the rates that were observed during the early 1990s. During 1991 to 1992 to 1994 to 1995, the CARG for ABN Amro was 32.23 per cent as against a high CARG of 71.29 per cent for all foreign banks. A similar trend is seen in reference to other attributes such as the advances, investments and total assets. This confirms our earlier statement that in the late 1990s the ABN Amro Bank became more aggressive in order to regain its position or rank among the other foreign players.

Post-1991 Strategies

The following discussion focuses on the various growth strategies adopted by ABN in order to face the increasing competition. It adopted a multi-pronged growth strategy by the way of restructuring and introducing new services/products through diversification, acquisitions, and joint ventures. Much of this took place in the late 1990s. This was in convergence with the decision taken by the parent bank to emerge as regional power in the Asian continent. The recognition of the importance of the Indian market motivated the Dutch banking major to build India as one of its strongest operations.

In order to increase its client base, the bank targeted both individuals as well as corporations. Two new services were introduced by 1998. These were the Savings Advantage Account for the individual and the Current Advantage Account. In addition, variants of credit cards and debit cards were also launched in the same year. The bank also tried to widen its branch network. Besides its branches in metro areas, the bank decided to open new branches in middle level cities. In 2001, ABN Amro had seven branches, all in metro cities. With historical offices in Mumbai and Kolkata, new branches were opened in Delhi (1991), Chennai (1994), Pune (1997), Baroda (1999) and Hyderabad (2001). However, later it decided to have only 10 to 12 branches across the country to reduce costs while increasing its reach through a powerful network of direct selling agents. Thus, it introduced a concept of doorstep banking.

The bank enhanced its reach to the customers by introducing the concept of doorstep banking, a national call centre, internet banking and setting up Any Time Money counters. The courier service system was made to deliver cash and drafts in minimum time at a nominal charge more efficiently. Further, the tele-service networks were strengthened to provide round-the-clock information and service to the account holder.

Acquisition
Aspiring to strengthen itself in the consumer banking segment, the global ABN Amro Bank, Amsterdam, decided to increase its focus on the consumer banking segment world-wide. It planned to generate as much as 40 per cent of its revenues from this activity by the year 2008. Considering the importance of the Indian market in the Asian continent, a similar emphasis was put on the Indian branch of ABN to enhance its presence in the consumer-banking segment. Consequent to this, in 1999, the ABN bank in India took over the retail business of another international bank in India, the Bank of America.

This acquisition was a quick step towards capturing a hold on the desired segment, and the banks' portfolio widened. At an acquisition price of Rs12 billion[13] the Dutch bank gained control over the four offices of the Bank of America across the country. As part of this deal, the deposit and loan portfolio of the Bank of America worth nearly Rs8 billion was taken over by ABN Amro Bank. In addition, almost 90 per cent of its retail assets of the Bank of America were transferred to ABN Amro. They thus got a readymade retail market of more than 100,000 customers. One of the critical issues in this acquisition deal were the employees of Bank of America. ABN Amro agreed to absorb half of the workforce of the retail segment of Bank of America, thus the acquiring bank absorbed 250 employees.

Subsequent to the takeover, the total assets of ABN Amro grew by 88 per cent during 1998-99 to 1999-2000. The total assets increased to Rs75.17 billion in 1999-2000 from the level of Rs39.77 billion in the previous year, whereas the total assets of Bank of America decreased from the level of Rs72.35 billion to Rs. 56.79 billion during the same period. Thus, the acquisition contributed to a more than twofold increase in the total assets of ABN Amro Bank. This was also reflected in the growth of sales of the ABN Amro in India.

The acquisition is best viewed in the context of the global strategies of the two banks. Bank of America was keen on exiting from this line of business in India, despite a reasonably well-performing operation. ABN Amro, with consumer banking being one of its global thrust areas, was looking to expand its relatively small Indian operation. It could, of course, have chosen an organic growth strategy, but preferred the acquisition route for some simple economic reasons. It saw consumer banking as an investment-intensive area, with long gestation periods and, therefore, slower growth prospects in the short-to-medium term. On the other hand, wholesale banking, targeted at corporate clients, justifies an organic strategy. When the opportunity to acquire a going consumer operation came their way, they took advantage of it.

Of course, there was a trade-off in terms of organisational compatibility, particularly when, as mentioned above, so many old employees remained in the new structure. An explicit integration strategy was put in place, which was referred to in our interview as the 'grafting model'. The respective strengths of each organisation were analysed. ABN Amro came out strong on the fronts of cost management, cross-selling capabilities across its different business lines and transparent human resource practices. Bank of America, on the other hand, was perceived to have been strong on internal processes, good process–business interface leading to high service efficiency and, very importantly, superior consumer risk management practices. The integration process basically aimed at retaining these process and risk management capabilities in the new organisational structure.

Diversification
Apart from expanding the capacity of existing product lines through acquisition, ABN Amro has also diversified its product lines through greenfield investment and joint ventures. It has diversified into debt market financing segment by setting up a non-bank finance company (NBFC) in 1999. This was set up in the name of ABN Amro Asia Corporate Finance Limited with an inflow of foreign investment of Rs23 million. It was immediately followed by the policy changes adopted by government in order

to encourage the new financial services activities. This firm aimed to undertake fee-based activities such as corporate finance advisory services. The ventures' debt financing portfolios include short-term debt instruments such as call money-linked debentures and other such products. It also provided general liaison marketing and representation services to the corporate sector mainly to foreign companies setting up shop in India. While ABN Amro has 75 per cent equity stake in this fund-based joint NBFC venture, the remaining 25 per cent is split into three local partners including the Burmans of Dabur, a relatively large pharmaceutical and consumer goods company in India.

It also used the joint venture as part of its diversification growth strategy. This joint venture was in the name of Lease Plan Fleet Management (India) Private Limited. The ABN subsidiary i.e. ABN Amro Lease Holding Company, had 51 per cent control while giving 49 per cent to its Indian partner i.e. International Travel House (ITH). It introduced a concept of fleet management to undertake the business of leasing and fleet management of company car fleets. Further, Lease Plan offered a solution that overcame the problems associated with traditional forms of buying, lease managing and disposal of fleets of vehicles.

The ownership structure of both these ventures was motivated predominantly by regulatory constraints. ABN Amro, as a global policy, prefers to maintain 100 per cent ownership of its overseas (certainly, in emerging markets) operations. Its choice of joint ventures or alliances is determined simply by whether the line of business is within its strategic priorities and the constraints that the host country regulations impose on ownership and structure. For that matter, even the separation between the banking and the securities business in India into two distinct entities is in response to regulatory requirements. As regulations permit, the organisation will converge to the global structure of business groupings, exiting all its joint ventures and alliances.

With respect to its partners in these ventures, there is a clear perception that they are passive or sleeping partners. There is no expectation that they bring any real resources to the operation and there is a clear understanding with them that changing regulations will immediately result in restructuring.

ABN Amro's Key Competitors

The overall strategy of ABN Amro, which could reasonably be termed 'universal banking', is being followed to a significant degree by a number of other organisations in India. From the management's vantage point, there are three foreign companies and one Indian company that are comparable in terms of strategic scope and scale of operations. The foreign companies are Citigroup, HSBC and Standard Chartered. The Indian company is ICICI

Table 6.2 ABN Amro's key competitors

	Deposits	Advances & loans	Total assets	Investments
Business Volumes (Rs bn)				
ABN-Amro Bank NV	581.54	939.71	1,715.98	260.73
HSBC	3,844.38	2,145.89	5,216.24	1,471.80
Standard Chartered Bank	2,738.57	2,018.46	4,193.88	883.36
Citibank NA	6,775.19	3,478.64	8,642.77	2,316.55
ICICI Bank Ltd (domestic)	2,984.78	15,582.81	24,481.11	4,036.69
Compound annual rates of growth (%) 1995–96 to 2001–02				
ABN-Amro Bank NV	42.48	30.48	28.14	41.91
HSBC	21.46	24.09	24.19	27.34
Standard Chartered Bank	17.60	28.30	28.54	41.26
Citibank NA	14.47	21.85	16.40	17.21
ICICI Bank Ltd (domestic)	48.56	20.22	27.46	43.93

Source: Prowess and Company reports

Bank. All of these have gone through significant mutations in the past few
years as they have acquired other companies, started off new lines of
business, reverse merged (in the case of ICICI). It is therefore difficult to
make comparisons of their performance over time. Nevertheless, in Table
6.2, we present a summary comparison between ABN Amro and these
institutions.The comparisons show that ABN Amro was the smallest member
of this group about five years ago, but it has been amongst the fastest
growing, both through organic growth and acquisitions. Interestingly, some
of the other firms, which were far larger to begin with, have also been able to
sustain relatively high rates of growth, which indicates that overall market
penetration for their portfolio of services is relatively low. This reflects back
on an important structural characteristic of the Indian financial sector – the
continuing significance of government-owned companies and the
organisational and strategic constraints they operate under.

   This backdrop explains a perception on the part of ABN Amro's
management that the Indian market remains a highly contestable market for
all the services that these organisations offer. Where there is high penetration,
e.g. in savings and chequing accounts, improved technology provides a
competitive edge. ABN Amro is actively discouraging visits by customers to
its branches for routine transactions as a cost-saving measure. This option is
not yet available to its public sector competitors. Further, there is also a
perception of an absence of first mover advantages in such a market, so there
is no compulsion to race into a product or service. Later entry with better
preparation is also a viable strategy. The perception that emerged from the
interviews was one of extreme contestability of the Indian market for a whole
range of financial services. In activities in which the market appeared
relatively well-penetrated, superior technology, which contributed to lower
transactions costs and better service quality, was a viable competitive
strategy. In segments in which penetration was low, the strategy was to use
the most 'appropriate' organisational form, which included joint ventures.
These would simultaneously neutralise entry barriers imposed by the
regulatory framework and leave the field open for complete control if and
when these barriers were removed. The driving force of the strategy was to
gain entry in all the segments in the Indian market, which its global strategy
warranted. The nature and scale of the entry, however, was dictated by local
conditions.

The Value of Local Resources

The picture emerging from the discussion in previous sections points to an
entry strategy that is completely driven by the business and organisational
priorities of the global entity. Country specifics in terms of joint ventures or
alliances are entirely dictated by regulatory constraints. There appears to be
no value contributed by the domestic partner, though it contains some very

prominent people on the Indian business scene, who are expected to remain passive through the duration of the alliance.

However, there is a very high dependence on local resources with respect to human capital. The current proportion of expatriate managers is very low and the bank has never had a significant number of them. While some of the senior managers have foreign degrees, the CR himself has been entirely educated in India. The management's characterisation of their relationship with the parent is 'global strategy, local operations', meaning that while the broad parameters of business are set by the parent, the country managers have considerable autonomy with respect to local priorities in terms of business lines in response to domestic opportunities. There is very little day-to-day supervision of the country business heads by their superiors in the global organisation (some report to the HQ in Amsterdam, while others to the regional HQ in Singapore). As an example of this autonomy, the securities company took significant local initiatives in setting up a bond house and a custodial service.

It should be kept in mind that it is not entirely appropriate to categorise local managers as a local resource. They are increasingly entering the global workplace from their initial local employment. If one were to view this resource in its global dimension, then one would have to conclude that the organisation really has no dependence on a non-tradable local resource. In ABN Amro, as in the other multinational banks operating in the country, it is quite feasible for managers to move from one country to another. However, when we view the bank's market strategy in conjunction with its human resource strategy, the predominance of local managers perhaps reflects the emphasis on identifying and responding to local opportunities. This would put some premium on familiarity with the local conditions and ways of doing business. In this respect, it is perhaps reasonable to conclude that the bank has tried to find complementarity between global marketing strategies and local human resources. On all other fronts – internal processes, risk management and so on, the company basically follows global templates with whatever local adaptation is necessary.

Spillovers

Spillovers from foreign investment are typically categorised into two types – efficiency gains that accrue to the entire domestic industry from the increased competition and efficiency gains that accrue to domestic firms from proximity to a technologically superior foreign firm. From the description of the strategic group in which ABN Amro operates, it is quite clear that most of its direct competitors are also multinationals with similar strategic objectives. There is only one domestic member of this group. Others may aspire to it, but are some way off from achieving the kind of significance in each segment that this group collectively has.

Given this, the 'competition' spillover is very likely to have been realised. The significance of the presence of a particular player in any segment and its willingness to enter new lines of business consistent with its global strategy would clearly keep all the competitors in the group on their toes. The speed with which all these players introduce new products and services and the aggressiveness with which they market them is clear evidence of the competitive pressure in this segment.

On the more conventional technology and knowledge-related spillovers, the bank's strategy seems designed to minimise them. Its joint venture strategy emphasises relationships with partners who are in entirely different businesses. Joint ventures, which are generally seen as having high potential spillovers in the right conditions, clearly do not generate anything more than peripheral benefits to the partners. The second channel for these spillovers is the mobility of human resources. The interviews suggested that exits among senior managers of the Indian operations were relatively low, but the financial sector in India, particularly the strategic group in which ABN Amro operates, is known for relatively mobile human resources. To the extent that these movements are restricted to the group, as is quite likely to be the case, the spillover benefits are internalised to a few players. Mobility outside the group will obviously bring knowledge and experience to other players in the financial sector, but, by most accounts, it is far more limited at this stage in the evolution of the sector.

Concluding Comments

ABN Amro's Indian operations began in 1921, but it was only in response to the opportunities provided by the liberalisation of the early 1990s that it manifested the strategic behaviour that this overall study is concerned with. In seeking to establish itself as a universal bank in India, it followed both the acquisition and joint venture route. Its acquisition decision, in which it took over Bank of America's consumer banking activities, was clearly seen as a way to bypass the time and costs associated with greenfield investment. In the process, it had to go through a complicated assimilation and adjustment process, but this has generally been perceived as successful.

Its joint venture decisions were motivated not by any need to leverage local resources, but purely by regulatory restrictions, which prohibited it from entering these activities by itself. Its partners were, typically, prominent players in other fields, who had no strategic interests in financial services. ABN Amro believed that it had all the process and skill capabilities to go it alone in these businesses if the opportunity were to present itself.

While it put virtually no premium on local resources in terms of the broader business processes, it has relied quite heavily on local managers to implement its strategy. This is consistent with assessments made during the interviews. Although the decisions on which business to enter were based on the organisation's global strategy, there was a fair degree of local autonomy in terms of deciding timing, scale and other details related to entry. In this context, there would be some premium on knowledge of the local conditions and business practices, which would justify an emphasis on local over expatriate managers. Finally, with regard to spillovers, the most likely source of positive spillovers is the increased competitive intensity within the strategic group in which the bank was operating.

References for Indian Case Studies

ABN Amro Bank, India, corporate website (http://www.abnamroindia.com/).

Prowess database, Centre for Monitoring Indian Economy.

RBI (2001), *Report on Trends and Progress of Banking in India, 1999-2000*, Reserve Bank of India.

7. Foreign Direct Investment in South Africa

Stephen Gelb and Anthony Black

INTRODUCTION

This chapter presents a descriptive overview of the survey results in South Africa (SA). The chapter starts by providing the background to FDI inflows into South Africa during the 1990s, and then turns to a discussion of the survey results, focusing on the sample and the parent firms first, then turning to entry and resource mobilisation, performance and impact of foreign investment.[14]

Foreign direct investment has a long and complex history in South Africa. Foreign corporations have been present since Britain established a colony early in the 19th century. Until the 1870s, the economy was focused on agricultural exports to Europe, but the financial system was dominated by branches of London-based banks. Industrial development was initiated by the discovery of major mineral deposits from the 1860s, first diamonds and later gold. Effective exploitation of the resources required large capital-intensive operations, and was made possible by both direct and portfolio investment flows from Europe, particularly London. This contributed to the early development of a domestic stock exchange in Johannesburg. Domestic economic growth and the re-investment of mining profits stimulated manufacturing development from the turn of the 20th century. Direct investment from the UK, the USA and Europe[15] was important in the establishment and growth of new industrial sectors during the five decades from the 1920s. Domestic manufacturing development was accelerated by exchange rate deprecation after the Gold Standard collapsed in 1933, by demand growth and import difficulties during World War II, and by import-substitution policies commonly found in developing countries during the 1950s and 1960s. Although some FDI continued to flow into mining, during this period it went mainly to manufacturing and services. By the early 1970s, 40 per cent of the FDI stock was in manufacturing and 25 per cent in financial and business services, with only 15 per cent in mining.

From the early 1970s on, new FDI flows into South Africa slowed appreciably. There was a shift in the composition of international capital flows from direct to portfolio investment, but more important, foreign investors in South Africa were increasingly subject to political pressures in their home countries by the growing international campaign against apartheid. During the 1980s, this campaign intensified appreciably as political instability in South Africa increased, and economic conditions also weakened. Foreign direct investors began to exit from SA, with about 225 US corporations, and about 20 per cent of UK firms, departing between 1984 and 1988. Nonetheless, there were still more than 450 foreign firms with direct investments in South Africa in 1990. Total foreign direct investment liabilities in South Africa at the start of the 1990s amounted to US$7.94 billion (at current exchange rates), of which 85 per cent was from Europe and 13 per cent from North America. From 1985, portfolio inflows also ceased, as foreign bank creditors imposed a debt repayment schedule on the South African government and public sector borrowers. The resulting capital outflows and further economic contraction were significant in shifting white political sentiment, especially within business, against apartheid.

Political changes – the unbanning of proscribed organisations and the initiation of constitutional negotiations in 1990, leading to a democratic election in 1994 – ended the disinvestment pressures and direct and portfolio investment inflows resumed. Like the other three countries in the CNEM study, and other emerging markets, South Africa had a 'new dawn' of foreign investment during the 1990s. At the same time, the substantial stock of existing FDI and the very highly-developed domestic capital market[16] – the legacies of prior investment – heavily influenced the level and composition of inflows during the 1990s, and the mode of entry of FDI.

Starting even before 1994, there was a commitment to lowering the fiscal deficit and price inflation, reducing tariffs and liberalising the capital account and the financial system. Through the 1990s, the policy regime became far more liberal and outward-oriented, with the explicit aim of attracting new foreign investment. Direct investment in particular has been identified by many policymakers as 'the' key to improved growth, as illustrated by the single most important economic policy statement since 1994 – the Growth, Employment and Redistribution (GEAR) policy announced in June 1996. The argument was largely macroeconomic – low domestic savings were identified as the binding constraint on growth, to be alleviated by net capital inflows. Since GEAR was formulated partly in response to a capital account shock, FDI was seen as far preferable to volatile portfolio flows as a route to address savings shortages (Govt of SA, 1996).

The fiscal deficit was 3.2 per cent of GDP in 1990 but ballooned to 10.1 per cent in 1993. It was brought below the 3 per cent target by 1998, where it has remained. CPI inflation was 11.3 per cent in 1990, but had been lowered to 6.7 per cent in 2000. But GDP growth has been disappointing, averaging only 0.1 per cent per annum from 1990 to 1994 as contractionary macroeconomic policies were used to lower inflation, and only 2.6 per cent from 1995 to 2001, equivalent to a bare 0.5 per cent per annum on a per capita basis.

South Africa became a GATT signatory in 1994, and average tariff levels were reduced from 27.5 per cent in 1990 to 7 per cent by 1997, while nearly 60 per cent of imports faced a zero tariff in 2000. Both imports and exports grew rapidly, and the current account deficit averaged just over 1 per cent of GDP during the five years to 2000.[17] South Africa also signed the GATS, TRIPS and TRIMS agreements on joining the WTO in 1995. Commitment to services liberalisation under GATS was limited up to 2000, but has since been extended in communications, transport and energy. Intellectual property legislation exceeded the minimum TRIPS standards before SA signed in 1995, though enforcement has been less effective.

Turning to the capital account and financial system, the two-tier currency in place for most of the period since 1961 was abolished in March 1995, and three-quarters of the foreign exchange control regulations in 1994 had been eliminated by 1998. In 1995, branches of foreign banks were allowed to operate and the Johannesburg Stock Exchange had a 'little bang', admitting foreign brokers and scrapping fixed commissions. By 2000, there were 12 foreign bank branches and 61 representative offices in South Africa (see Chapter 8).

There has been considerable success in attracting portfolio inflows, reflecting the developed financial markets, and progress with macroeconomic stabilisation. By 2000, gross non-resident transactions (purchases plus sales) represented 52 per cent of turnover on the equity market, and 23 per cent on the bond market (SA Reserve Bank 2003). Between 1995 and 2002, South Africa received two-thirds of gross market-based capital flows to sub-Saharan Africa, and 101 per cent of net portfolio equity flows. South Africa's share of all developing countries flows were 3.3 per cent and 22 per cent respectively (World Bank 2003, Tables A30 and A37).

The downside of financial liberalisation has been significant exchange rate and capital account volatility, reflected in three exchange rate crises since 1994. Against the US dollar, the rand has depreciated from around ZAR2.60 in 1990 to ZAR7.60 in 2000 to ZAR11.00 at the end of 2001. followed by an appreciation back to around ZAR7.50 by mid-2003. The substantial currency depreciation and associated capital outflows have offset the solid domestic macroeconomic performance reflected in the fiscal and inflation outcomes.

Notwithstanding an explicit commitment, privatisation has been slow and inconsistent, due to domestic political opposition as well as global market conditions since 1999. Just under half the capital stock was in public ownership at the end of 1994, but this had barely dropped to 46 per cent by 2001. The single largest foreign investment since 1994 was the 1997 sale of

30 per cent of equity in Telkom, the state-owned telephone company, to a strategic partner. But the IPO of a further 25 per cent of the stock was delayed by well over a year, and eventually occurred only in 2003.

Investment facilitation agencies have been established since 1994 nationally and in most of the nine provinces. These administer a large suite of more than 35 investment incentive schemes to national and foreign investors on a non-discriminatory basis. The TRIMS agreements requires equal treatment between national and foreign investors (with respect to importing, exporting, and access to foreign exchange), as well as free repatriation of capital and dividends. Reinforcing these commitments, SA has also concluded over 30 bilateral investment treaties since 1994, including with most OECD countries.

FDI INFLOWS IN THE 1990s: AN OVERVIEW

As implied above, the policy focus has been on the financial and macroeconomic dimension of capital inflows, resulting in a 'beauty contest' approach, with a narrow concern as to whether the country is receiving 'enough' investment, and what measures are necessary to get more foreign companies 'through the door'. There is little interest in foreign companies' mobilisation of non-financial resources at entry or after, or of their impact on the economy's growth and development.[18] For example, a recent official statement on industrial policy mentions FDI only once in forty pages, arguing that 'the promotion of domestic and foreign direct investment is critical given the low savings and investment rates in the economy' (Govt of SA 2002, p.32).

Notwithstanding this, FDI performance has been disappointing in quantitative terms. Between 1990 and 1993, total inflows averaged US$46 million per annum. Inflows rose rapidly after the transition in 1994, averaging US$1.861 billion per annum to 2002 (UNCTAD). This is equivalent to just over US$41 per capita (based on the 2001 population), 1.4 per cent of South Africa's per capita income. For comparison, average FDI inflow per capita for the developing world as a whole was US$40.42, equivalent to 3.5 per cent of per capita income (see also Table 1.2).

Between 1995 and 2002, net inward FDI to South Africa was 1.5 per cent of the total for all developing countries, though the country received 12 per cent of net inward FDI flows to sub-Saharan Africa (World Bank 2003, Table A29).[19] These shares are significantly lower than the corresponding proportions for portfolio flows cited above, reflecting much greater success in attracting the latter form of foreign investment.

Two other developments are worth noting. First, several major South African corporations in resource industries and financial services, have relocated their head offices to the UK or the US. This has led to capital flows formally defined as FDI, but more akin to portfolio flows in their economic effects, such as the Anglo American-de Beers unbundling of 2001 (see note 1).

Secondly, South African firms have become significant foreign investors themselves. The large mining houses have retreated from the conglomerate structure that was tied to operating in a relatively closed economy, selling off domestic non-core assets and making significant mineral investments internationally.[20] In addition, sub-Saharan Africa has opened up to South African firms since 1994. The stock of South African direct investment assets in Africa grew 18 per cent per annum between 1995 and 2001 (SA Reserve Bank 2001, 2003). Investment into Africa is concentrated in resource extraction and market-seeking activities, notably mining, finance, retail and infrastructure (EDGE Institute, African Investment Database, 2003).

THE CNEM/EDGE SURVEY

The CNEM/EDGE Institute survey was the first in South Africa since 1994 to examine foreign direct investment across more than one home country or economic sector. The population list was compiled by the EDGE Institute from an initial list of 3,500 firms which consolidated several sources, including market research lists, media reports, and lists provided by foreign trade missions, embassies and international chambers of commerce. Of these, 516 firms which fit the four project criteria[21] comprised the sample frame for the project, and the survey sample in South Africa numbered 162 firms, 31.4 per cent of the population. The distribution of the sample by sector and by parent's home region – shown in Tables 2.1 and 2.4 above – matches that of the population.

Firm Size

The size distribution of the firms' labour force and capital stock were provided in Table 2.2. Table 7.1 gives additional data on size distribution by sector in 2000. As discussed in Chapter 2, the firms are small: the medians are 90 workers and US$1.94 million capital stock for the sample as whole. Only 10 per cent of the firms have a labour force above 1,000 workers. This suggests FDI is unlikely to be a vehicle for either large capital inflows or for significant direct employment creation.

Only the primary and the trade tourism and recreation (TTR) sectors have significant shares of large firms, but both contain few firms. The primary sector is export-oriented, while market growth in TTR has been rapid. In the three manufacturing sectors, firms focus on the domestic and regional (Southern African) markets. Nearly one-third of the sample is in skill- or knowledge-intensive sectors – financial and business services (F&B), IT and pharmaceuticals – where size is not correlated with turnover. Nearly 40 per cent of firms with fewer than 50 workers are in the top 60 per cent of firms by value of turnover, while a quarter of the firms in the top quintile for turnover have fewer than 250 workers. A significant proportion of affiliates were found to be outsourcing much of their operation, especially production, while they focused on strategic management, marketing and technical services. In some cases, this was in contrast to other affiliates of the parent firm or a shift from their intention on entry to South Africa. This is a response to risk, including political and social risk (a new and unknown government, HIV/Aids, crime), currency risk (secular depreciation of the rand), and market risk (slow economic growth in both South Africa and most of the region).

Table 7.1 Affiliate size in 2000, South Africa

	Median No. of workers	Median capital stock ($m)	No. of firms
Primary	1500	24.50	5
Basic consumer goods	78	0.65	20
Intermediate goods	8	2.45	27
Machinery & equipment	100	2.00	31
Infrastructure & construction	147	0.22	18
Trade, tourism & recreation	220	13.69	7
Financial & business services	70	0.86	33
Information technology	55	1.01	12
Pharmaceuticals	23	0.08	5
All sectors	90	1.94	158

The Investors

Table 7.2 shows the sectoral distribution of each region's investors. The European firms are distributed evenly in basic consumer goods, intermediate goods, machinery and equipment (M&E), infrastructure and financial and business services. The North American firms are concentrated in intermediate goods, F&B and IT. East Asian firms are concentrated in manufacturing, particularly intermediate goods and M&E.

The parent firms (87 per cent from developed economies) cover the spectrum from small companies with operations in three or four countries to global giants (though South Africa had many major global corporations present prior to 1990). The median number of affiliates in the sample is 20.

Though nearly half the affiliates contribute a tiny share (less than 0.5 per cent) of parents' global turnover, for another quarter of the sample, the affiliate provides more than 5 per cent of global sales. Median global labour force size of the parent is 10,250 workers. Mean spending on advertising and on R&D both lie within 1 to 2 per cent of global turnover. Only 15 per cent of the sample had no emerging market experience at all, while more than half were already in three or more emerging market regions. Over one-third were elsewhere in Africa before entry to South Africa.

There is significant sector variation amongst parent firms. The basic consumer goods sector is dominated by European mid-size firms which have only recently started to expand into developing economies internationally –

Table 7.2 Geographic distribution of SA parent firms (No. of firms)

	North America	Europe	East Asia	MENA	Other	Total
Primary	3	1	1	0	0	5
Basic consumer goods	1	17	2	0	1	21
Intermediate goods	8	10	9	0	0	27
Machinery & equipment	5	16	9	0	1	31
Infrastructure & construction	1	15	2	0	1	19
Trade, tourism & recreation	2	6	0	0	0	8
Financial & business services	10	17	2	0	4	33
Information technology	6	6	0	0	1	13
Pharmaceuticals	0	4	0	0	1	5
All sectors	36	92	25	0	9	162

they have a small number of affiliates, mainly in Central and Eastern Europe and Asia, and would see South (or Southern) Africa as a potentially promising market. Intermediate goods firms – originating in roughly equal numbers from Europe, North America and East Asia – are somewhat smaller than the sample median and the local affiliate provides a relatively large share of turnover. The M&E firms by contrast are large, with the South African affiliates insignificant. Perhaps because their products are better suited to economies of scope, they tend to have a larger number of affiliates with more diversified presence in emerging markets than in intermediate goods, where economies of scale might be more relevant (and the affiliates' capital stock is larger). Both intermediate goods and M&E firms spend heavily on R&D.

Most infrastructure firms have extensive emerging market experience, possibly related to the growing involvement of the private sector in infrastructure provision in developing countries. In F&B, firms have many widely-dispersed affiliates with small employment. Firms in this sector provide fairly standardised services in which trust and personal networks are important, and spending on both R&D and advertising is relatively low. The South African affiliates contribute a very small share to global revenues. Finally, IT firms have a relatively large number of affiliates and substantial emerging market experience and spend a large share of turnover on R&D.

Mode of Entry

South Africa was the only country in the survey with a significant proportion of acquisitions. Table 7.3 shows that 31 per cent of the sample were full acquisitions and another 14 per cent partial acquisitions. The proportion of acquisitions is particularly high in Intermediate goods and in IT. Acquisitions are low in infrastructure, perhaps due to regulatory restrictions. In F&B, greenfield entry is more common – Chapter 8 suggests regulation is a factor here.

Table 7.4 shows entry mode by affiliate size in 2000 (rather than at entry). Full acquisitions are over-represented amongst medium-size affiliates (101 to 1000 employees), while partial acquisitions are more common amongst the largest firms. Amongst the largest group of parents, joint ventures are common.

Greenfields on the other hand are more prominent amongst small affiliates (fewer than 100 workers). Indeed, most greenfields have been very small: 71 per cent of greenfield entries had fewer than 100 workers in 2000, and 50 per cent of greenfields had a capital stock value at start-up of less than US$1 million. Smaller parent firms usually opt for greenfield operations. Tables 7.3 and 7.4 not only underline the maturity of South Africa's market for corporate control, but also show that many medium to large domestic firms are potential targets for foreign investors, who clearly feel comfortable and familiar in South Africa's corporate environment. This is underlined by most foreign investor risk assessments, which identify South Africa as very low risk on issues such as legal and taxation systems and operations (see Table 1.3 in Chapter 1). The frequent use of acquisition as entry mode suggests that FDI is more likely to improve domestic firms' international competitiveness and exports via spillovers from new foreign partners, than to contribute directly to employment creation via the establishment of large new operations.

Resources for Success

Table 7.5 presents the sectoral distribution of firms' three choices of critical resources for entry,[22] The 'All firms' column indicates that managerial capabilities was identified by the largest proportion of firms as a critical

Table 7.3 Distribution of entry mode by sector, South Africa (% of sector)

	Greenfield	Acquisition	Joint Venture	Partial Acquisition	No. of firms
Primary	0	0	60	40	5
Basic consumer goods	19	33	29	19	21
Intermediate goods	19	41	15	26	27
Machinery & equipment	32	32	26	10	31
Infrastructure & construction	53	16	26	5	19
Trade, tourism & recreation	13	13	50	25	8
Financial & business services	52	30	6	12	33
Information technology	15	46	38	0	13
Pharmaceuticals	40	40	20	0	5
All sectors	31	31	23	14	—
No. of firms	51	50	38	23	162

Table 7.4 Distribution of entry mode by affiliate size in 2000, South Africa (% of employment category)

Employees	Greenfield	Acquisition	Joint Venture	Partial Acquisition	No.of firms
10 - 50	38	22	31	9	55
51 - 100	43	27	10	20	30
101 - 250	20	50	23	7	30
251 - 1000	29	39	21	11	28
More than 1000	0	27	27	47	15
All sizes	30	32	23	15	
No. of firms	48	50	37	23	158

resource, followed closely by brands and technology, the two firm-specific assets most often argued to provide advantages to foreign investors. Marketing capabilities and business networks, also prominent across the full sample, impact (together with managerial capabilities) upon the integration and coordination of firm-specific assets with location-specific factors, which comprise most of the other resources prioritised.

Half the sixteen resources were chosen by the overwhelming majority of firms as critical – the five mentioned, and distribution networks, machinery and licences. Licences were ranked 5th as first choice, but few firms ranked them 2nd or 3rd. Marketing, machinery and distribution networks are complementary to the others, being more common as second or third choice than first.

The sectoral breakdown is suggestive. Technology is the most important resource in intermediate goods, M&E and IT when the 'first three' ranking is used, but the most common first choice only in intermediate goods. Surprisingly, distribution networks were the top choice of the largest number of M&E firms. But a substantial number in M&E ranked brands first, as did the largest group in IT, and significant numbers in F&B and consumer goods. All four are sectors where product quality is important. Managers are important in labour-intensive sectors, including the relatively high-skill IT sector.

Basic consumer goods, M&E, F&B and IT all have a similar profile: brands and managers are most important, complemented by technology in IT and M&E where production involves high capital- or skill-intensity, and by product distribution resources – marketing and distribution networks – in consumer goods and F&B, where products are standardised and the market more homogeneous.

Equity was significant for the large capital-intensive firms in the primary and TTR sectors. Though machinery is more important in the three manufacturing sectors than others, it was not especially prominent relative to other resources even there.

Although mode of entry was not important generally for understanding firms' resource choices, partial acquisitions do stand out as a mode of entry requiring a distinct combination of resources. Brands are less important since the foreign investor has less control over the disposition of firm-specific assets. The other major firm-specific asset, technology, is a top three choice for only a quarter of partial acquisitions. But technology ranks high amongst first choice resources for PAs and JVs, suggesting parents' willingness to transfer proprietary technology when it is crucial to the affiliates' success, even if ownership is partial. Managers, marketing, machines and business networks, all important 'top three' resources for PAs, all lower transaction and integration costs of entry.

If strong in the local partner, these may be a source of attraction for the foreign investor. On the other hand, if these resources are inadequate in the acquired firm, it is essential for the entrant to strengthen them in the short term.

A pivotal question in the survey asked firms where they sourced the critical resources for their South African operations. The long-held standard view is that foreign investors combine firm-specific assets with location-specific advantages sourced in local markets, implying Greenfield entry is

Table 7.5 Three key resources by sector, South Africa (% of firms within sector choosing resource in top three)

	Primary	Basic consumer goods	Inter-mediate goods	Machinery & equipment	Infrastructure & construction	Trade, tourism & recreation	Financial & business services	Infor-mation technology	Pharma-ceuticals
Brand	20	38	22	45	37	13	46	46	20
Business network	20	19	19	35	58	0	49	23	60
Distribution network	20	29	30	42	16	38	9	8	60
Equity	60	24	15	3	11	38	15	0	0
Licences	20	14	7	3	16	50	12	0	40
Machines	0	33	33	32	16	13	0	15	0
Managers	60	57	37	35	21	25	46	46	40
Marketing	20	43	37	19	37	38	28	31	60
Technology	20	14	59	48	37	25	28	77	0

Table 7.6 Source of three key resources, South Africa (mean % of resource)

Resource	Local partner	Foreign parent	Domestic markets	Foreign markets	Other	% of firms choosing resource	No. of firms
Managerial capabilities	46	28	24	2	0	40	65
Technological know-how	23	63	8	6	0	39	63
Brand names	20	69	9	2	0	36	59
Business networks	37	31	28	4	0	34	55
Marketing capabilities	38	34	27	1	0	32	52
Distribution networks	56	11	27	3	3	25	41
Machinery & equipment	41	28	8	22	2	19	31
Licences	20	23	29	8	20	11	20

If strong in the local partner, these may be a source of attraction for the foreign investor. On the other hand, if these resources are inadequate in the acquired firm, it is essential for the entrant to strengthen them in the short-term.

A pivotal question in the survey asked firms where they sourced the critical resources for their South African operation. The long-held standard view is that foreign investors combine firm-specific assets with location-specific advantages sourced in local markets, implying greenfield entry is optimal. More recently, mergers and acquisitions have become common options for developed country firms entering other *developed* countries, as firms attempt to leverage their existing strengths by integrating successful foreign firms into their operations. In many emerging economies, incomplete domestic markets for essential resources and high transaction costs may push foreign firms to source location-specific resources by linking with a local partner, either via acquisition or JV.

Table 7.6 – in which resources are ranked according to their scores in Table 7.5 – presents the relative importance of alternative sources for the key resources. The provision by parent firms of brands and technology is confirmed, contributing 69 per cent and 63 per cent respectively of these firm-specific resources. Local firms are significant contributors of managerial capabilities (possibly including high-skill employees for some respondents). Local firms were the major source of distribution networks, while foreign parents were insignificant, probably reflecting the domestic market orientation of most affiliates. Foreign markets were insignificant for all resources other than machines.

For managers, brands and technology (the top three resources), as well as distribution networks (ranked sixth), Table 7.6 suggests strong complementarities between local and foreign firms in sourcing critical resources. For business networks and marketing capabilities, there are few complementarities, and it is difficult to distinguish amongst foreign parents, local partners and local markets.

Looking at the mode of entry in Table 7.7 clarifies the sourcing of business networks and marketing.[23] Local partners supply a significantly larger share of business networks in full acquisitions than partial acquisitions, which source business networks similarly to JVs. Business networks, providing access to critical inputs for operations, is a strongly location-specific asset. But foreign parents and local markets contribute larger shares where the parent has less control (partial acquisitions and JVs). This counters the view that foreign firms enter via acquisition rather than greenfields to obtain location-specific assets at lower cost, in a context of incomplete markets.

It is possible that full acquisitions are successful local firms with well-functioning business networks, while partial acquisitions and JVs may

Table 7.7 Source of three key resources by mode of entry, South Africa (mean % of resource within mode of entry)

Resource	Source	Greenfield	Acquisition	Joint venture	Partial acquisition	All firms
Brand	Local partner	3	32	10	62	20
59 Firms	Foreign partner	88	66	68	22	69
	Local markets	10	3	20	0	9
	Foreign markets	0	0	1	17	2
Business networks	Local partner	9	76	44	41	38
54 firms	Foreign partner	45	11	26	30	31
	Local markets	45	8	19	29	28
	Foreign markets	1	5	11	0	4
Distribution networks	Local partner	13	80	65	75	56
41 firms	Foreign partner	9	13	5	25	11
	Local markets	60	7	30	0	27
	Foreign markets	10	0	0	0	3
Machinery	Local partner	0	48	43	69	39
31 firms	Foreign partner	68	12	37	4	29
	Local markets		13	3	11	8
	Foreign markets	29	27	8	17	22

Managers 65 firms	Local partner	6	62	47	66	46
	Foreign partner	62	11	31	14	28
	Local markets	31	23	22	21	24
	Foreign markets	2	4	0	0	2
Marketing capability 52 firms	Local partner	9	58	38	68	38
	Foreign partner	47	24	27	28	34
	Local markets	43	15	33	4	27
	Foreign markets	1	3	2	0	1
Technology 63 firms	Local partner	8	28	24	52	23
	Foreign partner	75	52	69	42	63
	Local markets	6	18	3	0	8
	Foreign markets	11	3	4	7	6
Licences 20 firms	Local partner	17	47	9	25	20
	Foreign partner	21	43	14	25	23
	Local markets	41	0	34	25	29
	Foreign markets	6	9	0	25	8

involve less successful and untested operations respectively, so that the investor lowers risk by bringing in assets.

There is a predictable difference between existing and new operations acquiring marketing capabilities: acquisitions, full and partial, rely substantially on contributions from the local partner, while new operations (greenfields and JVs) source much more heavily in local markets.

The local firm retains its own brand far more in partial than full acquisitions. This cannot be explained by brand familiarity, which would not necessarily differ, but the parent may be less willing to risk its own brand, an important firm-specific asset, without full control.

Business networks and marketing capabilities are both potentially separable into domestic and international resources, and so could be sourced independently. Firms which sell most (but not all) output (75 to 99 per cent) into the domestic market obtain three-quarters of their marketing capability from local partners, but firms selling either all output domestically, or less than three-quarters, only obtain about one-third from local partners, and the rest from the parent and local markets.[24] In other words, there is no apparent correlation between domestic sales and domestic marketing capability, and the mode of entry is the salient factor rather than destination of sales.

Institutional and Market Environment

Tables 7.8 and 7.9 report affiliates' perceptions of the availability on domestic markets of 'unbundled' inputs critical for performance. Table 7.8 indicates that foreign affiliates are not concerned about the commonly-expressed view that the South African labour market has a binding skills constraint (Lewis 2001). The mean scores for the full sample are 3.84 at entry ('then') and 3.87 at the time of the survey ('now'), both very close to 4.0, meaning 'mostly available'. All the means are greater than 3.0, or 'sometimes available'. The small changes for all sectors from 'then' to 'now' mask bigger changes in some sectors individually.

Suitable executive managers (in terms of quality and price) are the most difficult employees to find, though in some sectors – machinery and equipment, trade, tourism and recreation and pharmaceuticals – there was a significant improvement after entry. By contrast, professionals are easiest to find (their scores were highest both at entry and 'now'), though there was some decline in their score, mainly in basic consumer goods. This sector and F&B were above average at entry, but declined subsequently. By contrast, trade, tourism and recreation improved substantially, and machinery and equipment, IT and infrastructure also improved.

Looking at skilled labour availability by mode of entry, Greenfield firms were generally most pessimistic at the time of entry, but perceptions improved after greater exposure to the local market, with substantial increases in three of the four occupational categories. Interestingly, partial

Table 7.8 Labour market: availability of suitable skilled labour by sector, South Africa (means)

	Primary	Basic consumer goods	Intermediate goods	Machinery & equipment	Infrastructure
Exec. manager now (then)	3.60 (4.00)	3.62 (3.74)	3.56 (3.54)	3.58 (3.16)	3.47 (3.35)
Professionals now (then)	4.40 (4.40)	3.90 (4.26)	3.96 (4.04)	4.13 (4.03)	4.16 (4.11)
Ops. manager now (then)	4.20 (4.20)	3.90 (4.17)	3.74 (3.62)	3.58 (3.58)	3.33 (3.39)
Skilled workers now (then)	4.20 (4.20)	4.14 (4.26)	4.15 (4.00)	4.10 (4.06)	3.74 (3.63)
All labour now (then)	4.10 (4.20)	3.89 (4.09)	3.85 (3.80)	3.85 (3.71)	3.71 (3.64)

	Trade, tourism & recreation	Financial & business services	Information technology	Pharmaceuticals	All sectors	No. of firms
Exec. manager now (then)	3.75 (3.25)	3.42 (3.64)	3.38 (3.23)	4.40 (4.00)	3.56 (3.48)	160 (157)
Professionals now (then)	4.50 (4.38)	4.13 (4.28)	4.15 (4.00)	4.40 (4.40)	4.11 (4.16)	161 (158)
Ops. manager now (then)	4.00 (3.63)	3.97 (4.03)	3.58 (3.50)	4.20 (4.00)	3.76 (3.76)	159 (156)
Skilled workers now (then)	4.13 (3.63)	4.06 (3.94)	3.50 (3.58)	4.40 (4.40)	4.03 (3.96)	161 (158)
All labour now (then)	4.09 (3.72)	3.90 (3.97)	3.67 (3.56)	4.35 (4.20)	3.87 (3.84)	162 (159)

Note: Scale of 1 – 5, 1 = 'never available', 5 = 'always available'

Table 7.9 Inputs: availability of suitable inputs by sector, South Africa

	Primary	Basic consumer goods	Intermediate goods	Machinery & equipment	Infrastructure
Utilities now (then)	4.40 (4.00)	4.62 (4.68)	4.89 (4.65)	4.58 (4.48)	4.32 (4.26)
IT and telecom now (then)	4.00 (4.20)	4.19 (4.16)	4.52 (4.19)	4.45 (4.13)	3.84 (3.63)
Prof. services now (then)	4.20 (4.40)	4.52 (4.53)	4.52 (4.50)	4.55 (4.48)	4.37 (4.37)
Real estate now (then)	4.20 (4.20)	4.59 (4.67)	4.58 (4.61)	4.44 (4.44)	4.19 (4.19)
Machines now (then)	4.80 (4.80)	3.42 (3.65)	3.85 (3.76)	3.57 (3.40)	3.88 (3.76)
Intermediates now (then)	4.75 (4.75)	3.50 (3.92)	3.50 (3.72)	3.21 (3.11)	
All inputs now (then)	4.37 (4.37)	4.19 (4.29)	4.32 (4.25)	4.16 (4.02)	4.11 (4.04)

	Trade, tourism & recreation	Financial & business services	Information technology	Pharmaceuticals	All sectors	No. of firms
Utilities now (then)	4.38 (4.38)	4.59 (4.53)	4.77 (4.77)	5.00 (5.00)	4.62 (4.54)	161 (158)
IT and Telecom now (then)	4.25 (4.25)	4.15 (3.91)	4.23 (4.00)	4.60 (4.60)	4.26 (4.05)	162 (159)
Prof. Services now (then)	4.63 (4.50)	4.42 (4.39)	4.46 (4.38)	4.40 (4.40)	4.48 (4.45)	162 (159)
Real Estate now (then)	4.50 (4.50)	4.59 (4.38)	4.62 (4.54)	4.80 (4.80)	4.51 (4.47)	142 (139)
Machines now (then)	3.38 (3.00)	4.22 (4.13)	4.64 (4.45)	3.33 (3.33)	3.85 (3.77)	142 (139)
Intermediates now (then)	4.50 (3.50)	3.50 (3.50)	3.33 (2.67)	3.00 (3.00)	3.46 (3.51)	84 (81)
All inputs now (then)	4.18 (4.04)	4.37 (4.25)	4.47 (4.34)	4.37 (4.37)	4.27 (4.19)	162 (159)

Note: Scale of 1 – 5, 1 = 'never available', 5 = 'always available'

acquisitions, who have local knowledge prior to entry, moved in the opposite direction, being most optimistic at entry but then declining significantly in all four categories. It may be that foreign companies entering via greenfields have modest expectations based on experience in other developing or middle-income economies, while investors establishing partnerships with South African companies form expectations based on developed country norms, as is common in South Africa.

Table 7.9 looks at production inputs and transactions costs. Once again, the essential point is that the overall mean scores are very high, at well over 4 ('mostly available'), and indeed are higher than those for skilled labour inputs.[25] IT and telecoms lag behind other transactions costs inputs, though they improved post-entry. Direct inputs into production – machinery and intermediate goods – scored somewhat worse than transactions inputs, possibly due to the exchange rate depreciation during late 2001 just as survey fieldwork got underway. However even these means are between 3.5 and 4, that is, between 'sometimes' and 'mostly' available, and do not indicate a significant problem. The sectoral means in Table 7.9 show a significant decline in basic consumer goods' scores for direct production inputs, while the TTR and IT sectors both show significant improvements for these categories. But the variation in input ratings across either sectors or modes of entry is too small to be of significance.

The administrative and institutional (official) environment shown in Table 7.10 affects transactions costs for the acquisition of key location-specific assets required to establish the operation (as distinct from transactions costs for production and sales activities). If these transactions costs are high, it could impact on the choice of entry mode itself, by discouraging greenfields in favour of linking with a local firm. The official environment also influences the firm's perception of country risk. Firms included in the survey have obviously not viewed this risk as an insurmountable barrier to entry, but risk perceptions nonetheless might have encouraged entry in an easily reversible form, such as limiting the stock of fixed assets or arms'-length operations (outsourcing). The means are – with a single exception – well above the scale's mid-point of 3.0, but there is a small decline post-entry for several indicators. The first and second sets of indicators, for public institutions and official procedures, score better then government policies, but there is little difference between levels of government. Comparison with Tables 7.8 and 7.9 (strictly speaking not allowed) suggest that the official environment could be seen as a more significant constraint than skilled labour or operational inputs, though such an inference must be treated with caution.

The table underlines the well-known concerns about immigration barriers for foreign workers. This indicator is the only one with a mean less than 3.0, is ranked worst in seven of nine sectors, and declines post-entry in eight sectors. Unofficial payments are also of concern, deteriorating noticeably.

Table 7.10 Institutions: perceptions of official environment by sector, South Africa (means)

	Primary	Basic consumer goods	Intermediate goods	Machinery & equipment	Infrastructure
Licences now (then)	3.00 (3.60)	4.00 (3.82)	3.96 (3.67)	3.81 (3.81)	3.59 (3.59)
Real estate now (then)	3.80 (3.80)	4.38 (4.45)	4.00 (3.95)	4.24 (4.24)	3.73 (3.10)
Visas now (then)	1.75 (2.50)	2.44 (2.93)	2.68 (3.00)	2.81 (2.77)	2.95 (3.33)
Environmental regulations now (then)	2.80 (3.60)	3.58 (3.90)	3.48 (3.61)	3.84 (3.76)	3.36 (3.23)
All procedures now (then)	2.88 (3.43)	3.62 (3.72)	3.63 (3.60)	3.61 (3.61)	3.48 (3.41)
Law enforcement now (then)	2.80 (3.40)	3.52 (3.74)	3.15 (3.69)	3.19 (3.45)	3.21 (3.11)
Unofficial payments now (then)	3.40 (4.00)	4.30 (4.35)	4.00 (4.25)	4.24 (4.18)	3.72 (3.94)
Stability of rules now (then)	3.20 (3.60)	3.90 (3.68)	3.59 (3.77)	3.47 (3.37)	3.37 (3.56)
All institutions now (then)	3.13 (3.67)	3.90 (4.00)	3.56 (3.89)	3.63 (3.65)	3.39 (3.51)
Central govt now (then)	2.00 (3.00)	3.35 (3.39)	3.44 (3.25)	3.37 (3.43)	3.00 (3.27)
Prov govt now (then)	2.00 (2.80)	3.44 (3.50)	3.35 (3.26)	3.45 (3.55)	2.92 (3.27)
Local govt now (then)	1.80 (2.60)	3.39 (3.44)	3.58 (3.61)	3.55 (3.60)	2.85 (3.08)
All government now (then)	1.93 (2.80)	3.29 (3.34)	3.41 (3.28)	3.41 (3.44)	2.86 (3.17)

	Trade tourism & recreation	Finance & business services	Information Technology	Pharma-ceuticals	All sectors
Licences now (then)	3.57 (3.38)	3.96 (3.79)	3.83 (3.62)	2.40 (2.80)	3.67 (3.80)
Real estate now (then)	4.00 (3.86)	4.26 (4.30)	3.71 (3.71)	5.00 (5.00)	4.10 (4.04)
Visas now (then)	2.63 (2.88)	2.79 (2.86)	3.31 (3.62)	2.33 (2.50)	2.76 (2.99)
Environmental regulations now (then)	3.33 (3.50)	3.64 (3.67)	4.00 (3.75)	3.67 (3.67)	3.56 (3.63)
All procedures now (then)	3.24 (3.27)	3.60 (3.61)	3.58 (3.66)	3.03 (3.13)	3.52 (3.55)
Law enforcement now (then)	3.50 (3.38)	3.36 (3.39)	3.85 (3.92)	3.20(3.20)	3.33 (3.49)
Unofficial payments now (then)	4.71 (4.71)	4.48(4.38)	4.17 (4.25)	5.00 (5.00)	4.19 (4.30)
Stability of rules now (then)	3.63 (3.63)	3.52 (3.73)	3.85 (4.00)	3.40 (3.40)	3.57 (3.64)
All institutions now (then)	3.85 (3.90)	3.74 (4.82)	3.94 (4.04)	3.87 (3.87)	3.68 (3.51)
Central govt now (then)	3.25 (3.38)	3.31 (3.38)	3.42 (3.33)	2.60 (2.60)	3.32 (3.25)
Prov govt now (then)	3.50 (3.50)	3.29 (3.29)	3.56 (3.44)	2.67 (2.67)	3.27 (3.35)
Local govt now (then)	3.14 (3.43)	3.14 (3.29)	3.67 (3.44)	3.00 (3.00)	3.27 (3.38)
All government now (then)	3.33 (3.46)	3.24 (3.33)	3.38 (3.36)	2.87 (2.87)	3.27 (3.34)

Note: 1 = 'not conducive at all to profitable business operations', 5 = 'very conducive'

In two sectors with large proportions of the sample and where the regulatory framework is important – infrastructure and F&B – scores are well below the sample means on most indicators, and also decline after entry.

JVs and partial acquisitions scored the official environment far lower 'now' than at entry, reinforcing the earlier argument that these firms enter with unduly high expectations. National origin was not a source of significant differences amongst firms.

Firm Performance in South Africa

Table 7.11 and 7.12 present responses on the affiliate's performance relative to the investor's original objectives, averaging profitability and revenue growth.[26] These tables suggest that firms entering South Africa are by and large satisfied with their investment. The expectations were 'all or mostly' met for 46 per cent of the sample, and 'partially' met for 43 per cent of the sample. Only 11 per cent of firms felt disappointed. Firms' views of their performance were unaffected by mode of entry.

Table 7.11 Affiliate performance by mode of entry, South Africa (% firms in mode)

Expectations met	Greenfield	Acquisition	Joint venture	Partial acquisition	All firms	No. of firms
Poor (0 – 2)	8	16	8	17	1	19
Satisfactory (2.5 - 3.5)	47	36	45	43	43	69
Good (4 – 5)	45	48	47	39	46	74

Table 7.12 shows some sectoral variation, with primary, infrastructure and F&B performing somewhat better than the other sectors. The export-oriented primary sector has gained from currency depreciation over the decade, while infrastructure and F&B have both been strong growth sectors partly in response to liberalisation and related regulatory shifts. With the partial exception of intermediate goods (also export-oriented), the manufacturing sectors performed poorly. In IT, market growth both domestically and regionally was combined with a strong competitive response from domestic firms, as discussed below.

Table 7.13 investigates possible correlation between firms' performance and their perceptions of the operating environment, showing the aggregate indicators from Tables 7.8, 7.9 and 7.10. Intensive statistical analysis of the data for all four countries concluded that the business environment had no impact on affiliates' performance. However, looking as the South African

Table 7.12 Affiliate performance by sector, South Africa (% firms in sector)

Expectations met	Poor	Satisfactory	Good
Primary	20	20	60
Basic consumer goods	19	48	33
Intermediate goods	4	56	41
Machinery & equipment	23	45	32
Infrastructure & construction	0	32	68
Trade, tourism & recreation	13	38	50
Financial & business services	9	33	58
Information technology	0	54	46
Pharmaceuticals	40	40	20
All sectors	12	43	46
No. of firms	19	69	74

data only, good performers rated institutions (law enforcement, unofficial payments, stable rules, etc.) and government much better than satisfactory performers, but procedures (licences, visas, etc.) worse. Satisfactory performers also rated institutions worse than did poor performers, though they were better on the other sets of indicators. This may imply that institutions can constrain performance in South Africa, given an acceptable business environment for operational inputs and transaction cost issues. If confirmed by further investigation, this conclusion would place South Africa at odds with the other three countries with respect to this crucial issue.

There was little correlation between performance and the degree of market competition (data not shown). Some firms with over 75 per cent domestic market share were more satisfied than those with smaller market shares, but firms with a monopoly were less satisfied with their performance, perhaps because growth in the aggregate, and of firm revenues, was slower than hoped.

Impact on the South African economy
In theory, foreign firms impact upon domestic welfare and growth in five broad areas: capital markets and finance, international trade, domestic goods markets, technology and labour markets and employment. In each of these areas, there are a number of different possible channels, and the impact may be either positive or negative.[27] The survey addressed issues in each of these areas. The financial issue has already been discussed (Table 7.1).

Table 7.13 Performance by perception of business environment, South Africa

Expectations met	Poor	Satisfactory	Good	All firms
All skilled labour now (then)	3.79 (3.70)	3.91 (3.79)	3.85 (3.92)	3.87 (3.84)
All inputs now (then)	3.99 (3.98)	4.29 (4.21)	4.32 (4.23)	4.27 (4.19)
All procedures now (then)	3.28 (3.48)	3.59 (3.62)	3.55 (3.53)	3.52 (3.55)
All institutions now (then)	3.72 (3.81)	3.55 (3.71)	3.79 (3.89)	3.68 (3.80)
All government now (then)	2.93 (3.04)	3.22 (3.26)	3.31 (3.42)	3.27 (3.34)
No. of firms	19	69	74	162

Domestic market versus Exports

Table 7.14 presents the distribution of affiliates' sales into four distinct markets: domestic; regional (referring to either Southern Africa or sub-Saharan Africa, depending on the firm); exports to global markets; and non-arm's-length exports to other affiliates of the parent.[28] The latter reflects affiliates' integration into international production chains and networks. The distinction between regional and global exports is important. The former are often a 'vent-for-surplus' and fluctuate inversely with domestic demand, whereas the latter involve 'learning-by-exporting' and enhance productivity, at least for domestic firms (Rankin 2001). For foreign affiliates, the distinction may be important in relation to parent firms' supply of up-to-date technology, and to spillovers to domestic suppliers and competitors.

The table shows that except for primary and infrastructure firms, foreign firms entered South Africa for market-seeking purposes: on average, 81 per cent of starting sales went to the domestic market. Expansion into the domestic market has long been the major motivation for FDI in South Africa, at least for manufacturing and services. The table suggests that this pattern has undergone an important extension since 1994, as many affiliates have expanded into regional markets. Though regional shares were initially very low, eight sectors increased their regional share, with IT and M&E particularly significant (the latter because of its very low starting point).[29] In five of these sectors, the increase in the regional share was at the expense of the domestic share. In four sectors with domestic and regional share together over 85 per cent – consumer goods, M&E, F&B and pharmaceuticals – South Africa and the region appear to be a single market.

Only 15 per cent of firms' sales are in global markets, including the majority of sales from the small number of primary sector firms, which was the one sector to shift away from regional and domestic markets. Firms in intermediate goods, TTR (which includes tourism) and infrastructure entered with some intention of selling into global markets, but in the latter two sectors the global markets' share declined. Global markets have become a more significant destination for consumer goods and IT, possibly assisted by rand depreciation.[30]

South African affiliates are selling to other affiliates to a very limited extent, suggesting that direct equity links are not a common means to extend global chains into South Africa, at least for firms with no prior presence. This does not necessarily mean that the economy is not being integrated into global chains and networks, since the project excluded non-equity hierarchical links between foreign and domestic firms, such as outsourcing or franchising. There is also evidence – from the auto industry, for example (Black 2001) – that firms established in South Africa before 1990 have incorporated their local operations into global chains.

Other data confirm that foreign investors entered during the 1990s primarily for market-seeking, rather than efficiency-seeking, reasons.

Table 7.14 Market orientation by sector, South Africa (% of affiliates' sales)

Sector	Domestic market		Regional market		Global market		Other Affiliates	
	Start	Latest	Start	Latest	Start	Latest	Start	Latest
Primary	17	13	10	0	73	87	0	0
Basic consumer goods	94	85	5	7	1	8	0	0
Intermediate goods	84	73	1	6	15	19	0	1
Machinery & equipment	86	77	2	10	6	8	7	5
Infrastructure & construction	67	69	3	7	24	22	6	3
Trade, tourism & recreation	80	82	1	2	19	16	0	0
Financial & business services	84	78	6	10	6	8	5	3
Information technology	85	53	1	26	8	14	7	7
Pharmaceuticals	96	87	4	11	0	0	0	1
All firms	81	73	3	9	12	15	4	3

The National Enterprise Survey of 1,425 firms in South Africa carried out in 1999 included 68 firms that fit the four criteria for the CNEM/EDGE survey. In this sub-group, the mean share of domestic sales was 68.5 per cent, close to the figure of 73 per cent in Table 7.14, while 15 per cent of turnover was exported to Africa, compared with 9 per cent in Table 7.14 (Gelb 2001).[31]

Examining market orientation on the basis of sales-weighted data provides an important corrective to Table 7.14. Firms in all turnover categories focus on the domestic market, though four of the five size classes sold smaller shares of output domestically in 2000 than at entry. Firms with small turnovers have shifted mainly into the regional market, but this group comprised only 0.3 per cent of the total value of sales in 2000. The 17 firms with sales above US$100 million, which comprise over two-thirds of the total turnover of the sample and are spread across all sectors except pharmaceuticals, sell nearly 20 per cent of output in global markets, compared with none (reported) at entry. The increase in total exports is partially offset by firms in the second highest turnover category selling a slightly larger share domestically.

Domestic market competition
The impact of foreign firms on concentration and competition is hotly debated. Competition from more efficient foreign firms can pressure domestic producers to lower costs, but could also crowd out domestic firms, leading to an anti-competitive outcome. The survey focused on 'horizontal' effects in the goods market, that is effects on competitors, and excluded 'vertical' spillovers to suppliers or customers.

Table 7.15 confirms that market-seeking foreign investors enter markets in which a significant share is on offer: the mean market share at entry was 26 per cent, and this rose to 30 per cent in 2000. The markets which investors entered had fewer than five firms on average. In TTR and IT, with only 2.5 competitors on average, initial market shares were especially high. In seven sectors, market share increased after entry, significantly in infrastructure and TTR. Rising sectoral means were due to firms with low initial shares (below 20 per cent) increasing their share.

Several IT firms had very high market shares on entry, monopolising their market niche, but dropped market share later, possibly indicating technology spillovers. In F&B, domestic firms held their own, with average market share and the number of competitors both rising slightly. This is confirmed in the ABN Amro case study (Chapter 8).

In the three manufacturing sectors, the sectors' performance scores (in Table 7.13) were below average, notwithstanding the increase in market share, and the number of competitors was constant post-entry, suggesting that market growth disappointed firms.

Table 7.16 shows that foreign entrants look for South African partners with significant market shares – the three modes involving local firms had

Table 7.15 Domestic market share by sector, South Africa (%)

	Market share 1st year operations	Market share 2000
Primary	8	23
Basic consumer goods	21	27
Intermediate goods	28	35
Machinery &equipment	22	26
Infrastructure & construction	18	28
Trade, tourism & recreation	49	61
Financial & business services	19	22
Information technology	67	52
Pharmaceuticals	31	13
All sectors	26	30

substantial market shares at entry, while greenfields' shares were only 12 per cent, in line with their small size (see Table 7.4). Greenfields and partial acquisitions increased their market shares by about 50 per cent, suggesting the benefits brought by foreign firms. This reinforces the earlier point that full acquisitions may involve already successful local firms, whereas partial acquisitions are more likely to be under-performing local firms.

Table 7.16 Domestic market share by mode of entry, South Africa (%)

	Market share 1st year operations	Market share 2000
Greenfield	12	19
Acquisition	34	35
Joint venture	31	33
Partial acquisition	25	37
All firms	26	30

Comparison with local industry

Foreign affiliates were asked to rate domestic competitors on five dimensions: product quality and range, management capabilities, marketing capabilities, level of technology and labour productivity. The 5-point Likert scale interpreted 3 as 'local industry almost as good as affiliate', and 4 as 'local industry as good as affiliate'. The change from entry to 2000 indicates local industry's improvement or deterioration in the presence of the foreign affiliate, though clearly causality cannot automatically be attributed.

In Table 7.17, the means cluster close to 3, with only marketing capabilities being higher, though still well below 4. This is consistent with Table 7.7 showing that marketing was acquired predominantly from local partners. Marketing in consumer goods and pharmaceuticals declined, in contrast to strong increases in TTR and IT. Local firms fare worst on issues of product quality and technology.

The service sectors – infrastructure, TTR, F&B and IT – were seen as comparatively weaker at entry than the three manufacturing sectors. But local service firms improved, particularly in IT, reinforcing the suggestion in Table 7.15 that IT affiliates' drop in market share reflects greater competitiveness of domestic firms. In contrast, domestic firms in manufacturing fell further behind foreign investors in almost all dimensions, consistent with Table 7.15. The improvement in technology in seven sectors provides tentative support for spillovers from foreign to domestic firms.

Table 7.17 also shows that in six sectors, local management capability was 'almost as good as affiliates' at entry, consistent with Table 7.7, where local partners were identified as the predominant source of management capabilities.

However, in these six sectors, there was no improvement in local management capabilities after entry, indeed two manufacturing sectors had a significant decline. By contrast, in the three services sectors (TTR, F&B and IT), local firms' management was lower at entry but there was substantial improvement post-entry.

Table 7.18 shows local industry comparisons by mode of entry. There are important differences between new operations (greenfields and joint-ventures) and existing operations where entry was via acquisition. Local firms were 'almost as good' as greenfields at entry, in four of five dimensions (product quality excepted), and moved closer to the affiliates after the latter's entry, significantly in product quality, but also in management and technology. JV respondents (of whom two-thirds were South African) saw local industry as even closer at entry, but with less improvement subsequently. In contrast, acquisitions, particularly partial acquisitions, felt local industry had declined since entry, or rather that the acquired firm moved ahead of local firms, presumably a consequence of the acquisition.

Grouping affiliates by performance, good performers felt that local firms had more or less held their own but poor performers felt they had moved ahead relative to local firms, suggesting that performance is linked to broad economic conditions rather than competition from local firms. Satisfactory performers saw significant improvement in local firms, especially in the key dimensions of product quality and technology.

Table 7.17 Comparison with local industry by sector, South Africa

	Primary	Basic consumer goods	Intermediate goods	Machinery & equipment	Infrastructure
Product quality now (then)	2.80 (3.80)	3.15 (3.33)	2.85 (2.92)	3.07 (3.20)	3.17 (2.61)
Management now (then)	3.40 (3.40)	3.00 (3.67)	3.35 (3.32)	3.37 (3.60)	3.33 (3.18)
Marketing now (then)	2.60 (4.00)	3.50 (3.83)	3.04 (3.00)	3.57 (3.53)	3.44 (3.41)
Technology now (then)	3.75 (3.50)	3.00 (3.39)	2.85 (2.72)	3.20 (3.03)	3.50 (3.12)
Labour now (then)	3.25 (2.75)	3.11 (3.82)	3.36 (3.38)	3.28 (3.28)	2.78 (2.65)

	Trade, tourism & recreation	Financial & business services	Information technology	Pharmaceuticals	All sectors
Product quality now (then)	3.00 (2.43)	3.06 (2.88)	2.83 (2.00)	3.40 (3.60)	3.03 (2.95)
Management now (then)	3.00 (2.43)	3.06 (2.91)	3.50 (2.56)	3.60 (3.60)	3.25 (3.23)
Marketing now (then)	3.57 (3.14)	3.58 (3.48)	3.50 (3.00)	3.40 (3.80)	3.42 (3.43)
Technology now (then)	3.29 (3.00)	3.31 (3.06)	3.08 (2.56)	2.80 (3.20)	3.17 (3.03)
Labour now (then)	3.67 (3.17)	2.89 (3.00)	3.67 (2.89)	3.25 (3.75)	3.18 (3.20)

Notes: Scale of 1 – 5, 1 = 'local industry far inferior to affiliate', 3 = 'local industry almost as good', 4 = 'local industry as good as affiliate'

Table 7.18 Comparison with local industry by mode of entry, South Africa (means)

	Greenfield	Acquisition	Joint venture	Partial acquisition	All firms
Product quality now (then)	3.12 (2.92)	3.06 (2.98)	3.11 (3.09)	2.62 (2.76)	3.03 (2.95)
Management now (then)	3.37 (3.14)	3.15 (3.20)	3.36 (3.42)	3.00 (3.24)	3.25 (3.23)
Marketing now (then)	3.76 (3.57)	3.29 (3.41)	3.47 (3.39)	2.81 (3.19)	3.42 (3.43)
Technology now (then)	3.35 (3.06)	2.98 (2.80)	3.37 (3.25)	2.80 (3.10)	3.17 (3.03)
Labour now (then)	3.15 (3.11)	2.93 (3.14)	3.55 (3.23)	3.21 (3.47)	3.18 (3.20)

Human capital accumulation

Training spending provides a suggestive indicator of investment in human capital, but tells us nothing about the quality of the training, whether it is firm-specific, or spillovers to other workers and firms. Table 7.19 shows that just under one-third of firms spend below 0.5 per cent of turnover on training, and another third between 0.5 per cent and 2 per cent. Given the widespread perception of skills shortages, training expenditure seems low, though foreign affiliates probably spend slightly more than domestic firms on training.[32] As noted in Table 7.8 affiliates are not concerned about shortages of high-skill labour, though correlation between firms' training expenditure and skilled labour availability is low.

It is surprising that a higher percentage of affiliates in consumer goods are spending more than 4 per cent of turnover, and a smaller share in M&E. In services, many infrastructure and IT firms also spend over 4 per cent, but only one TTR firm is investing in its labour force. There is little variation by firm size, though the largest firms (labour force over 1,000) spend less on training, possibly reflecting the predominance of lower skill occupations in their workforce, but a concern in terms of skills upgrading.

There is a strong positive correlation between parent firms' global R&D expenditure levels and affiliates' training expenditure, presumably because the returns on R&D depend in part on employees' ability to use technology. There is also a correlation between human resource investment and performance (revenue growth and profitability compared with expectations). Better performing firms spend more on training than poor performance firms, and it seems reasonable to hypothesise that causality runs from investment in human resources to performance, rather than the reverse.

Technology transfer

Asked about the ease of obtaining technology from parent firms, 83 per cent of affiliates indicated they were 'usually' or 'always' able to do so. A larger portion of firms in M&E are always able to do so, but surprisingly a lower share in IT. Parent firms are much less willing to provide technology to partial acquisitions.

Black economic empowerment

In 1994, equity ownership and management of South African firms were overwhelmingly white, and the need for 'black economic empowerment' (BEE) obvious. Supplementary questions ere added to the survey to investigate BEE amongst foreign investors. The survey shows that foreign entry has not been a significant vehicle for expanding BEE ownership, the share of black owners being 2 per cent at entry and rising only to 3 per cent in 2000. In contrast, affiliates have been fairly effective in promoting black participation in high skill job categories, black executive managers rising from 5 per cent at entry to 11 per cent in 2000, and operational managers

Table 7.19 Training expenditure by sector, South Africa (% of affiliates in sector)

Training as % of sales	Primary	Basic consumer goods	Intermediate goods	Machinery & equipment	Infrastructure
0 - 0.5	20	22	33	35	21
0.5 – 2	40	28	33	45	32
2 – 4	20	6	19	10	5
4 – 8	0	22	7	6	11
8 – 15	0	22	0	3	21
Over 15	20	0	7	0	11

Training as % of Sales	Trade, tourism & recreation	Financial & Business services	Information Technology	Pharmaceutical	All sectors
0 - 0.5%	38	33	15	0	28
0.5 - 2%	38	24	38	20	33
2 - 4%	13	12	8	60	13
4 - 8%	0	18	31	0	12
8 - 15%	0	12	0	0	8
Over 15%	13	0	8	20	5

from 14 per cent to 28 per cent. There is significant sectoral variation, with TTR performing best (perhaps due to regulatory and public sector procurement requirements), and F&B and IT surprisingly poorly, though the latter have increased rapidly from a low base. Investors' home country matters: firms from English-speaking countries have transferred ownership and executive management positions, but not done well in other high-skilled jobs, whereas East Asian firms have transferred no equity, but have numerous blacks in the latter job categories. Small firms (fewer than 100 employees) have done far better than large in all the skilled job categories, including executive managers.

CONCLUSIONS

The majority of new foreign investors entering South Africa during the 1990s established small or medium size affiliates with limited impact on employment creation or capital inflows. Nearly half the entries involved acquisitions of existing operations, rather than greenfields or JVs setting up new enterprises. Many investors mitigated risk by limiting the irreversibility of their investment, by outsourcing production and focusing on services.

Most entry is market-seeking, though 'the market' should be understood as encompassing both the domestic economy and the region. Many entering firms have linked with local partners with substantial market share, also as a risk-mitigation strategy. Investors with very large affiliates have opted for partial acquisitions, providing established market share while limiting the initial investment.

The entering firms are by and large well-established but mid-size multinationals with significant experience in developing economies. Some may have delayed entry to South Africa until the 1990s because of political factors. The South African operating environment holds few surprises for entering firms. On the contrary, the high proportion of acquisitions and the lack of concern over skilled labour shortages suggest entrants see factor markets as above par by developing country standards. This is further underscored by the strong complementarities in sourcing critical resources, with local partners providing a significant share of key location-specific assets, in particular managers and distribution networks.

Mode of entry is correlated with several variables. It influences affiliates' ranking of the eight critical resources identified by most respondents. In sourcing these critical resources, there were strong complementarities between local partners and foreign investors for the top three – brands, technology and managers – but mode of entry helped to distinguish alternative sources for the others.

Affiliates also varied by mode of entry in perceptions of labour and operational inputs. Greenfields became more positive, while affiliates with local partners were optimistic initially but then were disappointed, possibly because their initial frame of reference was inappropriate, rather than actual conditions deteriorating. The official environment is arguably a more serious constraint than labour or input markets. The restrictions on foreign worker entry to South Africa are clearly a significant problem for investors, but not the only issue of concern. In sectors where regulation is significant, firms rated the administrative environment poorly at entry, and their anxieties increased later. But affiliates satisfied with their performance were positive about official procedures, while strong performers were happy with governance.

The mode of entry may also impact upon spillovers to domestic firms. Domestic firms acquired by foreign entrants improved in most dimensions relative to local firms. When Greenfield or JV entry involves a new operation, however, local industry has narrowed the entrant's initial advantage, Horizontal spillovers via competitive pressures may be limited in the case of entry by acquisition, and more likely when the either of the latter two entry modes is adopted.

An exceptional share of affiliates have met all or most of their own expectations at entry: even discounting for respondents reluctant to give themselves a bad 'report card', South Africa should be a very attractive destination for potential foreign investors.

Sectoral location also matters. In manufacturing, there is a high percentage of less satisfied firms, even though market shares increased and domestic firms were thought by affiliates to have deteriorated since entry. Performance rating here is probably linked to slow overall growth, and there are some grounds for concern about foreign investors squeezing local firms out of the market.

A different picture emerges in services. Affiliates' market share declined in IT, though this was offset by rapid sectoral growth domestically and regionally. The IT sector presents strong evidence for spillovers from foreign to domestic firms, since the latter gained market share and were also rated as having improved substantially, relative to foreign affiliates after entry.

The survey suggest that South Africa is not yet deeply integrated into global production processes, at least not on the basis of equity linkages with foreign companies. Although a large share of total sales of foreign affiliates is exported to global markets, this involves a small number of firms. Most affiliates are not exporting substantial shares of their output to global markets or to other affiliates of their parent company. The impact of these exports on domestic firms' efficiency via backward linkages, and South African firms' non-equity links with foreign companies, will have to be explored in future research.

8. South African Case Studies

Stephen Gelb and Anthony Black[33]

INTRODUCTION

This chapter presents four recent foreign entries into South Africa. Section 1 covers two automobile component companies: NGK Ceramics (catalytic converters), which entered as a greenfield and Behr (radiators and airconditioners) which entered via an acquisition. Both entries were in response to significant changes in the sector's policy environment, but NGK focuses on exports while Behr supplies the domestic market. The next case is concerned with the unusual occurrence of technology-seeking investment in an emerging market context. It involves the acquisition of a South African industrial equipment firm – Ziton – by a US corporation (EST) because of the former's superior fire detection technology. The final case is the entry of the Dutch bank, ABN Amro, to South Africa in response to financial sector liberalisation after 1994. Three different entry modes were used for the bank's three divisions – greenfield for banking, partial acquisition for securities trading and full acquisition for vehicle leasing. This case also illustrates the implications for emerging markets of major corporate strategic shifts by global giants.

AUTOMOTIVE COMPONENTS–NGK CERAMICS AND BEHR

In this automotive components case study, two contrasting firm types are examined. NGK Ceramics is a recently established greenfield plant that produces the ceramic substrate that is part of a vehicle emission control system. The plant is an example of a new type of export oriented investment in the automotive industry and is part of a very rapidly growing sub-sector. Behr South Africa produces automotive radiators and air conditioners and was acquired by the Stuttgart based Behr Group in 1999. It has very different origins. Production was established as early as the 1960s under South Africa's local content programme and the firm developed to supply the domestic market both for original equipment (OE) and aftermarket components.

Foreign Investment in the South African Automotive Components Industry

Prior to the 1980s, a rapidly growing domestic vehicle market together with high protection had acted as a magnet to foreign firms, which invested extensively in the South African automotive industry. Most of the main vehicle makes were assembled in South Africa although some of these operations operated under licence. Local content requirements, which were introduced from 1960 and gradually extended, ensured that firms sourced a certain portion of components locally. Exports of both vehicles and components were negligible.

In spite of the rapid influx of foreign investment in previous decades, by the late 1980s levels of foreign ownership were relatively low both among vehicle manufacturers and component producers. At this stage, only three of the seven vehicle manufacturers in SA had majority foreign shares. Many of the largest component groups were also locally owned and listed on the Johannesburg Stock Exchange. The relatively low share of foreign ownership was a function of a number of factors. The 1980s had been a period of economic stagnation and political turmoil unattractive for foreign investment. Japanese firms had for many years been prohibited by their government from making direct investments in apartheid South Africa although many had licence arrangements and there was large scale two-way trade. In addition, in the 1980s an active international campaign encouraged disinvestment from South Africa, which was particularly effective against American firms: both Ford and General Motors transferred ownership to local interests during this time. In any event, the industry was highly inward oriented so that access to export markets was not a critical consideration for South African firms.

The Impact of Government Policy

The South African automotive industry has been through wrenching changes over the past 15 years as it has opened up to international competition (Black 2001). Liberalisation began in the late 1980s and accelerated in the 1990s partly as a result of major changes sweeping the global automotive industry over this period but also reflecting the opening up of the South African economy with the demise of apartheid and important changes to government trade policy relating to the automotive industry.

The first major change to the protectionist trade policy in the automotive industry was in 1989 when the introduction of Phase VI of the local content programme signalled a partial shift from protection to export orientation. The Motor Industry Development Programme (MIDP) introduced in 1995 continued the direction taken by Phase VI and entrenched the principle of import–export complementation by which exports could earn import rebate credits. It also introduced a tariff phase down at a steeper rate than required in terms of South Africa's WTO obligations.

Import–export complementation enables automotive firms to use import credits to source components and vehicles at close to international prices. There is, therefore, considerable pressure on assemblers and distributors to gain access to import credits via exporting. Assemblers can, of course, achieve this through exporting vehicles and vehicle exports have increased from an average of less than 15,000 units per annum for the years 1992 to 1994 to approximately 110,000 units in 2002. But vehicle producers have also played a major role in expanding component exports either directly through subsidiary companies or through facilitating major contracts into their parent company global networks. This has encouraged large investments in certain components, the most important of which has been catalytic converters,[34] the industry in which one of the case firms operates.

The change in trade policy and resulting internationalisation of the industry manifested in growing exports and imports has had major implications for ownership. With the domestic market under pressure from imports and the introduction of an import–export complementation system, which effectively supported exports, it has become increasingly important for local firms to have links to international markets. This could most easily be achieved by establishing relationships with foreign firms. Thus a key potential asset brought in by a prospective foreign shareholder or owner is the access to markets, which they could provide. Recent foreign investment has, therefore, frequently been linked directly or indirectly to export production.

The access to international networks, which foreign owned firms could provide, is complemented by their control over the technology necessary to supply export markets and to meet the increasingly demanding requirements of domestic vehicle assemblers. In South Africa, before the recent influx of foreign investment in the automotive industry, the technology used and products produced by local firms were, however, generally licensed from major European, American or Japanese suppliers. While the South African plants may have had many features in common with that of the foreign licensor there were also significant differences. These differences were typical of manufacturing firms developing under import substitution policies. Firms in protected developing country markets tended to operate at much lower scale, were highly flexible and oriented to the domestic market (Katz 1987, Black 1996).

The pressures on SA firms to break into export markets and therefore to secure a foreign partner, have been complemented by the rapid internationalisation that has taken place in the world automotive component industry. Trends towards 'global sourcing' and 'follower sourcing' have had major implications in emerging markets where the trend is towards fewer first tier suppliers. In South Africa, and indeed in other emerging markets,[35] assemblers increasingly prefer to source components from joint ventures and wholly owned subsidiaries rather than from domestically owned firms. This is not only to achieve economies of scale but also to achieve quality levels in accordance with that achieved in the home plant.

As indicated in the following case studies, the particular dynamics of the industry have had important implications for the form that FDI has taken and for the outcomes that have resulted.

NGK Ceramics South Africa (Pty) Ltd

NGK Ceramics (South Africa) operates a recently established plant in Cape Town, which produces the ceramic substrate for catalytic converters, which form part of the emission control equipment in modern vehicles. It is 100 per cent owned by the Japan-based firm NGK Insulators Ltd.

The catalytic converter

The catalytic converter industry is growing rapidly worldwide. The use of converters has been a standard requirement for many years in the case of vehicles operating in developed countries but increasingly stringent legislation requires the use of numbers of catalytic converters in both petrol and diesel vehicles.

The production of a catalytic converter essentially requires three steps. The first is the manufacture of the ceramic monolith or substrate, which is a high technology product made of special clays with a very large internal surface area due to its honeycomb structure. This step is in itself divided into two processes, the extrusion of the monolith followed by firing at very high temperatures. NGK (Japan) and Corning (USA) are the two main suppliers worldwide accounting for 90 per cent of global supply and 95 per cent of South African supply. NGK has plants in Japan, Belgium, the USA, Indonesia and South Africa.

The second phase in the production of a catalytic converter involves the coating of the honeycomb monolith with a solution of platinum group metals, which create the filter effect. In the third phase, the ceramic monolith is 'canned' or packed into a stainless steel pressed casing.

In South Africa, the industry has seen dramatic growth of production. Nearly all of the production of catalytic converters[36] is destined for the export market once they have been coated and canned and exports have increased from ZAR197 million in 1994 to ZAR4,683 million in 2001 and the country now supplies approximately 12 per cent of global supply.

The South African based industry is for the most part foreign-owned and started with the establishment of plants, which undertook the coating and canning of the imported ceramic substrate. Backward integration into the ceramic substrate is a more recent development with the two world leaders,

Corning and NGK Insulators itself, recently establishing plants in South Africa.

The NGK investment

NGK Insulators Ltd is a large Japan-based multinational with sales in 2000 of US$2.978 million and 11,900 employees. While the company has production capacity in many countries, it is still very much dependent on the Japanese market which accounts for 72 per cent of sales. The ceramic products division, under which the South African subsidiary falls accounted for 17 per cent of turnover in the year ending 2000 (NGK Insulators 2000).

As indicated above, by the late 1990s, South Africa had become a leading global producer of catalytic converters with a number of coating and canning plants in operation. The announcement of major export contracts provided a clear indication of further expansion and provided additional justification for further backward integration through the establishment of production capacity in the ceramic substrate (BT 8 August 1999). In 1999, NGK's major international rival, Corning, announced that it was to build a new plant in Port Elizabeth to fire ceramic substrate and this forced the hand of NGK. The Japanese firm ran the risk of losing market share to Corning and it also faced requests from its customers operating in South Africa to open a facility.

The new facility was established according to very tight deadlines, with construction beginning in May 2000 and the start of commercial production in January 2001. Capital invested in the plant is approximately US$20 million including working capital. The plant has a capacity of 6 million pieces per annum and employs 90 workers. The plant technology itself involves firing of the substrate and testing of the product. These are sophisticated processes. The two huge kilns are state of the art, each with many individually controlled burners to allow for very precise and even control of temperature throughout the kiln. Each kiln has a capacity of 30,000 pieces which are fired for 60 hours at carefully regulated temperatures of up to 1,400 degrees Celsius. Testing is extensive involving dimensional integrity, isostatic and compressive strength, web thickness, water absorptiveness and expansiveness. While most of this is selective testing, each product is laser tested.

The plant has made extensive use of expatriate personnel. The managing director is British and in the early stages of establishment there were up to eleven Japanese technical and managerial staff at the plant. This has now been reduced to four and is likely to be reduced further.

Since production started the plant has met all output, quality targets and achieved a 100 per cent delivery rate. In March 2002 it was running at the optimal level of over 90 per cent of capacity and the kilns were in operation around the clock while other sections of the plant operated on a two shift basis for five or six days per week.

The phenomenal growth of the South African industry can only be understood in the context of South Africa's automotive policy. As explained above, the policy enables exporters of automotive products to rebate import duties on both vehicles and components. This has encouraged carmakers to establish export production in order to offset the duty burden on imports of both vehicles and imported CKD components. Producers of the ceramic substrates do not receive import credits but have benefited from the desire by vehicle manufacturers to increase export volumes of completed converters and to raise local value added.[37] Catalytic converters have been the component of choice and virtually all vehicle assemblers have arranged large-scale exports to their parent plants. Catalytic converters had certain advantages in this respect, not least that they are high value products as a result of the precious metal content. Furthermore, in spite of the fact that they are high value components, catalytic converters have relatively few components and production can therefore be established with relatively little labour and ancillary investment. Independent vehicle importers such as Peugeot have also set up contracts of this sort in order to rebate import duties. The import rebate system is now being phased down rapidly and industry growth rates are likely to slow.

The rapid expansion of this sub-sector has, however, created sufficient critical mass to attract investment in ancillary industries, which now provide significant agglomeration advantages. There now exists a large network of companies linked by a sophisticated logistics infrastructure and with a well established reputation in international markets. Arguably the industry has now created sufficient critical mass in terms of both volume of output and the localisation of the bulk of the value chain to make it internationally competitive. An important next step could be the localisation of the extrusion process, which would involve large capital investment and the importation of very sophisticated technology.

More conventional advantages include the fact that South Africa is a major producer of stainless steel and has considerable expertise in precious metals technology. More recently a further factor has undoubtedly been a 'bandwagon' effect. Foreign firms scouting South Africa for component export opportunities cannot fail to notice the country's leading position in this sector and have been quick to emulate their competitors.

Behr South Africa

The Behr Group is a large German multinational firm with global sales of €2.31 billion and 13,400 employees in 2000. Its major products are vehicle air conditioning and engine cooling systems which together account for over 85 per cent of turnover. Twenty per cent of the vehicles built in Europe use Behr cooling equipment but in common with many other German suppliers, the share of production outside of high-cost Germany is growing. Production (as opposed to sales) outside of Germany accounted for 49 per cent of total sales in 2000, up from 37 per cent in 1996. In emerging markets Behr has plants in Brazil, India, the Czech Republic and South Africa. The Behr Group is growing rapidly with total sales having increased by 82 per cent between 1996 and 2000.

Reasons for the acquisition
The Behr Group acquired its South African operation from the US firm, Federal Mogul, in May 1999. Federal Mogul had itself purchased the firm as part of a worldwide deal when it took over T&N plc, the UK based component supplier, a year earlier. T&N plc held a 51 per cent stake in T&N Holdings, a company listed on the Johannesburg Stock Exchange. The latter firm's divisions were friction materials; pistons, bearings, gaskets and heat transfer equipment. The T&N Heat Transfer division did not fit into the Federal Mogul structure as the latter company was not involved in this sector and this relatively small acquisition would not have given it critical mass in the sector.

As the South African automotive industry has become more internationally integrated, foreign-owned vehicle manufacturers have become drawn more closely into the networks of the parent company. This increasingly meant that they wanted selected suppliers to be located in South Africa. The Behr Group faced these pressures from key customers (BMW, Daimler Chrysler and VW) who were looking to expand vehicle production in South Africa. In particular, the Mercedes C Class export project offered the prospect of large contracts in the form of the air conditioner, radiator and condensor for this vehicle, which was to be built in volumes of 50,000 per annum in South Africa. According to the managing director of Behr (SA), the German group was faced with three alternatives. The first option was to invest in a greenfield facility. A second alternative was to purchase an existing firm and the third possibility was to simply continue their licence arrangements with existing firms operating in South Africa.

Essentially the decision on mode of entry revolved around risks and resources. The greenfield route was considered to be very demanding in terms of resources and also involved fairly high levels of risk. Maintaining a licensing arrangement was seen as risky because it involved losing control of core technology. T&N (and then Federal Mogul) had already been supplying the BMW 3 Series under licence but this was on an assembly basis and Behr was reluctant to licence its core technology. A licence arrangement which involved assembly would allow only low value added in South Africa.

Investing in emerging markets fitted with Behr's expansion strategy. While it was a multinational firm, it was very much German based and 'there was a perceived need to have a global footprint' (interviews). For this reason Behr had invested in Brazil in 1992. It also has an operation in India and is looking to integrate this more closely into the Behr network.

From the side of the South African operation, it was important to have a global partner. In the words of local management, 'the MIDP was starting to bite' and without a foreign investor the company 'could have stagnated into the aftermarket or even died'. The Behr Group proved to be an ideal candidate. Not only was Behr actively looking for an investment in SA as a result of pressure from its customers but it already had a well developed relationship with the South African company because of technology developed by the latter, which had been licenced to Behr. The Behr Group purchased 100 per cent of Federal Mogul Heat Transfer in May 1999 for an amount of €25 million, roughly equivalent to net asset value.

Performance of the subsidiary
Behr (SA) produces radiators, automotive air conditioners and condensers. Half of sales are original equipment and the remaining half are to the aftermarket. Direct exports account for a third of sales and are nearly all to the aftermarket. While the company does not export significant volumes of original equipment components, it supplies domestically assembled vehicles, many of which are exported. The basic strategy of the South African subsidiary has been to focus its activities in selected core areas. Turnover doubled between 1998 and 2001 to approximately ZAR620 million. Rapid growth is expected over the next few years and the SA firm is highly profitable.

It is clear that this investment has been advantageous for the local operation, which faced the prospect of cutting production and increasingly competing on price in the aftermarket. Local management expect that employment would have fallen and the company would have struggled to maintain its technological edge. Since the acquisition, in each business division there have been productivity and efficiency improvements. By 2001, Behr (SA) had 1,100 employees in four sites, up from 1,000 three years previously. Prior to this, the firm had been experiencing 'jobless growth' as it restructured in the face of tariff reductions and growing export opportunities.

As has been typical in the component sector, perhaps the most important contribution of the investor has been to facilitate access to key automotive customers. The Behr Group is one of the largest worldwide suppliers to the three major German automakers (VW, Daimler Chrysler and BMW) all of which have plants in South Africa, which increasingly act as a base for export. The export drive has necessitated the introduction of new technology on a large scale and the car firms have actively promoted investment and joint ventures by German component suppliers. In the Port Elizabeth airconditioner plant, production has been greatly increased through obtaining the contract to supply the C Class Mercedes. The Durban plant produces the radiator for the C Class but has also seen an expansion of exports into the aftermarket. The copper-based radiator plant at Silverton, Pretoria, which was looking at reducing production because of the transfer of technology to aluminium-based radiators, has attracted additional business. Production from a recently closed copper-based plant in Spain has been transferred to Behr (SA) and the same was expected to happen with a copper-based plant in the USA.

A few years prior to being acquired by Behr, the South African heat transfer division was spending 4 to 5 per cent of turnover on R&D. This was significantly higher than most component producers in South Africa and the firm was doing fundamental research and development. The South African operation had even developed innovative production technology, which had been licenced to the Behr Group. This process involved a new method of braising aluminium radiators using a specially developed powder. But this innovative capability was not a significant factor in the decision to make the acquisition and the situation has now changed radically. After the acquisition took place, all R&D activity in South Africa was transferred to Germany or shut down. The South African subsidiary now only does development work although its capability for this is expanding partly due to the high cost of assistance from the parent company.

South African management sees this development as positive for two reasons. Firstly, the South African subsidiary is now able to focus to a greater extent on its core activities. Secondly, they now have access to cutting edge R&D. A recent example of access to this know-how was a huge saving achieved in the course of a short visit from the parent company by a specialist in furnace technology. The Durban plant was set to invest ZAR13 million in a new furnace to increase capacity but by reorganising the spacing of parts and the adjustment of heating elements they were able to increase the capacity of the existing furnace with no additional investment.

Since the acquisition the management team is virtually unchanged and there have been no expatriate staff introduced with the exception of technical staff seconded for relatively brief periods. Some of the plants have not changed very much since the acquisition. The biggest change has been at the Port Elizabeth air conditioner plant, which put in a new more automated line to supply components for the Mercedes W203 vehicles.

Other changes have been in purchasing where the company is now able to source sub-components much more effectively and at world prices. Significant savings have, for instance, been made on aluminium tubes. Savings on sourcing components are particularly important in the air conditioner plant where imported content is as high as 65 per cent.

The South African location offers a competitive source of supply into the Behr global network. Labour, tooling costs and some overheads such as buildings are very cheap in South Africa. An area where Behr (SA) is particularly competitive is in small batch production for the aftermarket. This is because levels of automation are relatively low and the South African subsidiary has considerable expertise in rapid changeovers and low volume production. This cost advantage has become increasingly realised by the parent company and the South African subsidiary is 'playing an important role in the development of the worldwide spare parts business, as a supplier of heat exchangers' (Behr 2001).

Conclusion

With the liberalisation of the South African automotive industry, there has been a shift in the rationale for FDI. Previously a sheltered but growing domestic market provided attractive opportunities for foreign firms. The orientation was mainly towards the domestic market and there was some scope for domestic adaptations. Local companies also invested in this sector and were able to operate on the basis of licenced technology.

The basis of expansion has now become much more export oriented and it is increasingly important for component firms to have either direct or indirect access to export markets. The major asset contributed by foreign vehicle producers and component suppliers has undoubtedly been access to international networks. Carmakers have actively sought out component suppliers who are able to export and to supply components which meet the increasingly exacting standards of their own increasingly export-oriented assembly operations.

Foreign firms have played a major role as conduits between domestic firms and the international market in four main ways. Firstly, they have arranged large export contracts for component suppliers by facilitating access to their global networks. Secondly, they have brokered new investment by encouraging foreign suppliers to establish joint ventures with foreign firms or to set up new plants. Thirdly, they have brought in new technology and, fourthly, they have frequently accelerated the transfer of industry best practices in production organisation to their suppliers. One of the main factors leading to the perceived success of the MIDP therefore, is that it has facilitated the increased internationalisation, which has underpinned growing exports and investment in the industry. Thus the spillovers resulting from foreign investment in the vehicle industry have mainly been of a vertical nature accruing to those suppliers who have had greater access to markets and technology as a result of being drawn into the international networks of multinational car companies (Saggi 2002).

The mode of entry (acquisition or greenfield) has tended to be a function of conditions in the particular sub-sector concerned. Where local firms operating in the sector have been available, a joint venture or outright acquisition has been favoured on the grounds that this was a cheaper and faster way into the market and also brought in local expertise and know-how. In some instances this would involve a South African firm, which was already using licenced technology from the prospective investor. The latter case clearly reduces transaction costs for the prospective investor, as there would already be an existing relationship and possibly some commonality in the equipment and processes used. This clearly enhances the benefits of an acquisition relative to a greenfield investment. In the case of acquired firms the result has been a reorientation of production and incremental additional investment rather than wholesale changes to the plant and organisation, as would be the case in the extreme brownfield example. Greenfield investments have been pursued primarily in sub-sectors where there has been no domestic capacity.

INDUSTRIAL MACHINERY – ZITON

Recently, outward investment by firms based in emerging markets has become of increasing importance. In spite of being a developing country, outward FDI from South Africa has exceeded inward FDI over the last decade (Nordas 2001). Firms of this type clearly are likely to offer a range of additional assets, which may be attractive to foreign buyers. Such assets may include advanced process and product technology as well as international distribution capabilities. The second case, Ziton, provides such an example. The company had developed from small beginnings into the world's twelfth largest producer of fire detection equipment with an international distribution network. It then attracted a buyer in the form of a US firm, which was interested in its technology and also wanting to expand its market share in Europe.

Background to the Acquisition

Ziton was acquired in 1999 by US-based Edwards Systems Technologies (EST), itself a subsidiary of SPX Corporation, a Fortune 500 listed company with a turnover of US$2.7 billion, 23,000 employees and operations in 21 countries. SPX Corporation pursues a strategy of expanding businesses, which have scale and growth potential. It has four major divisions: technical products, industrial products, flow technologies and service solutions. EST is one of nine groups within the technical products division. It has 500 employees in the USA alone and has historically produced mainly for the US market.

The worldwide fire detection equipment market is growing fairly rapidly and is also experiencing rapid technological change. The global market is worth approximately US$600 million and growth prospects are good especially as legislative requirements for fire detection equipment continue to be tightened around the world. Competition is based on technology and features rather than simply on price. The requirement for approval by a recognised agency is a significant barrier to entry as this is expensive and time-consuming and raises risks for new entrants.

The early growth of Ziton

From its roots as a small family owned company engaged in installing fire detection equipment in 1969, Ziton (originally called Firefite) developed into a major company with proprietary product technology and a global market. Ziton products are in the mid-range in terms of price and quality and the company is a system producer providing full service support. At the time of the acquisition in 2000, Ziton had 450 employees in South Africa and also had a distribution and marketing office in the UK. Its 3.5 per cent world market share for fire detection equipment included 10 to 15 per cent of the UK and Australian markets, significant shares in a range of other European markets and 90 per cent of the South African market. Exports accounted for 80 per cent of annual sales of ZAR400 million.

In the early stages of its growth, Firefite began to import equipment on behalf of other suppliers. Initial production was crude and took place in the home of the founders, using the kitchen oven to fire the parts used! The first products designed were conventional detectors and reverse engineering was used extensively. From the start because it 'insisted on a high degree of home-grown components, Firefite established a fertile platform for encouraging rapid learning in-house in the area of production processes' (Wood 2000).

International operations started in 1984 with the opening of its UK office. In the same year, Ziton's first major technological breakthrough was the development of an analogue fire detection system, the first in the world. At the time of the sale to EST, 80 per cent of the product range was proprietary and the firm remained a world leader in analogue-based fire detection equipment. The company has grown through organic learning and at the time of the purchase had an R&D staff of 50 – very large for a company of this size. Such has been the success of Ziton that it has been used as a case in business school courses on the development of indigenous technological capability (Wood 2000). The early emphasis on being close to the market has been retained and the firm developed a large international marketing and service back up capability with specialist representatives in over 30 countries.

The Acquisition and Recent Developments

EST took control of Ziton in October 2000 after a lengthy due diligence process. A previous potential buyer, which planned to shut the South African operation and transfer all the technology to the USA, was rejected and the founders of Ziton have negotiated an arrangement by which the local operation had to be maintained. In fact EST are gradually transferring more production to Cape Town and all staff have stayed. EST has made a small injection of capital but as yet has not made major changes to the company.

Under the circumstances it is highly unlikely that EST would have established a greenfield plant in South Africa. It appears that even if Ziton had not been available, another acquisition elsewhere would have been the preferred option. EST had also considered a greenfield operation in Malaysia. There were four main factors motivating EST to acquire Ziton:

Relatively low cost producer
EST found that Ziton's production costs were relatively low. The managing director estimated that they were 75 to 80 per cent of US production costs and in some cases the cost differential was even greater. The main cost advantages over the US are in labour and overheads. Labour costs are a third of the US cost and with labour efficiency being a third less than the US, unit labour costs are approximately half of the US level.

Overhead costs are much lower in South Africa – in most cases between a third and 60 per cent of the US cost. This was evident in a number of detailed cost comparisons, for instance dollars per line of computer code, and in the case of injection moulding, the cost per injection and per mould. In the case of an engineering document change, costs in South Africa were only 18 per cent of those in the US. Overall, overheads were 40 per cent of US level and total production costs (labour and overheads) are 50 to 60 per cent of the US level.

Surprisingly, there also appeared to be some savings in procurement costs compared to the US for products such as electronic components. Ziton also claimed that in some cases they were able to secure lower prices for major capital equipment items being imported from Europe and Japan. Management cited the case of pick and place robot imported from Japan at a price 20 per cent lower than EST had paid some 6 months previously. The electronics, plastics and metals being used are mainly locally sourced with circuit boards produced in China.

The reasons for the company being competitive are a combination of the technology they have as well as high volume production. While Ziton produces a wide range of products, a few account for the bulk of output. Four detectors and two bases account for 85 per cent of turnover and are each produced in volumes of approximately a million per year.

The previous owners took a conscious decision to avoid high levels of automation partly because they considered this to be cheaper in the South African environment but also because they felt it important to create employment. This philosophy combined with the rapid growth of the firm meant that they never had to retrench staff. Because of Ziton's low production costs, the new owners plan to relocate a third of US production to Cape Town. But they will also be introducing higher levels of automation so employment is not expected to rise significantly.

The technological capabilities of Ziton
According to the co-founder of the company, one motivation of EST was to gain access to world leadership in certain types of technology especially as

EST lacked cutting edge technology, which would enable it to compete effectively in the European market.

Indeed Ziton's technology and low engineering costs were such that in the due diligence process, EST decided that it would make sense to establish Cape Town as a base for its third engineering centre. EST's established engineering centre is in Sarasota, Florida and it has recently made an acquisition of a California-based company, which will provide the engineering centre for gas detectors. Cape Town will be the third centre, involving an expansion of the existing Ziton research centre. More ambitious plans to develop a new type of detector in Cape Town were reversed in the face of the perceived political risk of investing a large amount of intellectual capital in South Africa.

The managing director's view was that while Ziton has some useful technological attributes, these were not critical determinants of the investment:

> The product line was in fact remarkably similar to what EST was producing but was just a lot cheaper. Having said that, Ziton had a unique combination of design and manufacturing....the whole style of the thing. Unlike some acquisitions where (the acquiring company) might have said 'that is a brand name or that is a product or a patent which we have to have at all costs', it was a basket of things that they looked at including some key personnel.

Although Ziton now has access to EST's engineering centres, the operations manager felt that to date there has been a greater transfer of technology from South Africa to the US than vice versa although there had been some sharing on a number of projects. EST have brought no new expatriate staff into Ziton although a number have visited on short assignments.

A well established market and distribution system in Europe

An important aspect of EST's strategy is expansion in Europe taking advantage of Ziton's established marketing and distribution system. The objective here is to take advantage of the expected expansion of the European market as legislation changes. Current legislation in Europe is far more lax than in the United States with fire detectors only required in public buildings such as schools, hospitals and old age homes and it is expected that European legislative requirements along the lines of the US standard will lead to a rapid expansion in demand in other European countries.

Complementarities between the two companies

There is considerable complementarity between the two companies. EST supplied at the top end of the market while the Ziton range was in the middle or lower end. EST plans to expand its market share in the US by introducing the Ziton range through its own distribution network.

Conclusion

The acquisition of Ziton represents a fairly unusual case where a foreign firm has invested to purchase technology and an international distribution and marketing network from a company based in a developing country. Before the acquisition, Ziton was considering a stock exchange listing and both the co-founder and the current managing director felt that expansion would have continued if the acquisition had not taken place.

It appears that Ziton has been an attractive acquisition for EST. It has been able to obtain a firm, which is operating profitably, with a significant share of markets in which it is only weakly represented. Ziton also has products, which may enable EST to raise its market share in its home (USA) market. The combined group is now the third or fourth largest producer of fire detection equipment worldwide. In addition EST has secured a low cost production base as well as a firm with high levels of expertise.

The link to SPX provides access to capital as well as markets in new areas. This particular example of FDI has much in common with a normal acquisition but there has been a substantial rearrangement of the assets. The European distribution network is now an integral part of EST giving the US company direct access to an established network in a major and fast growing market. At the same time EST appears set to make much greater use of the low cost production and engineering capability of the South African operation, a benefit which appeared to have been much enhanced by the depreciation of the rand in late 2001.[38]

Ziton is a firm that could fit quite easily into the operating environment of a first world multinational firm. It was export oriented, had operated without significant protection and its own production operations were of a world class standard albeit significantly more labour intensive than would be the case in an advanced country. In addition the firm was profitable and could have continued to expand possibly with additional funding obtained through a stock exchange listing. All these competitive attributes make a brownfield investment less likely in the sense that the complete reorganisation of assets, as has been common in cases of 'deep restructuring' in Eastern Europe (Meyer and Møller 1998), would presumably have been both wasteful and expensive. Nevertheless, it is clear that the purchaser valued the assets of Ziton somewhat differently to its original owners. A key objective for EST was the European distribution arm, whereas the original owners appear to have placed more value on Ziton's technological capabilities. EST appears to have come to a later realisation of the Cape Town plant's low cost production and engineering capabilities.

In the more developed emerging markets, particularly where economies have not been unduly protected, it seems likely that foreign acquisitions would be less likely to take a brownfield form because potential takeover targets are likely to operate in ways that are familiar to potential multinational buyers.

FINANCIAL SERVICES – ABN AMRO

Because services are produced and consumed simultaneously, internationalisation in the services sector traditionally has involved 'market-seeking' direct investment to establish a commercial presence in foreign markets. Many multinational corporations in producer service sectors undertook substantial FDI during the 1990s aiming to construct 'global service networks'. Increasing competitive pressures in existing markets led these firms to offer corporate clients a 'global package deal' involving both product diversification and a wider geographical spread of operations (Dicken 1998, p. 393).

In the financial services industry, foreign entry facilitated integration into global financial markets and enhanced access to capital. During the early 1990s, host governments and international banks therefore had a mutual interest in deregulating and removing entry barriers to emerging market financial systems, and foreign banks became major players in many countries, especially in Central and Eastern Europe and Latin America (Roldos 2001, Clarke et al. 2003, Dicken 1998). Financial system health is critical to aggregate economic stability and growth, with the trade-off between promoting market competition and avoiding potentially costly bank collapses especially important. National financial regulation and the strength of domestic banks are crucial factors in relation to foreign bank entry.

This case study examines ABN Amro's entry into, and presence in, South Africa, which has been shaped by three factors: the bank's efforts to create a global services network, the powerful competitive threat of South Africa's major domestic banks in the context of the liberalisation of the financial system, and the impact of the global financial market downturn from March 2000. ABN Amro established a branch in South Africa in June 1995, one of the first four to do so after banking was liberalised. The greenfield banking entry was soon followed by a partial acquisition in securities trading. In November 1995, the Johannesburg Stock Exchange was liberalised, and in June 1996 ABN Amro purchased 40 per cent (jointly with local and foreign partners) of Huysamer Stals, a South African stockbroker.

Entry Driver I: ABN's Global Strategy

ABN Amro was formed in September 1991 through a merger of Algemene Bank Nederland (ABN) and Amsterdam-Rotterdam Bank (Amro). Both banks had reached their limits of expansion, but were confronted with rising competitive pressures. Both had relatively small shares (between 7 and 9 per cent) of the Dutch retail market, but limited M&A options, so that their merger was a 'marriage of necessity' (Evans 1997, also de Vries et al. 1999). Though Amro was successful in the Dutch corporate market, its corporate clients were increasingly expanding beyond Holland, especially into Europe, and needed a bank with a substantial international network. Amro's international business was small, contributing only 11 per cent of profit in 1986. Like many other mid-size European banks, it had begun looking for a partner amongst its European peers as '1992' loomed (Economist 26 March 1988).

ABN, on the other hand, was small in the Dutch domestic corporate market, but a bigger player than Amro internationally, earning more than one-third of its profits outside Holland. It was long-established in South Asia and Latin America, and entered the US retail market (focusing on the Mid-West) in the late 1970s. During the 1980s, it successfully pursued a strategy of acquisitions in many countries. Continued international expansion was essential for future growth, but by 1990, ABN needed a capital infusion to strengthen its balance sheet for further acquisitions. A share issue was unattractive because it would dilute ownership, merger with a major European bank would (it was feared) lead to loss of the bank's identity, and the major Dutch insurers had significant US interests so that a merger was ruled out by the Glass-Steagall Act. This left only another Dutch bank as a possibility, with Amro as the leading candidate for organisational culture reasons. After the Dutch central bank relaxed its restrictions on mergers between Dutch banks from 1990, with its own eye on '1992' and the ongoing evolution of the European Union, the ABN–Amro merger moved ahead quickly.

At the merger, the new bank had operations in 48 countries, with 375 foreign branches, and was ranked 18th globally, in terms of total assets. The bank was organised into four autonomously operating divisions: the Netherlands Division; the International Division, supplying banking and financial services to both multinational corporate clients and consumers outside Holland; the Investment Banking Division, engaged in securities issuing and trading; and the Lease Holding Division, supplying fleet and equipment leasing services.

The merger sparked aggressive international expansion, and the bank's geographical spread and product diversity grew very quickly. By 2000, ABN Amro was in 74 countries, and had 2,709 branches and 76,140 employees outside of Holland (ABN Amro Annual Report 2001).[39] It had retail banking activities in 23 countries. Aiming to be a universal bank, it had begun investment banking only in 1992, but subsequently moved strongly into this area (Evans 1997).

Expansion was mainly via acquisitions, with an emphasis on relatively cheap targets that could be incorporated into the ABN Amro network and grown from within. There were two broad thrusts to the strategy. One focused on retail operations within national economies, with an emphasis on large domestic markets such as the US, Brazil and India. ABN Amro hoped to establish a second 'home market' in Europe, but failed in this ambition. The second arm of the strategy aimed at a global financial services operation, with a multinational corporate client base. Based in a medium-sized financial centre, ABN recognised the limits of its investment bank prospects in the major financial centres of London, New York and Tokyo. 'We're not an investment bank, we're a universal bank. We want a balance [between] the more volatile profits in investment banking [and] the far more stable return from commercial banking' (Evans 1997).

Rather than the more intensive, lending institution-focused operational structure of investment banks in the first-tier centres, ABN Amro's strategic orientation was customer-focused and extensive. Adopting the slogan 'the network bank', it aimed to provide 'relationship' banking on a global scale, offering corporate clients as wide as possible a range of services in as many markets as possible. 'In the overall relationship [between bank and client], we have more to offer than a Wall Street firm, because they can't do business with a multinational in Ecuador or Taiwan' (Evans 1997, also Els).

Entry into a market for ABN Amro thus involved not only market-seeking, to acquire new corporate clients in the new market, but also market-sustaining motives. Entry was intended also to expand the (geographical) scope of the bank's network, to benefit existing clients investing in or trading with the newly-entered market. These clients in effect obtained network externalities, contributing to brand loyalty. In many countries, ABN Amro established large local branch networks to attract new clients: 'we're also interested in providing commercial banking services to [national] tier-two and tier-three companies, so we need a presence in ....secondary centres' (Evans 1997).

Entry into a new country was seen as a very long-term commitment: 'We're here to stay. We don't close down branches easily' (Evans 1997). Furthermore, the bank aimed to build on local strengths in order to secure domestic markets. The standard entry strategy was via partial acquisition of a well-established domestic institution. ABN Amro was cautious and risk-averse in selecting acquisition targets, avoiding expensive high-fliers in favour of modestly-priced middle-of-the-road respectability. The bank did not rush to impose its own identity or full control: it delayed re-branding to retain customer loyalty, and delayed acquiring outstanding shares especially from local managers. The bank emphasised its respect for local culture, and used local senior managers to provide continuity for domestic business networks and employees: 'The key is having the right local guy. .. a top manager who knows the market in, say, Delhi. If you just send someone from Bombay, you can forget it. ...If you start by hiring second-tier local people, you're never going to be successful' (Evans 1997).

ABN Amro's strategic approach would be fundamentally transformed from 2000, as discussed below. But first we look at the opening of the South African market to foreign banks.

Entry Driver II: Financial Liberalisation in South Africa

Before 1995, foreign banks could enter South Africa only as representative offices (agencies performing administrative and marketing functions only) or subsidiaries, which could take deposits, but were incorporated locally and got a South African rating. At end-1994, there were 40 foreign representative offices and six subsidiaries in the market. The major step liberalising the sector internationally was to allow foreign banks to open branches from May 1995. Branches are subject to the same operating conditions and capital requirements as subsidiaries and domestic banks. They are licenced to take deposits and deal in the forex and securities markets, and face the same liquid asset and minimum reserve balance requirements. Branches were barred from simply trading off their parent's balance sheet – as with subsidiaries, the foreign parent bank had to establish a strong balance sheet for the branch via a substantial infusion of 'endowment' capital. Initial endowment capital was a minimum of ZAR50 million (US$6.25 million),[40] with operating capital to be maintained at 8 per cent of assets, risk-weighted as for domestic banks. The initial endowment has now been raised to ZAR250 million (US$31.25 million). But there are two important differences between subsidiaries and branches. Firstly, branches have the same international rating as the parent bank, allowing them to borrow more cheaply. Secondly, foreign branches were effectively excluded from the domestic retail market, since the minimum deposit by a natural person was set at ZAR1 million (US$125 000), a limit dropped in 2001.

South Africa's banking system is highly concentrated – at the end of 1994, the four largest banks (all privately-owned) held 80 per cent of the banking assets and 82 per cent of deposits. The capital and deposit requirements imposed on foreign branches provided significant protection for the major domestic banks, which were already under pressure in the retail market from non-bank competitors, particularly consumer goods retailers, and from the rising costs of their branch structure. Lack of access to their parent's balance sheet was a further disadvantage for the foreign banks. But the ability of branches to use their parents' rating created strong incentives for banks to opt for a greenfield entry by establishing a branch rather than a subsidiary. This further protected domestic banks from becoming acquisition targets, though foreign banks until recently expressed little interest in acquiring domestic banks, given the small retail market and high purchase price (Euromoney, September 1998). Price : earnings ratios for small South African banks were 14 to 18 during this period, but the large banks with extensive branch structures had ratios between 30 and 45. An acquisition would also have required regulatory approval, raising the transaction costs and delaying entry.

Liberalisation in the securities market followed a different pattern, in which domestic firms received little protection. In 1992, the Johannesburg Stock Exchange (JSE) began investigating regulatory reform, leading to new legislation implemented in November 1995. Similar to the 1986 'big bang' on the London Stock Exchange, the JSE's 'little bang' permitted limited liability and foreign membership, and introduced negotiated commissions and proprietary dealing by member firms together with capital adequacy requirements. Commissions dropped from 65 basis points to 25 between 1998 and 2001. Until 2002, foreign entrants were required to set up subsidiaries rather than branches. Domestic brokers were required to adapt to the new regulatory environment while simultaneously facing new competitive pressures from foreign investment banks seeking a share of an attractive new market. Given their distribution and sales networks, domestic firms were attractive acquisition targets for foreign firms.

Following liberalisation, entry into both the banking and securities trading market segments followed rapidly. In the mid-1990s, the South Africa financial services market was attractive for both market-seeking and market-sustaining investment. Growth in real output in the FIRE (Finance, insurance, real estate) sector has averaged 5 per cent per annum since 1994, compared with 2.7 per cent for the economy as a whole, and financial sector employment has increased significantly, in contrast to the decline in the rest of the formal economy. There were 638 companies listed on the JSE at the end of 1995, and in 1996, JSE market capitalisation ranked 14th globally (JSE Annual Report 1996), suggesting a large base of potential domestic clients, themselves increasingly engaged in cross-border operations. There was also a very strong foreign presence in industry and services – in 1994, over 550 foreign direct investors (firms with more than 10 employees) and nearly 1,000 more, smaller agencies and representative offices of foreign firms (Chapter 7). Activity on the JSE was expanding quickly, trading volume rising from 2.2 billion shares in 1992 to 5.15 billion in 1995. The political and economic changes in South Africa also promised a wave of privatisation and 'black economic empowerment (BEE)' deals for investment banks.

The number of foreign banks grew rapidly: before liberalisation, there were 40 representative offices, which grew to a peak of 61 in 2000, while 15 branches were established during the period, though only nine are major international institutions. Seven smaller foreign banks have established subsidiaries. These numbers reflect that for many banks, entering the South

African market was attractive, but not sufficiently so to justify the costs and risks of establishing a branch. Half of the entrants limited themselves to a representative office, and others entered in this form first, later establishing a branch. In the equities trading market, there have been approximately twenty foreign entrants of whom twelve remained in January 2003, when the JSE had 59 members.

ABN Amro's Entry: Choosing the 'right local guy'?

ABN Amro sought early-mover advantage in the banking sector by opening a branch immediately (Els). Greenfield entry via a branch (rather than a subsidiary) was predictable, given the incentive structure facing foreign banks, as discussed. The timing reflected ABN Amro's 'extensive network' approach at the time: an ABN Amro SA manager pointed out that 'South Africa was the last big sophisticated market in which [the] bank did not have a presence' (Euromoney, September 1998).

The target markets were the South African operations of its corporate clients elsewhere in the world, and the 'top 100' South African companies, particularly those with cross-border activities. The latter were offered access to off-shore borrowing in addition to banking services, and by May 1996, ABN Amro had been lead arranger on three large loans (each over US$100 million) for major South African corporates. 'Expansion into Africa [was] a large part of the bank's South African strategy' (Euromoney, September 1998). The bank also expected large FDI inflows into South Africa from Europe and the USA.

ABN Amro also moved early into the bond market, issuing a four-year bond in October 1995 in the new Eurorand market, and taking on a market-making role in the domestic bond market as soon as private institutions were allowed in 1997. Though it requires a strong capital base and returns are low, the attraction is that dealers (predominantly foreign banks) build reputation and can generate new business in the secondary market.

ABN Amro's entry into securities trading in South Africa appears less well-planned, even though entry via partial acquisition of a mid-size firm was on the face of it more in keeping with the bank's standard approach than the greenfield entry into banking. In May 1996, ABN Amro and NM Rothschild had begun a joint venture in global securities trading. In South Africa, Rothschild was setting up Kagiso Financial Services (KFS) as a merchant bank focusing on privatisation and corporate finance, with the Kagiso Trust (a 'black empowerment' group) and Huysamer Stals (HS).[41] ABN Amro seems to have 'tagged along' with Rothschild and joined the deal, which involved the 40 per cent partial acquisition of Huysamer Stals in November 1996, with ABN Amro's stake 15 per cent.

But, as discussed below, HS was a poor choice of target, given ABN Amro's objectives in South Africa. Although HS was a well-established broker, in business for about 30 years, its base was the retail segment of the white Afrikaans-speaking community. It had an extensive branch network in South Africa and Namibia, serving large towns in addition to the main cities. It focused on private clients rather than the institutional investors which ABN Amro sought.

In March 1998, ABN Amro purchased the outstanding 60 per cent of HS, the other 25 per cent still held by Kagiso Trust. It stated publicly it was raising its stake two years earlier than planned. Additional staff were hired to serve private clients, though the eponymous Werner Stals claimed that ABN Amro was aiming for significant market share from the major savings institutions: 'there will be six to eight really global players in the local market [after a shake-out], the rest will [be] discount brokers or serve private clients' (FM 6 March 1998). Reflecting similar confidence, HS was rebranded in August 1998, and the firm committed to moving in November 2000 to a branded building immediately adjacent to the new JSE building, as Johannesburg's financial district migrated from downtown to the northern suburb of Sandton. The re-branding would have raised customer expectations of performance standards to international levels.

ABN Amro Lease Holding NV, the independently managed subsidiary of ABN Amro, acquired in full the fleet management operation of Investec, a South African bank, at the end of 1997. The cost was ZAR500 million, and was the 16th largest acquisition in South Africa (Euromoney, September 1998). In April 2001, this division employed 65 people, an increase of five since its acquisition. Like the international leasing division, the South African operation has been run separately from the local banking and securities divisions.[42]

The entry into South Africa was a departure from the bank's standard strategy going into a new market, in which local banking expertise was a key resource providing client and business networks as well as local risk management expertise. Perhaps because the bank branch was a greenfield, a large group of ten expatriates was used, who had no South African, and limited emerging market experience. Nonetheless, there were still four expatriates in South Africa six years later, while Werner Stals had been appointed head of the overall operation in June 1999, even though his banking experience was limited to his time with ABN Amro. Early re-branding was also unusual for the bank: for example, several longstanding acquisitions in the US and Europe (including LaSalle bank acquired in 1979) were rebranded only in early 2003 and even then retained their own names (www.abnamro.com).

It is possible that the sophistication of South Africa's financial services sector and the strength of the local institutions (at least in the domestic market) were underestimated at the time of entry and South Africa was treated as 'just another' emerging market. But the lack of local banking experience and business networks was felt later when the bank was forced into the medium-size corporate market in search of clients, and several loans went sour. The local partner – a securities broker – was relied upon for distribution and business networks, a second key resource, but this was inadequate. On the securities side, furthermore, only a single expatriate was brought in, despite a trading skills shortage, and there was little integration with the bank's wider trading culture and systems.

The HS research team was a third key resource for entry, identified (again in hindsight) as a major reason for acquiring an equity broker, which could provide information on local corporations to increase the domestic investment banking market share. But according to a member of the securities research team, there was almost no contact with the local branch of the bank before November 2000, when the two divisions moved into the new building. On the other hand, the South African research team supported global equities research in London, having ongoing contact on resource companies (Kruger). In other words, South African research supported the investment banking operation, rather than either the market-seeking or the market-sustaining activities which had ostensibly motivated entry to South Africa.

ABN Amro's Performance: Progress followed by Retreat

Given the sub-optimal nature of the key resources for entry, it is perhaps unsurprising that, while early entry initially paid off, the local operation faltered badly after 1998. The optimism reflected in the early expansion of the stake in HS and the brokerage's re-branding was not realised.

Tables 8.1 and 8.2 provide indicators of ABN Amro's market penetration and competitive position. Table 8.1 shows total assets (including domestic and foreign assets) for ABN Amro and a 'peer group' of six other foreign banks: Citibank, Commerzbank, ING Barings, JP Morgan Chase, Credit Agricole and Deutsche.[43] During the first three years, ABN Amro outperformed the peer group, but as the number of foreign banks increased from 1998, ABN Amro grew slower than the others. The table may underestimate the banks' South Africa-based business: according to ING, as much as two-thirds of loans may be booked off-shore, and fee-based income up to 60 per cent of total earnings (FM 25 April 1997).

Opinion of ABN Amro in the market was initially favourable: an annual survey of financial directors of 100 large multinationals operating in South Africa placed ABN Amro as the top foreign financial institution in 1997 and 1998, ahead of both Commerzbank and Citibank (PMR Review, December 1997, Oct 1998). An annual 'peer review' of banks saw ABN Amro improve its ranking amongst foreign banks steadily between 1996 and 1998 in the corporate banking and treasury categories (PriceWaterhouseCoopers, various years). ABN Amro's excellent reviews in the latter two functions in 1998 was not matched in securities dealing or corporate finance, a possible indication of the securities division's future difficulties (Table 8.2).

Table 8.1 ABN Amro Total assets in South Africa, compared with peer group

End of	Total assets (ZAR bn)	ABN Amro asset growth (% p.a.)	Peer group asset growth (% p.a.)	ABN Amro rank	No. of banks
1995	102	n.a.	n.a.	3	3
1996	1,620	1,488	164	3	4
1997	2,995	85	76	3	5
1998	3,414	14	43	4	7
1999	3,300	-3	11	4	7
2000	3,851	17	19	4	7
2001	7,177	86	133	5	7
2002	5,179	-38	-45	4	7

Source: SA Reserve Bank. The figures for 2001 and 2002 partly reflect currency fluctuations as the ZAR was very volatile during these years; these of course affected all banks. The rank in Column 4 is by size of assets.

From 1999, the steady progress slowed and then reversed, and by 2003, the bank was in retreat in South Africa, as reflected in Tables 8.1 and 8.2, notwithstanding the imperfections of the indices.[44] In a separate rating of forex dealers, ABN Amro dropped from 6th in 2002 to 10th in 2003 in the ZAR market (Euromoney May 2003).

Several medium-sized domestic corporates to whom the bank had made loans ran into financial trouble, with associated fraud allegations.[45] Though there was no suggestion of any impropriety by ABN Amro, this raised questions about the bank's risk management. In 2003, the (Dutch expatriate) Country Manager acknowledged that there were still 'echoes' of these problems, which he argued were a consequence of acquiring the 'wrong' equity broker: HS links with 'quality' South African corporations were inadequate, pushing the bank into a lowermarket bracket with less rigorous business ethics. In other words, the lack of South African banking experience was telling.

In 2002, ABN Amro management claimed that '30 of the top 50, and 50 of the top 100, listed South African corporations use ABN Amro for the services it offers, together with around 60 multinationals'. Nonetheless, in corporate finance, the bank retained 'only one or two professionals to source business, flying in their overseas team when necessary' (BD 13 March 2002). By 2003 non-core services had been abandoned or outsourced to domestic banks, including local cash management and clearing functions.

Table 8.2 Competitive position ABN Amro's ranking in peer review

	No.	Equities	Bonds	Treasury	Corporate banking	Corporate finance	Project financing
1996	25			3	6		
1997	31			3	3		
1998	28	7	6	2	1	7	5

	No.	Institutional brokerage	Retail brokerage	Money market	Corporate banking	Corporate finance - M&A	Structured finance - projects
1999	26	10 (6)	7 (4)	11 (4)	6 (2)	13 (8)	7 (2)
2000	30	n.r.	n.r.	n.r.	n.r.	n.r.	n.r.
2001	27	n.r.	n.r.	n.r.	9 (4)	n.r.	n.r.
2002	32	n.r.	n.r.	n.r.	n.r.	n.r.	n.r.
2003	22	n.r.	n.r.	n.r.	n.r.	n.r.	n.r.

Source: PriceWaterhouseCoopers, various years. Respondents were asked to identify the top three banks in each category. From 1999, some ranking categories changed. Before 1999, local and foreign banks were surveyed and ranked independently; after 1999, they were combined. Brackets indicate ABN Amro's rank amongst foreign banks. n.r. = not ranked, ie. none of the respondent banks rated ABN Amro in the top three (local and foreign).

In the bond market, the lack of benefits to dealers started becoming a source of concern in early 1999 (FM 26 February 1999, BD 27 July 2000), and ABN Amro retrenched its bond team and withdrew from this market in August 2001. In mid-2002, a senior ABN Amro manager wrote this off as part of the 'learning process' in South Africa, and insisted the capacity would be rebuilt, though the market view was that this would require a substantial premium on salaries (BD 9 July 2002).

Reversal in securities trading was most dramatic. In Dec 2000, just 28 months after the re-branding, the bank withdrew from the South African retail market, selling the private client business (which had 23,000 clients and ZAR2 billion in assets) to Gensec, an offshoot of the largest Afrikaans financial institution (BD 21 December 2000). In May 2001, the rest of the division was closed, with the loss of 35 jobs. At the time, there were an estimated 72 brokerages in the South African market, of which only 15 were profitable. The top eight firms, six of them foreign, held 85 per cent of the local market. ABN Amro was outside the top ten (BD 2 May 2001, FM 11 May 2001). Management argued in 2002 that by 2001 (before the global strategic shift discussed below), 60 per cent of South African equities trading was out of London, making it more efficient to use London-based research. But in closing, the bank lost its local partners: Deon Huysamer resigned when the private client business was sold, and Werner Stals after the securities trading division was closed.

Its reputation as an employer in the domestic financial services industry was severely dented (Kruger). This was most uncharacteristic, given the emphasis previously on being a good employer: 'the perception is that ABN Amro is a bank that's good to work for. ...That lets us attract good local people...We don't lose many people' (Evans 1997). Employment in South Africa had grown from 30 in 1996 to 75 in 1998 and 320 in 2000, but then shrank to 96 in 2002 and 45 in mid-2003. At this time, most of the ABN Amro building in the heart of Johannesburg's new financial district was rented out.

ABN Amro's profitability in South Africa was low. According to data from then-Country Head Werner Stals, South African (after-tax) profits in 1999 were less than 1 per cent of ABN Amro's global profits. In 2000, this dropped to below 0.5 per cent. The banking and leasing divisions each had profits of around ZAR4-5 million in 1999, and ZAR6-7 million in 2000, but the securities division went from profit of ZAR10 million in 1999, to losses of over ZAR2 million the following year (before the financial market downturn). These numbers seem extraordinarily low even in local currency terms, given the size of the banking assets (over ZAR3 billion) and the cost of acquisition of the fleet management division (ZAR500 million). The contribution to global earnings was further reduced by substantial ZAR depreciation from 1996.

Accounting for the Retreat: Strategic and Systemic Factors

By 2003, the bank's South African operation had limited visibility in the domestic market, its staff was small and earnings were negligible. There is no evidence of the original securities acquisition, or the fixed-income trading presence. Management now present the acquisition of HS as, in effect, part of a brownfield entry, arguing that the equity market link was a useful mechanism for expanding the bank's global network in both investment and corporate banking. But a brownfield implies a conscious strategic choice at entry, whereas ABN Amro South Africa clearly looks very different from what was envisaged in 1995, or even 1998. As already noted, the bank's initial loss of momentum is attributable to its abandonment of its standard entry strategy, which in turn was partly a consequence of regulatory constraints in South Africa on entering foreign banks. The ongoing retreat from the South African market is similarly due to a combination of the firm's global strategic choices and broader developments in the domestic and global financial services industry, in particular intensified competition in the domestic industry and the global financial downturn from mid-2000.

The bank underwent a fundamental strategic reorientation at the global level from May 2000, when a new chairman – Rijkman Groenink – was appointed. The organisational structure shifted from a geographic to a product basis, with three autonomous divisions established for wholesale clients, retail clients, and private clients and asset management respectively. In addition to the Netherlands, the bank identified the US Midwest and Brazil as 'home' markets for the retail division, and retail operations in 26 countries were closed. Wherever their location, staff now reported directly to division heads in either Amsterdam or London, and the independent authority of country managers was severely downgraded. 'The main driver for the re-organisation [was] the external perception of ABN Amro as indicated by the share price, rather than a belief within the bank that the [existing] structure was fundamentally wrong. ...compound average total shareholder return of 31.9 per cent per annum has been achieved throughout the last 5 years...[but the price : earnings ratio is] barely more than half of other banks in the sector' (FV 30 May 2000).

Characterised by top management as a bigger change than the 1991 merger, the restructuring aimed to create a network which is investor institution-focused, (capital) supply-driven, and vertically-integrated, in sum, intensive rather than extensive, and similar to those of banks in the first-tier financial centres. Groenink said that 'the bank no longer aimed to be all things to all people .... universal banking is dead within ABN Amro . . . [He] identified two main weaknesses: no focus on investor value as the ultimate driver . . . [and] the structure was too complex, [with] fuzzy responsibilities and no accountability' (FT 31 May 2000). A group of 20 'peer' banks in the US and Europe was explicitly identified, with the goal of putting ABN

Amro's shareholder return in the top five of the peer group by end-2004 (FV 17 August 2000). In mid-2003, the bank was at number 12 out of 20, and it had not been in the top 10 since January 2001.

The promotion of shareholder value up the list of priorities inevitably involved a relative downgrading both of customer service and of employee voice and security. ABN Amro management continue to insist that 'the total network philosophy remains important . . . our clients will decide where we are, not us . . .[but] if we come to the conclusion that we are number 33 on the banking list of a major global corporate, we think that we would both agree that there is no relationship. In the old days, corporates would have more than a hundred banks. Now they are looking for fewer but closer relationships' (Euromoney October 2001).

The South African securities and bond market divisions were clearly victims of the restructuring and securities trading in all emerging markets except China, India and Brazil is now run directly out of ABN Amro's London offices. Decision-making became much more centralised and country managers with a local orientation found their strategic approach rejected. Stals argued that 'value was destroyed by poor decisions at the centre'.

According to South African managers more supportive of the shift, the new structure makes it inappropriate to evaluate the bank on a country basis: 'the entire concept of a branch is gone...the focus now is on client profitability, and no longer on product profitability'. 'The bank is not interested in country market share, but in 'client's wallet' share'. The South African operation reports to the Wholesale Client Services unit (WCS), which is divided into five sectors on the basis of clients' industrial activity. Capital is allocated to clients centrally, and return per client must clear a globally-defined risk-adjusted hurdle rate. Risk management is done on a client basis, taking country and internal risk into account. As a result, profit earned in South Africa, however small within the overall bank picture, is not relevant, say local management: 'South African companies do a lot of varied business [with us] in Europe, though not in South Africa.'

It seems that the bank's global service network has lost its 'grounding' in South Africa, and its current operations appear more of a representative office, a 'listening post'. With local activities barely served, and client service managed abroad, it is hard to assess the value added by activities *in* South Africa. The distinction between direct investment and imports has become blurred, as often the case in services. Nonetheless, the board has decided to maintain the branch, rather than scale back to a representative office, because South Africa represents the bank's last remaining presence in Africa.

ABN Amro's attempt to abandon geographical structure can be contrasted with alternative approaches to vertically-integrated global service networks. A senior South Africa manager of another major (London-based) bank.[46] indicated that the South African operation is 'one hundred per cent' integrated into the global operations of his institution, which also uses global risk management and capital allocation procedures, which are 'very conservative with strict global procedures from which South Africa can't deviate.' However, clients are defined on a country basis, so that all services to a South African-based client are evaluated as 'South African product', even if the services were provided (and billed) outside South Africa. The relationship managers for all South African corporations are part of the bank's 'SA team', even if not physically based in South Africa. This bank thus distinguishes its internal market evaluation processes from accounting for tax and regulatory purposes. This bank has introduced many new products into its South African operations, using a thousand-strong international managers group on a short-term basis to train local employees in internal risk and credit procedures.

ABN Amro's strategic decisions were reinforced by the collapse of the 'dotcom' bubble which coincided almost exactly with the bank's strategy change. The added pressure on profitability reinforced the decision to focus on shareholder value, with several major international banks (particularly in Europe) starting to look for fresh capital (FT 27 November 2002). Necessary increases in loan loss provisions, tighter management of risk and cutting of costs were much easier to implement in a centralised, vertically-integrated network. Mid-size international banks like ABN Amro, which had tried to break into a range of high-margin, high-cost services in global competition with 'bulge bracket' banks like Citibank, Deutsche and JP Morgan Chase, were forced to cut back as the downturn deepened and their volumes could not support the high costs of these services, leaving them over-extended. The impact spread throughout the global network: operations in small markets such as South Africa became expendable early on (BD 9 July 2001), but later even large market activities had to be cut, such as investment banking in the US (BT 14 April 2002).

In South Africa, foreign banks were caught in a local cost squeeze in relation to the international pressures. The rapid influx of foreign banks from 1995 increased competition dramatically, but market growth failed to meet expectations. GDP growth between 1997 and 2002 averaged 2.3 per cent per annum, and privatisation, FDI acquisitions and 'Black Economic Empowerment' deals all slowed. The result was a heavily overtraded market, pushing margins to low, developed country, levels: South African banking margins of 3.42 per cent are comparable to the US (3.65 per cent), the UK (2.66 per cent) and Australia (2.78 per cent) (KPMG 2002), while brokerage commissions are now at 0.15 per cent for institutional clients, down from 0.35 per cent five years ago (FM 24 January 2003). The ZAR depreciation further cut returns in home currency terms.[47]

Modest revenue streams in South Africa are not offset by low costs. The regulatory requirement that foreign branches maintain their own balance sheet imposes a significant cost on South African operations. Externallysupplied capital carries a country risk premium due to South Africa's 'emerging market' rating. Even sovereign South African assets require 'full solvency' capital backing, demanding returns 75–100 basis points higher than margins allow. SA corporate hurdle rates within ABN Amro are at the same levels as US blue chips and 50 basis points higher than competitors for capital such as Central European companies.

Secondly, financial sector depth – part of the attraction for foreign banks – results in high operating expenses. The foreign banks' entry created skill shortages and high labour turnover in the sector and salaries costs rose. By 1998, foreign banks felt that 'expatriate employees [were] becoming cheaper than the locals' (Euromoney, September 1998), though relatively few expatriates seem to have been brought in. A 2001 survey reported that foreign and local financial services salaries were close to par in nominal terms, though living costs are far lower in Johannesburg (FM 25 May 2001). Before '9/11', the financial services industry had the highest pay structure in South Africa, even non-professional staff being paid more than elsewhere. According to a sector human resources consultant, banks would headhunt and pay whatever was demanded and the foreign banks tended to poach staff from each other. After '9/11', salaries stopped rising, but Citibank, the only bank still expanding in 2003, continued to pay a premium of 30–35 per cent to attract staff from rivals.

Facing both global and domestic cost pressures, many second-rank international banks have cut back or withdrawn entirely from South Africa since mid-2001, though ABN Amro is thought to have retrenched more South African staff than others (BR 14 November 2001).The list includes ING Barings, International Bank of Southern Africa (the local arm of Banque Paribas), CSFB, Sociètè Gènèrale, Credit Lyonnais and Merrill Lynch, which sold its bond dealing and private client business in November 2001, reducing employment from 230 to 90, even though it was in the top six South African brokerages. The first-rank banks – Citibank, JP Morgan Chase, Deutsche and HSBC – have been able to raise their global market shares in investment and corporate banking by maintaining high-cost international operations, and have maintained a strong presence in South Africa, though they have also come under some pressure (FM 24 January 2003).

The major domestic banks have reasserted their dominance in the sector, and are now in a very strong position competitively. The top five South African institutions controlled 86 per cent of total banking assets and 88 per cent of corporate loans at end-2001, after slipping back to 76 per cent of assets in 1998 (KPMG 2002). All but one second-tier domestic banks have either been absorbed or collapsed over the past 2 years, the number of South African banks dropping from 44 to 33 during 2001. Though the 'big five' domestics remain worried, about Citibank in particular, they believe they have 'seen off the foreign competition' (Euromoney, September 2002) and that they are relatively invulnerable to foreign takeover (BR 29 May 2003).

Because they are relatively small in the international arena (ranked between 146 and 331 globally on Tier 1 capital at end-2001), they have been protected from the gales of the global financial market downturn. Furthermore, the country and currency risk premium offer them some degree of protection in the domestic market, where their dominance of the local interbank market allows them to obtain funds cheaply. They have addressed high cost–income ratios by cutting back in the retail market via branch closures, and have thus far avoided the costly investments required to extend financial services to South Africa's large mass of poor people. However, they remain relatively unprofitable – average after-tax return on equity for the three years 2000-2002 was 9.2 per cent, while the CPI averaged just over 7 per cent – and concerned about slow market growth.

Impact on Development

Spillovers of technology, productivity and skills from foreign firms to local competitors, suppliers, customers and employees are generally used to motivate foreign investment, but it is notoriously hard to find strong empirical justification for their existence, and especially difficult when considering a single firm. However, ABN Amro have undertaken some specific training activities, and skills transfer would also have occurred in the context of ongoing operations. Research staff in ABN Amro's securities trading division participated in workshops and conferences with bank staff and were sent on at least one internal training course per annum in Europe. As part of the global research team, they also participated in joint projects with internationally-experienced colleagues (Kruger). On the banking side, ABN Amro worked to familiarise South African corporate treasurers with new products and approaches by holding training courses for clients run by ABN Amro staff brought in from abroad. In addition, local banks have drawn on ABN Amro expertise by seeking cooperation on projects in specific sectors where the Dutch bank is known to be strong, such as energy and telecoms.

More generally, it is argued that the entry of foreign banks and brokerages has improved efficiency in the banking and securities markets, by importing standards and quality measures from parent companies and developed-country markets in research, regulation and risk management. Foreign banks have also introduced new products to South Africa, such as warrants (introduced by the local Deutsche branch), derivatives in interest rates and currencies and asset securitisation. These have led to marginal reductions in the cost of capital. Though foreign bank pressures on the 'big 5' domestic banks led to reduced costs and increased efficiency, the level of competition now is arguably lower than five years ago. Cost-cutting was in part at the expense of domestic consumers, so the net welfare impact is unclear. As already noted, foreign bank entry led to a skills shortage and a 'once-off' rise in wages and salaries in the sector, even for non-professional staff. Again the consequences for overall costs and efficiency are unclear.

Conclusions

Several conclusions can be drawn. First, the standard distinction between market-seeking and resource-seeking motives for entry into foreign markets does not always apply in services, particularly producer services. There is often a more complex mix of motives between market-seeking and 'market-sustaining', that is, establishing a presence both to acquire new domestic clients in a target country but also to consolidate the firm's *existing* base of foreign clients trading with or operating in the target country.[48] As the foreign firm aims to create a global network, market conditions and growth of market share amongst domestic customers may not be the only consideration in the firm's strategic approach.

For these reasons, the drive to expand the network can dominate other considerations in the corporate entry strategy, leading to costly errors even in large corporations. This is illustrated by ABN Amro's abandonment of its emphasis on selecting the right management and ensuring a cultural fit. ABN Amro has not established the intended presence in South Africa, but it has expanded its customer base in existing European markets by picking up South African corporate clients, and has sustained its existing customer base of large multinational clients by offering services in South Africa.

Second, the case illustrates the limits of the 'global service network' model. An extensive network is extremely costly, requiring a presence in many small markets, and this cost structure pushes firms towards more intensive, centralised, structures. Furthermore, when service corporations with global networks face competitive pressures in major markets, the firm is able to cut back in less important markets, rather than where the pressures actually appeared. Thus, market-focused service corporations can react in similar 'footloose' fashion to resource-seeking manufacturing investors with commodity value chains. Incorporation into global networks is not an unambiguous benefit to the host country, notwithstanding improved access and efficiency.

Third, although foreign entry has further integrated South African *markets* into global financial markets, local financial institutions are not fully integrated: the domestic banks are still protected by country risk and by regulation, and competition in financial services has declined. The case study also confirms evidence from the FDI survey (chapter 7), which suggests that South African service firms have reacted vigorously to the threat posed by foreign entry.

Fourth, the domestic response is linked to the regulatory environment: an effective regulator shapes entry strategies of foreign investors and influences their prospects for success. But is the regulatory focus 'development', or simply the protection of domestic firms? In South Africa, foreign entry has contributed to an 'overdeveloped' financial services sector, that is, a sector where the top end of the market is high-tech, efficient and competitive, but at the bottom end services are underprovided and very costly to consumers.

References for South African Case Studies

ABN Amro, Annual Reports & other documents, www.abnamro.com

Adele Slotar, P-E Corporate Services (HR Consultants)

Alexander Krivosh, Testing engineer, Ziton

Anon, Senior Manager, Johannesburg Office of London Bank

BD, Business Day (Johannesburg), www.bday.co.za

Behr (2001), *Annual Report 2000*, Stuttgart: Behr GmbH.

BNA, Business News Americas, www.BNamericas.com

BR, Business Report (Johannesburg), www.iol.co.za

BT, Sunday Times Business Times (Johannesburg), www.suntimes.co.za

De Vries, J., W. Vroom and T. de Graaf (1999) Wereldwijd Bankieren [Worldwide Banking]: *ABN Amro 1824-1999,* Amsterdam: ABN Amro.

Don Glass, Managing Director, Ziton

Elize Kruger, economist, formerly with Huysamer Stals & ABN Amro

EST, Edwards Systems Technologies, www.est.net/est_history.html

Euromoney (1998-2003), various issues.

Evans, G. (1997), 'The Kalff interview', Euromoney, October.

FM, Financial Mail (Johannesburg), www.fm.co.za

FT, Financial Times (London), www.ft.com

FV, Futurevantage (Germany), www.futurevantage.co.za

Gavin Simkins, Financial Director, Behr SA

Greg Els, Senior Manager, ABN Amro SA

JSE, Johannesburg Stock Exchange, www.jse.co.za

Jurgen Schwalbe, CE, International Bank of Southern Africa

KPMG, *Africa Banking Survey 2002* (www.kpmg.co.za).

Loet van Kniphorst, SA Country Manager, ABN Amro

Margaret Macfarlane, co-founder, Ziton

NGK Insulators (2000), *Annual Report*, Nagoya: *NGK*.

Nordas, H (2001), 'South Africa: A Developing Country and Net Outward Investor', mimeo, SNF, Bergen, Norway.

Posthuma, A. (1995), 'Restructuring and Changing Market Conditions in the Brazilian Auto Components Industry', Unpublished paper, Economic Commission for Latin America and the Caribbean, Industrial and Technological Development Unit.

PriceWaterhouseCoopers, *Strategic and Emerging Issues in South African Banking*, annual publication, published each year since 1996 (www.pwcglobal.com)

Professional Management Review (1997-2001), various issues.

Republic of South Africa, (2001), Current Developments in the Automotive Industry, Department of Trade and Industry: Pretoria.

Richard Chase, Operations Manager

SA Reserve Bank www.resbank.co.za

Steve Bates, Managing Director, NGK SA

Ted Waldburger, Managing Director, Behr SA

The Economist (London), www.economist.com

Waldburger, T. (2000), '*Behr*, a Multinational Supplier's Experience in South Africa', unpublished report, *Behr* (SA).

Werner Stals, then-CE, ABN Amro SA

Ziton, www.ziton.com

9. Foreign Direct Investment in Vietnam

Ha Thanh Nguyen, Hung Vo Nguyen and Klaus E. Meyer

ECONOMIC OVERVIEW

Macroeconomics

Vietnam, in 1986, embarked on a path of reform, known as 'doi moi' (renewal), a comprehensive change by restructuring the economy from a planned economy to a market economy. Since then, the Vietnamese economy had shown a remarkable performance as one of the fastest growing economies in the world. GDP per capita increased from US$100 in 1990 to US$448 in 2002; real GDP based on the constant prices of 1994 increased from VND109.2 trillion in 1986 to VND313.1 trillion in 2002. Despite a global economic recession in 2001, real GDP growth in 2002 was 6.4 per cent. Annual inflation fell from 67.5 per cent in 1990 to 0.4 per cent in 2001, and 4 per cent in 2003 and the fiscal deficit fell from 6.7 per cent of GDP in 1990 to 3.5 per cent of GDP in 2002 (CIEM 2002, ADB 2004).

Vietnamese businesses include three distinct categories: state enterprises (SOEs), domestic private enterprises (PEs) and foreign investment enterprises (FIEs). Agriculture and industry still had an important role in the economy, and in recent years, the services industry had emerged as an important sector. SOEs have been growing slowly, yet their relative contribution to gross industrial added value had been declining in recent years, from 52.6 per cent in 1994 to 41.3 per cent in 2001, due to the rapid growth of PEs and FIEs. PEs, which include small-scale industry such as handicrafts and household businesses, accounted for approximately 21.5 per cent of Vietnam's industrial gross added value in 1994 and 21.8 per cent in 2001. The fastest growth had been in FIEs, whose contribution to Vietnam's industrial gross output increased from 25.9 per cent in 1994 to 36.9 per cent in 2001.

International Trade

Before 'doi moi' in 1986, Vietnam's international trade was restricted to commodities exchange programmes with other, former Socialist countries. High tariffs and numerous non-tariff barriers governed the trade. During the economic reform, international trade had become an increasingly important part of the Vietnamese economy. In order to promote trade, Vietnam had implemented trade liberalisation, including tariff reductions and other measures designed to relax import and export restrictions. In addition, Decision 46 of the Prime Minister, which became effective in May 2001, provides a roadmap for future trade liberalisation. This Decision has led to a reduction of non-tariff barriers and more transparent and predictable import and export regulations.

Further trade liberalisation will result from bilateral and multilateral commitments. Currently, Vietnam had signed bilateral trade agreements with more than 60 countries, including a treaty with the USA that came into force in December 2001. Vietnam is also formally committed to implement reform to integrate into The ASEAN Free Trade Area (AFTA), with detailed plans for reducing tariff rates and removing other non-tariff barriers. Vietnam expects to fulfil all the obligations necessary to substantially comply with AFTA by 2006, and to completely comply by 2010. Vietnam negotiated accession to the WTO, with the objective of entering the WTO as early as 2005. Moreover, the quantitative restrictions on steel and edible oil were removed by the end of 2002 to fulfil commitments to the IMF.

As a result of liberalisation, international trade had been expanding rapidly since 1990. Exports grew at an average annual rate of 11.2 per cent for the period from 1990 to 2002, (ADB 2003). Total exports reached US$16.7 billion in 2002 and total imports US$16.200 million in the same year. Vietnam exports crude oil, textiles, footwear, seafood, and agricultural commodities such as rice, coffee, vegetables, rubber etc., while it imports oil and gasoline, travel vehicles, fertilizers and other chemicals for agriculture, steel, plastic in primary form, and various kinds of consumer goods. Export earnings from the 10 largest export commodities account for 72 per cent, with crude oil alone accounting for 20 per cent of export earnings.

The FIE sector emerges as an important exporter. Its share in total exports increased from 27 per cent in 1995 to 47 per cent in 2002. This trend in accordance with a boom in export-led FDI projects, including Taiwanese projects in Binh Duong and Dong Nai provinces.

The majority of increased imports were inputs for production, such as raw materials and machines and equipment, whilst the proportion of consumer goods declined dramatically from 15.2 per cent of imports in 1995 to only 5.1 per cent in 2002. Amongst the imported goods, materials accounted for a large share (62.9 per cent in 2002), reflecting the fact that some export industries in Vietnam were processing imported materials such as textiles, footwear, and electronics, and took advantage of cheap labour and availability of land. The FIE sector was also a significant importer, accounting for 30.8 per cent of total imports, however as this was much less than its share of exports, this sector was a net exporter.

Human Resources

In 2002, Vietnam had a workforce of 40.7 million people over the age of 15, of which women accounted for 49.4 per cent. The workforce was distributed unevenly with 23.9 per cent in urban areas and 76.1 per cent in rural areas. Correspondingly, only 15.4 per cent were employed in the industry-construction sector and 60.7 per cent in agriculture.

The general education level of the workforce was quite high with illiteracy of only 3.8 per cent. However, this was distributed unevenly between regions. The labour force was highest educated in the Red River Delta which includes Hanoi, and in the South East Region which includes Ho Chi Minh City, while the levels of education were lowest in remote regions.

Whilst the general education level of the workforce was considered to be relatively high, its professional qualifications were not. The majority of the workforce did not have professional qualification (83 per cent) and for those who had, for many it was in the form of an informal 'professional' qualification (without certification). It was reported that many employers had to spend a great deal of effort and energy retraining their workforce at all levels. One US software company estimated that it took about 4-6 months to train a distinguished graduate to work effectively. A motorcycle part-maker reported that it had taken more than six months to reduce the deficiency rate of a new worker from 50 per cent to 2 or 3 per cent.

In response to that situation, many efforts were made in recent years to improve the professional qualifications of the workforce at both national and local level. Some provinces were willing to cover the whole or part of training costs incurred by FDI companies as a means to attract foreign investment into their province, with a shift in the structure of the education system giving more attention paid to professional training. These policy measures were hoped to upgrade the professional qualifications in the workforce to the levels expected by foreign investors.

From State to Market

The establishment of a modern enterprise system was an important objective of Vietnam's overall reform programme. Traditionally, SOEs played a leading role in Vietnam's economy. Vietnam had approximately 5,700 SOEs, employing 1.7 million people in various industries. SOEs contributed 40.5 per cent to GDP in 1997 and 38.3 per cent in 2002. However, most SOEs suffered from inefficiency, outdated technology, non-competitive products, poor management and an inability to respond to market demands. The

Government estimated that about 40 per cent of SOEs were profitable on a stand-alone basis, 40 per cent break even and 20 per cent consistently incurred losses. In order to realise the goals of the 'doi moi' policy, an SOEs restructuring programme had been initiated with assistance from the World Bank, Asian Development Bank and other foreign donors. The principal objective of the SOE reform included:

- Restructuring SOEs, primarily though equitisation, a multi-step approach in restructuring SOEs. For political reasons, the term 'equitisation' is preferred over privatisation;
- Reducing the dependence of the overall economy on SOEs and the dependence of SOEs on Government's support; and
- Restructuring the non-performing loans of SOEs.

Equitisation converts SOEs into joint-stock companies. This involves the issue of new shares by an SOE, or the sale, by the government, of an equity stake in an SOE to outside or inside investors. As a result of the restructuring efforts, the total number of SOEs decreased from about 12,300 in 1990 to 5,700 in 2001. However, the remaining SOEs grew sharply in terms of both capitalisation and gross revenues. In the 1997/2001 period, 886 SOEs were equitised, mostly in the trading, services and manufacturing sectors. They were believed to have now become more profitable.

The Government made commitments to multilateral lenders regarding the pace of SOE reform, concurrently with a transparent and competitive legal environment for SOE operations. Direct subsidies are only provided to SOEs in public services, particularly in the agricultural sector. However, indirect subsidies are still available for SOEs in the form of preferential loans, energy cost subsidies, and subsidies for interest payments.

The legal environment for small and medium sized enterprises (SMEs) had been improved to some extent and this was expected to continue. Private businesses were historically not allowed and were subject to significant discretionary restrictions in their operations. Under the Enterprise Law of 1999, numerous discretionary licensing requirements imposed by administrative agencies had been replaced by more common licences that could eventually be replaced by a system of legal supervision. The government thus significantly shifted its policy towards the private sector by supporting the establishment and operation of private enterprises. To implement this policy, Vietnam intends to reform and liberalise the non-state economic sector, principally by:

- Enhancing the legal environment for SMEs;
- Increasing access to capital for SMEs;
- Establishing an institution to promote SMEs; and

- Continuing trade promotion and export development efforts.

Consequently, about 34,000 new enterprises with registered capital equivalent to US$2.1 billion have been registered under the Enterprise Law of 1999, a huge number compared to the numbers in the past.

Fiscal and Financial System

Fiscal policy underwent an important reform that aimed at delegating more autonomy to local governments. This autonomy included responsibility to collect revenue and self-finance for local expenditures. This meant local authorities had more responsibility to balance their own budgets. Amendments of the Budget Law had been prepared to improve the budget and the public debt management system, as well as to increase transparency in enforcing the fiscal policy.

The tax system in Vietnam had also undergone a significant reform. The period from 1986 to 1995 was characterised by remarkable efforts to make taxes a significant source of budget revenue. The following period was characterised by refinements of the tax system with the introduction of VAT, company income tax, and individual income tax. Further tax reforms are expected to include a gradual reduction of tax rates, more uniform tax ranges and improvements in the tax collection mechanism.

The banking sector includes the State Bank of Vietnam, six state-owned commercial banks (SOCB), various joint-stock commercial banks, foreign bank branches, and foreign-invested joint-venture banks. The goal of the banking sector reform was to strengthen the financial position of, and public trust in, the banking system, and bring it closer to international standards. Banking sector reform included:

- Reforming the regulatory framework for banking with increased transparency;
- Promoting risk-based commercial lending;
- Recapitalising and restructuring SOCBs and joint-stock banks;
- Improving the balance sheets of banks by restructuring non-performing loans;
- Separating policy and commercial lending;
- Improving accounting standards;
- Liberalising interest rates and foreign exchange transactions; and
- Modernising banking technology.

The government also planned to reform the organisation of the State Bank, including the reorganisation of State Bank departments to suit their functional activities.

INSTITUTIONS GOVERNING FDI

The first Law on Foreign Investment in Vietnam was passed by the National Assembly of Vietnam on 29 December 1987. This law was amended several times before being replaced by a new Law on Foreign Investment in Vietnam in 1996. Recently, that was amended on 9 June 2000. The law provides general regulation for setting up a foreign invested company in Vietnam, as well as for its operation. More detailed regulations and FDI incentives are specified in various kinds of documents, at both central and local government level.

In the 1987 law, a private organisation alone was not allowed to enter a joint venture with a foreign partner. It had to have joint capital with a state-owned organisation to be acceptable, but since 1992, private organisations are entitled to set up a joint venture with a foreign partner.

Regulation of Investment Mode

Vietnamese FDI law considers three modes of FDI: (i) business cooperation contract (BCC); (ii) joint venture; and (iii) 100 per cent foreign-owned. In the late 1980s and early 1990s, high transaction and establishment costs made the 100 per cent foreign-owned option prohibitively expensive in many sectors, leaving JVs as the only realistic choice for many investors.

From 2000, enterprises with foreign-owned capital, and parties to BCCs, have been allowed to change the mode of investment, and to split, merge and consolidate enterprises. Recently, there have been several cases of a joint venture being converted to a 100 per cent foreign-owned enterprise, although the bureaucratic procedures are complex. In these cases, foreign investors in a JV acquired the share of its local partner to make their own firm.

Procedures for granting Investment Licences

Before 1996, pre-licensing evaluation procedures applied to all foreign investment projects. During the evaluation process, the Ministry of Planning and Investment (MPI) could request any 'necessary' documents apart from those stipulated by law. The time it took to acquire an investment was supposed to be three months from the date of receiving a completed application dossier. However, in reality this usually took much longer, possibly even years.

Since 1996, procedures for granting investment licences have been gradually streamlined, and authority to issue investment licences for projects, up to specified sizes, had been delegated to local governments.

Before 1996, many issues, including many day-to-day operation issues in the joint venture, had to be decided on the principle of unanimity by the Board. Since 2000, the scope of issues needing to be approved on the principle of unanimity had been reduced significantly. Now, only key issues of (1) appointment, dismissal of the General Manager (GM), or the first deputy GM and (2) amendments of, and additions to, the Charter of the joint venture require the unanimous decision of the board of directors.

Land Lease

Access to real estate is a major concern for foreign investors as they cannot buy land as they might in other countries. Since the amended FDI Law of 2000, the Vietnamese side bears the responsibility for site clearance, including the necessary compensation payments. More precisely, nowadays, in those joint ventures where the Vietnamese party contributes capital in the form of the value of the land-use right, the Vietnamese party shall be responsible for site clearance, compensation and completion of procedures to obtain the land-use right. In cases where the state leases out land, these responsibilities fall to the provincial People's Committee wherever the investment project is located. Previously, the foreign investor might have had to do all this to obtain land.

Special Economic Zones

Vietnam had created different types of industrial zones that offer special investment conditions for foreign investors. Export processing zones (EPZ), industrial zones (IZ), hi-tech zones. The first regulation on EPZs was issued by the Government in 1991. An EPZ specialises in the production of goods for export and in the provision of services for the production of export goods and export activities. It had specific geographic boundaries and is open for both foreign and domestic investors. Enterprises operating within EPZs enjoy a profit tax rate at 10 per cent, 15 per cent in respect of production and service enterprises.

IZs have been established since 1994. An IZ is a concentrated zone specialising in the production of industrial goods and services for industrial goods production. Enterprises operating within IZs enjoyed profit tax rates of 18 per cent in respect of production, 12 per cent if exporting at least 80 per cent of its products, and 22 per cent in respect of service enterprises. From 1997, these rates are 15, 10 and 20 per cent respectively. There may be EPZs and export processing enterprises in an IZ and these enterprises shall enjoy tax rates applied to EPZs.

A hi-tech zone is a zone where hi-technology industrial enterprises and units providing hi-technology development services, including scientific technological research and development, training, and other related services, are concentrated. There may be an EPZ in a hi-tech zone. The profit tax rate applied to enterprises operating in the hi-tech zone is 10 per cent after an eight-year tax holiday from the first year in which the company is profitable.

Regulation of Recruitment and Salary

In the late 1980s and early 1990s, all foreign-invested enterprises had to recruit their workforce through labour supplying centres. In the late 1990s, although the procedures for recruiting employees had been simplified, the stipulation for recruiting employees through labour supplying centres still created disadvantages for foreign-invested enterprises. From 2003, foreign-invested enterprises have been entitled to recruit their employees directly.

Taxation

From 1987, the enterprises with foreign invested capital and foreign partners, operating under business cooperation contracts, were liable to pay a corporate income tax ranging from 15 to 25 per cent of earned profits. From 1996, these enterprises have been subject to corporate income tax at 25 per cent on the profit earned. If the investment was located in those priority areas, this rate was 20 per cent. If the investment satisfied certain investment promotion criteria, the rate was only 15 per cent, and if the investment was strongly encouraged, the rate was 10 per cent. These enterprises were exempted from corporate income tax for a maximum period of two years, commencing from the first profit-making year, and were entitled to a 50 per cent reduction of corporate income tax for a maximum period of two successive years. Since 1996, in cases where investment is strongly encouraged, exemption from corporate income tax had been allowed for a maximum period of eight years.

When transferring profits abroad, a foreign investor had to pay an amount of tax equal to 3, 5 or 7 per cent of profits transferred. This imposition was lower than the rates of 5, 7 and 10 per cent payable under the 1996 law, and lower again than the rates of from 5 to 10 per cent under the law of 1987. Vietnamese citizens permanently residing overseas who invested in Vietnam were entitled to a holding tax rate of 3 per cent of the profits transferred abroad, marginally lower than the 5 per cent imposed on other foreign investors.

Banking

Under the 1987 FDI Law, an enterprise with foreign invested capital could open Vietnamese and foreign currency bank accounts at the Bank for Foreign Trade of Vietnam, or at a branch of a foreign bank established in Vietnam. This would need approval from the State Bank of Vietnam (SBV).

In the 1992 Law, these enterprises were able to open bank accounts at any banks operating in Vietnam, and could open loan capital accounts at overseas banks with approval from the SBV. From the year 2000, in special cases approved by the SBV, an enterprise with foreign-owned capital was permitted to open an overseas account, and mortgage assets attached to the land and use the value of the land-use rights as security for borrowing loans from credit institutions permitted to operate in Vietnam.

Informal institutions

As the formal above-mentioned institutions governing FDI have been established quite recently, it is no surprise that informal institutions have significant effects on the FDI in Vietnam. Some of most notable informal institutions are the following.

First, there was a strong departmentalisation and a high degree of centralisation, which is the legacy of several decades of the command centrally planning economy. As a result, although the official FDI policies and regulations had been considerably liberalised and decentralised, it was still costly and time-consuming, especially for small investors, to do business in Vietnam. Therefore, in provinces where such top provincial leaders actively worked to implement streamlined FDI regulations and promotion, for example in Dong Nai, FDI inflow was higher.

Second, there was a preference at all levels of the Government for Western European and North American investment, with the belief that it brought along more advanced technology and management. However, most FDI continued to come from Asian countries where businesses maintained personal and professional networks with Vietnam.

Third, the attitude toward merger and acquisition by many government officials and some businesses was still negative. For them, it was the result of some 'unfair' competition. At least, it was not in the interest of weak, failing businesses, a legacy of the many years of egalitarian society. It was partly because of this that many foreign investors chose a greenfield investment.

TRENDS OF FDI

Joint Venture versus Greenfield

In Vietnam, there were effectively only two main modes of entry, greenfield and joint venture. Acquisitions of partial stakes in existing firms had been permitted since 1994, yet due to the lack of supporting institutions, they remained rare and almost always between foreign investors. Thus, the statistics did not record them as new FDI projects. Local sources moreover often referred to certain forms of non-equity cooperation as foreign investment, but this was not FDI as defined by, for example the OECD, and thus not a subject of this study.

JV was the dominant mode of investment in the early 1990s, while greenfield was the preferable choice later on. This pattern had been reversed over time. In 1991, more than 80 per cent of FDI projects were JVs; while in

2000, more than 80 per cent of newly established FDI projects were greenfield. However, the average size of the new greenfield projects was small.

Investors

In terms of a cumulative number of projects in 2002, Asian investors were dominant in Vietnam with more than three out of four projects according to official statistics. Taiwanese investors were leading (21.4 per cent), followed by Japanese (8.6 per cent) and Koreans (12.2 per cent). ASEAN investors also accounted for a large proportion (14 per cent). Europeans were important investors and accounted for 16.9 per cent, while North American investors made up a moderate proportion of 5.3 per cent.

Since 1998, Taiwanese investors have become most active. They accounted for more than 40 per cent of new FDI projects in 2000 and fell back to 26 per cent in 2002. The proportion of Japanese investors was much higher in the 1995 to 1997 period, compared to other periods. The proportion of Hong Kong investors was high in the early 1990s, but fell to a moderate level in later years. The share of Korean investors had been at a more stable level over time.

In terms of mode of entry, greenfield was very popular among Taiwanese investors. This popularity was also observed among Japanese and North American investors but at a lower level. In the case of Taiwanese investors, many came to Vietnam when greenfield was more feasible and located in the Ho Chi Minh City area where favourable conditions were provided by the local authorities.

A large proportion of investors invested in basic consumer and intermediate goods and machinery. However this was more obvious with Taiwanese and Korean investors. The proportion of European, North American and other Asian investors that invested in business services (including IT) was higher than with the other investors. The proportion of projects in trade and tourism was highest for Hong Kong investors.

Location

Over time, Ho Chi Minh City and environs are still leading in attracting FDI projects into their provinces. With respect to the number of new FDI projects, the trend of FDI locating in these provinces, had, in fact, determined the FDI trend for the whole country. The number of new projects coming to Hanoi is more stable over time. Ho Chi Minh City (HCMC) and environs became the most favourable destination for Taiwanese investors, while Hanoi attracted more European investors. Japanese and Korean investors did not seem to have any particular favourite location.

While manufacturing accounted for most of the FDI projects in HCMC and HCMC areas, the proportion of project in trade and tourism and business services was exceptionally high for Hanoi. The primary and trade and tourism sectors also accounted for a relatively large entry of FDI projects in other provinces, including many remote provinces.

FDI SURVEY IN VIETNAM

Table 9.1 Sector and size of FDI firms, Vietnam (No. of firms)

Local sectors	Employment in FDI firms					
	10-50	51-100	101-250	251-1000	>1000	Total
Primary	0	3	2	0	0	5
Basic consumer goods	4	5	11	20	6	46
Intermediate goods	15	11	8	11	1	46
Machinery & equipment	4	2	3	4	0	13
Infrastructure & construction	5	4	2	2	0	13
Trade, tourism & recreation	1	2	1	1	0	5
Financial & business services	6	5	2	1	0	14
Total	35	32	29	39	7	142

To further investigate the pattern and contribution of FDI in Vietnam, we conducted our own survey. The base population had been defined as FDI establishments that were set up during the period from 1991 to 2000, with at least 10 employees and registered capital of at least US$100,000. We used the database of the Ministry of Planning and Investment, but excluded contractual co-operations, such as those in the oil and gas industry. This yielded a population of 2,454 FDI establishments. We used random sampling to construct a list of 900 firms, of which 731 actually had usable contact information, and were contacted for an interview.

We expended considerable efforts to get a large return rate from major business centres, and across groups of foreign investors. The questionnaire was translated into Vietnamese, and back into English, as is common practice in management research. Moreover, we prepared a Chinese translation using a similar procedure to target firms with Chinese origins, as they are known to be reluctant to complete questionnaires in English or Vietnamese. It was in most cases necessary to contact firms in person, by meeting face-to-face or by telephone. This process led to 171 completed questionnaires, 23.4 per cent of the firms contacted. Comparing the base population and the sample, we could confirm that the sample is representative by all major criteria, including country of origin, industry, location, mode and registering authority in Vietnam.

Introduction to the Firms in the Sample

The survey confirms that FDI in Vietnam is strongly concentrated on the manufacturing sector, and this is reflected in our survey dataset. Most investors are in the light industries, which for this analysis are divided into basic consumer goods and intermediate products (Table 9.1). Few investors are in service industries, as Vietnam opened up manufacturing sectors earlier, and for many services the local demand is low due to the comparatively low level of income. There are only a handful of firms in financial or IT related services, which are all included in financial and business services. Two pharmaceutical firms are included among intermediate products along with other chemical industry firms as most sales are to government authorities or other businesses. Hence, there is little FDI in typical high-tech sectors in Vietnam at this stage.[49]

Table 9.1 reports the variation of the size of the local firms across sectors. The largest firms are mostly in consumer goods industries, i.e. 6 out of 7 firms with over 1000 employees. In contrast, service FDI is often small. FDI in infrastructure is relatively small reflecting the fact that many investors in this sector employ local subcontractors for their operations. The majority of FDI firms in Vietnam had capital stock of less than US$20 million.

Distribution among sectors did not fluctuate much over the decade, albeit the relative importance of FDI in intermediate goods and in business services increased slightly. Recent projects have much smaller registered capital than in earlier years. In terms of total registered capital, 1996 was a peak, and it dropped dramatically thereafter.

The survey data confirm that FDI was strongly concentrated on the two main business centres in the North and in the South, Ho Chi Minh City and Hanoi, and provinces in their immediate vicinity. This unequal distribution, and the different development between the North and the South was of considerable concern to policy-makers and business people in Vietnam. The destinations within Vietnam were relatively stable despite the volatility of overall in inflows. Over time, there had been a trend towards the provinces neighbouring the cities of Hanoi and HCMC. However provinces further away from the traditional business centres continued to receive little FDI.

Introduction to the Investors

In Vietnam, Asian investors dominated, accounting for more than 3 out of 4 FDI projects. They took advantage of lower psychic distance, which facilitates marketing and operations, as well as lower transportation costs and, compared to the USA, less complex political relationships between countries. The home countries varied little across sectors, except that North American FDI is concentrated on business services with information technology and insurance companies, possibly a long-term effect of the trade embargo lifted in 1994 – yet the absolute numbers are too small for more detailed inferences (Table 9.2).

Table 9.2 Sector by home country region, Vietnam (No. of firms)

Sector	North America	Europe	Asia Pacific	Other	Total
Primary	0	1	4	0	5
Basic consumer goods	0	9	43	1	53
Intermediate goods	1	8	41	0	50
Machinery & equipment	1	1	14	0	16
Infrastructure & construction	1	4	8	1	14
Trade, tourism & recreation	0	0	3	1	4
Financial & business services	5	3	15	1	24
Total	8	26	128	4	166

Within Asia, Taiwan, Japan, Korea, and Hong Kong were the main investors. In the sample, Taiwan alone accounted for 25 per cent of projects, with 16, 15 and 7 per cent for Japan, Korea and Hong Kong respectively (Figure 9.1).

The development of FDI over time indicated that there had been a peak in 1995, and a subsequent decline even before the Asian crisis of 1997. The data show a slight increase in the year 2000, which corresponds to a similar modest increase shown in official records. The first peak was particularly noticeable for Japanese firms and for ASEAN firms. A wave of Japanese FDI in 1995/1996, was followed by a sharp decline thereafter, with a small recovery in 2000. Hong Kong firms had been more active before 1995, while Taiwanese investors had been growing gradually in numbers. European investment had been more stable over time with a slight anti-cyclical tendency, that is Europeans participated less in the 1995 boom.

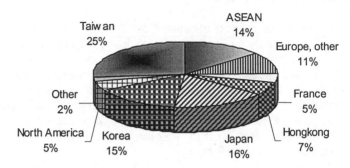

Figure 9.1 Distribution by home country

Foreign investors in Vietnam were overwhelmingly small and medium size firms, with few very large firms (Table 9.3). The median employment of the parent firm was about 2,000 employees. Across sectors we find that FDI in business services came from, on average, slightly larger firms, while light-manufacturing FDI included many small parent firms (Table 9.3). Taiwanese parent firms were often very small, whereas some European and North American parent firms employed more than 100,000 persons worldwide.

Table 9.3 Parent worldwide employment by sector (No. of firms)

	Parent size (worldwide employment)				
	<1,000	1,001-10,000	10,001-100,000	>100,000	Total
Primary	1	—	—	1	2
Basic consumer goods	17	13	6	1	37
Intermediate goods	16	12	8	—	36
Machinery & equipment	3	5	5	2	15
Infrastructure & construction	1	2	2	2	7
Trade, tourism & recreation	—	1	—	—	1
Financial & business Services	2	7	7	—	16
Total	40	40	28	6	114

Correspondingly, many investors had a very high proportion of their global business in Vietnam. As a corollary of having many small parent firms, the local affiliate was often relatively important for the parent. The relative size of the Vietnamese operations showed a bimodal distribution with more than a fifth of the investors reporting more than 20 per cent of their turnover in Vietnam. This contrasted with the pattern observed in Egypt and South Africa, but resembled the pattern found in India (though there were fewer individuals as investors). Hence, many FDI projects in Vietnam resembled entrepreneurial firms, or small and medium size firms, rather than the large multinational firms of the FDI literature.

This included firms, notably with Taiwan or Hong Kong origins, that appeared specifically set up to operate in Vietnam, and FDI owned by individuals rather than parent firms. More than half of the Taiwanese investors had more than 20 per cent of their turnover through the Vietnamese affiliates, which included about eight firms owned by individuals rather than firms. On the other hand, Japanese and Korean firms were most likely to have only a relatively small operation in Vietnam.

Local policy-makers were concerned about the small size of investment. Following continuous efforts to improve the investment environment in Vietnam, the country had expected investments from large multinational firms. In fact, a recent study considered FDI environment in Vietnam quite competitive relative to other countries in the region. This had however so far not led to increased FDI capital inflows, contrary to predictions by some policy advisory organisations.

R&D intensity of the parent firms was generally low, but higher for light manufacturing compared to service industries. For advertising intensity a similar but weaker pattern could be observed. Low advertisement expenditure in the manufacturing industry reflected the fact that many investors were sub-contractors for larger companies and their investment in Vietnam served their production network in the region.

Most investors in Vietnam had other operations in emerging Asian economies, which may have included their country of origin. However, there were very few investors that had experience on other continents. Some French, Japanese and Australian investors engaged in their first-ever FDI in an emerging market in Vietnam. International experience was especially low among manufacturers of basic consumer goods.

The pattern of global experience and diversification of the parent firms showed that late entrants were all small focused firms with little international business experience. On the other hand, large multinational firms, which we could call global players, seemed to have lost interest in new FDI in Vietnam. This also strengthens the argument that new investors often were entrepreneurial firms and businesses relocating production because of rising costs in their home country.

In concluding the review of investors, there were very few 'global players' among the foreign investors in Vietnam. Many of the investors were not only small but had little international experience outside Asia. The median investor had other overseas affiliates in only two other countries, which was far lower than the values for the other countries in this study. There was little variation of investors across sectors of industry, with small differences between light-manufacturing and service industries. However, we noticed some features with substantial variation across countries of origin:

- Taiwanese investors were small but plentiful, often with high export orientation. Their location tended to follow earlier Taiwanese FDI, notably to HCMC and surrounding provinces.
- Japanese and Korean investors included both big multinationals and small firms. They also attracted their traditional parts and components makers to invest in Vietnam.
- ASEAN and Hong Kong businesses appeared to be neighbours expanding into Vietnam, yet the numbers may include FDI, particularly from Singapore, Hong Kong and Malaysia, that was undertaken by regional headquarters of MNCs from Europe or America. To the extent this was evident from the data, we have reclassified the observations to the ultimate headquarter as requested in the questionnaire.
- The French lead among European investors. They mainly invested in light industry.
- North Americans can best be described as 'non-investors' with only eight firms, of which five were in business services.

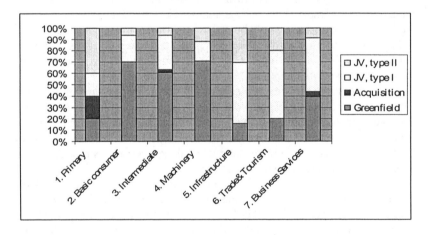

Figure 9.2 Entry modes by industry, Vietnam

Entry Mode Choice

In Vietnam, there were effectively only two main modes of entry, greenfield and joint venture. Our results corresponded to other studies and official statistics that distinguished only between JV and wholly owned firms. In the early 1990s JVs accounted for more than 9 out of 10 business licences, yet the relative number of greenfield projects had been steadily increasing. In 1998 for the first time more licences were issued to greenfield ventures than to JVs.

This trend is related to the liberalisation of FDI regulation in Vietnam. As mentioned earlier, 100 per cent foreign ownership was permitted, only on a case-by-case approval basis, which created transaction costs that were prohibitively high in some sectors in the early 1990s. These costs have been reduced over time and thus the share of greenfield projects had increased.

In Vietnam, we distinguish two types of joint ventures. The type I is what is commonly called a JV, a new firm established with contributions by both partners. The JV type II is a venture where the local firm contributes its existing assets to the JV. The local firms continues as a legal entity, yet primarily as a shell company owning the shares in the joint venture. The three cases studies of this research illustrated the different uses of joint ventures (Chapter 10). In 1993 Carlsberg established a brewery joint venture that in most ways resembled a normal joint venture where both firms contributed assets, and the JV was run and controlled jointly. Yet both firms developed their other business activities independently. Honda established a joint venture to manufacture motorcycles with a local partner that mainly contributed land use rights, but was not actively involved in the running of the JV. These two ventures would be classified as JV type I. On the other hand, ABB formed a JV with a local firm, which transferred all existing assets and liabilities to the JV. ABB was in control of most operating management issues, but local stakeholders could, by way of the local JV partner firm, influence strategic issues. In all three cases the local partner was a state-owned firm.

Across sectors, it appeared that JVs were more common in service sectors and greenfield projects in manufacturing sectors (Figure 9.2). Across provinces, greenfield had been particular common in the provinces neighbouring HCMC, while JV had been more common in the more remote 'other' provinces.

Resources for Success

We asked respondents, which resources would be most crucial for their competitiveness. The priority of resources showed considerable variation across sectors, but no clear pattern emerged (Figure 9.3). In the basic consumer goods industry, brands were relatively unimportant, which may have been due to a large number of textile and clothing firms that were mainly subcontractors of an international retailer. As a result, production capacity was more important than brands for these investors. In the intermediate goods industries, equity and distribution networks were most important, in the machinery industry, machinery was important, while

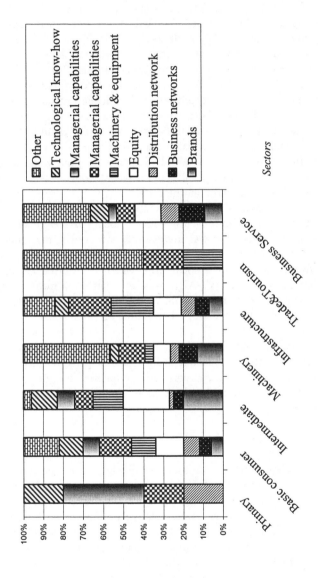

Figure 9.3 Key resources for successful performance, Vietnam (firms which ranked resource as the first choice)

Table 9.4 Percentage of Vietnamese firms that selected the resource as being of primary importance (by source of resource)

Resources for success: Source of resource:	Brand	Business network	Distribution network	Equity	Machinery & equipment	Managerial cap.	Marketing cap.	Technological know-how
Local parent firm	13	15	23	11	4	11	13	11
Foreign parent firm	78	53	46	76	78	67	44	72
Local source	2	21	23	4	9	14	20	11
Foreign source	7	11	0	9	7	6	14	6
Other	0	0	11	0	0	0	9	0

marketing and technology was considered less important. In businesses services, managerial capabilities were most important.

In acquisitions, managerial capabilities were named as important by more than half of the respondents, followed by machinery. Joint ventures type I reported more items from the lists that were not in the top eight contributions. Joint ventures of type II were in this respect more like greenfield projects as managerial capabilities and machinery were most important.

Smaller firms were more frequently reporting brands, marketing and technology among their top resources, while larger firms named managerial capabilities and machinery, and to a lesser extend business networks.

In Table 9.4, we report who contributed the resources considered most important. The foreign parent firm was the most important source for all resources. Local parent firms were relatively important with respect to distribution networks, while other local sources matter for business networks, distribution, and marketing.

Institutional and Market Environment

The institutional and market environment for FDI had undergone substantial change in the second half of the 1990s. Most notable was the change in the licensing regime, which had been decentralised, and administrative procedures that had been simplified. A lot of restrictions on the operation of FDI, e.g. on foreign exchange control etc., were also deregulated. At the same time, as the domestic private sectors developed, it had become easier for FDI to source intermediate products and supplies within Vietnam. These changes were reflected in the respondents' assessment of the business environment, which overall pointed to improvements facilitating the operation of business.

Across industries, most respondents give the most favourable assessment to availability of business licences (Table 9.5). This criterion along with access to real estate also saw the largest margin of improvement. The worst assessment had in most industries been given to the general legal framework and the predictability of the legal framework. The variation across industry may reflect the industry's exposure to different types of regulation or bureaucracy. For example, infrastructure and construction was most negative about environmental regulation, and had a considerably weaker assessment of local government, compared to their view of the central governments.

Across entry modes, the assessment of the institutional framework showed little variation. Acquirers provided more favourable assessments, but there were very few of them. JV type II firms seem to get along best with local governments.

Within Vietnam, businesses in the vicinity of HCMC gave the best ratings of the business environment by most crieteria, followed by HCMC itself (Table 9.6). Only on environment regulation did Hanoi get the best rating.

Table 9.5 Evaluation of institutional environment, Vietnam (by industrial sector)

Institutional environment	Primary		Basic consumer goods		Intermediate		Machinery & equipment		Infrastructure & construction		Trade & tourism		Business services	
	Initial	2001	Initial	2001	Initial	2001	Initial	2001	Initial	2001	Initial	2001	Initial	2001
Business licence	2.60	4.00	3.31	3.75	3.54	3.00	2.79	3.50	3.57	3.93	2.81	3.53	3.00	3.75
Real estate acquisition	2.00	3.20	3.02	3.27	3.32	2.75	2.37	3.67	3.00	3.61	2.69	3.07	2.64	3.36
Visa & work permit	3.20	3.40	3.36	3.73	3.42	3.25	3.04	3.50	3.65	3.71	2.62	3.12	2.79	3.82
Environmental regulation	3.20	3.25	3.32	3.52	3.34	3.00	3.08	3.50	3.57	3.47	3.31	3.44	3.29	3.08
General legal framework	2.60	2.80	2.98	3.31	3.04	2.75	2.71	2.75	3.35	3.38	2.56	2.87	2.64	2.92
Predictability of rules	2.40	2.40	2.96	3.33	2.86	2.50	3.04	2.75	3.35	3.04	2.50	2.87	2.64	3.17
Central government	3.00	3.20	3.17	3.51	3.34	3.50	3.04	4.00	3.57	3.68	2.94	3.31	3.43	4.00
Provincial government	2.80	3.00	3.22	3.50	3.43	3.25	2.96	3.75	3.48	3.71	3.00	3.33	3.33	3.64
Local government	2.80	3.00	3.19	3.48	3.24	3.25	2.75	3.67	3.27	3.48	2.87	3.20	3.14	3.45

Notes: on scale from 1 to 5, 1= not conducive at all
by industrial sector of the respondent

Table 9.6 Evaluation of institutional environment, Vietnam (by province)

Institutional environment	HCMC		HCMC region		Hanoi		Hanoi region		Other provinces	
	Initial	2001	Initial	2001	Initial	2001	Initial	2001	Initial	2001
Business licence	3.03	3.66	3.70	4.07	2.95	3.68	3.20	3.89	2.93	3.29
Real estate acquisition	2.77	3.30	3.29	3.53	2.63	3.26	2.80	2.89	2.92	3.23
Visa & work permit	3.15	3.72	3.51	3.78	2.89	3.33	3.00	3.50	3.13	3.20
Environmental regulation	3.22	3.41	3.38	3.52	3.74	3.89	2.90	3.10	3.14	3.29
General legal framework	2.65	3.19	3.35	3.63	2.63	2.95	2.44	2.78	3.07	3.20
Predictability of rules	2.69	3.18	3.00	3.19	2.89	3.16	2.22	2.56	3.00	3.29
Central government	3.13	3.60	3.43	3.70	3.32	3.58	2.89	3.33	3.29	3.43
Provincial government	3.21	3.61	3.42	3.69	3.21	3.47	2.44	2.89	3.27	3.40
Local government	3.01	3.35	3.48	3.68	3.05	3.32	2.33	2.89	3.08	3.31
No. of observations	73		47		19		10		15	

Note: On scale from 1 to 5, 1= not conducive at all

On the other hand, the weakest rating was reserved for the Hanoi region and the 'other' provinces. Comparing the ratings given to central and local governments, investors in HCMC region gave almost the same score, while investors in the Hanoi region rated the local government considerably less conducive.

Thus, the business environment in Vietnam showed encouraging trends in the assessment of foreign investors, as both the resource endowment and the institutional environment have improved. The assessment varies however within Vietnam, and to a lesser extent across industries, yet not between investors who came by different entry modes.

Firm Performance

ASEAN and European firms were more likely to report above average financial performance, while Taiwanese and Japanese firms were more likely to under-perform (Table 9.7). Within Vietnam, investors in HCMC were more likely to report above average performance, while investors in Hanoi and in 'other' provinces perform below average. Hence, it appeared that new investors preferred those areas where existing investors reported good results. However, the performance data require more detailed analysis to provide policy advice.

Impact on the Host Economy

Export contribution

Producers of basic consumer goods were most likely to export to global markets, and to deliver products to other affiliates of the parent firms. Vietnam thus attracted many investors in traditional light industries with labour intensive production that took advantage of comparatively low production costs. Domestic market orientation was much higher in business services than in the manufacturing sectors. Trade and tourism firms, for which we have data for only four firms, appear most oriented towards regional markets.

The domestic focus was much higher among joint ventures than among greenfield projects, which supported the contention that local joint venture partners were crucial to provide access to local markets. The import-substitution policy had apparently encouraged joint ventures that were oriented towards local markets.

Market orientation varied across home countries, with most investors serving in the initial year either only the local market, or only the export market. About half of the investors from Japan and Taiwan were exporting all their output, compared to an average of 36 per cent. The labor cost differences combined with moderate geographic distance made the

Table 9.7 Performance across source countries and host regions, Vietnam (No. of firms)

Source	Low	Middle	High
ASEAN	7	7	7
Europe	7	7	9
Hong Kong	3	4	3
Japan	9	12	2
Korea	3	16	4
North America	2	2	2
Taiwan	16	17	3
Other	1	1	2
Province			
HCMC	19	31	17
HCMC region	13	19	6
Hanoi	8	8	3
Hanoi region	2	5	2
Other	6	3	4

establishment of production sites in Vietnam attractive for investors from these two economies. On the other hand, 40 per cent of investors were selling only in the local market. This included all American investors and the majority of French and ASEAN investors. Domestic market oriented investors were distributed across all provinces, while export oriented investors were concentrated in HCMC.

Initially there seems to have been a clear either/or distinction between exporters and firms selling in the local market. This distinction blurred after 1995, as more recent entrants served both domestic and export markets.

Spillovers to the local industry
We expected that foreign investment might create positive spillovers that support the development of the local industry in the same sector. If this was true, then it should have been reflected in positive changes in the assessment of the local industry at the time of entry and at the time of the survey. Comparing the assessment of local industry at the time of entry and at the time of the survey, we noted an improvement in the local industry, which was fairly consistent across sectors, and for different aspects of the local industry.

Outliers and large margins of change emerged only for industries with few observations: The local trade and tourism industry, was improving by a large margin, followed by machinery and equipment. On the other hand, the local primary sector industry was by some criteria even declining. Marketing capabilities increased by a relatively large margin, but as an outlier they appeared to be declining in the infrastructure and construction sector.

Joint ventures were generally more favourable about the local environment, and they reported a larger improvement of their assessment. This indicated a positive spillover favouring institutional development, but it may also have been due to the fact that joint ventures had on average been in existence for a longer time.

Human capital accumulation

The main contribution of foreign investment was often seen in the transfer of knowledge from the parent firm to local affiliates. We thus asked respondents about the foreign investors' training expenditures. We found that these expenditures were on average higher in business services, while they were lowest in the machinery industries. However, there was no clear relationship between employment in the local firm and training expenditures. The relationship between training expenditures and financial performance appears U-shaped as training expenditures were higher in both the above and below average performing firms.

The training expenditures appeared weakly related to the R&D intensity of the parent (Table 9.8). The highest training expenditures (over 15 per cent) were incurred by parent firms with R&D expenditures of more than 4 per cent of sales. On the other hand, of firms with less than 4 per cent R&D expenditures, more than half spent less than 0.5 per cent on training. Hence there appears to be some support for the notion that attracting R&D intensive firms generated more knowledge transfers. In the current policy debate in Vietnam, this result provides support for policy to provide favourable treatment to FDI with R&D intensive operations.

CONCLUSIONS

Following gradual liberalisation over 15 years, FDI had surged in Vietnam, and foreign investment firms made a major contribution to the domestic economy in terms of for, instance, output and exports. Our survey provides new insights in the nature of this foreign investment and its potential contribution.

Foreign investors in Vietnam, especially more recent entrants, were often small focused firms with little international business experience. In contrast, most large multinational firms, which one could call global players, had little interest in FDI in Vietnam. Our data illustrate several features that vary substantially across countries of origin. For instance, FDI from NICs appears to show different characteristics such as labor intensity, export-orientation, and regional clustering. Rising costs in some of the neighbouring countries appear to be an opportunity for Vietnam to attract FDI. Thus country-of-origin influences on FDI were an area requiring further investigation, while sector variation seems to have little explanatory power.

Table 9.8: Training relative to R &D expenditure, Vietnam (No. of firms)

Local training (%)	R&D expenditures							Total
	0-0.5%	0.5-1%	1-2%	2-4%	4-8%	8-15%	Over 15%	
0-0.5	18	7	5	6	4	3	5	48
0.5-1	6	2	2	3	3	2	1	19
1-2	1	2	2	1	1	3	0	10
2-4	1	0	0	0	1	0	1	3
4-8	0	0	1	1	0	0	0	2
8-15	0	0	0	0	1	1	2	4
Total	26	11	10	11	10	9	9	86

Notes: R&D expenditures = worldwide R&D expenditures as percentage of sales; local training = training expenditures as percentage of subsidiary sales.

Entry modes available to foreign investors in Vietnam are more constrained than in other emerging economies, such that there are no partial acquisitions and very few full acquisitions in our sample. In part, foreign investors have used joint ventures to effectively acquire control of an existing operation, which we classify as JV type II. Over the decade of the 1990s, there has been a clear trend from JV to greenfield entry, and to a very limited extent acquisitions. The entry modes also vary across countries of origin, and across locations within Vietnam. Hence, an analysis of entry mode in Vietnam has to pay careful attention to the institutional context prevailing at the time of entry.

Foreign investors in Vietnam report managerial capabilities and machinery as their most important resources, ahead of both technology and networking assets. This applies in particular to large and wholly-owned affiliates. Managerial capabilities appear important across all industry sectors, while machinery and equipment is naturally more important in the manufacturing and infrastructure sectors. This pattern suggests a traditional pattern of competition, as few references are made to intangible assets such as technology and marketing assets. This ought to be investigated further in relation to the changing patterns of globally integrated operations of MNEs.

10. Vietnamese Case Studies

Ha Thanh Nguyen, Hung Vo Nguyen and Ca Ngoc Tran

INTRODUCTION

This chapter presents three cases of foreign investors in Vietnam. All established joint ventures, yet their roles in them vary considerably. The Danish Carlsberg Breweries established an early foothold in the Vietnamese market in 1993 via its Thai affiliate, with a conventional joint venture structure. The joint venture has been operating fairly successfully, and extensive training of staff improved the productivity of both the joint venture and other operations of the local partner. The Swedish engineering giant ABB accessed the local markets by establishing a joint venture that effectively took over an existing local firm. Hence, ABB had to take responsibility for restructuring and technological upgrading of the company. The leading Japanese motorcycle brand, Honda, moved from imports to local production in a joint venture with a largely passive state-owned enterprise. The new operation built a local supplier network, with potentially considerable spillover effects, yet not involving its local joint venture partner.

SOUTH EAST ASIA BREWERY

Introduction

With beer consumption remaining static in traditional markets, expansion into new markets is the growth engine for many international breweries. Unlike strategy on other continents, affiliates of Carlsberg in Asia are usually joint ventures with local partners. In Vietnam, Carlsberg established a joint venture, Southeast Asia Brewery (SEAB), with a local state company, Halimex, in 1993. Competitive conditions and past experience had a strong impact on Carlsberg's choice of partner and location. Carlsberg contributes capital, technology and machines, as well as extensive staff training. Sharing management between Carlsberg and the local partner works quite well; however, it does create some inconsistency in management style. The business is considered successful, although it is not the sales of the Carlsberg brand that earns money, but the local brand, Halida. Marketing and distribution of this local brand utilises primarily knowledge of the local partner.

Industry

Brewing is a mature industry. In many traditional markets, beer consumption has been static, or perhaps even declining, thus limiting further growth for European brewers. However, a great potential exists in emerging markets where beer consumption is presently comparatively low, and economic growth prospects are considered bright. During the past two decades almost all the international breweries have found their way into these new markets, and this has triggered an intense competition in an already highly competitive industry.

Five breweries are emerging as global players: Heineken, Interbrew, Carlsberg, SAB, and Anheuser Busch. Their brands are well recognised internationally and their sales have grown mainly through overseas operations. Regionally and locally, the competition is even stronger amongst many strong local and regional brands.

In Vietnam, the international brands, Carlsberg, Foster, Tiger, and San Miguel are considered as premium beers and compete fiercely for the tiny, and slow-growing premium market (less than 30 per cent of the total market). Many strong brands of local standard beers compete quite well in their traditional mid-range markets. The Vietnamese beer industry is still considered to have great potential in the coming years as annual per capita consumption is still relatively low at 9 litres.

The Investor: Carlsberg

Carlsberg A/S traces its roots to 1847 when brewer J.C. Jacobsen introduced Bavarian-style lager beer and new brewing technologies. Carlsberg Breweries soon became one of the most successful Danish businesses, first establishing the leading brand domestically, and later in many surrounding European markets.

Over the last two decades of the 20th century Carlsberg acquired a number of breweries in both Western Europe and the emerging markets, and it established 'Carlsberg' as one of the best-known brands worldwide with the very effective slogan, 'probably the best beer...'. In the 1990s Carlsberg expanded primarily in Central and Eastern Europe, where it has become the leading brand in some countries, notably in Russia. Central and Eastern Europe contributed almost 18 per cent of Carlsberg's worldwide turnover in 2003, compared with 5 per cent in Asia.

Its products were present in about 150 markets worldwide, and more than 94 per cent of beer sales were generated outside Denmark. Its products were then brewed at 90 production sites in 45 countries. Over the last few years Carlsberg Breweries has been pursuing acquisitions and joint-ventures, especially in emerging markets. In Western Europe, Eastern Europe and Asia, the main markets in which Carlsberg is active, the company has achieved market shares of 10, 22.4 and 9.1 per cent, respectively.

Carlsberg has been active in Asia for almost 30 years, often in joint ventures with local partners. Given the stagnant situation in its traditional markets, finding new markets is the main motive for Carlsberg to expand further into Asia, with its large populations and currently low per capita beer consumption levels. In this respect, Vietnam is not an exception.

With a predominantly young population of about 70 million people by the early 1990s, low annual per capita beer consumption (3 litres), no cultural restrictions on beer consumption, out-of-date local production facilities, and positive expectation of economic growth, Vietnam is considered a prominent potential market.

Entry into Vietnam is also part of Carlsberg's competition strategy to maintain its image in Asia, a high growth region where Carlsberg has always been in a strong position in competition with its international rivals. It is significant that in the early 1990s, almost all breweries operating in the region started to develop simultaneous investment projects in Vietnam. First-mover advantages were obviously the driving force of these projects. These early entries were also considered as a means to occupy a potentially limited number of seats in the beer business. This subsequently turned out to be the right move when the Government later decided to stop issuing investment licences for new FDI projects in the brewing industry.

The beer business is an advertising-intensive industry, especially for premium brands like Carlsberg and Heineken. Access to (or control of) a distribution network is considered critical for beer sales, and a deep understanding of the local market with its various cultural mores is also very important.

The art of brewing beer is not too difficult to transfer between organisations and over long distances. In order to maintain consistent beer quality, Carlsberg has reorganised all of its technical activities under a department called the Corporate Supply Chain, which includes Operational Control, Innovation, Quality Assurance and Process and Quality Audit. Training is the main channel through which technology is transferred.

The Local Partner: Halimex

Halimex (the Hanoi Union of Microbiological Products Enterprises) was a state-run enterprise established in 1966. At that time, Halimex was a group of enterprises producing several types of foodstuffs for local consumption, including baker's yeast, soy sauce, frozen meat, instant noodles, and later, beer and soft drinks.

Except for the brewery that Halimex bought from Danbrew in 1990,[50] most of its products were produced by conventional labour-intensive processes that were perceived as far below international standards. Compared with other similar local companies in the early 1990s, however, Halimex was relatively keen to conduct R&D, develop new products and processes, etc. It also had tried to work closely with local R&D institutes and university departments to support its activities.

A turnkey project was supplied by Danbrew for Halimex to produce Halida beer. The technology level of Danbrew plant was much higher than the technology used in the old breweries at that time. Halimex and its canned beer, Halida, quickly became a success. This was partly due to the superior technology that it acquired, but managerial competence also contributed an important part. Five different purchasers of largely similar turnkey-projects from Danbrew, with basically the same terms and conditions, created very different breweries and beers. Among them, Halimex had been the most successful, developing Halida as the strongest local brand at that time.

Halimex was very careful in assigning teams of engineers and technicians to accompany Danbrew experts all along, so as to learn and acquire new skills. This helps explain why, after only three trials by Danbrew experts, the Halimex technicians could start to brew by themselves. In several instances, this close working relationship helped solve problems that were new even to the Danbrew experts.

In addition to technical knowledge in the narrow sense, Halimex acquired new knowledge of management techniques, such as systematic planning of repair and maintenance. It was generally believed that Halimex had gained support from Hanoi's politicians to obtain a loan from the State commercial bank for its investment.

Obviously there is a huge difference in culture between Vietnam and Nordic countries in terms of beliefs, behaviour, attitudes, language, etc. However, the relationship between Vietnam and Nordic countries has been developing since the 1970s, beginning with the support by Sweden during the Vietnam War and the years that followed. Typical of this was the Swedes' building of the Bai Bang Paper Mill in Vinh Phu Province. This is one of the many reasons for the very positive attitude of the Vietnamese towards the Nordic countries.

Performance

The joint venture was set up in 1993 with a registered investment of US$79 million and a planned production capacity, for the first phase, of 360,000 hectolitres (hl) per year. At the time of this research, Phase I has been completed with an implemented investment of only US$23.4 million.

Financially, the subsidiary started making a profit from 1998. Regardless of the financial crisis in the region and the difficult nature of the Vietnamese economy, it still managed to make moderate profits in the years 1999 and 2000, and to improve its position in the market, especially with the local brand, Halida.[51]

Although considered as a successful project, its managers (representing Carlsberg's interest) admitted that the joint venture had not fully met the investor's original expectation in reaching their objectives. Despite a high level of awareness (91 per cent in Vietnam), sales of the Carlsberg brand remains static while its local brand, Halida, enjoys a slight growth. The affiliate now aims to maintain second position in the premium beer market after Heineken and is aiming to become number one in the standard beer market in the North.

Counterfactual

It is believed that even without the joint venture, the local firm would have done well. This is also supported by the fact that the local brand, Halida, was very strong before the joint venture was set up, and has so far been contributing decisively to its financial performance.

From Carlsberg's viewpoint, it would enter the market the same way, making joint ventures with local companies to acquire the necessary local knowledge. If it had not been with Halimex, it would have been with some other brewery in Vietnam.

The Entry

The ownership of the joint venture was initially split 35/25/40 between Carlsberg Breweries, the Industrialization Fund for Developing Countries (IFU, a Danish State-owned investment fund) and Halimex, respectively. This is typical of Carlsberg initiatives in developing countries. In summer 2003, Carlsberg acquired the 25 per cent stake of IFU.

It was agreed that the top management will be switched every three years, and Mrs Nguyen Thi Anh Nhan, the General Director of Halimex, became the first General Director. This is striking, because the Danish partners, controlling 60 per cent of the equity, were entitled to hold the General Director post, as would usually be the case for foreign partners in joint ventures. Under the above arrangement, the control is shared between the two partners.

As mentioned earlier, Carlsberg considers having a partner with local knowledge of tastes, distribution networks, and political support as crucial for its operation anywhere in Asia, so building a joint venture with local partners was the entry mode of choice. However, why Carlsberg ended up having a joint venture with Halimex in Hanoi is worth further study because (1) the largest beer market (70 per cent) is in the South, and (2) Halimex was a relative newcomer to the beer business.

In explaining this decision, it has to be noted that by the end of 1991, Asia Pacific Breweries, Singapore, which produces Tiger and Heineken beer, had obtained a licence to build its brewery in Ho Chi Minh City, at a scale three times larger than SEAB later reached. Given the presence of its main competitor in the South, going North became a natural decision for Carlsberg.

Halimex was not the largest brewery in the North at that time. Hanoi Brewery was the largest and the oldest in the North; however, Halimex was seen as having the ability, skills and know-how to grow into a large brewery business, conscious of quality. It did not make any compromise on quality, which can be an easy temptation when a company is growing fast. This explains why the quality of Halimex beer is higher and more stable than that of the other breweries that had also bought Danbrew turnkey projects.

Resources of the New Venture

In the beer industry, both tangible and intangible resources are important. Most of the tangible assets in terms of equipment and machinery were provided by Carlsberg. Another important tangible asset in the beer business is the distribution network. With income per capita at a low level and a traditional custom of beer being consumed mainly (on more than 70 per cent of occasions) on public premises in Vietnam, having access to outlets like restaurants, pubs, bars, nightclubs, cafes, etc., is considered critical for beer sales at this stage.

Intangible assets are even more important. Among them, know-how related to the production of a high and sustainable quality, as well as efficiency in production, is critical. One example is the way of controlling temperature to add flavour to the beer, principally during the brewing and fermentation periods.

Other well-known important intangible resources in the beer business are brand management and marketing know-how. These skills help greatly to sell the product without changing its physical conditions. Management know-how and political 'savvy' (in dealing with authorities at all levels) are other important assets that help the business to operate smoothly and profitably.

Generally speaking, the local side contributed the land, its initial production facility including the building, equipment, distribution network, labour force, political connections, local brand prestige of Halida, and marketing know-how for this local brand. The foreign side provided capital, technical and management training for the workforce, some critical know-how in production, international brand prestige (Carlsberg) and marketing know-how for the Carlsberg brand.

Resource Transfer

Other than just capital, the investor also transferred technical, marketing and management knowledge by means of training. Training is an important investment, required to maintain the quality of products and efficiency of operation. Training occurred both in Vietnam, within the factory by on-the-job training, and also overseas.

A large number of senior technical and managerial staff from SEAB were sent for training in different countries. By 1996 most of the key personnel in SEAB had been trained abroad. In certain cases, for instance the chief of the laboratory, the training was focused on transferring in-depth, advanced knowledge. Whilst Halimex only required basic tests, SEAB's needs were more substantial. For instance, SEAB needs thorough tests not only on the ultimate quality of the beer, but also on the raw materials as well as regular intermediate tests on the product during the process.

Nonetheless, training was not limited to specific skills. For instance, the maintenance manager was sent to Carlsberg Breweries in Hong Kong and Malaysia with a view to expanding his knowledge and breadth of vision, giving him other perspectives on how things can be done as well as why, rather than just what needs to be done.

This can be exemplified in the understanding of the challenges of beer making. In the beginning, when a technical problem occurred, the Vietnamese staff would know that something was wrong, and they might find a solution. However, they might not know why it was wrong, and thus may not have been able to recognise the root of the problem and ways to prevent a recurrence. After continuing more in-depth training, studying technical documents and discussing them with foreign experts, they came to know better the underlying causes of the problems they were frequently faced with.

Training abroad was essential, but also costly, and could be made more effective if those trainees could maximise their knowledge after returning home by being able to use creatively what they had learned, by developing further skills from this knowledge base, and by being able to disseminate their new knowledge to others. Careful selection and preparation was therefore needed. The joint venture selected candidates for a certain job, provided them with prior knowledge, tested their ability and skills, and then came up with the person likely to benefit most from further training. They were also informed about the objectives of the training, along with the expectations of responsibilities and obligations after they returned. This was a process of local training *in preparation* for training abroad.

The lesson of training, both abroad but particularly at home, was that it was essential to enhance the knowledge of the staff so that they could understand what they were doing, or were meant to do. To give them meaning, rather than just giving them specific measures and telling them, step by step, what to do.

It is the joint venture's policy to localise management and senior technical staff. Even in the initial set-up, only three expatriates worked at the brewery. Three years later, only two expatriates remained (one as General Director and one as Brew Master). In 2003 only the Vice-General Director was an expatriate, though the arrival of a new export marketing director was expected.

A Vietnamese national has successfully replaced the Brew Master. Four candidates were selected and rotated through tasks and on-the-job training in different positions and operations, from the brewing house to fermentation, bottling and canning, etc. By so doing, the candidates were given broader knowledge and skills for their job input. This is important, because a brew master has to work with over 200 workers and in different departments, so is required to coordinate and manage different groups when problems arise.

A broader based knowledge was also needed. It was necessary for the entire workforce in the brewery to have a good knowledge of the brewery business and techniques. More than that, it was not only the knowledge of how to make beer, but also to make what was considered to be 'good' beer by different customers in different regions, or a 'beer culture' as it is put by some people. This was important for them because, in general, beer had not until recently been a common drink for many Vietnamese people, unlike in Europe, for instance. One typical example of this approach to broadening knowledge for everyone was the technical training for marketing and sales personnel. Sales staff were educated in various aspects of brewing techniques so they could understand why and how tastes become different, what makes 'good' beer, etc.

After many years of continuous efforts in training the staff, Carlsberg is very happy with the technical side of the operation. For example, quality is considered to be consistent, and the Vietnamese brew master is doing well.

Spillover Effects

A remarkable, yet lesser-known, development of the Halimex enterprise has been its attempt to produce draught beer by itself, capitalising on knowledge, skills and experience gained from the Danbrew turnkey project, and the joint venture with Carlsberg. This attempt led to the building of a brewery called Viet Ha, in which almost everything was planned and implemented by Halimex itself.

The brewery was modelled after the Danbrew line, and Halimex was to prepare all technical and project planning. To reduce costs, most of the equipment was designed and manufactured locally. A step-by-step approach was applied, starting with, an experimental design of the brewing oven. This oven was then put to work with the line supplied by Danbrew, to check that it was operating well and could match the quality and other specifications of brewing ovens produced by Danbrew.

The success in designing and manufacturing the brewing oven created confidence within the management and staff of Halimex, and led to the decision to design and manufacture locally a majority of the equipment needed. Only certain intricate equipment that was essential for the brewing technology or was difficult to manufacture locally, was imported. Halimex itself carried out the design part of the mechanical engineering, while some other design work was contracted out to appropriate local organisations.

A big challenge for the Vietnamese was to design and select the type of process and equipment feasible in the context of Vietnam in terms of the availability of suitable materials. Thus, because there were few suppliers of suitable mechanical parts, and it was difficult to find parts that were consistent in quality and with the required specifications, the process of freezing using salt water was chosen instead of freezing with glycol. This technique avoids the evaporation stage in the cooling process.

The quality of some local manufactured parts and equipment was not perfect. However, compared with other locally designed and manufactured breweries that also make draught beer, Viet Ha has many better features in the process techniques, and its overall product quality is thus better. For example, while the others have no appropriate equipment to control temperature during the fermentation, Viet Ha has a sensor that can automatically cut the power supply when the temperature reaches a certain level. Keeping a stable temperature ensures a stable and desirable product quality.

Overall, although the brewery was self-designed and constructed by Viet Ha, it was not as 'modern' as the Danbrew project. Nevertheless, it reflects the Halimex technological and managerial capabilities in planning, designing and implementing a project, manifesting as a spillover from its earlier experience.

In addition to adaptations in term of equipment, Halimex also pursued some technical developments specifically for its draught beer at Viet Ha, as well as other product lines. This was done in cooperation with the local Foodstuff Technology Institute, where research work had been done with the flocculant variety of yeast, in an attempt to make a sort of yeast similar to Danbrew's variety, but more suitable for Vietnam's conditions. In terms of management, the Viet Ha brewery, surprisingly, managed to retain a high level of autonomy, and copied some of the joint venture's management features in the later phase.

Most important for Viet Ha, according to its senior managers, was the close coordination between the technical departments and marketing/sales units. The latter were to seek out and observe all the reactions of clients, and channel them back to the technical departments for consideration. Similarly, they worked closely with the technical departments, especially the quality control unit, to evaluate the relevance of new sources or new types of raw material for the brewery.

Senior employees in Viet Ha were required to know more than just operational skills. Indeed, most of the middle and upper level staff were required to have a broader knowledge and understanding of a great variety of issues related to beer brewing. For example, two training courses, each lasting two and a half months, were organised for senior technicians, engineers, foremen and managers on the specific issue of tasting evaluation, with trainers from various organisations. This apparently helped enormously, and made possible the setting-up of the 'Taste Testing Committee', selected from personnel right across the brewery.

Since the commencement of operations of the joint venture, a small proportion of the local brand, Halida, has been exported to France and Japan. It is expected that in the future it can be exported to neighbouring countries, such as Laos and Cambodia.

The entry of Carlsberg into Vietnam's market is considered to have had an important influence on the development of the beer industry in the country. Among these influences, one can mention things like competition between breweries, both local and international, and raised standards of product quality and production practices.

Enterprise Restructuring

In general, it could be argued that the joint venture was an upgrade of the local brewery with the introduction of a new kind of beer, Carlsberg. Expansion of the production facility and improvement of technology and management accompanied this expansion. Since technical and technological issues have been discussed in the above sections, we concentrate here more on the restructuring of management.

Even after the joint venture was started, and operated rather successfully, the need for change in management was evident. It was also seen that this was not for the survival of the joint venture, but rather for maintaining its competitiveness and growth. Partly because of this, the General Director was replaced after her first term. It is obvious that the initial success of Halimex, and to some extent SEAB, had depended on her contribution.

However, as a business grows, changes are normally needed. Thus, when the brewery expanded from a small, independent unit to a large joint venture, and when the joint venture itself grew, her strong, commanding, egoistic style of management posed some difficulties. For obvious reasons, it was necessary to delegate power and decisions to departments and divisions within the expanded organisation, but this was not done effectively. Her replacement led to a more decentralised style of management, which also delegated more authority to people holding middle level jobs. This then allowed people who had trained abroad to experiment with new knowledge, and organise a formal dissemination of that knowledge and information to everyone in the joint venture.

One major change for the joint venture management was the move from a more or less top-down hierarchical approach to a more participatory manner.

Internal cooperation between different parts of the production line has been important for the brewery, as it is a continuous process, in which any flaw at one stage could undermine the quality and taste of all the beer. This was initially handled by the foreign brew master. Gradually, it was taken over by the Technical Deputy General Director, who coordinates all departments involved, especially the laboratory, the brew house and the fermentation facility.

Most critical for the brewery was the cooperation and constant feedback between the marketing/sales departments and the technical departments. With the trained background and awareness of this issue, the two departments kept up regular exchanges and discussions on various aspects of the product and the process – the colour of beer, its level of bitterness, level of foam, etc. In particular, whenever a bottle or package of beer had problems, it was quickly returned to the technical departments for examination and investigation.

The most difficult work for SEAB has been to build up an organisation that would ensure that all beer leaving the brewery had the same high, uniform quality, and keep SEAB competitive amongst the increasingly modernised breweries throughout the country. This has been a success. Its beers are now amongst the best of the 64 brewery facilities Carlsberg has around the world.

After almost 10 years of the join venture, regardless of the switch in the management team, the structure of the company is almost unchanged. The staff, however, are more confident in their jobs.

Concluding Remarks

Over the first half of the 1990s, as a result of regulations, joint venture was the only choice for entry into the beer market in Vietnam. However, this is also the strategy that Carlsberg has been pursuing in Asia generally.

Under the above condition, selecting a local partner and a location for the new affiliate becomes a strategic decision. Competition dynamics and past relationship seem to be the decisive factors. With its rivals occupying the Southern market and with a past relationship with Halimex (via the turn key project with Danbrew), developing a joint venture with Halimex became a natural move when Carlsberg considered entering Vietnam.

Unlike the majority of joint ventures in Vietnam where the foreign partners aim effectively to control the joint venture, management of SEAB is shared between the two partners. This, however, creates a change in management style every time the management is switched.

Carlsberg contributed capital, equipment, technical knowledge, know-how and international brand and training, whilst Halimex contributed access to land, machines, a distribution network, the local brand and political ties.

The affiliate sells two brands, Carlsberg and Halida, of which the local brand Halida performs very well in terms of market share. The substantial investments in training and knowledge transfers gave been crucial for the success of the JV with a state-owned enterprise (Nguyen and Meyer 2004).

The joint venture creates spillovers for the local partner. Jointly with other international breweries operating in Vietnam, it creates a new face for its beer industry.

ABB TRANSFORMERS VIETNAM LTD

Introduction

At the time of its establishment, ABB Transformer Vietnam was reported as a notable case of joint-venture businesses between foreign and local companies in Vietnam. It represented a number of features that were sought after by local government and businesses, e.g. substantial capital investment, transfer of modern technology and management, continued employment of all local staff, etc. However, the marriage turned sour a few years later for both external and internal reasons. The joint venture may be classified as one of the more successful foreign investments in Vietnam, but it has far to go before both parties are satisfied.

Manufacturing of electrical transformers is one of the key areas of electrical engineering, and has a strong effect on the efficiency of power distribution and consumption. Internationally, there are only a few large manufacturers who can compete in the world markets, such as General Electric, Siemens, Mitsubishi, Thompson and ABB.

As the markets in industrialised countries became more or less saturated in the 1970s - 80s, these big multinational companies became more interested in expanding into emerging and developing countries. Some of them also located manufacturing facilities in those countries.

In Vietnam, before 1990, all transformer manufacturers were state-owned enterprises, but managed by different ministries. Thus, there was some local rivalry, although only to a minor extent. The sub-sector was on the government's high-priority list for seeking foreign investment.

The Investor: ABB

The ABB group is a major multinational enterprises that specialises in global electrical industries. It is involved in the worldwide manufacturing and marketing of various kinds of power plants and equipment, as well as in servicing a wide range of electrical systems. These comprise power generation plants, power transmission and distribution, industrial installations, transportation and general applications of electricity.

The group is a federation of national companies and uses a matrix structure for its organisation. The whole group has approximately 214,000 employees in 1,300 independently incorporated units. ABB's worldwide activities are grouped into eight business segments comprising 65 business areas, each with its own profit-sensitive responsibility for product development, production and marketing. The group has some 5,000 autonomous profit centres.

In Vietnam, ABB has diverse business interests. In the beginning, power generation was its key business focus, and by 1996, ABB was involved in several key power-generation projects. In addition, ABB was also active in electrical engineering projects, supplying, for example, electrical machinery and equipment for large industrial projects. However, it was transformer production that ABB wanted to enter into as a joint venture for local manufacturing in Vietnam.

Acquired Local Firm: Hanoi Transformer Manufacturing Factory

The Hanoi Transformer Manufacturing factory (HTM), was established in the early 1960s, under the General Corporation of Electrical Equipment and Techniques, the Ministry of Industry, and was one of five major distribution-transformer manufacturers in the country. HTM enjoyed about 50 per cent of Vietnam's distribution-transformer market.

HTM manufactured a variety of products, for instance, various types of drying kilns and metallurgical kilns. In addition, because the networking of business and back-to-back integration was underdeveloped, HTM had to produce many types of intermediate products and components themselves. This forced HTM to acquire basic knowledge in rather broad areas of technical and production activities.

In the area of transformers per se, underlying production technologies, as well as product designs, were modelled after the then Soviet Union's products. In many ways, HTM had to adapt the Soviet and other technologies to Vietnamese conditions, as well as to develop some technologies of its own, and self-design and manufacture certain machinery itself. This experience in adapting and modifying foreign technologies became a conscious effort amongst HTM staff.

HTM already had a long tradition of reverse-engineering. It was active in the acquisition of technical literature, especially industrial catalogues, and using them as a reference source. HTM also had a long tradition of co-operation with technical universities and R&D institutes.

These technological endeavours were part of the reason for HTM's success in expanding production and market share. Compared with the design capacity of about 400 transformers of various sizes, during the early 1990s, its actual annual capacity was about 1,600 transformers, making it the biggest producer in Vietnam, accounting for about 50 per cent of market share. This success may be surprising, considering the fact that HTM was outside the aegis of the Ministry of Energy, which is responsible for installing the power distribution network and has two of its own transformer producers.

Performance

The joint venture's market share at present is about 30 per cent. ABB Transformer Vietnam Ltd initially achieved financial success very quickly. The joint venture broke even after only six months of operations, a record time compared with most of the ABB transformer joint ventures worldwide. However, later, while expanding into power transformer production, the joint venture began to make losses. This is partly because the market did not grow as quickly as expected, and partly because of heavy debt servicing. The joint venture has successfully managed to export to regional markets. So far, it has exported to India, Laos, Indonesia, and is preparing to export to Singapore.

Counterfactual

It seemed that the joint venture was, and remains, the best choice for both parties. For the local company, the joint venture seems to be the best way to retain its identity, obtain foreign capital and technology, and enter into international markets. If this ABB joint venture had not occurred, it is likely that HTM would have entered into a joint venture with a Japanese partner.[52]

For ABB, joint-venturing was also the best choice. The Government policy at the time did not encourage 100 per cent foreign-owned businesses. At the same time, because of the import substitution strategy, and because all customers of this industry are state-owned companies or entities, it would have been difficult for ABB to compete using imports. If this joint venture had not occurred, ABB would have sought a joint venture with another local company.

The Entry

Unlike many joint venture preparations, in which the Vietnamese party often played a passive role, the HTM factory acted enthusiastically to establish a genuine partnership. It was also actively involved in the discussions and formulation of the long-term plan for the joint venture (for example its insistence that power transformers be manufactured before the year 2000), together with product lines, distribution and marketing/sales strategy, etc. It was agreed that HTM and ABB were each to be primarily responsible for certain specific aspects (for example, HTM for sales and marketing, and ABB for production management), while at the same time both would contribute jointly to all other aspects. To avoid the paralysis incurred by some joint ventures due to lack of support from local employees, or lack of consensus between local and foreign staff, many issues were exposed to comment and discussion by various departments and units within HTM.

The Vietnamese factory had stronger bargaining powers than most Vietnamese enterprises seeking to establish a joint venture with a foreign company. HTM set some preconditions, most significant of which were: (1) to retain all existing employees of HTM within the joint venture,[53] and (2) to start with distribution-transformers, then quickly move to the manufacturing of power transformers so long as the distribution-transformer business was in normal operation.

Resources of the New Venture and Resource Transfer

HTM insisted that its contribution to the joint venture was its equipment, technical capabilities and human resources, not the land-use right conferred by the State. The main technical changes brought by ABB to the joint venture were in product design and management.

Surprisingly, getting new equipment and machinery for manufacturing transformers was not a top priority of the Vietnamese managers and engineers in the ABB joint venture, as was commonly demanded in other cases. Both ABB and the Vietnamese factory were very selective in their choice of equipment for the joint venture.

Both sides were careful in deciding what types of machine could be used second-hand, and what types should be new. All in all, existing equipment and machinery by HTM accounted for up to 10 per cent of the prescribed capital, valued at US$400,000.

ABB's contribution to the prescribed capital was also mainly in the form of equipment and machinery. This included a CNC machine for cutting high and low voltage, a winding machine, crane, oil pump, electrostatic painting system, and auxiliary equipment.

For the distribution-transformer phase, 28 persons in total were trained in courses overseas. To benefit most from this overseas training, careful preparation and selection was done. The first and most basic preparation was to provide prospective trainees with background knowledge about the subject in which he or she was going to be trained.

Second, intensive English training was provided for all employees, especially senior technicians and managers. The joint venture wanted to retain all existing staff, and wanted to retrain key personnel from the Vietnamese partner so that they could take up similar positions in the joint venture, which was preferable to recruiting already qualified managers and technicians from outside. This approach would build on the existing capability and human resource, and have an accumulative effect, but it required substantial English training because most of more senior managers and engineers had Russian as their first foreign language, unlike the younger generation.

The people selected for overseas training were then to be sent to the ABB facilities that would be providing technology to the joint venture. In addition to some classroom training, they were primarily assigned to work with ABB experts who would later come to work for the joint venture in Vietnam. This way, close working relations were initiated from the beginning.

In critical specialties or technical areas, at least two senior people were to receive in-depth training. One would learn specialist skills for a certain area, while the other would learn how to become a supervisor/trainer for that area.

Training on the spot, at the joint venture, was critical for the installation of equipment and the initial operation. In reality, both short-term consultants sent by ABB to the site, and resident engineers and managers, were required to train complementary Vietnamese staff. Moreover, this was considered to be one of their main tasks, not something incidental to be done in their spare time. Resident expatriates, including the Chief Technical Engineer, spent nearly five hours on training each working day.

Technology sharing and management localization
Rather than using the term 'technology transfer', ABB believed 'technology sharing' would be a more effective mode. Both sides considered this as one important part of the joint venture. Its main purpose was to help local managers build up competence and capability of their own, so they could act as independent experts, and could replace foreign experts.[54]

The technology-sharing programme did not run well at the beginning. One of the major problems was that most foreign experts were preoccupied with the performance of the joint venture, product quality and reliability, etc., and did not pay proper attention to this programme. There was also a problem of picking appropriate candidates: a very qualified engineer may not be suitable, or even interested, in senior engineering jobs that demand some management and supervision functions.

To improve the programme, several measures were undertaken by the joint venture. First, the human resource managers were required to be involved in the implementation of the programme, so that problems and difficulties could be identified early, and remedied in a timely fashion. Second, senior managers were to be more actively involved in the supervision of the implementation of the programme. Third, after each particular period envisaged in the Action Plan, Vietnamese persons subject to the programme were to make reports on its implementation, and come up with suggestions for improvement.

In practice, the joint venture expatriates are being replaced. When the joint venture started operations there were five resident managers and engineers. Two years later, only two were left, and one of those two is now preparing to go. This is claimed to be a rapid process, considering that even in ABB companies in the US, it normally takes five years to complete the substitution with local managers.

Two stages of overseas training were pursued. First, before the commencement of operation of the joint venture, staff were sent to ABB transformer manufacturing facilities elsewhere to learn basic operational knowledge and techniques. Later, when the joint venture had already been in operation for some time, and people had achieved a first-hand understanding of the ABB products and production, they were further trained for more in-depth knowledge, including underlying theoretical issues and wider practical experience. Thus, elements of education for 'know-why' capability were introduced more systematically in this second stage.

Tapping into ABB's regional and international networks

The in-depth knowledge and technology can also be upgraded via the regional forum, or common meetings, for people from all ABB facilities from different countries in each subject area. This type of meeting is organised regularly for each functional segment, such as purchasing, design and electrical engineering.

Vietnamese managers and engineers were exposed to, and actively involved in this forum. The joint venture's Vietnamese staff participated in the Asia-Pacific Training Programme, a programme in which managers from different ABB companies in the region are rotated to work at other ABB facilities on a cost-sharing basis, thereby gaining broader experience, as well as a new vision.

The impression of managers at the joint venture is that it is information and understanding about markets and management that was most beneficial for the Vietnamese in these forums. Surprisingly, the Vietnamese Deputy Technical Director stated that understanding from tapping this network 'is more valuable than specific techniques', and 'may be impossible to buy even if you had the money'.

Enterprise Restructuring

One of the many changes in management was its refocusing from day-to-day management to more strategic planning and monitoring. This required considerable training of middle-level staff.

As the market was still in the embryo stage, the network of agents and dealers had yet to be developed, and the joint venture had to do most of the sales function itself. Moreover, most orders for transformers were small, and the time lag from placing an order to expecting delivery was short, normally only 10-15 days.

This situation led to the necessity for close cooperation between various departments within the joint venture to respond quickly to an order. Thus, a new procedure was created, in which each department's role and functions were clarified: the sales department would inform the technical department about a new order; the technical department then chooses an appropriate design for the technical parameters, calculates material needs and then transmits these to the planning department for calculation of costs and suggestions for a price, which would be returned to the sales department to negotiate the final price with the customer. A production order would only be made after agreement had been reached with the client.

This procedure also led to changes in the method of placing a production order within the joint venture. For example, previously the technical department was responsible for making drawings and blueprints for transformers to be manufactured, and for suggesting the type of material. This was then sent to the shop floor and the rest of the specification calculated and final details decided by the shop floor manager. In the joint venture, however, after making detailed technical drawings, the technical department has also to prepare material bills, in which specifications and volumes of all materials required must be specified for each component of the transformer. These data will enable the planning department to finalise the remaining calculations quickly, and when the production order is obtained, all materials can be quickly made available according to those specifications. Thus, aside from close cooperation with other departments, the technical department was also required to be knowledgeable of broader issues, for example, an alternative material supply, so that they could work effectively with the other two departments.

By early 1997, the joint venture had four product/service areas, namely, (1) distribution transformer, (2) switch gear, (3) services, and (4) power transformers. The first three areas no longer needed ABB's expatriate experts, and by mid-1998, the first power transformers were being churned out by the joint venture, more than a year earlier than originally planned by the Vietnamese party and Government agencies.

However, it turned out to be inefficient for the joint venture to retain such a broad range of products, and they had to streamline by cutting the switchgear group, and reducing the services to only those directly required for distribution and power transformers.

The expansion to power transformers in 1997 was a controversial decision. ABB was a bit hesitant to move quickly to power-transformer production, mainly for commercial rather than technical reasons. In spite of the more complex and sophisticated nature of power transformers, ABB believed that the Vietnamese staff of the joint venture could handle it. Its hesitancy came mainly from cost-effectiveness considerations. For one thing, investments in additional manufacturing facilities are enormous: A new laboratory needing far more precise analysis and tight quality control, costs alone around US$2 million. Another reason was that the Vietnamese market for power transformers is still small, and can well be supplied by ABB's other facilities, in China or Thailand.

Unlike the production of distribution-transformers, the Vietnamese personnel had no previous experience with power transformers, so although the joint venture could rely to some extent on the experience with the distribution-transformers, it also had to invest substantially in training for power transformer production, costing the joint venture almost US$600,000 to do so.

Employment
In the beginning, the joint venture employed all the staff of the Vietnamese factory – 470 persons. In 1998, the joint venture started to downsize employment. Gradually, as productivity increased, the need for labour was also reduced. For instance, the design department had 30 persons in the beginning, but employed only four by early 2001. In addition, as the joint venture closed down non-core products, a number of redundant employees were also laid off.

By 2001, the joint venture employed only 260 persons, which meant that nearly half the original labour force of the Vietnamese side had been made redundant. The laying-off process was a strenuous one for the joint venture itself, and for managers from both parties.

Utilisation of equipment of the acquired firm
Some equipment for the Vietnamese side was retained and contributed to the joint venture, for the production of non-core products. However, five years later, most of it has been replaced by new equipment. It became evident that the ABB side had foreseen that such equipment would not last for long, but had had to accept it in the first place in order to reach the joint-venture agreement.

Most of the product adaptations took place in technical areas. These adaptations were made for two main reasons: one was the local market condition, and the other was to exploit the accumulated experience and expertise of the local partner. Yet there were two notable adaptations suggested by Vietnamese staff. First, the core of the transformer was modified to a new vertical design, so that it could be easily transported and handled safely under the rough transport conditions prevailing in Vietnam.

Second, an additional component to sustain the copper winding was added to the ABB standard design. This was a solution to the problem caused by the lowering of the winding, which resulted from the fact that due to high humidity, the tightness of the winding changed considerably after the drying, thus making it very loose. ABB's efforts to remedy this problem, which included drying for a longer period, brought little success because the constantly varying humidity made it difficult to have a standard measure for winding and drying.

Spillover Effects

There are several spillover effects from ABB Transformers Vietnam. It initiated the efforts to reduce no-load loss by 20-30 per cent across the whole industry. In relation to suppliers, the joint venture assisted in the specifications and technical assistance for them to supply parts and other inputs to ABB requirements. In general, ABB set new informal standards on manufacturing and management, which have later been adopted by many local firms.

The joint venture has managed to export to regional markets, and so far it has exported to India, Laos, Indonesia, and is preparing to export to Singapore. In the beginning, 100 per cent of inputs had to be imported. The local inputs now account for about 10 per cent. Potentially, these local inputs may eventually account for up to 20 per cent.

Competition

This joint venture has created waves of competition, and upgrading in technology and quality by other companies. Most notable was the imitation by some other local companies in choosing equipment and product design. The ABB joint venture reduced the no-load loss by 50 per cent within four years, so other companies had to reduce this also, and this has helped to reduce the no-load loss by 20-30 per cent across the whole industry.

Indirectly as a result of this joint venture, the industry became less concentrated. No company has a dominant position now, and the number of major companies increased from five to seven (all State-owned or joint ventures).

Concluding Remarks

The joint venture was the only mode of entry available to ABB at the time it entered the Vietnam market and it seemed to be a satisfactory choice for both sides in the beginning. Over time, however, many unexpected things happened, and both sides discovered that there are many problems with this way of doing business. In the summer of 2003, ABB acquired the stake of its local partner and thus attained full ownership and control over the venture.

Considerable resources were transferred from ABB, but intangible resources were the most appreciated, rather than the tangible equipment and hardware. Similarly, the intangible contribution by the acquired firm was more appreciated by ABB and the joint venture: human resources, government relations and understanding of local markets, etc., while tangible assets, including equipment, was not seen as important. (Nguyen and Meyer 2004.)

The integration process was fairly smooth in the beginning, when the joint venture basically retained the previous business of the acquired firm. However, when it needed to undergo substantial restructuring, the process was not easy, and many Vietnamese felt that they were being 'taken over' by ABB. The joint venture had a substantial positive impact on the local industry, although the financial prospects in the near to medium term were not bright.

HONDA VIETNAM

Introduction

The Government's protection of the motorcycle market has encouraged foreign investments in this sector. Honda's joint venture with a state-run company has been a political move. With its long-established reputation for quality, Honda quickly became the largest and most profitable producer, within a few years of its commencement. Production in Vietnam can be seen as an extension of Honda's operation in the region. The product and process technology are similar to its Thai factories. Training is critical to maintain specified quality and productivity.

Honda Vietnam was established in 1996 and started its operation in 1997. Its main business is the manufacture of motorcycles. The industry can be considered as mature. However, there is still some potential for growth, with shifts in market demand and the continuous development of motorcycle technology. This is also a very competitive industry, with several Japanese companies, especially Honda, dominating the market.

Industry

In Vietnam, as in many other Asian countries, the motorcycle is the main means of transportation. Before 2000, the market was dominated by international brands (Honda, Yamaha, Suzuki, SYM of Taiwan, Piaggio) which are assembled locally with many imported components, or are imported as whole machines. Honda has enjoyed the lion's share in the Vietnamese market, even though recently it has been seriously challenged by cheap locally-assembled motorcycles using imported components from China, as illustrated in Table 10.1. A jump in usage of motorcycles in recent years has illustrated the high demand-elasticity of price.

The industry has been protected by a high tariff on motorcycle imports. As a result, until 2000, the domestic price had been at about 1.5 times higher than the price of similar models in Thailand. The import of components is regulated by a sliding scale of duties linked to the assemblers' fulfilment of 'local content' conditions (Fujita 2003).

Table 10.1 Motorcycle market in Vietnam and Honda's share

Year	Cumulative units registered	Units registered in the year	Industry growth (%)	Honda Vietnam[2]	HVN's share (%)
1990	2,770,000	36,400	–	–	–
1991	2,806,000	36,000	-1.1	–	–
1992	2,846,000	40,000	11.1	–	–
1993	2,901,000	55,000	37.5	–	–
1994[3]	3,275,000	374,000	580.0	–	–
1995	3,678,000	403,000	7.8	–	–
1996	4,209,000	531,000	31.8	–	–
1997	4,827,000	618,000	16.4	–	–
1998	5,219,000	392,000	-36.6	81,000	20.7
1999	5,585,000	366,000	-6.6	96,000	26.2
2000	7,452,524	1,867,524	410.3	162,000	8.7
2001[4]	9,422,524	1,970,000	5.5	170,000	8.6

Notes: 1. Calculations based on various reports of the Ministry of Industry, and HVN.
2. Sale of HVN's products only, imported Honda products are not included.
3. The first FDI in motorcycle manufacturing was the 100% foreign owned project of Ching Fong Group, a Taiwanese conglomerate. It received its investment licence in 1992, and started production in late 1993.
4. Motorcycles originating from China account for approximately 86.5% of the Vietnamese market.

Transportation costs or other natural barriers to trade do not seem to have much effect on this industry.

The Investor: Honda Motor Co.

Honda Vietnam is a joint venture between Honda Group and Vietnam Engine and Agricultural Machinery Corporation (VEAM). Honda Motor Co., Ltd is the ultimate parent of all Honda subsidiaries throughout the world. It was established in Japan on 24 September 1948, and now has its office in Tokyo, Japan. Its main operations are the manufacture, sale, lease, and repair of motorcycles, automobiles and power products. The company is one of today's leading manufacturers of automobiles and the largest manufacturer of motorcycles in the world. By the end of March 2001, the company had a global network of 434 subsidiaries and affiliates, including 118 production facilities in 31 countries. Honda Motor Co., Ltd and its subsidiaries employed 114,300 workers, had total assets of US$45,741.8 million, net sales of US$52,169.7 million, a net income of 3.6 per cent of sales, and an R&D expenditure of US$2,847.7 million (Honda 2001). Worldwide, Honda sold 6.1 million motor cycles, of which 4.8 million in Asia.

Asian Honda Motor Co., Ltd is a 100 per cent Honda-owned operation in Thailand. It was established in 1964. In 1996, Asian Honda Motor Co., Ltd became the ASEAN regional headquarters and took responsibility for the coordination of operations of subsidiaries, and the import and distribution of Honda products throughout the ASEAN region. Honda's Thai operations are still the largest in Asia outside Japan, encompassing R&D, production and sales of motorcycles, automobiles, power products, and parts and accessories.

Motive for entering the country

The entry of Honda into Vietnam might be seen as a result of several forces, one of which is the size of the Vietnamese market. With a population of 74 million people and the motorcycle as the main transportation means, Vietnam is definitely an attractive market. However, this alone was not enough to justify the entry, because, given low transportation costs and similar conditions in the region, Honda could have effectively exploited the market by importation, as it had already been doing for a long time.

The second factor that had an impact on Honda's investment in Vietnam is the protection of the local market. A 60 per cent tariff rate applied on imported complete motorcycles is an effective incentive for a market-seeking FDI project. The third factor was the other attractive incentives that the Vietnamese government offers foreign investors with ambitions to develop the local automobile and motorcycle industry. Honda Vietnam Co., Ltd, for example, was granted a four-year corporate income tax holiday, followed by a further four years at half the normal rate, and after 15 years of operation, a rate stabilised at 25 per cent.

Characteristics

The motorcycle manufacturing industry is considered a mature industry. With advancement in engine technology, and advanced engineering safety and environmental regulations, the industry has been improving at a rapid pace. R&D expenditure in all business segments of Honda has been around 5.5 per cent of net sales during the last 10 years. In the financial year ended March 2001, expenditure for R&D in the motorcycle segment was about 8 per cent of sales worldwide.

With a 'market-in approach', which is (1) understanding each local market and (2) tailoring products to local needs, Honda has developed its five regions global strategy. The traditionally centralised R&D and engineering activities in Japan are now distributed amongst the main regions (Japan, North America, Europe, and Asia) to produce products that meet the local needs.

Advertising is an important activity in marketing Honda's products. However, the motorcycle industry is not considered to be advertising-intensive. We do not have any reliable estimate of Honda's advertising expenditure at this time.

Experience

Honda has been in Asia since 1964 with the establishment of Asian Honda Motor Co. Ltd, in Thailand. Since then, Honda has developed a comprehensive business in the region, making Asia one of five strategic regions in its global strategy. The Asian operations of Honda cover a wide range of activities, including R&D (just recently in 1997), production and sale of motorcycles, automobiles, power products, and parts and accessories. For motorcycles alone, Honda has 14 production sites in nine Asian countries, with a combined annual production of about three million units.

In 1996, the Asian Honda Co. in Thailand became Honda's headquarters for the ASEAN region. Its function is to support and oversee the strategic development and operations of all Honda operations in the region. Given a long-term serving of the Vietnam market from its production bases in Thailand, Honda has used its experiences in Thailand in applying production technology, product designs, and quality control methods in Vietnam.

With regard to mode of entry, the joint venture is typical of Honda (but not dominant) in Asia (rather than in the Pacific), while 100 per cent ownership is typical in North America, Europe, South America, and Japan. We do not know at this stage, however, if 100 per cent ownership is by means of M&A or of greenfield investment. The difference in mode of entry in Asia is probably due to regulations of the governments in the region, where joint ventures are more welcome.

Vietnamese Local Partner: VEAM

The local partner in Honda Vietnam Co., Vietnam Engine and Agricultural Machinery Corporation (VEAM), owns a 30 per cent share in the joint venture. VEAM is a State General Corporation that was set up in 1995 by merging (simply combining) activities of 15 individual State-run production/research units. The corporation is under the control of the Ministry of Industry. The Prime Minister assigns the General Director, the Minister of Industry assigns the Vice-General Directors, and the Minister of Finance assigns the Head Accountant.

VEAM's enterprises stretch all over the country and produce various things like multi-purpose engines, agricultural machinery, tractors, automobiles, motorcycles, equipment for on-land and water transportation. By 2002, it employed about 7,000 workers. It is also the local partner in some joint ventures with foreign investors such as Toyota, Suzuki, and Ford amongst others.

The main contribution of the local partner in Honda Vietnam Co. is property in terms of land-use rights, and its political position in the machinery industry. Informal regulations of this sector have changed over time. In the early 1990s, with the Government objective of attracting foreign investors into the automobile and motorcycle industry, few FDIs were allowed to take the form of 100 per cent foreign-owned. Later on, joint venture with Vietnamese enterprises was effectively the only choice for FDI in this sector. In this circumstance, VEAM emerged as the most politically suitable partner.

It is also a surprise that none of the 15 subsidiaries of VEAM could become a local parts-supplier to the joint venture. In fact, the joint venture has developed business relationships with other local producers for their components supplies.

Cultural Distance

Even though Japan and Vietnam are both in Asia, and both are influenced by Buddhism, their culture, tradition, and language are very different. However, the Japanese managers who currently work at Honda Vietnam do have some experience of working in the region. Regardless of all the differences, Japan is still amongst the top foreign investors in Vietnam, and is seen by many policy-makers as a major source of technology transfer.

Performance

Honda Vietnam Co. is considered to be a profitable FDI business in Vietnam. By the end of 2000, protected by a high tariff rate and efficient sourcing policy, Honda's accumulated production reached 339,000 units, and its accumulated profit was about US$65.8 million. HVN took just 15 months to reach its first 100,000 units of production, a further 11 months to reach 200,000, and only seven more months to reach 300,000 units of cumulative production. By that time, HVN had identified itself as the country's largest motorcycle producer. In general, the FDI has fulfilled the expectations of the investors in terms of its original objective.

Counterfactual

If this joint venture had not been established, Honda would have found another local partner to implement its entry plan. As for the current local firm, it would have survived with subsidies from the Government, as many other state companies have.

The entry of Honda into Vietnam has created many changes that have had a great impact on the Government's policy towards the motorcycle industry. So there is reason to believe that some actions of public sector institutions would have been different if Honda had not entered.

The Entry

Honda Vietnam Co. was legally established in March 1996 with legal capital of US$31.2 million. This is a joint venture in which Honda Group owns 70 per cent (42 per cent Honda Motor Co. and 28 per cent Asian Honda Motor Co.) and the Vietnamese partner owns 30 per cent. This rate allows Honda to have managerial control in the operation of the joint venture. On the management board, the Japanese side holds the post of General Manager and the Vietnamese side holds the post of Vice-General Manager.

HTM is located in Phuc Thang Commune, Me Ling District, Vinh Phuc Province, about 30 kilometres from Hanoi. This is essentially a greenfield project in which Honda takes the leading role. The Vietnamese partner contributes land-use rights, and the foreign partner contributes capital funds. Design capacity of HTM is 450,000 units/year and this is in line with the registered investment of US$104 million. By 30 October 2001, the accumulated investment was about US$134.4 million. By January 2002, HVN had 1,143 workers and a capacity of 450,000 units/year. By April 2002, it reached the capacity of 600,000 units/year with about 2,000 workers, a dramatic growth.

Resources of the New Venture

As a typical mechanical factory, manufacturing, assembling, and testing the final products requires a large area of land and an appropriate building configuration. Appropriate and reliable machinery, especially testing equipment, is also important to maintain consistent of quality and safety. In the motorcycle business, a manageable distribution network is important, because the distributors are not only the sales outlets, but also the service centres where customers can obtain after-sales services.

Concerning intangible resources, technology, brand name, managerial know-how, business relations, and motorcycle culture are all-important but for different reasons. Technology helps to attain product quality, as well as cost control. Even though there is nothing advanced in the technology to make standard motorcycle models, technological know-how, managerial know-how, and practical experience (reinforcing specific technology) are needed to obtain a consistent level of high quality and reliability.

Business relations are also vital for the new venture. The operation of Honda Vietnam Co. relies heavily on the Honda procurement-network in the region. This network has enabled HVN to become successful in a relatively short time. The establishment of HVN also brought with it many foreign parts and accessory makers into Vietnam, creating an array of satellite companies around HVN. Without strong business relations, Honda would not have been able to do this.

Honda has contributed almost all the resources necessary for the operation of the new venture and the local partner contributes only land and some political connections. Construction of HTM was also carried out in accordance with the development plan and engineering works of Honda. HVN is set to go through several phases, starting with assembling standard models with some parts produced and sourced locally, and sophisticated components (such as entire engines) sourced from overseas. It will then move up, producing these sophisticated components in Vietnam. Resource transfer is part of this development strategy.

Concerning the machinery and production-line structure, by the end of 2000, HVN had developed this structure with six production workshops, as follows:

- *Pressing Workshop* with a 200-ton and two 400-ton pressing machines, a CNC pipe-framing machine used to make frames, gasoline tanks, chain boxes, and other precision parts;
- *Welding Workshop* with five robots to ensure productivity precision and quality of components;
- *Plastic Object Workshop* with modern computer-controlled machines, which allow high productivity whilst providing endurance and aesthetics of plastic parts;
- *Paintshop* equipped with state-of-the-art technology (the first in use in the ASEAN region) to ensure the greatest possible surface protection for metal parts;
- *Engine and Frame Assembly Line* being a modern assembly line with a relatively high level of automation. It is also equipped with on-the-line testing facilities, which allow quality to be checked at every stage of production;

- *Quality Control Workshop,* which is equipped with modern state-of-the-art Japanese testing equipment operated by overseas trained staff. It also manages the 500-metre long test-runway, which is the longest in the ASEAN region so far. Recently, HVN has started to invest in manufacturing engine components locally. This might result in a totally new workshop.

Concerning the product range and quality as mentioned in the above sections, HVN started production with the 'Super Dream', and later the 'Future', a sports-type model. These models were both designed in Thailand and their quality was equivalent to similar models produced in Honda's Thai factories. Their prices were also close to similar models imported from Thailand. Facing challenges from cheap Chinese motorcycles, which were copies of the Honda products, in January 2002, HVN launched its Wave Alpha model, which was priced about 20 per cent higher than the Chinese ones, but perceived by Vietnamese customers as having superior quality.

So far, the technology transferred has been process technology, which means equipment and skills to operate and control the production-process smoothly. Product technology has not been transferred fully, since design and product development capacity is centralised in Honda R&D South East Asia Co., and Honda's factories located in Thailand.

The above-mentioned process technology is being transferred mainly through staff training. Before starting production, HVN had built up a core staff comprising engineers and technicians whom they sent to Japan and Thailand for training. There were six-month courses for production-line managers and three-month courses for managers at lower levels. In total, 100 people had this type of training. Once the production commenced, Honda sent its supervisors overseas on a regular basis to gain guidance in production activities.

Besides overseas training, on-the-job training has been in use since the start of operations in the form of short training courses provided by Japanese lecturers. This type of training aims at specific or problematic issues arising in the operation of the new venture. The training curriculum is based on the Honda Foundation Course, a programme used within Honda only. Teaching methods include classroom lectures, role-plays, scenario building, etc.

The above training is not restricted to technical issues, but also managerial and marketing issues. Here again, the typical formula is overseas training plus in-house training and on-the-job training as well as supervision and guidance by foreign staff. In the charter of the joint venture it is clearly written that in the long term, Vietnamese will eventually replace positions currently held by Japanese professionals. However, some Japanese managers say that it might take at least 10 years to complete this process, whereas Vietnamese staff in the company have a more optimistic outlook on this.

A general problem in Vietnam during its transition period is the shortage of managerial and technical skills. The market for raw materials and intermediate inputs is much more developed. As discussed earlier, given the ambition to develop the automobile and motorcycle manufacturing industry in Vietnam, the Government requires motorcycle assemblers (both FDI and domestic firms) to use some proportion of components made locally. The higher the local content, the lower the import duty rate for imported inputs. This 'local content' rate is required to increase steadily over time. In order to enjoy a better import duty rate, Honda has therefore focused on sourcing components locally, and this, in turn, has helped develop the local input market. By the end of 2001, Honda had localised more than 60 per cent of the two models, Super Dream and Future. The local content of Wave Alpha, the newly launched model, is targeted at an even higher level of localization.

By 1997, the FDI policy environment was quite favourable. However, in the case of motorcycles, there were some extra requirements, as well as incentives, in accordance with the 'local content' policy.

Regardless of the 30 per cent ownership held by the local partner, Honda keeps the leading role in this greenfield project. So far, there is not much said about integration of the local partner with the foreign partner in this case. As mentioned earlier, other subsidiaries of VEAM have been unable to obtain any supply contracts from Honda.

Post-Acquisition Development

The operation of Honda Vietnam relies heavily on the company's production network in the region. Its product designs and engineering works all originate from Thailand. The technical staff are also from other Honda operations in the region, many important components are sourced from Honda's affiliates or suppliers in the regions.

The entry of Honda into Vietnam had a dramatic impact on the development of the motorcycle industry. In order to meet the targeted rate of local content (so as to enjoy a lower rate of import duty for imported components), HVN had to develop a network of suppliers in Vietnam. This network is made up from domestic suppliers who have been selected by, and received technical support from HVN, and other FDI enterprises that in many cases are suppliers to Honda within the region. At the moment, Honda has about 20 local suppliers, of which 13 are Japanese firms who set up in Vietnam solely to serve Honda, a firm based on Thai investment that had been assembling Honda products before Honda came to Vietnam, and six domestic firms. Honda itself has entered into two more joint ventures with other local partners to produce motorcycle parts.

The process of seeking local domestic suppliers had an important impact on the awareness of many local domestic firms. By negotiating with Honda, they have learned a great deal about quality requirements and control, and management skills and philosophy. Those who failed to become suppliers to Honda learned, the hard way, how and why they had failed in their attempt to gain the prestige and profit the role would have earned them. Those who succeeded have improved greatly in the process of meeting the demanding requirements of their client. In many cases the link to Honda proved to be a valuable source of technical support and enlightenment.

The entry of Honda also changed the competitive behaviour in the local market. First, the importation of similar standard models from Thailand has been replaced by the importation of more expensive models aimed at the higher-end of the market. Secondly, Yamaha and some other assemblers also entered the market, making countrywide competition even more intense. Thirdly, the high price set by FDI firms (Honda is the most noted for this) has created opportunities for low-priced units to enter the market. Thus the emergence of so called 'Chinese motorbikes' (as most of the components are made in China) with prices which range from half to a third of that of Honda's standard products.

In responding to the challenge of these 'Chinese bikes', Honda launched its new model 'Wave Alpha', which is priced at about 20 per cent above the Chinese units. Very quickly after its launch, the new model gained a significant share in the low-end market. Many people had to wait in turn to buy one. Wave Alpha became a real threat to local assemblers who, so far, had enjoyed the surge of 'Chinese bikes' by assembling only those models. They fought back by criticising Honda, saying that they had used too many 'Chinese parts' in their new model, and that Honda had manipulated the local content rate for low tax benefits. The debate brought about an investigation by the Government, and the situation has become problematic.

After its investigations the Government realised that the 'local content policy', with its ambiguous method of calculation, is a paradise for rent-seeking activities and smuggling. Within the Government, ministries blame each other, and some corrections ensued. However, correction of a problem of this sort often creates new problems. As a result, years 2001 and 2002 showed repeated changes in regulations promulgated on the motorcycle industry. This created an unpredictable policy framework that led to considerable irritation among foreign investors (Fujita 2003). Honda, for example, at some point had to stop its operation for six months to wait for clearance from the Government on a particular issue. In 2003, 'local content policy' based on tax incentives is being eliminated.

Concluding Remarks

Market seeking or 'Jumping over the tariff' has initially been the main objective of Honda's investment in Vietnam. It started mainly with simple assembly operations and the production of some non-critical components, then moves up the value chain. Joint venture with a politically strong local company was the most suitable choice at the time Honda entered Vietnam.

Honda's operation in Vietnam has created a network of suppliers and thus has a strong spillover impact on the motorcycle industry. Standard equipment and training is critical in maintaining the quality of Honda's products. With an established reputation for quality, the affiliate enjoys high growth and profit.

The local partner is weak in exploiting its position in the joint venture with Honda and the evidence is that its enterprises have failed to become suppliers of Honda Vietnam. The affiliate is effectively under the full control of Honda.

References for Vietnamese Case Studies

Fujita, Mai (2003): Foreign direct investment and industrialization in Vietnam: New developments and remaining issues, mimeo, National University of Singapore and JETRO.

Honda (2001, 2002), *Annual Reports* (http:/world.honda.com/).

11. Conclusions for Management Research

Klaus E. Meyer

INTRODUCTION[55]

This research project has analysed foreign investors' entry strategies with particular attention to transactional, resource and institutional aspects. Our research focus has been on the adaptation of entry strategies to the local business context, in particular the institutional environment and local resource endowment. This chapter reviews emerging themes and implications of the research, and the case studies in particular, with relevance to the international management and strategy literature introduced in chapter 1.

To start, we revisit the global strategies of the investors and their implications for FDI in emerging economies. Global strategies are the prime determinants of entry strategies, and any analysis of entry has to take them into account. Secondly, I consider conceptual issues concerning entry strategies, and reflect over the appropriateness of the conventional classifications of joint venture versus wholly owned, and acquisition versus greenfield. The case studies reveal important features of modes that may go unnoticed with the conventional classification. I thus describe and classify the entry modes in more detail with the aim of enriching the conceptual analysis of entry modes, and to propose concepts for future research.

Thirdly, I review the crucial resource dimension of foreign entry in the spirit of recent literature on the resource-based view of the firm (Barkema and Vermeulen 1998, Anand and Delios 2002). Our study investigated what kinds of resources are crucial for success or failure of affiliates in emerging markets, and where FDI firms obtain these resources. The cases point in particular to the dynamics of resource contributions during the early years after the initial establishment. Eventually, we are concerned with the implications of mode choice for both corporate and societal performance: which local circumstances would suggest using either entry mode and when do for instance acquisitions perform better than greenfield projects? The main implication of the qualitative work is, however, that the design of the deal may be more crucial than the choice of mode: In practice, investors rarely face a choice between two clearly defined options.

Table 11.1 Overview of case studies

	Foreign Investor	Country of origin	Acquired firm	Industry	Objectives (main group of targeted customers)	Year of entry
SA	NGK Ceramics	Japan	–	Automotive suppliers	Global MNE (local & export)	2000
SA	Behr	Germany	Federal Mogul, SA			1999
SA	EST	USA	Ziton	Fire detection equipment	world-wide, mainly businesses	2000
SA	ABN Amro	Netherlands	–	Banking	Local businesses and individuals, global customers	1995
VN	SEAB	Singapore / Denmark	–	Beverages	Local individuals	1993
VN	ABB	Sweden / Switzerland	Hanoi Transformer	Electrical engineering	Local state-owned firms	1996
VN	Honda	Japan	–	Motorcycles	Local individuals	1996

IN	Bacardi-Martini	USA	Gemini Distilleries	Beverages	Local individuals	1998
IN	Packaging	n.a.	Unit of a conglomerate	Packaging	Local businesses	mid 1990s, 2000
IN	ABN Amro	Netherlands	Bank of America, IN	Banking	Local businesses and individuals, global customers	1920, 1998
EG	France Telecom, Motorola	France, USA	ECMS MobiNil	Telecom operator	Local individuals and businesses	1998
EG	GSK	UK	ABI, APIC	Pharmaceuticals	Medical practitioners in Arab countries, Africa & parts of Europe	1981, 1997
EG	Heinz	USA	–	Processed food	In Egypt and other Arab countries Individuals & restaurants	1992

GLOBAL STRATEGIES AND LOCAL ENTRY

Any explanation of foreign investment must start from an understanding of the global strategies pushing MNCs into emerging markets, including the impact of institutional changes at the global level such as membership in the World Trade Organization or regional integration. Most investors in our study focus on a particular industry aiming for global leadership in their chosen segment. FDI in developing countries can serve this objective by providing a global supply base or by extending market reach.

The case studies have been selected to cover a diversity of countries of origins and investment objectives as well as a diversity of industries, with emphasis on manufacturing (Table 11.1). All foreign investors have undertaken new FDI in the last 10 years; however two investors had operations in the host economy for many years before: ABN Amro in India and GSK in Egypt.

The home countries of the investors include Europe, USA and Japan. The foreign investor firms in the sample are mainly large MNEs with several operations abroad; some even have a worldwide presence. They thus undertake substantive projects with potentially large impact in terms of employment, capital and knowledge transfer. They are not 'average investors', who, as the survey data show, often are small and medium size firms that in case of Vietnam and Egypt may originate within the region.

The industries span a wide range of manufacturing with variations reflecting the host countries' industrial structure, plus a major business services case in three countries, respectively banking and telecommunications. To facilitate cross-country comparisons, we analysed ABN Amro in both India and South Africa; they do not have subsidiaries in Egypt or Vietnam.

Except for the South African manufacturing cases, all investors are primarily serving the local market. This corresponds to the pattern found in the survey, especially considering that the case-firms are at least medium size, while many export-oriented operations are small. The market-seeking cases cover both business-to-business industries, and manufacturers of consumer goods. In contrast, Behr and Edwards Systems Technologies (EST) invested in South Africa to acquire technological resources of local firms that are valuable not just in a local context, and moreover provided access to customers worldwide. GSK Egypt has for many years served primarily the Egyptian market, yet in recent years, it has grown into one of the five worldwide production and supply hubs of GSK, serving the Middle East, Africa and parts of Southern Europe.

None of our cases reports an investment that is solely established with the aim to exploit local labour cost advantages or raw materials. This is indicative of the fact that most FDI projects are driven by a mix of motives. Yet, global sourcing strategies lead to the transfer of supplier relationships, and thus local sourcing for local production. Manufacturing companies often prefer to use their same established suppliers worldwide, especially in the automotive industry. Thus, Honda's investment in motorcycle assembly in Vietnam triggered further investment by its Japanese suppliers, while Behr has reacted on requests by German automotive manufacturers in South Africa.

To explain the pattern of operations in emerging markets, one has to understand how global strategies drive international entry. Globalisation has led to the opening of many markets and thus increased competition not only in emerging markets, but also in developed countries. In consequence, rather than building a strong position in several markets in their home country, more and more companies pursue a global strategy that is focused on one particular industry. In recent years, many MNEs have gone through a process of 'globalfocusing', as they have shed peripheral product lines and expanded their core businesses, often by acquisition (Meyer 2003). As industry-specialists, they aim for global leadership positions in their chosen segment.

FDI in emerging economies can serve this objective by providing a global supply base, or by extending the market reach. Among the case firms, in particular Heinz, changed its strategy by refocusing on a narrower product line while strengthening its global operations, among other sites in Egypt. For companies aiming to become global leaders in their market segment, competitive interaction with global rivals may induce early entry in emerging economies in view of first-mover or fast-second advantages, as in the case of Carlsberg acting soon after Heineken entered Vietnam, and NGK Ceramics following competitor Corning into South Africa.

On the other hand, some firms have divested selected emerging market operations as part of a global restructuring, including ABN Amro. Moreover, two of the case-firms acquired emerging market affiliates of firms that wished to divest from certain industries, namely ABN Amro taking over Bank of America's Indian retail banking operation, and Behr taking over a South African division of Federal Mogul of the USA. Global mergers and acquisitions can also affect operations in emerging markets, yet in the cases we have only one example. Glaxo Egypt changed its name to Glaxo-Wellcome Egypt in 1995 and to GSK Egypt in 2001 as result of global mergers.

In conclusion, entry in emerging economies is to a large extent driven by changing global strategies. The globalisation of industries and competition can be expected to generate more MNEs that aim to exploit locational advantages worldwide, and which thus establish operations in emerging markets as part of their integrated global operations. Further research ought to investigate this trend and its driving forces. It needs to be incorporated into both strategic management research and policy analysis of FDI.

Table 11.2 Entry modes

	Firm	Mode	FDI ownership	Employment
SA	NGK	Greenfield	100%	90
Sa	Behr	Acquisition from another MNE	100%	1081
SA	EST	Acquisition of a firm with worldwide exports	100%	450
SA	ABN Amro	Greenfield, then grown through an acquisition.	Affiliate 100%, which owns some businesses as JV.	2000: 350, 2003: 120
VN	SEAB	JV with a SOE	35% (plus 25% investment fund up to 2003)	1995: 340
VN	ABB	JV with a SOE, but effectively a partial acquisition	65%	1998: 470 2001: 260
VN	Honda	JV with 'passive' SOE	70%	n.a.
IN	Bacardi-Martini	JV with local conglomerate	74%	n.a.

IN	Packaging	Stepwise acquisition from local conglomerate	Initially 51%, later 100%	n.a.
IN	ABN Amro	Organic growth, acquisition from another MNE & JV with passive partner in different segments.	Affiliate 100%, which owns some businesses as JV	n.a.
EG	ECMS MobiNil	Consortium-JV acquires a privatised firm	71.25% in JV, which owns 51% ECMS	1700
EG	GSK	Multiple acquisitions of private firms	(a) Stepwise to 87.8%, (b) 97%	1057
EG	Heinz	JV with a Kuwaiti firm	Initially 33%, now 51%	200

Note: In India, employment data are considered confidential and thus not readily available.

ENTRY MODES

Multinational firms normally prefer full ownership of their operations, as partial acquisitions and joint ventures with unequal partners are potentially subject to many conflicts. Exceptions are made for instance when a local partner is needed but cannot be incorporated in the firm, or when investment risk shall be shared. Moreover, expansion in industrialised countries is often in form of acquisition, while expansion in emerging markets is more frequently in form of greenfield or with shared ownership, as illustrated by our survey data (Chapter 2). The cases include many joint ventures and partial acquisitions, and show a variety of entry modes not just in terms of types as discussed in the scholarly literature, but in the ways that these modes are actually designed. This variation concerns multiple dimensions, including equity control and resource transfers.

In all our cases, the foreign investor has a dominant influence over the management at least on strategic issues. However, in most cases the foreign investor holds less than full equity (Table 11.2). The variations in equity ownership appear mainly country specific. In South Africa, the foreign investors hold 100 per cent where they wish to do so. In Vietnam, all investors have formed joint ventures with state-owned firms. In Egypt, all foreign investors also hold a majority stake in a JV, yet the partners are private firms, and the foreign stake has increased since the first entry in Egypt. In India, all three projects were initially established as JV, but two had been converted to 100 per cent ownership by 2002.

The cases include both acquisitions and greenfield projects, both among the fully foreign-owned firms and among those with shared equity. Only in South Africa, are full acquisitions common according to our survey data and they are represented in the cases. In the other countries, acquisitions occur as partial acquisitions, as in ECMS Egypt, or in the formal structure of a joint venture as in ABB Transformers, Vietnam or Bacardi-Martini, India.

The small number of full acquisitions may be surprising, considering that many investors need complementary local resources. In mature market economies, FDI capital flows from M&A account for more than 90 per cent of all FDI capital, while in emerging markets the proportion of FDI in form of acquisition fluctuate between a quarter and half of FDI capital (UNCTAD 2002). In our survey study, less than one in four FDI projects are in form of partial or full acquisition (Chapter 2). Our cases include several acquisitions, but also firms that might be expected to expand by acquisition, but didn't. This research points to two complementary factors that may inhibit acquisitions in emerging economies: potential acquisition targets are rare as resource endowment of local firms is weak, and relevant capital market institutions are not well developed.

The survey data show that large affiliates are more likely to be created by partial or full acquisition, while greenfield dominates among affiliates with (so far) less than 100 employees. Our cases show a similar pattern, as the only pure greenfield, NGK Ceramics in South Africa, is also the only subsidiary that has as yet less than 100 employees. The larger numbers of employees in the projects mostly originate from the acquired firm.

Another feature of the cases that has rarely been explored in the literature is the dynamics of ownership patterns over the lifetime of an FDI project (but see Gomes-Casseres 1987, Harrigan 1988). In our cases, foreign partners in Egyptian, Vietnamese and Indian cases increased their equity stake, but the survey data also show foreign investors reducing their stake. In some cases, these equity changes appear pre-planned, in other cases the change occurred in response to changes in the environment, notably the FDI regulation. A low level involvement moreover provides a foreign investor with a platform from which to expand if the business develops favourably, while at the same time retaining the flexibility not to commit further resources if prospects turn out to be less promising.

GSK took 11 years to increase its stake in ABI to 87.8 per cent in 1992, Heinz soon after the initial entry increased its stake from 33 to 51 per cent. In the ECMS case, one of the foreign partners in the original MobilNil consortium left and its shares were taken over by France Telecom. Increases of foreign capital were also observed in both Packaging and ABN Amro in India, where it appears closely related to the removal of legal constraints on foreign ownership in the pertinent sector. In Vietnam, increases of foreign equity stakes by ABB and Carlsberg occurred only in 2003, several years after the initial entry. In ABB Vietnam, the foreign partner had managerial control from the outset, while SEAB has a rotating management arrangement. It appears that as long as the established relationship is working, and the local partner serves a role in for instance maintaining relationships with authorities and local businesses, foreign investors do not wish to 'rock the boat', i.e. disrupt trust in the relationships by suggesting to change the ownership pattern.

Many foreign investors engaging in a partial acquisition aim at eventually attaining full control. This is illustrated by the packaging case. Lack of financial resources of the local partner to finance major restructuring or expansion became a trigger for change of ownership. However, it appears that both partners have considered the option of an eventually full acquisition early on. The local partners intended to exit the industry as part of a change in corporate strategy, and the foreign investor would prefer full control over its operation in an important and growing market. Similarly, GSK gradually increased it ownership in the Egyptian operation, yet this process stretched over a far longer period of time. In the Bacardi-Martini case, capital needs were met by issuing non-voting preference shares so that the local ownership stake remained at the legally required minimum of 26 per cent. However, Bacardi-Martini would increase its equity stake if it were permitted to do so.

Increases in equity have consequences for the interpretation of FDI statistics. As we experienced in our sampling in India, many projects registered as new FDI appear to be increases of the equity of the foreign partner in a joint venture. In practice, it has sometimes been difficult to distinguish between 'entry' and 'expansion' in the way the scholarly literature does. This is illustrated among the cases for instance by ABN Amro in India and by GSK in Egypt. They have been established in the host country for decades, but in the 1990s increased their operations using a variety of modes of expansion, or entry, into new segments. National statistics differ how they record expansion of existing FDI operations by either mode. Acquisition-based growth may require additional permits, and would thus be recorded, while statistics may not capture organic growth. Thus, FDI statistics may over-report the number of foreign investors that are new in the country, especially if incumbent investors expand by acquisition. However, foreign expansion and equity increases can be an important source of capital inflow to a country, and thus relevant for certain policy issues.

The role of local partners in the joint ventures varies greatly, as illustrated by the three Vietnamese cases: In the case of Honda, the local firm appears to play a largely passive role, helping to gain legitimacy, and providing land use rights. In the case of ABB Transformers, the local co-owner has transferred all its operations to the newly created joint venture and remained as a shell-firm owning equity in the JV. ABB has effectively taken over the existing operation, and the local state-owned co-owner provides a means through which the ministry aims to influence an otherwise privately-run firm, while facilitating access to other state entities that are important customers. SEAB/Carlsberg is structured as a conventional joint venture where both partners contribute resources, and share control. The local firm has also developed related business thus realising synergies and spillovers. Carlsberg Breweries of Denmark maintains control indirectly through its brand name, and by having a Danish financial investor as a partner that locals perceive part of the 'Danish side'.

Hence, Honda's local partner can be classified as silent, and at least one of ABN Amro's partners in India also falls in this category (Figure 11.1). ABB transformer Vietnam is best described as partial acquisition, and thus has much in common with Bacardi-Martini's investment in India, where the local partners also transferred a business unit to the JV. Carlsberg's relationship with Halimex represents a traditional JV, apart from the involvement of IFU as financial investor.

In Egypt, two local joint venture partners are operating on a pan-Arab basis, providing location-specific resources to several foreign investors. The Al Kharafi group originating in Kuwait is acting as local partner to a variety of foreign businesses in Egypt, among other businesses using the brand name Americana. It has operated in Egypt for many years prior to setting up the JV with Heinz, and serves as link to local customers and facilitates operating in the Arab cultural context. MobilNil was set as a consortium between two Western investors and a local firm to bid for ECMS. The local partner, Orascom Telecom, has subsequent expanded beyond Egypt, mostly through similar partnerships with Western partners in other Arab countries and in Africa, including in 2003, Iraq. The 'regional local partner' is contributing resources to a JV that are region-specific. As international business is often regional rather than global (Rugman and Verbecke 2003), this phenomenon may be of increasing importance in international business worldwide.

These diverse roles of local JV partners calls for a new terminology to analyse joint ventures. Figure 11.1 suggests a classification and concepts for joint ventures based on these types of observed joint ventures.

Role of Partner	Partner		
	Local firm	Regional firm	Global firm
Transfer of entire business unit	**Quasi-partial acquisition:** ABB (VN) Bacardi-Martini (IN)	–	–
Both partners make substantive contributions	**Traditional JV:** SEAB (VN)	**Regional specialist:** Heinz (EG) Al Kharafi ECMS (EG) Orascom	**Consortium:** MobiNil (EG): bid consortium
Partner is largely passive	**Silent partner:** ABN Amro (IN): leasing business Honda (VN)	–	**Financial investor:** SEAB (VN)

Figure 11.1 Role of partners in the joint ventures

The acquisitions vary in two important dimensions: the previous owner, and the pattern of ownership change. The literature to date mainly presumes that previous owners are private firms or individuals, while a separate literature analyses privatisation. However, the phenomenon of acquisition of a foreign-owned operation by another foreign investor seems quite common in emerging economies, but it has not yet been explored in the scholarly literature. Figure 11.2 suggests that these dimensions might be related, as state-owned firms appear more frequently to be acquired partially, while foreign owned affiliates change owner fully and in one transaction. This is plausible as the capital markets are typically more developed concerning foreign owned businesses than for state-owned businesses. However, the type of acquisition is highly dependent on the wider institutional context, which suggests that one should be wary of excessive generalisations based on Figure 11.2.

Type of Acquisition	**Previous Owner**		
	Foreign investor	Domestic private	State-owned firm
Full	Behr (SA) ABN Amro (IN)	EST-Ziton (SA) GSK (EG): APIC	–
Stepwise	–	GSK (EG): ABI Packaging (IN) ABN Amro (SA)	ABB (VN)
Partial	–	Bacardi-Martini (IN)	ECMS (EG)

Note: 'partial' includes firms that were in shared ownership by 2002, they might change into 'stepwise' at a later point in time.

Figure 11.2 Role of acquired firms in acquisitions

The case evidence moreover suggests that acquisitions from the state need more extensive restructuring, as do some of the domestic private firms. In the two cases of acquisition from the state, ECMS Egypt and ABB Transformer in Vietnam,[56] this restructuring occurred even with shared ownership and control. In contrast, the deep restructuring in Packaging appears to have been implemented only after the foreign investor acquired full ownership.

The dynamic perspective on entry taken in this research also reveals that decision-making processes concerning foreign entry strategies are not made as rationally as theoretical models may suggest. Foreign investors may, to a high degree, be simultaneously reacting to opportunities and designing entry strategies (Antal-Mokos 1998). Moreover, observed strategies may often be 'emergent strategies' (Minzberg and Waters 1985) that diverge from the originally designed strategy as decision-makers obtain new information and adjust strategy, or delegated decisions on lower levels of the hierarchy gradually change the overall direction that the firms is taking. For example, ABB Transformers Vietnam entered a new business segment earlier than planned, and engaged in deep restructuring with downsizing of the workforce, which in this form was not anticipated. ABN Amro gradually built its operations in India and South Africa, seeking new opportunities as they emerged, yet exiting other segments as result of changes in global strategy or unsatisfactory local performance.

Another important aspect of entry illustrated by the cases, is the dynamic interdependence of entry and exit. Foreign investors enter emerging economies to pursue business opportunities that extend their global strategies.

Yet, they may well leave when it suits them. Exit may result from changes in global strategies, as for ABN Amro South Africa. The global trend of firms focusing on more narrowly defined core lines of business, where they aim for global leadership, leads to divestment of non-core businesses. This may lead to divestment of affiliates in a peripheral emerging market, even if the business as such is profitable. Other exits arise from dynamics of the local industry. For instance, liberalization often leads to entry of many investors; yet the wave of entry may be followed by a period of consolidation when some competitors leave, for instance by selling their operation to another foreign investor.

In conclusion, we find a considerable variety of entry modes serving different needs and accommodating contextual idiosyncrasies. With respect to the received literature (see Chapter 1), this suggest that international business scholars may have been excessively concerned with the choice between stylised alternative entry modes, rather than studying the design and the dynamics of operation modes. Future research may thus aim to enrich concepts such as 'joint venture' and 'acquisition', and analyse further the adaptation of modes, rather than the selection between modes from a presumed set of alternative choices. It may thus integrate the work on mode combinations and mode switching (Benito and Welch 1994, Petersen et al. 2000).

RESOURCE-BASED PERSPECTIVES

Table 11.3 summarises the key resources that provide case firms with competitive advantages in their respective markets, and alternative sources for these resources, including the foreign investment firm and the local partner in cases of JV or acquisition. As would be expected, the most important resources are knowledge-based assets, including production technology as well as managerial and organizational capabilities. The pattern varies across sectors as technology is considered important in most manufacturing operations, while brand names and marketing are important for consumer goods manufacturers focusing on local markets, and some service industries. Many cases show a traditional pattern with foreign investors contributing technology and global marketing and management knowledge, while local partners contribute knowledge and network access related to the local business environment.

The local contributions vary across industries, with most investors setting up manufacturing operations citing human capital relevant to their particular type of operations as attraction of the location selected. Customer access can be provided by local JV partners or acquired firms in various forms, from existing customer base in the service industries (ABN Amro, ECMS) and

Table 11.3 Resources in the local firm

Firm	Key resources	Contribution by foreign firm	Contribution by local firm	Other local resources
SA NGK			n.a. (Greenfield)	Stainless steel, precious metal technology
SA Behr	Access to global customers	Technology, market knowledge, supplier relations with car industry	Industry-specific capabilities and facilities for lower cost production	–
SA EST	Cost, technology, distribution	Global operation in the up-market segment in the same industry.	Global brand & distribution, technology, low-cost production base	–
SA ABN Amro	Broad bundle of resources	Global network, brand, operational know how	Customer relations, retail bank network, market research	–

VN	SEAB	Technology brands	Technology and marketing know-how, machinery, global brand, capital	Educated workforce (absorptive capacity), distribution network, local brand, land and buildings, political know-how	Water quality
VN	ABB	Technology	Technology & management, especially production-process related knowledge, machinery, capital,	Staff, physical assets & liabilities, relationship with state-owned firms as customers, industry-specific human capital (absorptive capacity)	—
VN	Honda	Broad bundle of resources	Brand, technology, machinery, local sales network, capital, etc	Land use rights, political legitimacy	—
IN	Bacardi-Martini	Brand, technology	Brand, marketing, technology, e.g. waste treatment	Legitimacy, local knowledge concerning regulatory issues	Managerial resources, local farm produce (molasses)
IN	Packaging	Technology, location	Technology, financial capital	Existing operations, customer relations Organic n.a.	—

Table 11.3 (continued)

	Firm	Key resources	Contribution by foreign firm	Contribution by local firm	Other
IN	ABN Amro	Broad bundle of resources	Global brand, Organisational procedures,....	Acq.: retail network, organisational procedures JV: regulatory permit only	Managerial resource Network of base stations (newly created)
EG	ECMS MobiNil	GSM license, management	Industry specific management knowledge, technology	GSM license	
EG	GSK	Patents, human capital	Patents, capital, production technology	Existing market share, licenses, approvals, sales force real estate	---
EG	Heinz	Brand, recipes, quality of inputs.	Brand name, recipes, marketing & management knowledge, Machinery & technology.	Local & regional market knowledge, access to fast-food outlets.	Local farm produce (tomatoes)

manufacturing (Behr, EST, Packaging), to relations with authorities when aiming at public sector procurement contracts (ABB Transformers, GSK), and to distribution channels and local brand names for consumer goods (SEAB, Heinz). However, such contributions are not required by foreign investors with an already established brand name and distribution channel and service network, such as Honda in Vietnam.

Where the operation is export oriented, foreign firms mostly contribute access to export markets, especially to other units of the same MNE, and with their global brand and distribution network. An exception is Heinz, where the El Kharafi group as regional partner also facilitates accessing markets in other Arab countries.

The Carlsberg and ABB cases discuss the partner selection process, and thus illustrate the resources that the foreign investor has been seeking. Carlsberg had several cooperations in form of turnkey projects prior to establishing the joint venture in 1993. The chosen partner, Halimex, had demonstrated high 'absorptive capacity' (Cohen and Levinthal 1990, Steemsma and Lyles 2000), i.e. ability to adapt and apply received technology. This, and good political standing of the firm, compensated for the fact that it was a relative newcomer to the brewing industry. ABB chose a partner with a track record of production and innovation in the industry, including experience in reverse engineering. This firm thus was technologically advanced by local standards, and commanded a substantial market share.

A few years after the establishment, both joint ventures would primarily compete on the basis of the foreign investor's technology, thus it is correct that 'foreigners contribute technology'. However, at the outset the technological competence of the local partner is crucial for establishing the joint venture and being able to apply the transferred technology locally. The cases thus illustrate how absorptive capacity matters for technology transfer in joint ventures. High levels of education of individual employees, as well as organizational structures and cultures promoting learning, innovation, and flexibility, enhance the technological progress of the acquired business unit or the local joint venture.

Only in one case, ECMS, has the business licence been of prime importance, yet business licences have been a secondary resource in other cases as well. Various forms of 'assets' created courtesy of local regulation are mentioned in the cases. While it is apparent why licensing of GSM networks in necessary, it may be more surprising that state-owned firms are needed as a partner in Vietnam to access 'land use rights' due to restriction of private land ownership, or to obtain permission to engage in export and import (only in 1999, were private firms allowed to import and export directly, before that everything had to be handled by SOEs). In Vietnam, only state-owned firms have access to land, while private domestic firms do not, such that only state-owned firms are able to be partners for foreign investors.

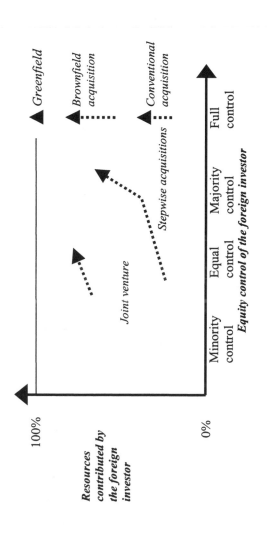

Note: Arrows represent possible evolutionary paths over the first years of operation of an FDI.

Figure 11.3 Evolutionary paths of FDI during the initial years

Beyond a formal requirement, local partners provide legitimacy that facilitates relations with authorities, which appears to be important for many businesses.

The type of resources sought from local partners is also a function of the corporate strategy. Market-oriented investors, such as Heinz, seek licences and marketing-related assets. Industry-specific technology that is competitive on the international stage has attracted foreign investors aiming to build an export base in South Africa. EST and Behr would probably not have invested in South Africa if it weren't for the specific acquisition opportunity. However, such organizationally embedded resources are unusual in emerging markets; South Africa is an exception to the rule and illustrates this point. In consequence, acquisitions of local firms are relatively rare, as shown in the survey data. This can be attributed to the weak endowment of local firms with internationally competitive resources. Thus, acquisitions and in consequence the volume of FDI capital that enters emerging markets is constrained by the lack of local firms with capabilities that are valuable in international competition.

Some cases also point to local resources other than those obtained from local partners, for instance quality of management, as stressed in the Indian cases, and industry-specific technological expertise such as precious metal technology for NGK. Moreover several investors depend on the quality of local raw materials, especially if transportation costs are high, for example stainless steel (NGK), or in the food and beverage sector relying on clean water (SEAB), and farm produce such as tomatoes (Heinz) and molasses (Bacardi-Martini).

The resource transfer from the foreign parent has been extensive in all ownership forms, and contributed substantially to organizational performance, as observed in earlier studies (Uhlenbruck and De Castro 2000, Steensma and Lyles 2000). In several cases of acquisitions, the resources transferred by the new owners quickly came to dominate over those of the acquired firm, such that they can be described as brownfield projects. The most important result here is that brownfield investments are found across emerging economies, and they are not specific to Central and Eastern Europe, where they have been described before (Estrin et al. 1997, Meyer and Estrin 2001). Fast restructuring and resource upgrading happened in particular in the two case firms that were previously owned by the state: ECMS Egypt and ABB Transformers Vietnam. However, it also happened in some acquisitions from private owners, such as GSK's acquisitions of ABI and APIC, though not in the South African acquisitions.[57]

The extent of the resource transfer appears to be related to the foreign equity stake, as transaction cost theory would lead us to expect (Figure 11.3). The more control a foreign investor has over local operations, the more it would be willing to transfer sensitive knowledge. In a shared venture, the possibility of local partners using received assets for unauthorised, competitive purposes is higher. However, the Vietnamese cases, in particular Carlsberg and ABB, illustrate that even without majority ownership, extensive knowledge transfer can take place, especially if the relevant technology is not considered 'leading edge' in terms of the foreign partners' global competition. In stepwise acquisitions, the resource transfer may set in soon after the initial entry, but the deep restructuring may also be delayed until the foreign investor attains majority control, as in the Packaging case.

A prime concern in these restructuring processes is human resources (Nguyen and Meyer 2004). Many MNEs compete on the basis of organizational or technological capabilities. New affiliates need to recruit employees that fit into their global organization, and train them accordingly. This is a particular challenge when acquiring an existing organization that may have a non-entrepreneurial or public sector style organizational culture. In some cases, investors may be able to select the employees whom they take over from the existing organization, as in ECMS in Egypt. Elsewhere, the employment restructuring has been more painful, as for ABB Transformers in Vietnam, where ABB took responsibility for the entire operation. However, layoffs at an early stage may be followed by employment growth. GSK Egypt made 380 of ABI's 741 employees redundant, but recruited 1,190 new employees. In part such shifts are due to the different skill profile expected by foreign investors, but it may also reflect deliberate focusing and outsourcing strategies that generate growth in the long-term.

Deep restructuring seems less complex where businesses were acquired from another foreign investor as for Behr South Africa and ABN Amro India. This apparent relationship between previous owner and intensity of restructuring arises from the competitiveness of firms in different forms of ownership: Foreign affiliates have an organizational structure and culture that serves most of the needs of a new owner, while state-owned firms often have a fundamentally different organizational logic, which may not be conducive to competitiveness. Hence the brownfield phenomenon appears to be associated with privatisation and weakly competitive local private firms, which may be found in many emerging economies. Empirical research may test if this relationship between types of previous owners and intensity of the restructuring can be generalised beyond our case studies.[58]

On the other hand, the cases do not support the notion that deep restructuring would require full ownership. In fact, the deepest restructuring is found in two partial acquisitions. Thus, the effective managerial control of the foreign investor over the operation seems to be more important than ownership. Consider the case of ABB Transformers in Vietnam: The formal structure and lack of local experience with deep restructuring and layoffs severely constrained ABB's management. However, they had managerial control and worked cooperatively with the relevant authorities to implement not only the technology transfer, but the organizational change in the jointly owned operation. In contrast, Packaging in India engaged in deep restructuring only after the foreign investor had established full ownership.

The transfer of knowledge, often the most important resource-transfer, occurs in multiple forms (Nguyen and Meyer 2004). Most important has generally been managerial training on the job with foreign advisers, or rotation of staff to other affiliates of the investor. In SEAB, Vietnamese employees were send to other Asian subsidiaries of their parent firm, as learning from the application of technology in other Asian contexts was deemed more conducive to transferring tacit organizational and managerial knowledge. ABB's Vietnamese employees were sent to Norway and Finland where the specific technological expertise was concentrated. Naturally, the success of such training depends on the individual and organization capabilities that the recipients can contribute. Hence, preparation and selection of individuals and groups from training is crucial, as is the creation of an organizational context in which trained employees can implement their ideas. Other means of technology transfer include transfer of machinery that embodies new technology, such as the turnkey arrangements that preceded Carlsberg's JV in Vietnam.

In conclusion, the management of resources is probably the most complex and challenging aspect of establishing operations in emerging markets. Crucial differences arise with both the resource needs in such environments, and their local availability embedded in local firms or otherwise. This suggests that the resource-based view of the firm may hold great potential as theoretical grounding for future empirical research aiming to explain the variations of entry strategies in emerging economies.

INSIGHTS FOR MANAGEMENT

This research aimed primarily at identifying relevant influences on entry mode choice, rather than the effectiveness of alternative strategies. Our performance indicators did not exhibit clear differences across entry modes, in part because entry mode choice is endogenous and observed performance differences would reflect primarily unexpected difficulties encountered post-entry. Hence our managerial insights concern primarily factors that decision-makers ought to include in their analysis when preparing an FDI in an emerging economy.

First, the analysis of alternative entry strategies has to start with the global strategy, which in turn determines the envisaged role of the new emerging market operation. In particular, which markets will be served by the new affiliate, which resources does the parent firm provide, and which resources need to be obtained locally. An understanding of these resource flows then allows an analysis of interfaces with local firms and other local agents, and thus alternative modes of operation, such as joint venture, acquisition of a local firm, or establishment of a greenfield operation without local partner.

Second, the types of entry modes are not fixed. Decision-makers thus ought to think creatively how to design an entry mode. Many obstacles may best be overcome by customising a mode to the local context, rather than opting for a second best mode. The contributions of local or regional partners can be arranged in many different ways, from contractual cooperation to full acquisition. Joint ventures allow for many different roles of the partners, and acquired firms play different roles in establishing a new operation. Figures 11.1 and 11.2 provide classification schemes that may be developed for managerial analysis. Moreover, the entry strategy should permit sufficient flexibility to be adjusted to a changing institutional framework.

Third, the resource contributions vary for each project, and they evolve over time. This change over time in some cases follows initial plans, but in many cases changes in the competitive environment or a reassessment of the affiliates own resources lead to unpredicted changes. Decision-makers thus need to analyse the resources needs, the investor's own resources, and the resources controlled by local firms. Complementary resources and objectives are essential. MNEs would normally know their own core competences, and their transferability. But they need to assess what complementary local resources they need to make best use of their core competences as these might vary from their experiences in mature market economies. As illustrated in Figure 11.3, the processes of transferring resource and of acquiring local resources stretch over several years, and may require continuous reassessment. Thus, any strategic design needs to be flexible to adjust to changing circumstances, for instance, by changing the equity stake in a JV.

Fourth, foreign investors need to analyse the institutional environment, paying special attention to industry-specific institutions, sub-national institutions, and (if an acquisition is considered) capital markets. It may be obvious that regulatory institutions and law enforcement are different in each emerging economy. However, even within countries there are more differences than many investors expect (Meyer and Nguyen 2003). Thus entrants have to invest in getting to know the local institutions and in network relationships. Moreover, they have to anticipate possible changes in the institutional framework. These issues are discussed in more detail in connection with the policy discussion in Chapter 12.

12. Conclusions for Economic Policy

Saul Estrin and Klaus E. Meyer

INTRODUCTION

In this final chapter, we analyse the interrelationships between FDI and economic policy. When interpreting the qualitative and quantitative data one has to keep in mind the sample of countries chosen for the study. All four are emerging markets, with institutional infrastructure and business environments less conducive than those of any developed economies. On the other hand, they have all consistently received significant amounts of FDI in recent years, and these FDI inflows have had important impacts on domestic investment and growth (see Table 1.2). This stands in contrast to the majority of developing countries, where FDI flows are usually very modest.

We concentrated our attention on firms that had made the decision to enter, rather than the full set of potential entrants. Nonetheless, our study sheds some light on these issues, particularly through the case studies that place examples of FDI into an evolving policy context. We also consider the relationship between the policy environment and entry mode, which the theoretical framework in Chapter 1 suggests will be important in determining the performance of foreign subsidiaries and the spillover benefits and costs for the host economy. We therefore start by summarising the main findings from the survey, and the implications for the policy environment and the spillover effects of FDI. We use the data to speculate on the reasons for the modest levels of FDI in our sample countries, and on the interrelationship between motives for FDI entry mode and the evolving policy environment.

Policy-makers in emerging markets are usually motivated to encourage foreign direct investment primarily because of the external benefits that they yield. FDI would be of less interest if it were merely an incremental form of investment finance, especially if domestic investment were thereby crowded out. Once again, the case studies provide a rich menu of spillover benefits from FDI to emerging markets, which we analyse and compare in the third section. These are often associated with particular entry modes and motives for entry, and there are also clearly important industry specific factors at work. Final conclusions to the study are drawn in the fourth section.

STRATEGY AND CHARACTERISTICS OF INVESTING FIRMS

Foreign investment is widely expected to have beneficial effects on host economies, yet the expectation is based on certain assumptions of what investors actually do. By incorporating strategic management and economic analysis, this study allows us to reassess whether the characteristics of inward foreign investment actually match the expectations of policy-makers and economic analysts.

It could be expected that much FDI into developing countries would take the form of outsourcing manufacture to low-cost suppliers and investing to exploit location specific assets, for example, natural resources. Such investments would primarily lead to enhanced exports and balance of payments benefits. The survey reveals that this is not an accurate description of FDI into our four host economies. Around three-quarters of FDI is 'market-seeking' – that is, aimed at supplying the domestic market in the host country – except in Vietnam where the proportion is around 50 per cent. Moreover, the survey reveals that most foreign direct investments are small; at the time of formation the median number of workers was 40 in Egypt, 30 in India, 76 in South Africa and 85 in Vietnam, although some have subsequently grown significantly. The median value of fixed assets was also modest, ranging from US$690,000 in India to $1.67 million in South Africa. Less than 20 per cent of FDI subsidiaries in each country employed fixed assets valued at more than US$10 million.

Global sourcing strategies lead to the transfer of supplier relationships. Manufacturing companies often prefer to use the same suppliers worldwide, especially in the automotive industry. Thus, Honda's investment in motorcycle assembly in Vietnam triggered further investment by its Japanese suppliers, while Behr moved to South Africa to supply the new overseas operations of its German customers. In recent years, many MNCs have shed peripheral product lines and expanded their core businesses, often by acquisition. They increasingly serve worldwide markets and reorganise their supply chain to take advantage of locational advantages worldwide (see Meyer 2003). For example, among our cases, Heinz changed its strategy by refocusing on a narrower product line but with a large international presence, including that in Egypt. For companies aiming to become global leaders in their market segment, competitive interaction with global rivals may induce early entry in emerging economies to reap first or second-mover advantages. This appears to be the motivation for Carlsberg acting soon after Heineken entered Vietnam, and NGK Ceramics following competitor Corning into South Africa. On the other hand, some firms, including ABN Amro, have divested from selected emerging market operations as part of a global restructuring.

One can infer some important lessons for policy-makers. Although many developing economies could provide low-cost settings for western firms, very few countries actually succeed in attracting significant numbers of MNCs. The investment that occurs often generates little local employment, and primarily focuses on meeting the needs of domestic markets, and therefore is concentrated in large or fast growing economies. Hence, even in countries like those in our sample, with quite significant FDI flows, policy-makers should not look to FDI primarily as a source of employment creation: the main benefits instead must derive from spillovers that improve competitiveness. Moreover, policy-makers need to create an infrastructure, such that investing firms can, with limited risk, take up the opportunities offered by the comparative advantage of potential host economies, for example, relatively cheap labour or raw materials.

The sectoral allocation of FDI to our sample of emerging markets was also somewhat surprising. Manufacturing accounts for only 41 per cent of entry into Egypt, 59 per cent into India, 51 per cent into South Africa and 73 per cent into Vietnam. Moreover, only in Vietnam does basic manufacturing predominate; in India and South Africa a significant proportion of FDI is in capital goods, including vehicles. Financial and business services and tourism are perhaps what one might have expected, accounting for 35 per cent, 14 per cent, 26 per cent and 20 per cent of entrants in our sample respectively.[59] Thus, when thinking about FDI, policy-makers should not only concentrate on the industrial sector; as the cases illustrate, spillovers often derive from developing capital markets or business services through foreign entry.

We also find that local familiarity, experience with emerging markets and integration into regional trading blocs plays an important role in the FDI process. This suggests that the problems for foreign firms operating in the more complex institutional environments of emerging markets must, to some extent, be mitigated by experience in similar economies. The case evidence confirms this finding, as we will see below. Moreover, many investors originate within the region, and regional trade and integration policies, as well as global ones, often influence location decisions. For example, we observe an increasing role of regional rather than global exports in the survey, especially in Vietnam and Egypt. Policy-makers may therefore want to think more carefully about how to develop their FDI strategies in the context of regional trade policies and the development of regional groupings.

Mode of Entry

We have seen that one can distinguish between three categories of FDI: 'efficiency-seeking', for example, for low-cost labour; 'resource-seeking', for example, for raw materials and 'market-seeking', for example, for enhanced sales and sales growth. Resource- and efficiency-seeking firms usually invest to export; market-seeking ones to supply the domestic market.

As noted above, a surprisingly large proportion of FDI in our sample has been motivated by market rather than efficiency- or resource-seeking reasons. Models of comparative advantage would instead lead us to expect efficiency-seeking investments, especially searching for low-cost labour, to predominate in such markets. But in South Africa and Egypt, only around one quarter of FDI entrants are efficiency-seeking. Investments into India follow a split pattern, with most FDI being of a market-seeking character but with a small yet significant efficiency-seeking sector, especially in IT. Vietnam however, has a much larger efficiency-seeking FDI sector, representing a majority of all investments. This is also reflected in the sectoral distribution of FDI to Vietnam, which is more concentrated in basic manufacturing, and in the regional character of FDI source firms, disproportionately based in South East Asia. Of the exports undertaken by foreign affiliates in our sample countries, in India and South Africa around half are destined for the global market by foreign affiliates, but, as noted above, in Vietnam the majority goes to regional markets. The proportion of regionally focused trade is also growing in Egypt.

Acquisitions are the most common mode of FDI entry in developed countries. They are also sometimes argued to generate the greatest technological spillovers through technology, skill transfers and backward linkages because they directly impact on a current firm in the host economy, and thus on its existing supply chains and distributing outlets. In our sample, we find the dominant entry mode to be greenfield and joint venture; acquisitions represent less than 5 per cent of FDI in Egypt, India and Vietnam. As discussed below, this is because appropriate acquisition targets are scarce and capital markets are less well developed. These factors may together explain the relatively low levels of FDI going to many emerging markets. However in South Africa, where the industrial and institutional structure is more mature, entry by acquisition has been more common. Compared to developed economies, foreign entrants also rely relatively more on their own resources than on what can be purchased in the local market place, either unbundled or as a bundle of resources, through acquisition. This is again a reflection of the weaker business environment in emerging markets and is correlated with the mode of entry.

We summarise the motives and entry modes among our 12 cases in Table 12.1. Nine of the 12 display a significant element of market seeking, while efficiency seeking unambiguously and solely motivates only one case firm. There are proportionately more acquisitions in the cases than the survey (five out of 12), but greenfield/joint venture predominate. Interestingly, many of the investing firms already had experience in other emerging markets. The cases clearly confirm that the business environment in the host

Table 12.1 Motives and entry mode of twelve studies

Name	Motivation	Mode of entry	Prior experience in emerging markets
NGK	Efficiency-seeking	Greenfield	No
Behr	Efficiency/market-seeking	Acquisition	No
ABN Amro	Market-seeking	Expansion/ Acquisition	Yes
SEAB	Market-seeking	Joint venture	Yes
ABB	Market-seeking	Joint venture	Yes
Honda	Market-seeking	Joint venture	Yes
Bacardi-Martini	Market-seeking	Joint venture	Yes
Packaging	Market-seeking	Joint venture	No
ABN Amro	Market-seeking	Greenfield	No
ECMS /	Market-seeking	Acquisition	Yes
MobilNil	Efficiency/resource-seeking	Acquisition	No
GSK	Market-seeking	Acquisition	Yes
Heinz	Market/resource-seeking	Joint venture	Yes

economies have a significant impact on the mode of entry, leading to relatively higher proportions of joint ventures and greenfields, and therefore upon the subsequent performance and impact of the investments on the host economy.

We have also explored the resources regarded by managers as important for their competitiveness. In all four countries, the three most important assets for success are found to be brands, management and technology. It is interesting, though perhaps not surprising, that these are provided primarily from the resources of the investing firm. The contributions of local firms remain largely in the province of local know-how; networks for business and distribution and marketing skills, assisting foreign firms in doing business in the host economy environment. Resourceful and entrepreneurial local firms are more attractive business partners, in whichever form of collaboration. They thus would not only attract more business relationships, but also be able to extract more spillovers from them. Policy-makers may thus aim to support local firm development as an indirect means to attract FDI by building local resources, especially through education and strengthening absorptive capacities. More attractive acquisition targets may then stimulate more FDI capital inflows.

THE INSTITUTIONAL AND POLICY ENVIRONMENT

This section aims to contribute to a better understanding of how business strategies and performance are influenced by the 'investment climate', more specifically the local institutional environment and the policy implications of the analysis. Overall, this task has been a considerable challenge because the relevant institutions seem to be very specific to each case, allowing for few generalisations (Table 12.2). We encountered a lot of discussion, or more precisely complaints, about general issues such as bureaucracy or corruption, yet the issues that actually impacted on business were often very specific to the industry, if not the firm. Arguably, this is a finding: which institutions really matter for an investment project is specific to each industry and each location, and how the specific context differs from the general norms established in mature market economies.

Before delving into specific aspects of the institutions, we discuss the assessment of the local business environment by survey respondents. In the further discussion, the institutional and policy influences on entry strategies and performance of FDI projects are grouped in three categories. First, as we have seen from the survey, formal institutions, such as the legal code, as well as informal ones, such as law enforcement, affect both foreign and local businesses. Second, capital markets are important when it comes to acquisitions as a possible entry mode. Third, the cases report several

Table 12.2 Institutional influences on establishment of the firm

#	Firm	Institutions influencing FDI	Impact on business strategy
	NGK		
SA1	Behr	Industrial policy to attract FDI to this sector	Motivated the FDI
SA2	EST	No institutional influence with crucial impact	---
SA3	ABN Amro	Financial sector deregulation	Timing of entry
VN1	SEAB	FDI laws	Need for local partner
VN2	ABB	FDI laws, public sector procurement	Need for local partner
VN3	Honda	FDI laws, tariff-barriers, fiscal incentives, local content requirements	May have motivated the FDI, the choice of partner and the extent of local sourcing.
IN1	Bacardi-Martini	State-level regulation of alcoholic beverages industry	Limited foreign ownership, 74%
IN2	Packaging	General FDI liberalization	Timing of entry, initial sharing of equity.

IN3	ABN Amro	Financial sector de-regulation	Timing of entry, sharing of equity for some business segments.
EG1	ECMS MobiNil	Telecom liberalization & regulation	Timing of entry, design of the bid for ECMS.
EG2	GSK	Regulation of pharmaceuticals industry: drug approval, pricing, intellectual property rights	May have motivated initial tariff-jumping FDI.
EG3	Heinz	Licensing of food products, investment incentives	No clear impact

incidences of sector-specific regulation being crucial for investors' entry strategy, not only in the financial sector and natural monopolies such as telecommunication, but also in manufacturing sectors such as pharmaceuticals in Egypt and alcoholic beverages in India, and almost all sectors in Vietnam.

Investor Assessments

The business environment is widely regarded as crucial in determining the scale and format of FDI, and we have seen considerable evidence of its relevance in determining the mode of entry and the balance of resources provided from the source firm or the host economy. In the survey, we explicitly investigated managers' perceptions of the quality of the host country's labour force, the quality of local inputs and the institutional and legal environment. We find managers' perceptions about many aspects of the business environment in our sample of emerging markets to be good. For example, managers' evaluation of local labour quality and availability in four skill categories from skilled manual workers to executive managers is relatively high, around or above 4, with little variation across countries or over time. Since developing economies often suffer from skill shortages this result is surprising. One interpretation is that foreign firms in our sample are sufficiently small, to avoid the labour supply constraints. Another is that they are able to attract the 'pick of the crop' by paying very high wages, and filling any gaps that emerge with expatriate workers. If this is the case, the foreign investors may simply be creating 'enclaves' in the host economy, and the spillover benefits for the host economy may be limited.

We have similar findings with respect to other aspects of the business environment; the quality of local inputs, in terms of raw materials and machinery; availability of real estate; the quality of professional services; and the reliability of telecommunications and utilities. The quality of most local inputs at the start of operations is evaluated modestly well, above 3 in Egypt, India and Vietnam and above 4 in South Africa. Once again, this may simply reflect the superior purchasing power of FDI firms. However it is encouraging to observe considerable improvement in the evaluation of the quality of local inputs by 2000 in the first three countries, though there is no change in South Africa. Given that all of our countries received reasonably significant flows of FDI over this period, we can infer from the data that ensuring a supply of reasonable quality inputs is a prerequisite for FDI to developing countries, and that policies with respect to labour skills and infrastructure, particularly of utilities, electricity and telecommunications are vital.

However, the survey reveals that managers' evaluation of the host economy's institutional and policy environment remains poor, with a high proportion of issues evaluated in the 2's (not very conducive). Moreover, except in Vietnam, there is no evidence of improvement in any of our countries. This is the area where our findings conform with external perceptions of doing business in emerging markets. The institutional environment, including the general legal framework, is typically evaluated below 3. The predictability of government policy is also evaluated very poorly. The conduciveness of central government to FDI is evaluated at 2.9 in Egypt, 3.3 in India and South Africa and 3.6 in Vietnam. Central governments are therefore regarded as failing to follow policies conducive to FDI, and the evaluation of provincial and local governments is even worse. Foreign investors do not regard many governments in emerging markets as business friendly, even in countries like those in our sample that have prioritised FDI, and the situation is not seen as having improved greatly outside Vietnam up to 2001. The survey suggests that institutional problems are concentrated in the public sector itself, and relate to unpredictability of policy, legal frameworks and complexity of the business environment. The survey only covers firms that have chosen to invest, many of which have managerial experience in similar business environments that has probably enabled them to develop mechanisms to cope with weak institutions. It seems likely that firms which are not able to manage the risks of operating in such environments instead choose not to invest.

The survey therefore suggests that the relatively weaker institutional environment in emerging markets distorts the choice of entry mode away from acquisitions and in favour of greenfields and joint ventures. The balance of resources critical to the success of the FDI is shifted away from firms and markets in the host economy, relying disproportionately on source firms. The difficulty for many western firms in resolving these problems, especially those with limited experience in emerging markets, probably helps to explain the relatively modest FDI flows to most emerging markets. For those firms that do enter, the critical issues remain the policy, legal and institutional environment, rather than difficulties in obtaining inputs.

General Institutional Environment: Formal and Informal

The 'institutional framework' is a broad concept that includes both formal and informal aspects (North 1990). It influences foreign investors in establishing the range of feasible strategies, the transaction costs of alternative modes, and the need for context-specific resources. Moreover, institutions are critical for political risk analysis as even small changes in pertinent legislation can have a major impact on profitability. For instance, local business communities dominated by state-owned enterprises, as in Vietnam, complicate business relations and may increase political risk as policy interventions may favour them in comparison to foreign investors.

The cases as well as the survey evidence point to a variety of aspects of the general policy framework that, although not aimed at FDI, are of major concern to (potential) investors (Table 12.2). Complaints about general issues such as bureaucracy or corruption were common but firms that had decided to invest (all of our sample countries) had found ways to address these. The institutional problems that really had an impact on our firms were instead very specialised to the industry, if not the firm itself. However, the cases do point to a variety of aspects of the general legal framework that are of major concern to investors. For instance, in Egypt and India the labour law has frequently been described as problematic, as foreign investors complain about the 'pampering of workers'. In India, laying-off employees appears almost impossible. Restrictive labour law inhibits FDI by acquisition as it inhibits the post-acquisition restructuring and modernisation of production processes. Bureaucracy in Egypt is still very difficult according to various studies (El-Mikawy and Handoussa 2001), which creates a need for a local partner. In South Africa, the visa and immigration regulations has been frequently mentioned as an obstacle. Yet overall, the cases make few references to institutional factors inhibiting entry strategies.

On the positive side, wider policies of liberalization affecting industry facilitate FDI, and in many cases crucially influence the timing of entry. Liberalisation also changes the competitive conditions for local firms who may in consequence actively seek a foreign partner to cope with the anticipated increase in competition. At the same time, when liberalisation is still partial, foreign investors are interested in partnering with local firms that can contribute location-specific capabilities, especially for those concerned with establishing a position in the local market (Packaging, SEAB, Bacardi-Martini, Heinz).

In setting up operations, our cases provide evidence that investors do consider the national institutional framework as well as institutions at the specific investment location. Industrial policy may ˙intentionally favour investment in special industrial zones by providing incentives such as tax and tariff exemptions, as in Egypt (Mikawy and Handoussa, 2002). Industrial parks providing infrastructure have been attributed a pivotal role for instance in the development of software clusters in India, Brazil and Israel (Commander, 2004). Moreover, the Indian and Vietnamese cases illustrate the importance of sub-national institutions at the level of states or provinces. In contrast, Egypt and South Africa are administratively more centralised such that this issue has arisen neither in the cases, nor in the domestic policy debate.

The Bacardi-Martini case illustrates the obstacles for businesses that operate nation-wide, if regulatory regimes and/or pertinent tax legislation vary within a country. The case also points to the potentially detrimental effects of sub-national competition for FDI (also see Oman (2000) who describes the situation for the Indian automotive industry). For foreign investors, complex regionally diverging regulation creates obstacles to FDI, increases costs of information gathering and negotiations, but also increases the need for local partners that help with these tasks. As a side effect, complex and de-central regulatory institutions also increase the scope for corruption.

In further analysis of the intra-country variation of FDI volumes and entry modes within Vietnam, we found a clear pattern of provinces that are more progressive in implementing liberalization and establishing effective law enforcement also attracting more FDI, in particular in form of greenfield projects (Meyer and Nguyen 2003). Formal rules are largely set at national level, but informal institutions, that is implementation of the law, vary within Vietnam and are influenced by local policy-makers. Licensing decisions are made by the Ministry of Planning and Industry, and may be influenced by politics on a national level, yet recent decentralization has given provincial authorities more authority. In this process, informal institutions at the local level have become more important, including FDI promotion, promotion of market institutions and access to industrial real estate. The ability to strike a deal at local level is often seen as a disadvantage because of the potential for bureaucracy and corruption. Yet, in Vietnam and China it may actually be an advantage because the overall framework is rather restrictive and entrepreneurially minded local authorities may use their leverage to improve the business climate. Local government taking a progressive approach to reform may thus facilitate foreign investment. Thus we conclude that, for foreign investors, complex and regionally divergent regulation creates obstacles to FDI, increases the costs of information gathering and negotiations and increases the need for local partners to help with these tasks.

The Supply Side: Capital Market Development

The development of capital markets is often considered a major facilitator of mergers and acquisitions, and in consequence companies are more likely to pursue acquisition-based growth strategies where capital market institutions are highly sophisticated. The difference in entry patterns that we observe between South Africa and the other countries of our study may be related to the larger and more developed capital markets (see Chapter 1), though better resource endowment of local firms provides an alternative explanation. The liquidity of capital markets, and markets for corporate equity in particular, is a function of the institutions governing capital markets, as well as the 'supply' by owners willing to sell their businesses, which in turn depends on institutions in the host economy.

Capital markets first of all may be the place where the deal is struck, as acquirers may acquire shares through the stock exchange before launching a bid to take over the firm. This did not happen in our South African cases, yet they appear to be indirectly facilitated by several capital market-related institutions:

334 *Investment Strategies in Emerging Markets*

- Stock markets provide benchmark prices for the valuation of corporate assets and entire firms.
- Information on firms is more readily available if accounting standards are sophisticated, and specialist intermediaries provide the required services, notably independent auditing. In the absence of information systems, information asymmetry between seller and buyer may create 'market for lemons problems' and inhibit efficiency of markets for corporate equity.
- Specialist intermediaries, such as investment banks, stockbrokers and even consultancies experienced with mergers and acquisitions are available to provide support services to any firm considering an acquisition. ABN Amro provides some such services in South Africa and India. Yet they withdrew from Egypt in the early 1990s and they do not have an operation in Vietnam, which is a symptom of the level of capital market development.

Apart from these capital market institutions, liquidity of markets for corporate control depends on owners of firms being interested in selling their businesses to foreign investors. This 'supply side' of markets for corporate control is created by those willing to sell a good company at an attractive price. In emerging economies, a high proportion of firms tends to be owned by state-entities, or by domestic family-controlled business groups, as in India. Hence, the availability of firms for possible acquisition depends on privatisation policies and on business groups' corporate strategies.

Policy has been important in determining the opportunities for potential foreign investors in partnerships with state-owned enterprises. Most important, naturally, is privatisation, which creates a supply of potential acquisition targets. Privatisation has played a substantive role in all four countries, yet not nearly on the scale as in Eastern Europe in the 1990s. Privatisation also explains a lot of the volatility of FDI capital inflows reported in balance of payment statistics (see Chapter 1). For instance, in Egypt the privatisation of telecommunications has been crucial for the establishment of ECMS and the takeover of mobile services from the state-owned service provider. In India, privatisation has been officially initiated in 1991, but the implementation has been slow (Chapter 5). Where there has been privatisation, local Indian business groups have participated as the main bidders, quite in contrast to Eastern Europe. Hence, few FDI projects (and none of our cases) are related to privatisation in India.

In Vietnam, state-owned firms dominate the local economy, and foreign investors until recently were dependent on cooperating with them to get access to resources such as real estate and export licences, or more broadly legitimacy with local authorities. Government policy recently encouraged state-owned firms to seek foreign partners, and thus created incentives to be proactive in building relationships with foreign investors, facilitating the creation of joint ventures in Vietnam in the 1990s (Chapter 9) and in Egypt in the 1980s (Chapter 3). There has been some privatisation, but not in forms that would allow foreign investors to acquire firms. However, the ABB Transformers case illustrates how a foreign investor can attain control over an existing operation in ways that resemble a partial acquisition, yet creating considerable challenges for management.

In Vietnam, acquisitions were not permitted until 1997. Initially foreign ownership was limited to 30 per cent of equity, with each foreign investor holding no more than 10 per cent; and this had to be approved on a case-by-case basis by the prime minister's office, making it practically impossible for most investors. Thus, acquisition was mainly an option for acquiring a firm previously established by another FDI firm.

Private ownership of local industry facilitates acquisitions, as foreign investors would negotiate directly with the owners without need to involve government authorities. Private owners may be willing to sell for a good price if as entrepreneurs they want to sell out their business, as Ziton to EST in South Africa and ABI and APIC to GSK in Egypt, or if business groups sell non-core business units, as in the Packaging case.

However, private ownership is no guarantee that local owners would be interested in selling the companies to foreign investors. For instance, many family-owned Indian business groups are not interested in selling their businesses. In consequence, they would have a strong bargaining position when negotiating with potential foreign investors and ask for high premiums for a local firm. The willingness of family-owned businesses to sell out is a function of their corporate strategy and performance. Where local conglomerates are restructuring, their divestment of peripheral businesses may create opportunities for increase of FDI, as for instance Thailand and South Korea after the Asian crisis of 1997 (Zhan and Ozawa 2001). Business groups in India do not yet seem to restructure on large scale to create more focused operations (Khanna and Palepu 1999), but the Packaging case illustrates that even in India, the divestment of business groups from peripheral operations can create opportunities for inward FDI.

Thus, capital market development influences opportunities for FDI by acquisition in various ways, both in terms of institutions and in terms of the 'supply' of attractive firms that might be acquired. Since FDI in form of acquisition tends to be larger, capital market development is in particular, related to the volume of FDI-related capital flows, rather than the number of FDI entries. Multinational firms preferring to grow internationally through acquisitions may choose not to invest where capital markets do not facilitate such entry, or choose an alternative mode of entry.

Thus, ironically, our study suggests that policy-makers wishing to facilitate enhanced FDI flows in emerging markets need to develop a vibrant domestic private sector economy, thereby creating acquisition targets as these can then act as vehicles for skill, technology and management transfers to the wider economy. They also need to strengthen capital market institutions, increasing liquidity and developing a market for corporate control.

Industry Specific Institutions

The cases frequently refer to industry-specific regulatory institutions, rather than general societal or national institutions, when discussing institutional influences on entry strategies and performance. Examples include the industrial policy in the automotive sector, regulation of the banking sector, licensing and pricing of pharmaceutical products.

The case of the South African automotive industry represents a positive influence of industrial policy. In fact, the automotive policy may have been absolutely critical for the establishment of the export-oriented automotive components industry (Chapter 8, also see Barnes and Lorentzen 2003). A key element of this policy has been a tariff regime for imports of cars and components based on local contents with import-export complementation. Local content is measured on a 'net foreign exchange usage' basis, which allows export revenues to be deducted from the value of imports on which tariffs were to be paid. This industrial policy succeeded in attracting foreign investors such as NGK Ceramics and Behr, and in creating an automotive (supplier) cluster in South Africa. Local content requirements have also encouraged the development of the local supplier network serving Honda's motorcycle manufacture in Vietnam, where Japanese foreign investors have established some key suppliers.

Other industry-specific policy influences arise from the removal of barriers to business. In particular, the timing of entry and the acceleration of resource commitments is determined by changes in the regulatory conditions and the liberalization of the industry (McCarthy and Puffer 1997). Where local firms control industry-specific 'rights' such as operating licences, these institutional arrangements can induce foreign investors to choose JV or acquisition as entry mode. The importance of business licences has declined in recent years with liberalization, yet path dependency leads to continued operation of businesses set up during the more protectionist period. In Egypt, GSK established local manufacturing at least in part to ease access to the local pharmacy market and to protect international patents through a local presence. As the intellectual property rights were strengthened and the market was liberalised in the context of Egypt's association with the WTO, there were some fears that local production would be reduced. However, in the case of GSK, the opposite happened; the operation was upgraded to become a regional supply hub for Africa, the Middle East and parts of Europe.

The banking sector is by necessity a highly regulated industry as sound banking practices are essential to ensure the functioning of the financial sector. This regulation also sets the conditions for foreign banks operating in the country, for instance by limiting the number of banking licences, or by requiring local equity ownership or local management. The step-wise liberalization of the banking sector in South Africa and India thus created the business opportunities ABN Amro has been pursing, gradually expanding into different newly liberalised segments of banking.

Industry-specific regulation also affects entry mode as remaining restrictions on foreign ownership are often limited to industries considered politically sensitive. In India, this includes alcoholic beverages, as illustrated by the Bacardi-Martini case where foreign ownership has been limited to 74 per cent. Liberalization of such industries would see new entrants establish wholly-owned affiliates, while existing JVs may, possibly after some time-lag, be converted to full foreign ownership.

For empirical analysis the industry-specificity of institutions creates a methodological problem. Since empirical studies normally control for industry-specific effects with industry dummies, these controls also capture for industry-specific regulation, or other institutional arrangements that affect the particular industry only. In this way, empirical studies may underestimate the impact of institutions.

In conclusion, institutions affect foreign entry and performance in multiple ways. Yet these influences are often specific to the markets in which firms act, including output, input and capital markets, as well as the specific site of the FDI. Further studies of institutions and FDI may thus focus on industries or locations.

CONCLUSIONS

Our hypothesis in this study has been that, given the characteristics of the source firm, the institutional environment of the host economy will influence the mode of entry of FDI, and through that the performance of the enterprise and the nature of the spillovers generated for the host economy. For example, weak institutions and supply-side constraints in terms of acquisition targets and capital market structures might distort entry patterns in favour of greenfield or joint venture entry modes. The literature suggests that the direct technological spillovers from these entry modes, might be more modest than from entry through acquisitions. If they acquire an existing firm, the source firm needs to work directly with existing employees, managers, technologies and supply chains, and is therefore more likely to be active in upgrading these. With greenfield entry, the source firm could instead set up systems of technology, management and input supply paralleling activities in other subsidiaries, but potentially with only limited impact on the host economy. Similarly, when JVs are created primarily to circumvent policy regulations or domestic ownership, the local partner may have little or no influence on the subsidiary which is formed, and may not have the capacity to absorb the transfers of technology and skill.

We find considerable evidence for these views in our survey. Regression analysis indicates that entry mode is associated with the business environment (see Bhaumik et al. 2003). Moreover, as we have seen, the bulk of entry outside South Africa is either greenfield or joint venture, and the source firm supplies the majority of the resources critical to success. These patterns of entry mode are counterintuitive given that entry is usually 'market-seeking', rather than representing efforts to outsource manufacture to low-cost supplies or investing to exploit location-specific assets, for example natural resources. With market-seeking entry, one would expect acquisitions as a predominant entry mode so the foreign firm could rapidly acquire market share and obtain knowledge of how to operate on local markets. The very low level of acquisition in our survey indicates that the supply-side constraints must be severely binding, and this is an issue of major concern for policy-makers who wish to enhance the flow of spillover benefits from FDI.

The quantitative survey provides little hard evidence on spillover benefits from FDI however. We included questions about the impact of FDI on domestic firms in the sector, or up and down stream, and on training, but were unable to identify any significant patterns of spillover benefit by sector or entry mode. It is likely that this reflects deficiencies in the data rather than a substantive conclusion from the study; missing values are prevalent in these questions. Unfortunately this means that the survey data are silent on the issue of spillover benefits and their relationship to entry mode. We systematise the evidence about spillovers from the cases in Table 12.3. It can be seen that there is a considerable variation in the main areas of spillover, from traditional benefits like training, knowledge and management to capital market development, creation of clusters and assisting competition. It is clear however that most entrants were in some ways influenced by the policy environment in making their investment decisions, and that in addition to the private benefits, each investment yielded some positive external benefits to the host economy.

Liberalisation has created many opportunities for FDI, and determines in particular, investors' choices of timing, equity stake and locations, including intra-country locational choices. In larger, decentralised countries like India and Vietnam, the institutions at the state or province level are often also crucial. Industry-specific policies are often more important than general FDI ones.

They may be actively promoting FDI in a sector, as in the South African car industry; neutrally regulating an industry, as in the financial sector; or inhibiting FDI by over-regulation, as in the Indian alcoholic beverages industry. The presence of FDI may itself create pressures on both local firms to upgrade their technologies and on local institutions to accommodate the needs of a market economy.

There are some interesting country differences in our survey data and cases. To a significant extent, efficiency-seeking Greenfield entry has been

12.3 Spillovers

	Firm	Entry Mode	Spillovers
SA1	NGK Behr	Greenfield Acquisition	Development of a new industrial cluster with strong supplier networks
SA2	EST	Acquisition	Improved export market access
SA3	ABN Amro	Greenfield	Efficiency of capital markets, competition; banking infrastructure for business
VN1	SEAB	Joint venture	Local partner use knowledge spillover to build new facility
VN2	ABB	Joint venture	Technical training, product improve local infrastructure
VN3 IN1	Honda Bacardi-Martini	Joint venture Joint venture	Waste treatment technology expected to create spillovers to local businesses
IN2	Packaging	Acquisition	n.a.
IN3	ABN Amro	Joint venture	Efficiency of capital markets, competition between foreign banks; banking infrastructure for business
EG1	ECMS MobilNil	Joint venture	Development of telecom industry, service to other businesses
EG2	GSK	Acquisition	Exports, from mid 1990s
EG3	Heinz	Joint venture	Training in technology and marketing; developing farming practices, exports

the predominant pattern in Vietnam and for a significant minority of investments in India, notably in the IT sector. The technology spillover benefits from this mode of entry to other firms in the industry, or up and down stream, are perhaps likely to be limited, though they help to integrate the host country into the global economy. In contrast, FDI in South Africa, Egypt and non-IT sectors in India has been primarily market-seeking and more likely to be through acquisition or the formation of joint ventures. Investments of this sort may improve business performance in the host economy by upgrading technologies, intangible assets, management capabilities and labour skills within existing organisations.

In environments where market-seeking investors predominate, foreign affiliates learn ways to operate in the local environment, often using know-how from acquired firms or joint venture partners. They may thus have little incentive to try to alter the business environment. This is perhaps the case for many firms in Egypt or India in our sample. If investment is efficiency-seeking and greenfield in form, so that success requires the investors to achieve more alone, and to operate competitively on global markets, this may create powerful lobbies supporting reform to the institutional and policy structure. This is consistent with the findings from our sample in Vietnam.

Notes

1. However, the high levels seen around 1999/2000, when this research was conceptualised, have not been maintained in all cases, notably Egypt. The high value of FDI for SA in 2001 is due to the unbundling of shareholdings between Anglo and de Beers, which generated a significant capital transfer into South Africa for the purchase of Anglo American shares from de Beers and its owners. But this was not FDI in the usual sense – these associated companies were both SA-based until 1997, when Anglo shifted its headquarters to London, and a large proportion of its activities remain in SA.
2. We thank Maria Bytchkova for assembling this information.
3. Some researchers include non-equity modes in a study of entry modes (for example Kim and Hwang 1991, Tse et al. 1997). We follow Pan and Tse (2000) who argue and show empirically that entrants first decide between equity and non-equity modes, and then decide the specific mode of their investment project.
4. This refers to studies using panel data. Older studies using cross-sectional data often found positive spillovers within the same industry. Yet this approach is methodologically problematic (Görg and Strobl 2001), and reverse causality is highly plausible (Fan 2002). Several studies suggest that the causality may be reverse because MNEs are found to transfer more technology when local industry is more competitive (Kokko et al. 1996).
5. The authors would like to thank all the members of the country teams, especially Sumon Bhaumik and Stephen Gelb, and also Maria Bytchkova, Caitlin Frost and Gherardo Girardi for their research assistance. Any errors are their own.
6. The story does not change if we use the proportion of affiliates that are efficiency-seeking in the sense that they export more than 50 per cent of their output. A majority of firms in Vietnam but fewer than 20 per cent foreign affiliates in Egypt and South Africa are efficiency-seeking using this definition. Indian foreign affiliates usually produce for the domestic market, but still some 35 per cent export a majority of their output, while around half of Vietnamese subsidiaries export most of their output. Of these firms, almost half send their exports to the regional market, as against fewer than one fifth of Indian ones. The Egyptian and South African firms that choose to focus on exports are also mainly orientated to global markets. Once again, we find that only in India does exporting to other affiliates represent a significant share of affiliate's activity.
7. The macro-economic policy environment is discussed in more detail in Louis et al. (2003) and El-Mikawy and Handoussa (2001).
8. Percentage of filed cases resolved.
9. However, private businesses prefer to settle disputes in court. The WEF report ranked Egypt 2 out of 59 in terms of preference for using the court system.
10. A second confirmation that the criteria were satisfied was made from the completed questionnaires:

1. Year of establishment: All 150 replied to the question concerning the year of operation, only 1 firm started operations in 1989.
2. Number of employees: Question 21.1 of the questionnaire confirms the number of employees. Eleven of the surveyed firms did not reply to this question, but confirmed that the number of employees met the minimum requirement.
3. Equity Share: The minimum of 10 per cent foreign equity share was confirmed in question 4 of the questionnaire. All, except two firms replied to this question.

11. For example, the number of foreign firms that work in the construction sector is 21, representing 14.3 per cent of total firms surveyed. In the base population, the number of foreign firms in this sector represents only 4.5 per cent of total foreign firms. But the sample includes infrastructure, contractors and construction activities. Table 3.2 shows that in 2001 this sector represented 7 per cent of total FDI stock in Egypt. The construction sector is probably increasing its long-run share because the government plans to increase the habitable area of the country from 3 per cent to 20 per cent by the year 2020. This has encouraged newly established firms to engage in construction activities. There is also growth in infrastructure; the government has approved projects in power generation, telecommunications, airports and highways. The other major anomaly is the service sector. In the base population, this includes financial services (excluding funding services, for example banks and investment firms), transportation, consultancy, health, petroleum services and other services. In the sample, it includes business services and real estate. Hence, it is not possible to compare the sample to the population. However, if we add the firms in the sector on transportation and communication to services (7 firms) the total number of services firms would be 26, representing 17 per cent of total number of firms in the survey. In 2001, the FDI stock directed to the services sector (excluding financial services) accounted for 3 per cent of total FDI stock, while the financial services FDI stock accounted for 18 per cent.
12. This finding is confirmed by another survey in which businessmen agreed that the most important gain in their linkage with their parent firm was technology acquisition. The second most important was the brand name, training came third and managerial capabilities came fourth.
13. In 2002, the exchange rate was roughly Rs. 47.5 to the US dollar. During the periods being discussed, the rate has varied between Rs. 41 to the dollar and Rs. 45 to the dollar.
14. A comprehensive discussion of the survey results is contained in S. Gelb, Foreign Companies in South Africa: Entry, Performance and Impact (EDGE Institute, Johannesburg, 2002, www.the-edge.org.za).
15. Particularly France and Germany after 1945. Many South African companies licensed technology from Japanese corporations, whose government barred direct investment in South Africa because of apartheid.
16. At end-1990, the Johannesburg Stock Exchange was the 9th largest in the world by market capitalisation.
17. From 1985 to 1993, the current account was maintained in surplus to finance a capital outflow to repay debt.
18. Empirical firm-level analysis of FDI has focused only on specific host countries, specific sectors, or as one aspect of broader studies of firms.

19. Given substantial outward investment by SA corporations, net inflow data mask significantly larger gross inflows, the relevant variable for evaluation of inward investment.

20. In 1994, about 84 per cent of capitalisation on the Johannesburg Stock Exchange was accounted for by five major conglomerates, whose share dropped to about 55 per cent by 1998. In 1999, South African firms were by far the largest net purchasers of foreign assets – in excess of US$4 billion – of all emerging markets (*The Economist*, 7 October 2000).

21. At least 10 per cent foreign ownership, at least ten employees in South Africa, initial entry to SA after 1990, and some value-addition in South Africa. Another 452 companies had first invested in South Africa before 1990, but met the other three criteria in 2002.

22. In Table 7.5, resources chosen as 1st, 2nd, or 3rd most important are weighted equally. The columns total to 300 percent because each firm identified *three* key resources. The 300 percent total includes responses for eight resources mentioned in the questionnaire but excluded from Table 7.5 – fewer than 12 per cent of firms chose each of these.

23. The number of firms in some cells in Table 7.7 is small, especially in the partial acquisition column. 23 firms entered via partial acquisition, but each resource is relevant to between a quarter and a third of this number. The columns do not always add to 100 per cent because the 'other' category has been omitted.

24. fifty-six per cent of firms sell all output into the domestic market, and the remaining 44 per cent are divided evenly between those selling more than 75 per cent into the domestic market, and those selling less than 75 per cent.

25. Firms' responses on skilled labour and production and on transaction inputs are not directly comparable, but the questions have the same format and the Likert scale the same meaning.

26. The objectives omitted are productivity and domestic market share.

27. For a thorough account of these channels of impact, see Dicken 1998, Chapter 8.

28. Since firms' entry dates differ, the change from 'then' to 'now' cannot be interpreted as a change in exports over a specified time period. Table 7.14 is not weighted by turnover.

29. The limited contribution to distribution networks by parent firms (see Table 7.7) reflects the focus of most affiliates on local and regional markets.

30. Rand depreciation reduced the weight of domestic sales in overall sales value expressed in dollars.

31. There were no primary sector firms in the National Enterprise Survey; 89 firms had more than 10 per cent foreign ownership but entered South Africa before 1990. These firms had a mean share of sales in the domestic market of 85.7 per cent, and 8.9 per cent to the region. Average turnover is much larger for the pre-1990 investors than for post-1990 group.

32. This is based on a crude comparison with the National Enterprise Survey (Gelb 2001).

33. Anthony Black is responsible for the automotive components and industrial equipment cases. Stephen Gelb is responsible for the financial services case.

34. Other important component exports include leather seating, tyres, exhausts, wheels, engine parts and wiring harnesses (Department of Trade and Industry 2001).

35. For South Africa see Barnes and Kaplinsky (2000). This development is apparent also in Brazil (Posthuma 1995), Argentina (Miozzo, 2000) and the Czech Republic (Meyer 2000) among other countries.
36. Catalytic converters are still not required on vehicles destined for the South African market although they are increasingly being fitted.
37. Only domestic value added to exported products qualifies for import rebates.
38. The exchange rate of the South African rand has been extremely volatile over the last few years. A major depreciation against the US dollar in 2001 has been followed by an equally rapid appreciation in 2002/2003.
39. In Holland, there was a 38 per cent decline in the number of branches between 1992 and 2000, though employment was relatively constant around 38,000.
40. Throughout this chapter, an exchange rate of USD 1 = ZAR 8.00 is used.
41. KFS was owned 42 per cent each by Kagiso Trust and NM Rothschild, and 11 per cent by Huysamer Stals.
42. In February 2003, the global leasing division was re-named Leaseplan Corporation, as the final step in the shift from a financial services provider to a financial group in the automotive services sector. This division is not discussed further in this case study.
43. Of course, all foreign banks' assets are small compared with those of the top six domestic banks.
44. Though the domestic banks dominated the ratings, several foreign banks do appear after this date.
45. ABN Amro was not the only foreign bank which experienced these problems. International Bank of Southern Africa (IBSA), a JV between BNP Paribas and Dresdner Bank, withdrew from South Africa at end-2002, the MD citing large losses due to 'lots of scandals' in South Africa. (See BR 14 May 1999, 7 July 1999, 11 November 1999, 30 November 1999, 10 January 2000, 12 April 2000.)
46. Anonymity was requested. This bank is ranked in the top ten globally by capital and assets, as well as in ABN Amro's own peer group system. It has maintained over 300 employees in South Africa since 1999.
47. The average effective nominal exchange rate was 46.18 in 2002, on a base of 100 in 1995.
48. The technological advances in communications (and transport) which have facilitated commodity chains in manufacturing have also enabled geographical dispersion within some value chains in services, such as the relocation of back office and call centre operations to low-wage economies in airlines, software and financial services. Thus recent FDI in service sectors has involved resource-seeking by multinational firms.
49. In the corresponding reports for other countries of this research, IT and pharmaceuticals are reported separately. Yet with only one and two incidences respectively, this was not sensible for Vietnam.
50. Danbrew is a 100 per cent owned affiliate of Carlsberg providing turnkey brewing facilities and associated services.
51. Due to the confidential nature of this kind of information, we are not sure of the exact year the affiliate started to be profitable. Some reported that it was 1998, others said it was 2000.
52. By 2001, there was another joint venture in transformer production in Vietnam with a Japanese company, Takaoka.
53. This was, and still is, an exception in Vietnam, where the majority of joint ventures employ only up to 70-80 per cent of employees of the Vietnamese

partners to the joint venture, and foreign partners often use examinations and other formalities to refuse to retain less-skilled or peripheral employees.

54. Partly because of this, and because of the confidence in this possibility, the ABB Country Manager was not so concerned about a Government regulation issued in late 1996, which permitted expatriate managers to hold jobs in joint ventures for not more than three years, a regulation that caused deep concern for many foreign companies, which normally expect expatriates to hold top jobs for most of the joint venture duration.

55. Collaborators and contributors to this research project are thanked for insightful discussions that contributed to this chapter. Many ideas have been developed in long discussions between the contributors to this book during seminars in London and Cairo, and many informal discussions. Valuable comments were also received from Zoltan Antal-Mokos, Bent Petersen and Freek Vermeulen.

56. ABB acquired the stake of its local partner in summer of 2003, after our case research has been completed.

57. The managers that had to implement brownfield acquisitions, did, at least *ex post*, not necessarily appreciate the experience. In both Egyptian cases, interviewees described the process as time-consuming and burdensome, especially when merging administrative structures, and in handling redundant labour and training needs. These operational managers thus recommended greenfield entry for future expansion.

58. Research in Eastern Europe suggests that there may be such a relationship (Uhlenbruck et al. 2003, Estrin et al. 1997, Antal-Mokos 1998, Meyer 2002).

59. Interestingly, foreign investments to the IT sector are rare except in India, where they account for almost 20 per cent of entrants. This rarity may be a cause for concern for policy-makers.

Bibliography

Aitken, B. and A. Harrison (1999), 'Do domestic firms benefit from direct foreign investment? Evidence from Venezuela', *American Economic Review*, **89** (3), 605-618.

Altenburg, T. (2000), 'Linkages and Spillovers between Transnational Corporations and Small and Medium-Sized Enterprises in Developing Countries: Opportunities and Policies', proceedings of the UNCTAD Special Round Table 'TNC-SME Linkages for Development', Bangkok, February.

Anand, J. and A. Delios (2002), 'Absolute and relative resources as determinants of international acquisitions', *Strategic Management Journal,* **23**, 119-134.

Anderson, E.M. and H. Gatignon (1986), 'Modes of foreign entry: A transaction costs analysis and propositions', *Journal of International Business Studies*, **17** (3), 1-26.

Antal-Mokos, Z. (1998), *Privatisation, Politics, and Economic Performance in Hungary*, Cambridge: Cambridge University Press.

Asian Development Bank (2004): Asian Development Outlook; Manila: ADB

Barkema, H. and F. Vermeulen (1998), 'International expansion through start-up or through acquisition: a learning perspective', *Academy of Management Journal,* **41**, 7-26.

Barkema, H., J. Bell and J. Pennings (1996), 'Foreign entry, cultural barriers, and learning', *Strategic Management Journal*, **17**, 151-66.

Barnes, J. and R. Kaplinsky (2000), 'Globalization and the death of the local firm? The automobile component sector in South Africa', *Regional Studies*, **34** (9), 797-812.

Barnes, J. and J. Lorentzen (2003), 'Learning, Upgrading, and Innovation in the South African Automotive Industry', paper prepared for Workshop on Understanding FDI-Assisted Economic Development, May 2003, TIK Centre, University of Oslo.

Basant, R. (2000), 'Corporate response to economic reforms', *Economic and Political Weekly*.

Belderbos, R., G. Capannelli and K. Fukao (2001), 'Backward vertical linkages of foreign manufacturing affiliates: Evidence from Japanese multinationals', *World Development,* **29** (1), 189-208.

Benito, G. and L. Welch (1994), 'Foreign market entry: Beyond choice of entry mode', *Journal of International Marketing,* **2** (2), 7-27.

Bevan, A., S. Estrin, and K. Meyer (2003), 'Foreign investment location and institutional development in transition economies', *International Business Review* 13, number 1, p. 43 - 64.

Bhandari L. and Goswami, O. (2002), *So Many Lost Years: The Public Sector Before and After Reforms*, New Delhi: NCAER.

Bhaumik, S., S. Estrin and K. Meyer (2003), 'Resources for Competitiveness in Emerging Economies, and Foreign Investors' Entry Mode Choice', CNEM Working Paper no.33, Centre for New and Emerging Markets, London: London Business School.

Birkinshaw, J. (2000), *Entrepreneurship in the Global Firm*, Thousand Oaks: C.A. Sage.

Birkinshaw, J., H. Bresman and L. Håkanson (2000), 'Managing the post-acquisition integration process', *Journal of Management Studies*, **37** (3).

Black, A. (1996), 'Learning, Technical Change and the Trade Regime in the South African Automotive Component Sector', Working Paper no. 7, Development Policy Research Unit, University of Cape Town.

Black, A. (2001), 'Globalization and restructuring in the South African automotive industry', *Journal of International Development*, **13** (6), 779-796.

Blomström, M. and A. Kokko (2002), 'FDI and Human Capital: A Research Agenda', Technical Paper no. 195, OECD Development Centre, Paris: OECD.

Brouthers, K.D. and L.E. Brouthers (2000), 'Acquisition or greenfield start-up? Institutional, cultural and transaction cost influences', *Strategic Management Journal*, 21, 89-97.

Buckley, P. and M. Casson (1976), *The Future of the Multinational Enterprise*, London: Macmillan.

Buckley, P.J. and M. Casson (1998), 'Analysing foreign market entry strategies: extending the internalisation approach', *Journal of International Business Studies,* **29**, 539- 562.

Buono, A.F. and J.L. Bowditch (1989), *The Human Side of Mergers and Acquisitions*, London: Jossey Bass.

Caves, R.E. (1971), 'International corporations: The industrial economics of foreign investment', *Economica,* **38**, 1-27.

Chatterjee, S. (1990), 'Excess resources, utilization costs, and mode of entry', *Academy of Management Journal*, **33**, 780-800.

Chen, H. and M.Y. Hu (2001), 'An analysis of determinants of entry mode and its impacts on performance', *International Business Review*, **11** (2), 193-210.

CIEM, Central Institute for Economic Management (2002), *Vietnam's Economy in 2001*, Hanoi: National Political Publishers.

Clarke, G. et al. (2003), 'Foreign bank entry: Experience, implications for developing economies and agenda for further research', *World Bank Research Observer*, **18** (1).

Cohen, W.M. and D.A. Levinthal,. (1990), 'Absorptive capacity: A new perspective on learning and innovation', *Administrative Science Quarterly*, **35** (1), 128-152.

Commander, S. (ed.) (2004), *The Origins and Dynamics of the Software Industry in Emerging Markets*, Centre for New and Emerging Markets, London Business School, forthcoming.

Danis, W.M. and A. Parkhe (2002), 'Hungarian-Western partnerships: A grounded theoretical model of integration processes and outcomes', *Journal of International Business Studies*, **33**, 423-456.

Dawar, N. and A. Chattopadhay (2002), 'Rethinking marketing programs for emerging markets', *Long Range Planning*, **35**, 457-474.

Desai, A. V. (2003), 'The Dynamics of the Indian Information Technology Industry', DRC Working Paper no.20, Centre for New and Emerging Markets, London: London Business School.

Dicken, P., Global Shift (1998), *Transforming the World Economy*, 3rd edition, London: Paul Chapman Publishing.

Dunning, J. (1993), *Multinational Enterprises and the Global Economy*, London: Addison Wesley.

EIU (Economist Intelligence Unit) (2002), *Country Profile 2002 South Africa*, London: EIU.

Edge Institute (2003), African Investment Database, Johyannesburg: Edge Institute.

El-Mikawy, N. and H. Handoussa (eds) (2001), *Institutional Reform and Economic Development in Egypt*, Cairo: American University in Cairo Press.

Estrin, S., K. Hughes and S. Todd (1997), *Foreign Direct Investment in Central and Eastern Europe*, London: Cassel.

Fan, E.X. (2002), 'Technological Spillovers from Foreign Direct Investment – A Survey', ERD Working Paper no. 33, Asian Development Bank.

Gelb, S. (2001), 'Fixed Investment in South Africa', Office of the President, Government of South Africa.

Gelb, S. (2002), 'Foreign Companies in South Africa: Entry, Performance and Impact', Johannesburg: Edge Institute.

Globermann, S. and D. Shapiro (2003), 'Governance infrastructure and US foreign direct investment', *Journal of International Business Studies,* **34** (1), 19-39.

Gomes-Casseres, B. (1987), 'Joint venture instability: Is it a problem?' *Columbia Journal of World Business,* **13** (summer), 23-32.

Görg, H. and E. Strobl (2001), 'Multinational companies and productivity spillovers: A meta-analysis with a test for publication bias', *Economic Journal,* **111** (November), 723-739.

Government of South Africa, Department of Finance (1996), 'Growth, Employment and Redistribution', Pretoria.

Government of South Africa, Department of Trade and Industry (2002), 'Accelerating Growth and Development: The Contribution of the Integrated Manufacturing Strategy', Pretoria.

Guisinger, S. et al. (1985), *Investment Incentives and Performance Requirements, Patterns of International Trade, Production and Investment*, New York: Praeger.

Haddad, M. and A. Harrison (1993), 'Are there positive spillovers from direct foreign investment? Evidence from panel data for Morocco', *Journal of Development Economics*, 42, 51-74.

Harrigan, K.R. (1988), 'Joint ventures and global strategies', *Columbia Journal of World Business*, 14 (2), 36-64.

Haspeslagh, P.C. and D.B. Jemison (1991), *Managing Acquisitions: Creating Value Through Corporate Renewal*, New York: Free Press.

Henisz, W.J. (2000), 'The institutional environment for multinational investment', *Journal of Law, Economics and Organization*, 16, 334-364.

Hennart, J.-F. (1988), 'A transaction cost theory of equity joint ventures', *Strategic Management Journal*, 9 (4), 361-374.

Hennart, J.-F. and Y.-R. Park (1993), 'Greenfield vs. acquisition: The strategy of Japanese investors in the United States', *Management Science*, 39, 1054-1070.

International Monetary Fund (2003), *International Financial Statistics*, Washington D.C.: IMF.

Jemison, D. B. and S. B. Sitkin (1986), 'Corporate acquisitions: A process perspective', *Academy of Management Review*, 11, 145-163.

Katz, J. (1987), *Technology Generation in Latin American Manufacturing Enterprises: Theory and Case Studies Concerning its Nature, Magnitude and Consequences*, London: Macmillan.

Khanna, T. and K. Palepu (1999), 'Policy shocks, market intermediaries, and corporate strategy: The evolution of business groups in Chile and India', *Journal of Economics and Management Strategy*, 8, 271-310.

Khanna, T. and K. Palepu (2000), 'The future of business groups in emerging markets: long-run evidence from Chile', *Academy of Management Journal*, 43 (3), 268-285.

Kim, W.C. and P. Hwang (1991), 'Global strategy and multinationals' entry mode choice', *Journal of International Business Studies*, 23 (1), 29-53.

Kogut, B. (1996), 'Direct Investment, Experimentation, and Corporate Governance in Transition Economies', in R. Frydman, C.W. Gray and A. Rapaczynski (eds), *Corporate Governance in Central Europe and Russia*, vol. 1, London and Budapest: Central European University Press, pp. 293-332.

Kogut, B. and H. Singh (1988), 'The effect of national culture on the choice of entry mode', *Journal of International Business Studies*, 19 (3), 411-432.

Kokko, A.R. Tasini, and M. Zejan (1996), 'Local technological capability and productivity spillovers from FDI in the Uruguayan manufacturing sector', *Journal of Development Studies*, **32**, 602-611.

Lewis, J. (2001), *Policies to Promote Growth and Employment in South Africa*, Informal Discussion Papers on Aspects of the Economy of SA, Washington DC: World Bank.

Louis, M., A. El Mahdy and H. Handoussa (2003), 'Survey of Foreign Investment Firms in Egypt', DRC Working Paper no. 3, Centre for New and Emerging Markets, London: London Business School.

Luo, Y. (2001), 'Determinants of entry in an emerging economy: A multilevel approach', *Journal of Management Studies*, **38**, 443-472.

McCarthy, D. and S. Puffer (1997), 'Strategic investment flexibility for MNE success in Russia: Evolving beyond entry modes', *Journal of World Business*, **32**, 293-319.

Meyer, K.E. (2000), 'International production networks and enterprise transformation Central Europe', *Comparative Economic Studies*, XLII (1), 135-150.

Meyer, K.E. (2001a), 'International business research on transition economies', in A. Rugman and T. Brewer (eds), *Oxford Handbook of International Business*, Oxford: Oxford University Press, pp. 716-759.

Meyer, K.E. (2001b), 'Institutions, transaction costs, and entry mode choice in Eastern Europe', *Journal of International Business Studies*, **32** (2), 357-367.

Meyer, K.E. (2002), 'Management challenges in privatization acquisitions in transition economies', *Journal of World Business*, **37**, 266-276.

Meyer, K.E. (2003), 'Globalfocusing: From Domestic Conglomerate to Global Specialist', DRC Working Paper no. 16, Centre for New and Emerging Markets, London: London Business School.

Meyer, K.E. and I.B. Møller, (1998), 'Managing deep restructuring: Danish experiences in Eastern Germany', *European Management Journal*, **16** (4), 411-421.

Meyer, K.E. and H.V. Nguyen (2003), 'Foreign Investor's Entry Strategies and Sub-national Institutions in Emerging Markets', DRC Working Paper no. 14, Centre for New and Emerging Markets, London: London Business School.

Meyer, K. E. and S. Estrin (1999), 'Entry mode choice in emerging markets: Greenfield, acquisitions and brownfield', *Journal of International Business Studies*, **32** (1), 575-584.

Meyer, K. E. and S. Estrin (2001), 'Brownfield entry in emerging markets', *Journal of International Business Studies*, **32** (3), 575-584.

Minzberg, H. and J.A. Waters (1985), 'Of strategies deliberate and emergent', *Strategic Management Journal*, **6** (3), 257-272.

Miozzo, M. (2000), 'Transnational corporations, industrial policy and the war of incentives: The case of the Argentine automobile industry', *Development and Change*, **31**, 651-680.

North, D.C. (1990), 'Institutions and their consequences for economic performance', in K.S. Cook, and M. Levi, (eds), *The Limits of Rationality*, Chicago and London: University of Chicago Press, pp. 383-401.

Oliver, C. (1997), 'Sustainable competitive advantage: Combining institutional and resource-based views', *Strategic Management Journal*, **18**, 697-713.

Oman, C. (2000), *Policy Competition for Foreign Direct Investment: A Study of Competition among Governments to Attract FDI*, Paris: OECD, Development Centre Studies.

Pan, Y. and D.K. Tse (2000), 'The hierarchical model of market entry modes', *Journal of International Business Studies*, **31** (4), 535-554.

Peng, M. W. (2000), *Business Strategies in Transition Economies*, Thousand Oaks, CA: Sage.

Penrose, E. (1959), *The Theory of the Growth of the Firm*, 3rd edition, London: Oxford University Press.

Petersen, B., D.E. Welch and L.S. Welch (2000), 'Creating meaningful switching options in international operations', *Long Range Planning*, **33** (5), 690-707.

PriceWaterhouseCoopers, *Strategic and emerging issues in South African banking*, Annual since 1996 (www.pwcglobal.com).

Rankin, N. (2001), 'Specialisation, Efficiency and Exports: Some Preliminary Results from South African Manufacturing Firms', Centre for the Study of African Economies, University of Oxford.

Roldos, J. (2001), 'FDI in Emerging Market Banking Systems', paper presented at OECD Global Forum on *New Horizons and Policy Challenges for FDI n the 21st century*, November.

Rugman, A. and A. Verbecke (2003), 'Regional and Global Strategies of Multinational Enterprises', paper presented at Journal of International Business Studies Conference, March, Duke University.

Saggi, K. (2002), Trade, foreign direct investment and international technology transfer: A survey, *World Bank Research Observer*, **17** (2), 191-235.

Sarkar, J. (1999), 'India's Banking Sector: Current Status, Emerging Challenges and Policy Imperatives in a Globalized Environment', in James Hanson and Sanjay Kathuria (eds), *India: A Financial Sector for the Twenty-First Century*, Oxford: Oxford University Press.

Sarkar, J. and P. Agarwal (1997), 'Banking: The Challenge of Deregulation', in Kirit Parikh (ed.), *India Development Report*, New Delhi: Oxford University Press.

Sinani, E. and K.E. Meyer (2002), 'Identifying Spillovers of Technology Transfer from FDI: The Case of Estonia', CEES Working Paper no. 47, Copenhagen: Copenhagen Business School.

Smarzynska, B. (2002), 'Does Foreign Direct Investment Increase the Productivity of Domestic Firms: In Search of Spillovers Through

Backward Linkages', Policy Research Working Paper no. 2924, Washington D.C,: World Bank.

South African Reserve Bank (2001), 'South Africa's Balance of Payments, 1946-2001', supplement to Quarterly Bulletin, June.

South African Reserve Bank (2003), *Quarterly Bulletin*, September.

Steensma, H.K. and M. Lyles (2000), 'Explaining IJV survival in a transitional economy through social exchange and knowledge-based perspectives', *Strategic Management Journal*, **21**, 831-851.

Subramanian, A. and M. Abd El Latif (1997), 'The Egypt-EU Partnership Agreement and the Egyptian Pharmaceutical Sector', in A. Galal and B.Hoekman (eds), *Regional Partners in Global Markets Limits and Possibilities of the Euro-Med Agreements*, ECES and CEPR.

Tse, D.K., Y. Pan and K.Y. Au (1997), 'How MNEs choose entry modes and form alliances: The China experience', *Journal of International Business Studies*, **29** (4), 779-801.

Uhlenbruck, K. and J. de Castro (2000), 'Foreign acquisitions in Central and Eastern Europe: Outcomes of privatization in transitional economies', *Academy of Management Journal*, **43** (3), 381-403.

Uhlenbruck, K., K.E. Meyer and M. Hitt (2003), 'Organizational transformation in transition economies: Resource-based and organizational learning perspectives', *Journal of Management Studies*, **40** (2), 257-282.

UNCTAD (United Nations Conference on Trade and Development) (1994, 1998, 2000, 2001, 2002, 2003), *World Investment Reports*, Geneva: UN.

United Nations Development Programme (2002, 2003), *Human Development Reports*, Oxford and New York: Oxford University Press.

Wells, N. (ed.) (1985), *Pharmaceuticals Among Sunrise Industries*, New York: St. Martin's Press.

Wood, E. (2000), *Managing Innovation at Ziton SA (Pty) Ltd*, University of Cape Town, Graduate School of Business.

World Bank (2000-2002), *World Development Reports*, Washington DC: World Bank.

World Bank (2002), *Telecom Infrastructure Development for Corporate Data in the MENA Region*, Report of the World Bank, Washington DC: World Bank.

World Bank (2002), *World Development Indicators*, CD-ROM.

World Bank, Global Development Finance (2003), *Striving for Stability in Development Finance*, Washington DC: World Bank.

WEF (World Economic Forum) (2000), *The Global Competitiveness Report 2000*, Oxford: Oxford University Press.

World Markets Research Centre (2002), *Country Analysis Report*, London: WMRC.

Zhan, J. and T. Ozawa (2001), *Business Restructuring in Asia*, Copenhagen: Copenhagen Business School Press.

Index

ABB 280–81, 301
chose partner with track record in the industry 316
multinational group in global electrical industries 280–81
new equipment in Vietnam 287
'technology sharing' 284, 319
US and substitution with local managers 284

ABB Transformers Vietnam Ltd 280
competition 288
counterfactual 282
employment 287
enterprise restructuring 285–7
entry 282–3
exports to regional markets 288
FDI laws, public sector procurement 328
foreign partner had control from outset 308
HTM and 281–3, 294
increases in foreign capital 308
JV and 288, 307
market-seeking 326
partial acquisition 335
performance 282
reduced no-load loss by 50 percent 288
resources in local firm 314
resources of the new venture and resource transfer 283–4
restructuring 311, 318–19
role of local firm 309–10
spillovers 288, 339
tapping into ABB's regional and international networks 285
technology sharing and management localisation 284–5
training 320
utilisation of equipment of the acquired firm 287

ABI, sold to Glaxo (1989) 103, 106–7, 308, 318

ABN Amro Bank (Amsterdam), 225, 302
acquired Alleghany Asset Management 163
consumer banking segment world-wide 166
divested selected emerging market operations 304, 323
expansion mainly via acquisitions 226
long-term commitment in new country 226
market-seeking 326
provides services in SA and India 334
strategic decisions and collapse of 'dotcom' bubble 237
strategic reorientation at global level (2000) 235
universal bank 226

ABN Amro Bank (India) 159–60, 165, 226, 303, 306, 337
acquisition 166–7
Bank of America and 166–7, 172
complementarity between global marketing and human local resources 171–2
conglomerate bank with international services 162
diversification 167–8
financial sector de-regulation 329
foreign competitors 165, 168
global strategy 162–4
increases in foreign capital 308
key competitors 168–70
market-seeking 326
multi-pronged growth strategy 165–6
non-bank finance company (NBFC) 167–8
post-1991 strategies 165–6